Praise for
RIVAL POWER

"It would be good to say that this book is a valuable addition to the canon. It is not. When it comes to the issue of Russia, the Balkans, and the wider region of Southeastern Europe, it is *the* canon, because no one else has written about it. Dimitar Bechev is the right author of the right book at the right time."

Tim Judah, Balkans correspondent, *The Economist*

"For the new 'Great Game' of geopolitical competition, look above all to the Balkans, a region where the impact of Russian energy, soft power, and covert operations are all at their strongest. This excellent book is the best primer yet to this unfolding struggle; a scholarly, sympathetic, and realistic analysis of the present situation and likely future developments that deserves to be read widely and carefully."

Mark Galeotti, head of the Center for European Security, Institute of International Relations, Prague

"Russia is back in the Balkans and ideology has little to do with it. In this engaging book, Dimitar Bechev argues that revival of Russia's influence in the region was made possible by its pragmatism and tough-minded pursuit of material gains. Those viewing Russia as the new ideological warrior will be challenged in their beliefs."

Andrei P. Tsygankov, professor of international relations, San Francisco State University

"This timely and insightful analysis takes the Russian challenge to the stability of Southeast Europe seriously, and shows its limitations, despite the abundant opportunities created by local miscreants."

Pavel Baev, Nonresident Senior Fellow, Brookings Institution, and Research Professor, Peace Research Institute, Oslo

"At the time when it is fashionable to sound alarmist on Russia's return to the Balkans, *Rival Power* provides a clear-eyed assessment of the opportunities and significant limits for Russia's power in the region."

Vladimir Frolov, foreign affairs columnist, Republic.ru

"Once written off as a fading actor in a region ever more integrated with the EU, Russia is now playing an increasingly disruptive role in Southeast Europe. Drawing on his innate understanding of the area, and an unmatched knowledge of the region's languages, Dimitar

Bechev looks beyond the stereotypical explanations for this Russian resurgence and investigates the hard political calculations at play. This is a truly excellent, and highly readable, account of how Moscow is trying to extend its influence across the Balkans, Greece, Cyprus, and Turkey."

James Ker-Lindsay, Senior Visiting Fellow, London School of Economics and Political Science

"Dimitar Bechev's book possesses the rare quality of being the work of a seasoned and insightful scholar, but also of someone who appreciates the exciting twists and turns of Russia's dramatic relationship with the Balkans. *Rival Power* is very well written and dispenses with several persistent myths, especially one that views countries of the region and their leaders as 'victims' of Moscow's preying. A thrilling and stark exposé of Russia's masterful use of a limited political arsenal to further its goals."

Konstantin Eggert, commentator and host, TV Rain, Moscow

"*Rival Power* is a very timely and comprehensive book, written by one of the most accomplished observers of the international relations of the Russian Federation since its inception. It is written in a concise and clear language, masterfully relaying the gradual reemergence of Russia as a new (old) challenge to the West in the Balkans and the Black Sea. A must reading for those who wish to make sense of the recent developments in international politics."

Mustafa Aydın, professor at Kadir Has University, Istanbul

"Dimitar Bechev's groundbreaking work on Southeast Europe vividly demonstrates how Vladimir Putin exploits the West's distractions. This book documents a revisionist Kremlin's efforts to disrupt the reform and integration process in the Western Balkans, and in turn sow doubts about the future of the European project and US leadership. Bechev's research also makes clear that Russia offers no viable alternative to the European Union and United States in Southeast Europe, while serving as a warning that, if left unchecked, Russian mischief-making could lead to conflict in the region."

Damon Wilson, executive vice president of the Atlantic Council

"In times when conspiracy theories are in full blossom, this is a sober, historically informed, cogently argued, and well-documented analysis of Russia's influence in Southeast Europe. Very much worth reading."

Loukas Tsoukalis, professor of European integration, University of Athens, and president of the Hellenic Foundation for European and Foreign Policy

RIVAL POWER

RUSSIA'S INFLUENCE IN SOUTHEAST EUROPE

DIMITAR BECHEV

YALE UNIVERSITY PRESS
NEW HAVEN AND LONDON

For information about this and other Yale University Press publications, please contact:

U.S. Office: sales.press@yale.edu   yalebooks.com
Europe Office: sales@yaleup.co.uk   yalebooks.co.uk

Set in Minion Pro by IDSUK (DataConnection) Ltd
Printed in Great Britain by TJ International Ltd, Padstow, Cornwall

Library of Congress Control Number: 2017943875

ISBN 978-0-300-21913-5

A catalogue record for this book is available from the British Library.

10 9 8 7 6 5 4 3 2 1

To my children, Emanuil, Anthony, and Sophia

CONTENTS

MAPS AND FIGURES

Maps

Figures

ACKNOWLEDGMENTS

This book is the product of more than three years of work. It was originally conceived after a research trip to Moscow in May 2013 that I took with a co-conspirator, Andrew Wilson, at the time we shared an affiliation with the European Council on Foreign Relations. Although our report on the decline of Gazprom never saw the light of day, much of the content ultimately found its way into Andy's masterful account of the Ukraine crisis and, now, in this volume. The idea of writing a book on Russia in Southeast Europe picked up speed only in the watershed moment that was the spring and summer of 2014. In the process of conducting research and drafting the text, I benefited from the incredible hospitality of a number of institutions, drawing vast amounts of knowledge and inspiration from fellow scholars across disciplines.

The project began in earnest in the academic year of 2014–15, which I spent as a fellow at LSEE, the unit at the London School of Economics specializing in the politics and economics of Southeast Europe. I owe a special debt to James Ker-Lindsay, Tena Prelec, and to Spyros Economides (who, many moons ago, examined my DPhil thesis at Oxford). Exceptionally kind hosts as well as dear friends, they all helped me reinvent myself as an academic, following a stint in the policy world. Together with James and Othon

Anastasakis of Southeast European Studies at Oxford (SEESOX), a program with which I was affiliated between 2002 and 2009, I had the pleasure to co-convene a conference on Russia's involvement in the Balkans.

The bulk of the writing was done at Harvard University, where I spent more than a year at the Center for European Studies. I am grateful to Elaine Papoulias, a long-time friend who shares my passion for the politics of Turkey and the Balkans, to the CES director Grzegorz Ekiert, and to all fellows of the center whose generosity was only matched by their intellectual depth. My gratitude extends also to the Davis Center for Russian and Eurasian Studies, whose seminar series provided an excellent opportunity to present my work. Many thanks to Mark Kramer, Rawi Abdelal, and to Lenore Martin who tirelessly co-pilots the Turkish Studies Seminar, as well as to the Post-Communist Politics Working Group, especially Dmitry Gorenburg and Nadiya Kravets. At Harvard, I was privileged to get to know Joseph Nye whose scholarship I have admired since my undergraduate days and who helped sharpen my thinking about the project I had embarked upon. Last but not least, I am thankful to the Center for Slavic, Eurasian, and East European Studies at the University of North Carolina-Chapel Hill, and particularly to Milada-Anna Vachudová and Adnan Džumhur.

The list of people to whom I owe thanks is unmanageably long and includes colleagues who invited me as a speaker, chaired my talks, or were fellow panelists; those who were kind enough to read the chapters and provide critical feedback and advice; and, of course, those who spared the time to talk to me about the multitude of subjects I address in the book. There follows a list of names, in no particular order: Tim Judah, Amanda Paul, Damir Marušić, Wojcieh Ostrowski, Eamonn Butler, Iver Neumann, Roy Allison, Florian Bieber, Kerem Öktem, Vladimir Frolov, Nicu Popescu, Kalypso Nicolaidis, Cahtryn Clüver, Mesut Özcan, Bill Park, Alina Inayeh, Suat Kınıklıoğlu, Paul Ivan, Plamen Petrov, Srdja Pavlović, Ioannis Grigoriadis, Illin Stanev, Tolga Bölükbaşı, Martin Vladimirov, Pavel Anastasov, Josip Glaurdić, Suat Kınıklıoğlu, Vassilis Petsinis, Filip Ejdus, Ivan Krastev, Ilian Vassilev, Michael Taylor, Peter Pomerantsev,

Konstantin Eggert, Miloš Damnjanović, Kyril Drezov, Margarita Assenova, Tom Junes, Andrey Makarychev, Hanna Shelest, Simon Saradzhyan, David Koranyi, John Herbst, Galip Dalay, Ulrich Speck, Ümit Sönmez, Angela Stent, Jeffrey Mankoff, Loukas Tsoukalis, Tolga Bölükbaşı, Orysia Lutsevych, Michael Werz, Dušan Spasojević, Şaban Kardaş, David Patrikarakos, and Julian Popov. Needless to say, the blame for any errors and omissions is all mine.

I would also like to extend my thanks to the anonymous peer reviewers at Yale University Press who read my proposal and then the final draft. This book owes a great deal to Taiba Batool, Senior Commissioning Editor at Yale, who supported me from the very outset and guided me through the process. A heartfelt "thank you" to her as well as to the rest of the production team, including Jennie Doyle, Melissa Bond, and Samantha Cross. My gratitude also goes to Richard Mason, who copy-edited the text with great care.

Lastly, this book would not have been possible without my wife, Galina, with whom I have been through a lot over those three years. It was she along my parents-in-law, Penka and Georgi, who shared the joy—and shouldered the demanding tasks—of raising three children and helped me see the manuscript through. I wish to dedicate this book also to our loving memory of Georgi.

A NOTE ON TRANSLITERATION

I have rendered Russian words and names using the Romanization rules of the Library of Congress. The only exception is made for names already popularized with an alternative transliteration. Therefore, "Yeltsin" rather than "El'tsin". The Library of Congress system is applied to Greek as well. Serbian, Croatian, Bosnian, and Montenegrin names appear with the original diacritics, as do the ones in Turkish.

ABBREVIATIONS

A2/AD	Anti-access/area denial
AES	Atomexportstroy
AKEL	*Anorthōtikó Kómma Ergazoménou Laoú*, Progressive Party of the Working People (Cyprus)
AKP	*Adalet ve Kalkınma Partisi*, Justice and Development Party (Turkey)
ANAP	*Anavatan Partisi*, Motherland Party (Turkey)
ANB	*Agencija za nacijonalnu bezbednost*, National Security Agency (Montenegro)
ANEL	*Anexártētoi Éllēnes*, Independent Greeks
bcm	billion cubic meters (natural gas)
BIA	*Bezbednosno-informativna agencija*, Security and Information Agency (Serbia)
BSEC	Black Sea Economic Co-operation
BSP	Bulgarian Socialist Party
BTC	Baku–Tbilisi–Ceyhan oil pipeline
CDR	Romanian Democratic Convention, *Convenţia Democrată Română*
CSDP	Common Security and Defence Policy (EU)
CEF	Connecting Europe Facility (EU)
CIS	Commonwealth of Independent States
CSTO	Collective Security Treaty Organization

DANS	*Dârzhavna agenciya za nacionalna sigurnost*, State Agency for National Security (Bulgaria)
DDoS	distributed denial of service
DEPA	*Dēmósia Epiheirēsē Parohēs Aeríou*, Public Gas Corporation (Greece)
DISY	*Dēmokratikós Synagermós*, Democratic Rally (Cyprus)
DS	*Demokratska stranka*, Democratic Party (Serbia)
DSS	*Demokratska stranka Srbije*, Democratic Party of Serbia
DYP	*Doğru Yol Partisi*, True Path Party (Turkey)
EC	European Community
EDF	Électricité de France
EEU	Eurasian Economic Union
EEZ	Exclusive economic zone
EPS	*Elektroprivreda Srbije*, Electrical Industry of Serbia
EU	European Union
FRY	Federal Republic of Yugoslavia
FSB	*Federal'naia sluzhba bezopasnosti*, Federal Security Service (Russia)
FSN	*Frontul Salvării Naţionale*, National Salvation Front (Romania)
FTA	Free Trade Agreement
GECF	Gas Exporting Countries Forum
GDP	Gross Domestic Product
GERB	*Grazhdani za evropeysko razvitie na Bâlgaria*, Citizens for the European Development of Bulgaria
GRU	*Glavnoe razvedyvateľnoe upravlenie*, Main Intelligence Directorate (Soviet Union/Russia)
HDZ	*Hrvatska demokratska zajednica*, Croatian Democratic Union
ICJ	International Court of Justice
ICTY	International Criminal Tribunal for Former Yugoslavia
IFOR/SFOR	Implementation/Stabilization Force (NATO)

IGA	Intergovernmental Agreement
IPAP	Individual Partnership Action Plan (NATO)
ISIS	Islamic State of Iraq and the Levant
JNA	*Jugoslovenska narodna armija*, Yugoslav People's Army
KAP	*Kombinat Aluminijuma Podgorica*, Aluminum Smelter Combine of Podgorica
KFOR	Kosovo Force (NATO)
KGB	*Komitet gosudarstvennoi bezopasnosti*, State Security Committee
KKE	*Kommounistikó kómma tēs Elládas*, Communist Party of Greece
KLA	Kosovo Liberation Army
KTB	*Korportativna târgovska banka*, Corporate Commercial Bank
LNG	Liquefied natural gas
LTC	Long-term contract
MAP	Membership Action Plan (NATO)
MFA	Ministry of Foreign Affairs
NATO	North Atlantic Treaty Organization
ND	New Democracy (Greece)
NGO	Non-governmental organization
NIS	*Naftna Industrija Srbije*, Petroleum Industry of Serbia
OAF	Operation Allied Force (NATO)
OHR	Office of the High Representative (Bosnia and Herzegovina)
OIC	Organization of Islamic Conference (formerly "of the Islamic Conference")
OSCE	Organization of Security and Co-operation in Europe
PASOK	*Panellēnikó Sosialistikó Kínēma*, All-Greek Socialist Movement
PDSR	*Partidul Democrației Sociale din România*, Social Democracy Party of Romania
PfP	Partnership for Peace

PIC	Peace Implementation Council (Bosnia and Herzegovina)
PKK	*Partiya Karkerên Kurdistanê,* Kurdistan Workers' Party
PSD	*Partidul Social Democrat,* Social Democratic Party
PYD	*Partiya Yekîtiya Demokrat,* Democratic Union Party (Syria)
RISI	*Rossiiskii institut strategicheskikh issledovanii,* Russian Institute for Strategic Studies
ROC	Russian Orthodox Church
RS	Republika Srpska
SFRY	Socialist Federal Republic of Yugoslavia
SNS	*Srpska napredna stranka,* Serbian Progressive Party
SPS	*Socijalistička partija Srbije,* Socialist Party of Serbia
SRI	*Serviciul Român de Informaţii,* Romanian Intelligence Service
SVR	*Sluzhba vneshnei razvedki,* Foreign Intelligence Service (Russia)
TANAP	Trans-Anatolian Pipeline
TAP	Trans-Adriatic Pipeline
TEP	Third Energy Package
TIKA	*Türk İşbirliği ve Kalkınma İdaresi Başkanlığı,* Turkish International Co-operation and Development Agency
UDF	Union of Democratic Forces (Bulgaria)
UN	United Nations
UNMIK	United Nations Mission in Kosovo
UNPREDEP	UN Preventative Deployment Force (Macedonia)
UNPROFOR	UN Protection Force (Bosnia and Herzegovina)
UNSC	United Nations Security Council
USSR	Union of Soviet Socialist Republics
VRS	*Vojska Republike Srpske,* Republika Srpska's Army
VTB	Vneshtorgbank

INTRODUCTION
An Empire Returns

Russia is back. The same line crops up over and over again in news-paper columns, think-tank papers or policy speeches dealing with post-communist Europe. The Ukraine crisis, the annexation of Crimea in March 2014 and the war in the Donbas, the ensuing confrontation between Russia and the West, have all fueled fears that tensions could spill over west of the former Soviet borders. "Serbia, Kosovo, Montenegro, Macedonia, other places. They're all in the firing line [together with] Georgia, Moldova, Transnistria," stated Secretary of State John Kerry before the U.S. Senate's Foreign Relations Committee on 24 February 2015.[1] To Kerry and others, Russia's revisionism posed a threat not only in the "near abroad" but also across former Yugoslavia where the wounds of recent wars still festered. The link to Ukraine does not appear to be arbitrary either. After all, Moscow justified the takeover of Crimea with the prece-dent set by Kosovo's unilateral declaration of independence in February 2008. Vladimir Putin himself constantly brings up Russia's humiliation during the conflicts in ex-Yugoslavia in the 1990s to chastise the perfidy of the West.

Kerry has not been alone in seeing danger in the Balkans. Senior figures from the European Union (EU) share his concerns. In March 2017, Federica Mogherini, the EU's High Representative for Foreign Affairs and Security Policy, singled out Russia as a troublemaker and a challenger. "The Balkans can easily become one of the chessboards where the big power game can be played," she observed during a meeting of the EU's twenty-eight foreign ministers. "So the concern is there ... and it is profound."[2] The German Chancellor Angela Merkel had voiced such apprehensions as early as December 2014. In an interview for *Welt am Sonntag*, she had accused Russia of "trying to make certain Western Balkan states politically and economically dependent."[3] Merkel issued those words mere weeks after Putin, the strongman whom Germany had once regarded as a credible partner, was accorded a royal welcome in Belgrade. Amidst Western sanctions, Vladimir Vladimirovich was showing everyone that Russia could not be easily reduced to a pariah state. A host of countries and nations in Europe, from Serbia to Cyprus, continued regarding Moscow as a time-tested ally, not as a rogue or a menace.

Putin did have a point. In April 2015, the Greek Prime Minister Alexis Tsipras paid a highly publicized visit to Russia to solicit economic assistance as the threat of bankruptcy and a forced departure from the eurozone ("Grexit") loomed large. Despite the sanctions, politicians in Croatia and Slovenia have been looking eagerly for business opportunities, not unlike their counterparts in Hungary, the Czech Republic or Austria. Even Turkey, Russia's one-time imperial rival and pivotal American ally, has been reluctant to censure Moscow and cut profitable ties. Once the European Commission hit the brake on the South Stream, Russia's landmark project for a gas pipeline project traversing the Balkans, Putin announced in December 2014 from Ankara that Gazprom, the Russian Federation's national gas company,[4] would be building an alternative gas pipeline through Turkey, TurkStream. The whole of Southeast Europe appeared to be Moscow's stomping ground—just like in the days when the Romanovs ruled in St Petersburg or at the height of the Cold War.

This book is an account of Russia's engagement with Southeast Europe since the early 1990s. It addresses two sets of questions. First, what has been driving Moscow's policy in the region? What are the strategic goals and objectives that policymakers, both before and after Putin's ascent to power in 1999–2000, have been pursuing? How effective is Russia in deploying its assets and instruments: military muscle, diplomacy, energy exports, and—not least—soft power to spread its influence. Second, what explains the attitude and responses of local states to Russia? Why have they engaged and curried favor with Moscow? How have they balanced extensive security and economic links with the West, EU and NATO in particular, with ties to the Russians? And, by implication, what is the strategic significance for the West of the fact that Russia appears to have carved a niche in the Balkans and the Eastern Mediterranean.

The Reign of Pragmatism

Pundits easily succumb to the temptation to explain Russia's influence and popularity through the bonds of identity, religion, language, culture, and shared historical memories. Of course, the argument goes, the likes of Serbia, Greece, Bulgaria or Montenegro should look up to the Russians. It was, at the end of the day, Russia that had been waging one war after the other on behalf of kindred Eastern Orthodox nations in the south. The empire had dispensed patronage at least since the days of Catherine the Great, and it even had its rights enshrined in the 1774 peace treaty of Küçük Kaynarca with the Ottoman Empire.[5] Russia had helped Serbs, Greeks, and Bulgarians break free from Ottoman domination and build their own states. The centennial of the outbreak of the First World War in 2014 presented an occasion to be reminded of the deep, emotive ties linking Russia to its Balkan brethren; or, depending on your view, of how recalcitrant Serbia dragged the mighty Russian Empire into a conflict of pan-European proportions that ultimately brought down the Tsars and triggered the Bolshevik revolution. In 2014, however, the theme of camaraderie forged in hardship trumped all else. To commemorate the anniversary of the Great War, the Belgrade municipality unveiled a monument to Nicholas II, the last of the Romanov autocrats. As in 1914, Russia comes to the rescue of Southern Slavs and Orthodox Christians, whoever their adversaries might be: the arrogant West or radical Islam, American imperialism, the Vatican, godless liberalism, and so forth. Tomislav Nikolić, Serbia's president (2012–17), calls that "the unbreakable bond of brotherhood" (*neraskidiva veza bratstva*). Russian leaders, from Putin to Patriarch Kirill, reciprocate, framing their country's actions in cultural and civilizational terms. Having seized Crimea, the site where Prince Vladimir the Great converted to Christianity and made a Byzantine princess his wife, Moscow has dusted off the ancient myths of the Third Rome. Southeast Europe forms the bridge to the Second Rome, Constantinople, which itself is the source of Russia's civilizational identity. "Russia was seen as the heir of the Byzantine Empire that fell in 1453," Foreign Minister Sergei Lavrov proudly noted in a 2016 article.[6] When Vladimir Putin traveled to the monasteries of Mount Athos in May 2016, the hosts honored him by seating him on the throne once reserved for the Eastern Roman emperor.

Yet historical symbolism, for all its significance, is only one part of the story. This book's core message is that pragmatism and calculations of interest inform Russia's moves as well as the response of local players. The permanent seat in the UN Security Council makes Moscow a desirable ally on vital issues such as the division of Cyprus, the status of Kosovo, or post-conflict Bosnia. In addition, political elites and their friends in business are attracted by Russia's massive energy deals because of the juicy payoffs they entail. Governments perceive ties to Russia as a hedge, looking for extra room for maneuver and bargaining chips vis-à-vis the EU and the United States. This is true for countries as dissimilar as Serbia, pursuing a policy of neutrality, and Turkey, a leading NATO member. Both chose not to support the Western sanctions imposed in response to the annexation of Crimea and the war in eastern Ukraine. They preferred to sit on the fence and juggle options in a manner reminiscent of the former Yugoslav leader Josip Broz Tito, eager to avoid negative fallout from the East–West standoff but equally keen to exploit opportunities.

The bulk of analyses err in treating states in Southeast Europe as Russia's pawns, victims or historical hostages. Empirical evidence suggests otherwise. Often finding themselves under pressure from Russia, for example with regard to the terms of gas trade, they have tried to reverse the game and squeeze out concessions. Their under-standing of partnership has been instrumental. What transpires behind the lofty rhetoric of fraternity, pan-Slavism, Orthodox soli-darity, and historical bonds is often crude opportunism.

The Russian Federation's approach can be deciphered in terms of hard-nosed material interests as well. To quote the political scientist Vladimir Gel'man, "ideology as such has probably been the least meaningful factor in Russian politics since the Soviet collapse."[7] The observation applies to domestic affairs but even more so to foreign policy. In dealing with Southeast Europe, the Kremlin seeks leverage deployable in its power contest with the West. It also fends for corporations such as Gazprom, Lukoil, and Rosatom, which are both tools and beneficiaries of its policies. Thanks to its pragmatic gene, Russia is perfectly capable of doing business with all countries and nations, irrespective of the predominant religion or ethnic makeup, their historical dealings with the Romanovs or the Soviet Union, the level of exposure to Russian culture, and so on and so forth. "Virtually anyone can be a partner, and practically anyone can be an opponent," notes the political analyst Dmitri Trenin.[8] In Southeast Europe, Russia has dealings with former communists and Islamists, with nationalists and pro-Western liberals, populists and technocrats, oligarchs and intellectuals. As long as there is a scope for the deal, the price is right, and the opposite party can deliver on commitments, Moscow is open to business.

Hard-nosed pragmatism and the absence of ideological scru-ples differentiate Russia from both the Soviet Union and the Tsarist Empire. That is hardly surprising. After all, Russia has a fraction of the military power and economic assets it wielded at the height of the Cold War. It keeps no boots on the ground in Southeast Europe nor is it willing or able to bankroll potential client countries in the area. From Cyprus to Greece to Serbia, states have discovered the hard way that cashing in on Russia's friend-ship does not always work. When Moscow is indeed prepared to spend vast amounts of money to facilitate huge projects such as South Stream, it does so from the premise that it will take the lion's share of the attendant benefits. Overall, as we shall see, Russia often opts for assorted soft-power stratagems: presenting itself as a credible counterweight to Western hegemony, planting its narrative of world politics into local media, appealing to historical sentiments. It is a low-cost approach that neither puts Russia's scarce resources under strain nor generates much risk.

Russia's moves are in accordance with the ebbs and flows of its relations with the West. On more than one occasion, Moscow has shifted gears from co-operation to competition and back again. A thaw under President Dmitry Medvedev (2008–12), defined by the reset (*perezagruzka*) with the United States and the so-called partnership with Europe, gave way to heated confrontation, if not a new Cold War, after Putin returned to the presidency. In Southeast Europe, relations have fluctuated too. At times, Russia co-operated—begrudgingly—with the West, as in the wake of the 1999 NATO intervention in Kosovo. The Yugoslav President Slobodan Milošević had to concede defeat after Russia joined forces with the United States and EU demanding a diplomatic solution. On other occasions, it opted for confrontation: for example, the anti-Western information campaign unleashed since 2014. However, Moscow accepts, tacitly if not directly, that the Balkans fall within the Western sphere of influence. It expects that, like Bulgaria, Romania, Croatia, or Slovenia, the entire region may eventually integrate into the EU—or whatever remains of it. In contrast to the Eastern neighbourhood, Russia is not in a position to roll back Western influence. What it is capable of, however, is to project influence, cultivate allies, and profit from opportunities as they arise.

Or indeed, stir trouble. "As well as being the EU's backyard, the Balkans are the underbelly of Brussels' diplomacy," wrote the Bulgarian analyst Ivan Krastev on the pages of *The Financial Times*. "This is the place to apply pressure, if Moscow wants to make Europeans feel uncomfortable."[9] Southeast Europe is the "weakest link in the EU", concurred another Bulgarian, President Rosen Plevneliev, pointing at "nationalists, oligarchs, corruption, propaganda and energy dependence" that, in his opinion, bolstered Russia's disruptive potential.[10] According to Kolinda Grabar-Kitarović, the president of Croatia, "Russia is waging a hybrid war in Bosnia".[11] In

October 2016, the Montenegrin government pointed a finger at Russia for plotting a coup d'état in league with rogue security operatives from neighbouring Serbia. More than that, Serbian Prime Minister Aleksandar Vučić's life was allegedly under threat. Whatever the truth about this murky affair—and there are many unanswered questions, to be sure—it is hard to deny that Moscow benefits from instability on Europe's periphery. And the fact that Montenegro and Serbia are in the crosshairs proves that even Russia's best friends are at risk of being double-crossed, as they engage in a precarious balancing act between East and West. Russia can reward but also make life difficult for Balkan politicians.

History Matters—or Does It?

The strong emphasis on present-day concerns, ideas, developments, movers and shakers is not to suggest that the past is irrelevant ("it is another country, they do things differently there", as the saying goes) and that the shadow of history should not be of much interest. This is clearly not the case. But what is worth remembering is that "history" is invariably more complex than the two-line version one gets from newspaper articles—for example, "Russia's traditional influence in the Balkans". A central theme in this book is the ambiguous legacy of the past. Despite cultural links and political alignments, Russia never had the benefit of a harmonious relationship with its clients, real or presumed. That was eloquently captured by Barbara Jelavich, an eminent scholar of Balkan history, in her first-rate study of Russia's entanglement in the region during the period from the early 1800s to 1914:

> With an attitude often characterised as heavy-handed benevolence, the Russian officials serving in the Balkans expected the local regimes to follow their leadership and treat their commands with respect and gratitude. ... Unfortunately for their success, no Balkan regime or political leader looked upon Russia, its tsar, or its representatives in this same manner. ... [T]he political leaders correctly judged that Russia was the

great power from which aid could most easily be obtained. Once Russian military and financial resources had been utilised, however, they wanted the benefactor to go home. They did not consider the fact that most debts, whether private or national, usually must be paid.[12]

Plus ça change plus c'est la même chose. Motifs like mutual misunderstandings, divergent interests, and betrayed expectations are as pertinent today as in the period surveyed by Jelavich. The romanticized reading of the past is an indispensable rhetorical tool in the hands of decision makers, but it also has the tendency to cloud judgment about current events. It is common for Russian commentators, particularly those with a nationalist bent, to insist that Balkan peoples owe a great debt to Russia, on account of the blood and resources spent for their liberation, most recently from Nazi Germany. "How could you join NATO and turn your back to Russia after everything we have done for you?" they reproach Bulgarians or Montenegrins. But to be sure, there are similar grudges heard on the other side. A widespread complaint in Serbia is that Russia, loved and admired though it is, has the penchant for putting its interests as a great power first, often at the expense of commitments made to its brethren in the Balkans.

Russian attitudes to the region and its peoples were just as ambivalent in the dominant era of the great powers, the nineteenth century. Romanticism and the lofty sentiments of solidarity with the suffering brethren cohabited with misgivings and an attitude of imperial superiority. Pan-Slavists of the 1860s and 1870s appealed to Mother Russia's calling as the protector of the enslaved Eastern Orthodox peoples. Yet conservative thinkers such as the novelist Fyodor Dostoevsky or the philosopher Konstantin Leont'ev harbored deep suspicions regarding the brotherly nations in Southeast Europe. They were fearful of the pernicious germ of European social and cultural mores and institutions spreading across the Balkans, a process well underway in the middle of the nineteenth century even in some remote corners of the Ottoman Empire. "Russia must seriously prepare herself to watch all these liberated Slavs rushing

rapturously off to Europe to be infected by European forms, both
political and social, to the point their own personalities are lost; and
so they will have to undergo a whole long period of Europeanism
before comprehending anything of their own significance as Slavs
and their particular Slavic mission amongst humanity."[13]

Strikingly, these lines imbued with pessimism were written in
November 1877, at the very height of pan-Slavic fervor. Following
uprisings in Herzegovina (1875–77) and Bulgaria (1876), popular
enthusiasm for the South Slavs had reached unprecedented levels,
fueled by the newspapers and by pressure groups such as the Slavic
Benevolent Society (*Slavianskoe blagotvoritel'noe obschestvo*) headed
by Ivan Aksakov. Defying his superiors in St Petersburg, General
Mikhail Cherniaev had joined the Serbian Army to lead its war
against the Porte in 1876, drawing scores of Russian volunteers under
his flag. In April 1877, Russia had declared war on the Ottomans and
by February 1878 its troops reached the gates of Constantinople—in
the vicinity of where Istanbul's Atatürk International Airport stands
today. Bulgaria was about to emerge as a state under Russian tutelage,
while Romania, Serbia, and Montenegro, allied with St Petersburg
during the war, would gain independence. And yet, Dostoevsky's
instinct—which certainly went against the grain of public opinion—
suggested that the *Drang nach Süden* was fraught with risks:

> Russia never will have and never has had anyone who can
> hate, envy, slander, and even display open enmity toward her
> as much as these Slavic tribes will the moment Russia liberates
> them and Europe agrees to recognize their liberation. ...
> I repeat: after their liberation they will begin their new life by
> asking Europe—England and Germany, for instance—for guar-
> antees and protection of their freedom and, even though Russia
> will also be a part of the concert of European powers, they will
> do this precisely as a means of defence against *Russia* [original
> emphasis].[14]

The same motifs of debt, ingratitude, betrayal, and misplaced syco-
phancy towards the decadent West may sound painfully familiar to

students of today's Russian foreign policy and the way in which the country's leaders regard its former satellites in Eastern Europe.

Leont'ev's critique was even more profound than that of Dostoevsky. His 1876 treatise *Byzantinism and Slavdom (Vizantinizm i slavianstvo)* staged a frontal charge against nationalism thriving among Balkan peoples, Bulgarians in particular, as an unwelcome import from the West, tearing apart the cherished principles of religious universalism and the unity of the Orthodox Church. To a Philhellene, or more properly a Philo-Orthodox, like Leont'ev, pan-Slavism constituted nothing more than a subversive doctrine of Western derivation that undermined the hallowed Christian tradition preserved over centuries in Southeast Europe by the Patriarchate of Constantinople and, by implication, eroded Russia's own moral foundations.[15]

Leont'ev's qualms were not completely groundless. The Russian Empire of Alexander II was itself in the business of spreading the Western gospel. In 1879, Sergei Lukianov, a Russian jurist attached to the governor of newly established Bulgaria, Prince Aleksandr Dondukov-Korsakov, drafted the new country's constitution enshrining principles such as the rule of law and universal male suffrage. This occurred at a time when Russia did not have a written constitution of its own, despite the era of reforms it was going through, including the abolition of serfdom in 1861. Furthermore, the Russian intellectuals and thinkers who would have the most lasting impact on Southern Slavs would not be those of conservative persuasion but the radicals opposed to Tsarist autocracy: the anarchists, the populists (*narodniki*), the socialists, the utopians, the Herzens and the Tolstoys, the Bakunins and the Lenins. To cut a long story short, there was an ill-concealed tension about the Russian presence and imprint on the Balkans—that of Russia as the Third Rome on a messianic quest to build a new Byzantium versus Russia as part of the West, a card-carrying member of the Concert of Europe and, in a sense, promoter of its *mission civilisatrice*.

Switching from the realm of ideology to the practice of foreign policy, Russia confronted tough dilemmas as regards intervention in the Balkans. During the Great Eastern Crisis of 1875–78, decision makers in St Petersburg came under sustained pressure from Slavophile public opinion. But appeals to the Tsar to fulfill his duty as protector of Orthodox Slavs and reclaim Constantinople and the Straits raised concern with risk-averse statesmen such as Prince Aleksandr Gorchakov, foreign minister between 1856 and 1882. He sought to avoid another debacle after the Crimean War (1853–56) and advised caution, a perspective shared by other key officials, the Minister of War Count Dmitrii Miliutin and even the Tsar himself. And although Russia "bumbled into war", to borrow a phrase from Robert Legvold, it stopped short of destroying the Ottoman Empire in 1878 or making a doomed bid to establish its hegemony over Southeast Europe.[16] The Treaty of Berlin brokered by German Chancellor Otto von Bismarck gave significant conces-sions to Austria-Hungary and Britain, thwarting the aspirations of Russia's Balkan allies. In other words, Realpolitik prevailed over messianism and the sense of moral obligation to fellow Slavs. By contrast, in the fateful summer of 1914, Russia chose to go beyond the brink in order to back Serbia—overestimating its chances in a military showdown against Germany and Austria-Hungary, with France and Britain as its allies. And it is not that Russian officials were oblivious of the risks. In 1912, a farsighted diplomat wrote:

> Russian policy was to a great degree guided by assumptions & catchphrases such as Russia's historic tasks, the balance of power ... natural obligations to the Slavs, the Straits were the key to Russia's home & must rest in Russian hands ... All these clichés were dangerous nonsense that were leading Russia toward a continental war in the near future that would serve the interests only of revolutionary socialism.[17]

All those dilemmas, tensions, conflicts, and points of ambiguity showcase the complexity of Russia's historical relationship with Southeast Europe. Sadly, they have mostly been erased from public memory, which by definition is selective. Both Russia and the bulk of Balkan countries privilege the moments of convergence over conflict. In Serbia, for instance, Nicholas II overshadows Joseph

Stalin and the schism with Tito in 1948, which limited Yugoslavia's social and cultural connections to Russia until the 1990s. In a sense, the link was stronger in the interwar period thanks to the White Russian émigrés who settled in Belgrade and other Yugoslav cities (as they did also in neighbouring Bulgaria, making an enormous contribution to society, cultural life, and science). Similarly, Bulgarians and Russians celebrate the memory of the 1877–78 war of liberation. Vladimir Putin timed his visits to Sofia in 2003 and 2008 around the anniversary of the 1878 Treaty of San Stefano (3 March/19 February in the Old Style), Bulgaria's national holiday. By contrast, there is rarely a mention of the First World War when the two countries clashed on the battlefield. In much the same vein, Greeks and Russians revel in the bonds forged by common faith. However, the longstanding rivalry between the Patriarch of Moscow and All Russia and the Ecumenical Patriarch in Constantinople over the leadership of the Eastern Church, seen recently in the Russian boycott of the Pan-Orthodox Council in Crete (19–26 June 2016), rarely comes to the fore.

A word must also be said about the Second World War and how it is memorialized in the present. Central to Russia's conception of itself post-1991, the memory of the war is often invoked by Moscow in its dealings with Southeast Europe. Not only did Russia liberate the region from the Ottomans but it also fought back Teutonic imperialists, first the Habsburgs and then Hitler's Third Reich, expelling the Nazis in the autumn of 1944. Yet, in Southeast Europe, the war opens up traumatic memories of deep divisions within and between countries. Although the Soviets are credited for their role in defeating fascism, there are nuances. For instance, in commemorating the war, former Yugoslavia celebrated indigenous resistance, the partisans, and Josip Broz Tito's leadership, less so the decisive contribution of the Red Army. The same is true of Albania. Elsewhere, for example in Bulgaria and Romania, the Soviet victory against Hitler is venerated by the left but questioned in other quarters. The post-communist right describes Nazism and Stalinism as two sides of the same coin, lamenting the decades of communist rule, the erosion of national institutions and sovereignty by Moscow and its local proxies. And, as elsewhere in Europe, there are no shortage of Nazi apologists on the extreme right end of the spectrum. In Greece, the Second World War is inextricably linked to the Civil War (1946–49) and the left-right polarization shaping politics and society decades thereafter, with old grudges and traumas still only partially healed.

The point of this brief historical sketch is that the past is not a monolith. Rather, it is a repository of multifaceted, often dissonant and conflicting experiences, events, and memories. As such, what we call "history" is susceptible to political distortion to the point of outright manipulation. Leaders, parties, intellectuals, journalists, foreign-policy pundits pick and choose those bits and fragments of the past that suit them best in the present, casting Russia as a hero or a rogue, big brother, a beacon of Orthodoxy, a European great power, heir to the almighty Soviet Union, or indeed an evil empire on the bounce back. Southeast Europe certainly boasts a long and distinguished Russophile tradition, which inevitably feeds into present-day politics. But the link between Russia and the Balkans was never as organic, unbreakable or intimate as many authors and commentators seem to believe.

What is Southeast Europe?

The focus of this study is Southeast Europe. That might seem a puzzling choice. To start with, what is "Southeast Europe", does it constitute a coherent whole, what makes it a region and therefore distinct from other regions? Secondly, how does the Russian Federation come into the picture? Why zoom in on this particular area, rather than take a broader perspective on Russia in the international politics of Europe?

As any "region", that of Southeast Europe is not immune to contestation. Scholars, pundits, and politicians have broken spears in debating where its borders lie, which country is in and which is out. This book takes an inclusive approach and defines the area as comprising the republics of former Yugoslavia, Albania, Romania, and Bulgaria. It also covers Greece, Cyprus, and Turkey, countries that did not experience communist rule during the Cold War. Having Cyprus and Turkey in justifies the use of "Southeast Europe", rather than "the Balkans", though the latter term appears throughout the book as well. One of the problems with the Balkans is that the great majority of Western policymakers along with many pundits treat it as synonymous with ex-Yugoslavia (or the "Western Balkans" if we are to use the EU nomenclature). Thus most writings on "Russia in the Balkans" are exclusively preoccupied with the successors of Tito's socialist federation but have little to say about the wider region. That hidden bias inhibits analysis. It is hard to gauge the significance and implications of cross-border energy projects promoted by Moscow without taking a broader view.

What then brings those countries, from Turkey to Croatia or even Slovenia, together? First of all, they have a shared past, having been, with some notable exceptions (Slovenia, the westernmost regions of Croatia, northwestern Romania, parts of the Montenegrin coast, Greece's Ionian Islands), provinces or protectorates of the Ottoman Empire. Second, the countries in question form a geographical continuum. This fact became patently obvious with the migration crisis of 2015–16 when vast numbers of refugees and asylum seekers from Syria, Iraq, Afghanistan, and other wartorn countries crossed from Turkey into Greece and ex-Yugoslavia en route to the core of Europe. Contiguity does not mean countries have no strong historical, spatial, societal, and human connection to other regions: Central Europe, the Black Sea, the Middle East (in Turkey's case), and so on. But what weighs in is of course politics. Having gained a name for turbulence and violent upheavals and having contributed a term as negatively laden as "Balkanization" to the vocabulary of international relations, the region boasts a decent record of multilateral diplomacy, some of which dates as far back as the 1930s. All the states covered in this book have been participants in a web of regional institutions and co-operation schemes that has grown thicker since the late 1990s, Cyprus being the only exception.

Both the Balkans and broader Southeast Europe have been defined and shaped by European integration. Starting with Greece in 1981, the EU has enlarged to cover parts of the region. The Republic of Cyprus joined in 2004 along with Slovenia, followed by Bulgaria and Romania in 2007, and Croatia in 2013. The rest are lining up at the gates of the Union. Even Turkey, with its membership talks grinding to a halt, is deeply enmeshed within the EU single market thanks to the customs union it has in place. The EU remains the principal trading partner for the region, accounting for between 40 and 80 percent of trade depending on the country (see Figure 1 below). The EU is also the main source of foreign direct investment (FDI), even for a major player like Turkey—seeking to diversify economic relations away from Europe—where the share is as high as 80 percent. The lowering of tariffs and non-tariff barriers conditioned by the EU has given an unprecedented boost to commercial ties within the region, blurring former divides. For instance, both Turkey and Greece have been trading heavily with their neighbours to the north. The EU provides the political and economic framework holding Southeast Europe together.

In the economy, Russia plays second fiddle (at best) to the EU. It is the main supplier of gas and oil but not a significant export market or purveyor of FDI. Virtually every country runs large trade deficits with Russia due to hydrocarbon imports and the premium prices charged by Gazprom. This is why governments have always struggled to balance the ledger, hoping to bring more Russian

	EU		Russia	
	Imports	Exports	Imports	Exports
Bosnia and Herzegovina	86.2%	81%	3.5%	1.5%
Bulgaria	63.4%	63.3%	12%	1.6%
Greece	52.7%	48.5%	10%	1.6%
Macedonia	76.6%	65.9%	1%	1.2%
Montenegro	42.3%	39.6%	>1%	
Serbia	62.5%	65.8%	9.6%	5.4%
Turkey	38%	44.5%	9.9%	2.5%

Source: European Commission, UNCTAD

Figure 1 EU/Russia share in external trade in goods, 2015

tourists to the resorts on the Aegean, Mediterranean, Adriatic and Black Sea coasts, to attract investment in strategic energy infrastructure, to slash natural gas prices, and to improve market access for agricultural products, manufactures (e.g. Fiat cars assembled in Serbia), pharmaceuticals, and so on.

This does not make Russia irrelevant—not at all. As a 2016 report by the Washington-based Center for Strategic and International Studies (CSIS) observes, its economic footprint is rather large—thanks to FDI, in some cases channeled through EU members such as the Netherlands, Austria, and Cyprus. According to the authors, Russia's share reaches a full 22 percent of GDP in Bulgaria and around 14 percent in Serbia. What is more, "Russian companies in [Central and Eastern Europe] have tended to be concentrated in a few strategic economic sectors, such as energy and fuel processing and trading, whereas EU countries have a more diversified investment portfolio that spans different manufacturing subsectors."[18] Consequently, Russia can get "the maximum bang for its buck" and harness economic links to serve political ends. Nor should we forget, moreover, the dependency of Russian energy firms on the state.

The EU has seen its clout eroding. Europeanization has proven both a blessing and a curse for the region. The financial, economic, institutional, and political crisis shattering the Union after 2008 has sent shockwaves to its periphery. Greece, the region's frontrunner, stands out as a cautionary tale of the pitfalls of halfway transformation coupled with the adoption of a transnational currency, the euro. Crisis in the eurozone has sapped demand for Balkan exports, led to a severe contraction of banking credit, FDI, and remittances. As a result, Serbia has actually gone through a triple-dip recession between 2009 and 2014. International indices suggest that democratization, Brussels' key political export item, has stalled too. In some cases, there has been a pronounced backslide towards authoritarianism. Turkey is the most prominent example but certainly not the only one. The migrant crisis, Great Britain's Brexit referendum, and the election of Donald Trump as U.S. president, putting in question security commitments to European allies, all have dealt further blows to the EU's "transformative power" over its periphery.

Russia's three moments

Economic stagnation, defunct democracies, and the weakening pull of Europe have all presented opportunities to Russia to come and fill the gap. The CSIS report quoted above contends, "Russia seeks to gain influence over (if not control of) critical state institutions, bodies, and the economy, and uses that influence to shape national policies and decisions. Corruption is the lubricant on which this system operates, concentrating on the exploitation of state resources to further Russia's networks of influence."[19]

Some analysts talk of "Putinization" or Putinism as a full-blown ideological alternative to Western liberal democracy. They assure us that the cult of the strong leader, holding the economy and the security apparatus in his iron grip, taming the media, corroding the rule of law, and stamping out dissent, is Russia's most successful export item. Such anxieties intensified after the annexation of Crimea, as testified by the quotations from American and EU dignitaries. In reality, most of those challenges appear to be homebred, rather than attributable to Russia's wrongdoing. From the rise of strongmen, to the decline in media freedom, to the difficulties in reforming judiciaries and uprooting corruption, pathologies in political development have deep roots in both the Balkans and Turkey.

This book argues that, unlike the EU, Russia has no grand plan and does not pursue an ideological vision, in contrast to the Soviet days. It is a power animated by the ambition to rival the West but it is also an opportunist. The essence of its policy is playing a weak hand the best possible way, taking advantage of others' weaknesses. While illiberal trends in domestic politics, the malfunctions of EU enlargement, and Turkey's pursuit of greater autonomy in international affairs are not of Russia's making, they have given wind to its sails. Russia's overarching goal has been tactical—improving its relative position in European politics—not the creation of a political and ideological order underwritten by its power and resources.

Russian policy in Southeast Europe has gone through three main stages. During stage one, coinciding with Boris Yeltsin's two terms in office (1991–99), Moscow tried to assert itself as a

power of equal standing with the United States and the principal
states of Western Europe as a co-manager of the region's security.
Having disbanded the Warsaw Pact and COMECON (Council for
Mutual Economic Assistance),[20] and having largely left Romania
and Bulgaria, Russia engaged diplomatically, politically, and militarily in former Yugoslavia in order to preserve its status as a senior
stakeholder in European affairs. In doing so, it had to strike a delicate balance between its ambitions and the imperative of maintaining good relations with the West. After setbacks in Bosnia and
especially Kosovo, this phase ended in 2003 when President
Vladimir Putin pulled Russian peacekeepers out of the Balkans.
The 1990s, particularly the perceived humiliation in Kosovo, left a
deep psychological scar in Moscow. The trauma informed the
Kremlin's pushback against the West in the post-Soviet space.

In the second stage, ushered in by the first gas crisis with Ukraine
in 2006, Russia made a comeback. This time round, it returned in the
guise of a hydrocarbon superpower. Southeast Europe turned into a
centerpiece of the strategy to diminish dependence on transit routes
through the former Soviet Union. Russia's intention was not to roll
back the EU but rather to obtain a foothold and shape Europe's
energy policies according to its own needs and preferences. That
period witnessed the peak of Moscow's influence. The list of achievements included the reinvigorated alliance with Serbia following
Kosovo's unilateral declaration of independence, the broad coalition
of states rallying behind South Stream, and the unprecedented
rapprochement with Turkey underway since the late 1990s.

The Ukraine crisis of 2013–14 came as a game-changer. The
standoff with the West made Russia opt for confrontation in
Southeast Europe as well. It has sought to undermine EU policies
there, oppose NATO enlargement and the Western sanctions, acting
as a spoiler. Russia has interfered more directly in the domestic
politics of a number of countries too, playing on anti-Western
resentment. Yet, at the same time, its energy clout has been degraded
with the cancellation of South Stream, which epitomized the
resulting collateral damage of rising tensions with the EU. The new
Russian strategy falls back on soft power through the use of media

and strategic communications. The policy has been partially successful: a number of governments have refused to sign up to the sanctions. However, even Moscow's best friends in the Balkans continue to see the EU as their principal partner.

Overview of the Chapters

The book is divided into two parts. Part I is mostly historical and recounts the development of Russia's political and economic relations with countries or closely related clusters of countries in Southeast Europe. Chapter 1 traces involvement in the Yugoslav wars between 1991 and 1999. Shaped by distinguished figures such as Foreign Ministers Andrei Kozyrev and Evgenii Primakov (prime minister in 1998–99), the Russian Federation played an active role pursuing recognition as a key European power by the West. However, the conflict in Bosnia and especially NATO's Operation Allied Force (OAF) in Kosovo witnessed the failure of the policy.

Chapter 2 deals with Russia's relations with post-Yugoslav republics since 2000, telling the story of its alignment with Serbia over Kosovo and the growth of its economic and political footprint across the Western Balkans.

Bulgaria and Romania, two former satellites of the Soviet Union, are the subject of Chapter 3. Viewed respectively as a pro-Russian and a diehard Russophobe country, both have toed a pragmatic line, balancing their interests against those of Moscow but also engaging with it. Much like in the Western Balkans, Russia has been successful in influencing domestic politics in Bulgaria.

Chapter 4 looks at Greece and Cyprus. Russia's alleged "Trojan horses" inside the EU have cultivated ties with Moscow over many decades, as a security hedge against next-door Turkey. However, neither Athens nor Nicosia has been able to fully capitalize on their friendship with the Russians and accrue significant benefits, especially in a time of sharp economic downturn.

Part I finishes with a chapter on Russian–Turkish relations. It follows the origins and course of the unprecedented political rapprochement between Moscow and Ankara based on economic interdependence, the short-lived crisis erupting in the autumn of 2015 with the downing of the Russian Sukhoi Su-24M bomber and the speedy reconciliation that followed, as well as the impact on Turkey's neighbours in the Balkans and the Black Sea area.

Part II takes a thematic approach and discusses Russia's presence and influence across three fields or dimensions: security, energy, and soft power. Chapter 6 argues that the annexation of Crimea and the consequent militarization of the Black Sea has changed defense relations between Russia on one side, and NATO members Turkey, Romania, and Bulgaria on the other. Elsewhere in Southeast Europe, in the Western Balkans and the Aegean, Russia's role remains more limited yet the presence of neutral states such as Serbia and Cyprus plays to its advantage.

Chapter 7 contends that Russian energy clout is in decline in comparison to the golden era in the 2000s. EU policies and rules regulating cross-border infrastructure and trade in natural gas have tipped the balance of power away from the Kremlin and Gazprom and in favor of consumers.

Chapter 8 contains an appraisal of Russian soft power. Moscow enjoys success because it preaches to the converted, taking advantage of deeply ingrained anti-Americanism and Islamophobia in a number of societies. It has invested in media and strategic communications, and in links with political parties and civic groups.

The Epilogue recaps the main themes and arguments put forward in the chapters. It also takes a broader look at Russia's complex relationship with the West since the onset of what many have described as "a new Cold War" and discusses its repercussions in Southeast Europe.

PART I

RUSSIA AND THE COUNTRIES OF
SOUTHEAST EUROPE

CHAPTER 1

THE BALKANS REDISCOVERED
Russia and the Breakup of Yugoslavia

Regular contacts between Moscow and Belgrade seem to be enabling Russia to play the role of mediator between the West and the Serbs as well as to show the opposition at home its international influence. Though, we must admit that the "special relations", "historical links" and Moscow's "strong influence" on Serb leadership could have yielded a greater effect. Unfortunately, one can speak now not only about Moscow influencing Belgrade, but also about Belgrade and Pale manipulating Moscow for their own ends. The attitude to Russia is modified by both the historical tradition of Russian–Serbian rivalry in the Balkans (their "being allies from the start" is a historical-political myth) and the undeniable weakening of Russia's position, whose power and influence cannot be compared with those of the Russian Empire or the Soviet Union.

—Editorial comment, *Kommersant*, 29 July 1995[1]

Yugoslavia's violent implosion in the 1990s may now be consigned to the realm of memory, but it is a piece of memory that resonates to this day in Russia. Vladimir Putin, his entourage, nationalist opinion makers, and intellectuals regularly invoke the humiliation at the hands of the United States and its allies in Kosovo. "Russia was pretty close to following the Yugoslav scenario [of disintegration]," the president remarked in April 2015, reflecting on the turbulent 1990s.[2] "Lessons learned" in the Balkans fed into the push to harden control over "the near abroad" in the mid-2000s and more recently, in Putin's third term in the Kremlin. The recognition of Abkhazia and South Ossetia as independent states and the annexation of Crimea have all been framed as a response to the precedent that the West set unilaterally in Kosovo.

In its day, the Yugoslav conflict[3] presented a formidable challenge to President Boris Yeltsin. The question of how post-Soviet Russia would respond polarized its nascent politics. It prompted fervent debate about the country's path after the collapse of empire, its relationship with the West and its place in the post-Cold War order. Moscow's policy fluctuated, pulled apart by competing demands. Yeltsin and his team prioritized good ties with the West essential for Russia's transition to a market economy and political pluralism. They also wished to preserve the country's influence over European and global affairs, defusing nationalist opposition at home. After a liberal prelude, Russia chose to be a tough partner and occasional naysayer to the United States and its European allies. The outcomes were disappointing. The war in Bosnia and Herzegovina exposed Moscow's weakness, while Kosovo was nothing short of a fiasco. On both occasions, Russia was left with no choice but to adjust to the consequences of NATO's actions.

Moscow's presumptive local allies in Belgrade and Bosnia's Republika Srpska (RS) also caused a headache. (Republika Srpska was the self-proclaimed state of the Bosnian Serbs that became in 1995 one of the two constitutional and legal entities of Bosnia and Herzegovina; the other is the Federation of Bosnia and Herzegovina.) They never baulked at opportunities to harness Russian policy and make it work for themselves. They created *faits accomplis* and seized on opportunities to influence Russia's domestic politics. Aligning with the Serbs did grant Moscow leverage but it imposed costs at the same time. Appeals to religious and ethno-cultural solidarity empowered Slobodan Milošević and the Bosnian Serbs and could threaten, if pushed to the limit, an all-out confrontation with the West, damaging Russian interests. In parallel, post-Yugoslav leaders had no qualms in using ties to Moscow as a bargaining chip to pursue separate deals with Western powers.

The Yugoslav (Dis)connection

In the course of the 1990s many came to believe that the Soviet Union and, later on, Russia and (former) Yugoslavia had strong connections and that what happened in one of those countries would affect the other. That was true only in part. The Yugoslav conflict happened as Moscow was radically downscaling its presence in East-Central Europe, dismantling "the outer empire" and the Warsaw Pact. On balance, the Russian Federation continued to view itself as a pivotal European power, having inherited the USSR's permanent seat on the United Nations Security Council (UNSC) along with the bulk of its military and diplomatic assets. Even if it had chosen to stay out of the Yugoslav quagmire, Moscow would have been drawn in by default.

But the prevalent view at the time was that Russia's interest in Yugoslavia, and Southeast Europe as a whole, ran much deeper. Apparently it was the call of blood, faith, and history, not the cold, impersonal logic of power politics, that was in motion. The Western media bought fully into that viewpoint. For instance, in August 1994, *The New York Times* piece remarked casually that "[t]he Russians have for centuries been allies of the Serbs, who share their Eastern Orthodox religious tradition."[4] Nationalists and conservatives in Russia, Serbia, and elsewhere happily echoed similar views. It felt as if the Russia of the Romanovs had awakened, by a magic spell, from seven and a half decades of sleep to re-embrace its loyal ally from 1914. The time in between was of lesser significance. Seemingly, the rift dividing the Soviets from both royalist and socialist Yugoslavia counted for little.

In actual fact, the intervening decades had left their indelible mark. After the 1948 split between Tito and Stalin, Yugoslavia built its appeal on the insistence that it was *unlike* the USSR. It developed a more liberal interpretation of Marxism-Leninism, introduced a mix of market policies and central planning in the economy, and adopted a non-aligned course in foreign affairs. While political and economic relations with Moscow went through multiple ups and downs, personal and cultural links remained tenuous. Yugoslav citizens could travel to the Soviet Union but the opposite was not true. Only in the 2000s did Russians start flocking to the Adriatic beaches, long popular with Western tourists, in any significant numbers. Bulgarians, Romanians or Hungarians could tune their antennas to Yugoslav television but Soviet viewers could not. Beyond the academic or expert *milieux*, it proved hard for most people to gain much familiarity with the intricate history, model of governance, and ethnic or confessional makeup of the Socialist Federal Republic of Yugoslavia (SFRY).[5] As a Russian journalist put it, "Hardly anyone could tell a Serb from a Croat back then."[6]

The chasm narrowed only after Mikhail Gorbachev came to power as General Secretary of the Communist Party of the Soviet Union in March 1985. *Perestroika*'s project of rejuvenating socialism and giving it "a human face" could draw lessons from the Yugoslav experience with self-management and decentralization. Gorbachev would later write that his much-publicized tour across Yugoslavia (14–18 March 1988) "closed the period of hostility and disintegration".[7] Sadly, those embryonic trends towards convergence did not last long. It was not for Yugoslav democrats and reformers like the last prime minister, Ante Marković, to forge a common cause, but rather for the ultranationalists.

In the late 1980s and early 1990s, Moscow's relations with Serbian communist party leader and president Slobodan Milošević were anything but a foregone conclusion. Neither Gorbachev nor Yeltsin, who oversaw the Russian Federation's journey to independence, had reasons to sympathize with the strongman in Belgrade. The mix between communism and ethno-nationalism and the bid to "save" Yugoslavia by recasting it as a Serb-dominated state found little approval in Moscow. At the same time, Gorbachev opposed secessionism and did not shy from using force to crack down on pro-independence rallies in Tbilisi (April 1989), Vilnius and Riga (January 1991). That is why the Soviet media instinctively sided with Belgrade as hostilities broke out in Slovenia and Croatia during the summer of 1991. In March, the Yugoslav defense minister, Veljko Kadijević, had made a surprise visit to Moscow. Reportedly, he discussed plans for a Soviet intervention with his opposite number, General Dmitrii Iazov, an event that would have turned decades of Yugoslav security policy on its head.[8] Yet talks were inconclusive. As much as he frowned upon Croatian and Slovenian separatism, Gorbachev could not find common ground with an aspiring autocrat like Milošević. His only plausible interlocutors were the protagonists of the August putsch, including Iazov and the head of the KGB, Vladimir Kriuchkov. But the Soviet hardliners were not keen to intervene either. The most they could give Kadijević and Borisav Jović, the Serbian member of the Yugoslav presidency, were assurances that the West would not step in either.[9] As the dramatic events of August 1991 unfolded in Moscow, Milošević kept a low profile, busy with issues closer to home. However, the lingering sentiment in Moscow a year afterwards is that he was on the side of the would-be junta. At any rate, that is how Milošević was seen by Yeltsin, who led the effort to resist the coup attempt.[10]

"Our task is to show that we are with you"

From the outset, Yeltsin wanted to avoid a Yugoslav scenario. Contrary to both Milošević and Gorbachev, he subscribed to the idea that republics, Russia included, should be allowed to make a free choice and therefore live in peace. He came out strongly about the military clampdown in the Baltic States, which in all likelihood emboldened the JNA (*Jugoslovenska narodna armija*, or Yugoslav People's Army) to strike against Croatia and Slovenia later in 1991.[11] After the USSR unraveled, Yeltsin did not question the legitimacy of the old republican boundaries, incite ethnic Russians from Crimea, Kazakhstan, and the Baltic countries to pursue self-determination or endorse the nationalists' calls for a Slavic union led by Russia. The Russian Federation was constitutionally defined as the state of all its citizens (*rossiane*), not just the ethnic Russians (*russkie*). Just as the SFRY was the direct opposite of the USSR,

Russia was very much unlike Serbia and the constellation of break-away ethnic enclaves in its orbit.

Differences aside, the violent dismemberment of Yugoslavia commanded attention across the Soviet Union at the moment of its extinction. What went on in the Balkans presented a dangerous precedent, which could potentially affect events and processes thousands of kilometers to the east. There had to be a different way to part ways and dismantle a multi-ethnic federation. The Russian foreign minister, Andrei Kozyrev, presented the Belavezha Accords replacing the USSR with the loose structure of the Commonwealth of Independent States (CIS) as "the last opportunity to avoid the Yugoslav option."[12] Yet the specter of "Balkanization" continued to haunt his Soviet successors, with conflicts flaring up in Transnistria, Nagorno-Karabakh, and Georgia. And as the case of Chechnya suggested, Russia itself was vulnerable to the centrifugal forces of secessionism.

The Yugoslav wars left their deep imprint on Russian politics, having become the rallying cry of the anti-Yeltsin opposition keen to wrest power away from the Kremlin. From early 1992 until its forced closure in October 1993, the Congress of People's Deputies (*S'ezd narodnykh deputatov*), Russia's legislature, spared Kozyrev no criticism. The "Red–Brown" coalition (*Krasno–korichnevaia koalitsiia*) of communists and nationalists upbraided the foreign minister for siding with UNSC Resolution 757 (30 May 1992) imposing sanctions against rump Yugoslavia.[13] In defiance, Evgenii Abramtsumov, head of the Supreme Soviet's foreign affairs committee, went to Belgrade to meet the Serbian and Yugoslav leadership together with Radovan Karadžić, president of the self-proclaimed Republika Srpska (RS) in Bosnia. The opposition turned Belgrade and RS into sites of pilgrimage. According to one estimate, one in ten opposition deputies made the journey between late 1992 and October 1993.[14] Amongst others the list of visitors included General Vladislav Achalov, military advisor to the Supreme Soviet's chairman Ruslan Khasbulatov, the founding father of Neoeurasianism, Aleksandar Dugin, and the maverick writer Eduard Limonov, future leader of the "National Bolshevik Party." Russian volunteers poured into

Bosnia too. One of them was Igor Girkin, known by the *nom de guerre* of Strelkov ("Shooter"), who would rise to international prominence with the seizure of Crimea and the war in eastern Ukraine in 2014.

Hard-line views permeated the media too. In January 1993, the chief editors of *Den'*, *Sovetskaia Rossiia*, *Nash sovremennik*, and *Literaturnaia Rossiia* signed an appeal to the Supreme Soviet (a parliamentary body elected by the Congress of People's Deputies) asserting that "[i]f the Serbs [were] denied the support of Russians [*russkie*], they [were] fated to disappear from the face of the earth, because they [would] defend themselves against the interventionists until the last man. And then it [would] be the turn of the Orthodox Russians, Ukrainians, Belorussians."[15] One of the signatories was Gennadii Ziuganov, who, as leader of the Communist Party of the Russian Federation (CPRF), would later become Yeltsin's chief rival in the 1996 presidential election.[16]

Yeltsin's suppression of the recalcitrant parliament and the adoption of a new constitution at the end of 1993 made no difference. The tug of war continued into the new Duma (lower legislative chamber) dominated by Vladimir Zhirinovskii's ultranationalist Liberal Democratic Party (LDP) and the communists.[17] The Red–Browns went on to slam Kozyrev for kowtowing to the West and abandoning brotherly Serbs in their valiant struggle against the two-headed monster of American hegemony and Islam. Greeted by a 50,000-strong crowd in the Montenegrin capital of Podgorica, in February 1994, Zhirinovskii offered "brother Serbs" his version of what Yugoslavia's demise was about:

> The world wants to divide the Balkans into many little statelets, so that the West can Catholicize half the peninsula, and Islamize the other half. They are trying to destroy our Orthodox religion, and your only fault is that you are on the border with the West, and therefore the attacks on you are all the fiercer.[18]

To be sure, the sympathy for the Serbs had purchase amongst Russian centrists and even reformers as well. Vladimir Lukin,

co-founder of the pro-reform Yabloko party and influential chair
of the Foreign Affairs Committee in the first (1993–96) and second
(1996–99) Duma, was frequently in Belgrade. "Our task," he
remarked in September 1995 to Serbian diplomats, "is to show that
we are with you. And as long as your country faces a military threat,
Russian deputies will stay on duty in Yugoslavia. If the Americans
want to bomb this country, let them drop bombs on me, the former
ambassador to their country."[19] Such opinions had strong traction
amongst many Balkan experts in Moscow—for example, the historian Elena Gus'kova. As wryly observed by Sergei Romanenko,
Gus'kova's colleague at the Russian Academy of Sciences, their "irrational Yugoslavophobia" gave way "no less irrational Serbophilia."[20]

In reality, what Russian political and intellectual elites were
battling was not Yugoslavia, Milošević, the Serbs, the Croats or the
Bosniaks. At stake was the future of Russia itself. Would it "join the
West," as the heirs of Gorbachev's New Thinking aspired to do while
transplanting democratic and market institutions onto Russian soil?
Kozyrev, for one, perceived the Yugoslav conflict as a humanitarian
concern but also as an opportunity for Moscow to reinforce ties
with the United States and Western democracies. On the other
side of the barricade were those taking a somber view of America
and disapproving of the changes carried out by Yeltsin's early
reformist cabinets. Communists and ultranationalists agreed that
Russia's harmful obsession with the West contradicted its calling as a
great nation and center of a unique civilization. Whether venerating
Stalin, quoting the émigré exponents of Eurasianism of the interwar
years, Orthodox theologians, and the nineteenth-century Slavophiles,
the anti-Westerners believed that the Serbs were waging a battle for
which the stakes were global. It was their fight too. "Thank God that
in contrast to Yeltsin's Russia, Serbia has not left these Serbs [beyond
the borders of Serbia] in the lurch," editorialized the communist
daily *Pravda* in January 1992.[21] To reclaim its rightful place in the
world, Moscow had to challenge the post-1991 borders in the CIS.
Under the cover of human rights, the United States was meddling in
former Yugoslavia so as to encircle and stifle Russia. The wounded
giant had no choice but to strike back.

E pluribus unum

With such a public mood at home, Yeltsin and Kozyrev were walking a tightrope. As much as they believed that their country's interest lay in working with, not against, the West, they had to reassure domestic audiences that Russia was being respected. Public opinion was initially amenable, pressing issues near to home and drawing attention away from the Balkans. A poll in July 1992 found that 25 percent favored the UN sanctions against Milošević, 16 percent were against, and a whopping 60 percent remained undecided.[22] But with time things changed. Opposition in the Duma and pressure from senior officials to take a tough line (presidential foreign policy advisor Sergei Stankevich, Defense Minister Pavel Grachev, security services chiefs, and top brass) compelled Kozyrev to backtrack from his initial pro-Western stance.[23] By 1994, the so-called statists (*gosudarstvenniki*), middle-of-the-road pragmatists who believed in assertive foreign policy, became dominant. The first war in Chechnya and the NATO enlargement of post-communist Europe ratified their ascendance.

The emergent consensus positioned itself at an equal distance from both the ultranationalists and the pro-Western outlook of *perestroika* liberals, some of whom were co-opted into the *gosudarstvenniki* ranks. Russia would strive to preserve its great-power status by balancing or conditionally co-operating with the United States and its allies. Yeltsin himself shifted to the center ground, gradually willing to work with the Duma rather than fight it. The war in Bosnia offered an opportunity. In the words of Paul Goble, the president could "kill two birds with one stone—he could appease the still-strong nationalists at home and he could reaffirm his status as an international good citizen in the eyes of the West."[24]

With Friends like These . . .

One of Russia's chief handicaps in former Yugoslavia was placing nearly all bets on Slobodan Milošević. Moscow ignored everyone else, including a traditional friend such as Montenegro that was treated as little more than a Serbian province within the Federal Republic of Yugoslavia (FRY). Such a one-sided approach was not inevitable. In 1991–92, a more inclusive policy was tried out. Near the end of his term, on 18 October 1991, Gorbachev mediated between Milošević and Franjo Tuđman in Moscow. The Soviet Union applied an informal arms embargo of its own. Franjo Gregurić, who served as Croatian prime minister between July 1991 and August 1992, later stated that Russia played a central part in pressuring the JNA to terminate the airstrikes against Zagreb in October 1991.[25] Following the EU and the United States, the Russian Federation recognized the independence of Bosnia and Herzegovina on 27 April 1992, three weeks after the outbreak of war, having already done so for Slovenia on 14 February and Croatia three days later. Remarkably, Russia became the first major power to extend recognition to Macedonia on 4 August. Yeltsin made the decision in Sofia at the request of Bulgarian President Zhelyu Zhelev, who had resolutely condemned the 1991 putsch. By supporting Macedonia, Moscow could claim it had taken a principled stance. The Badinter Commission[26] deemed the Yugoslav republic to have met the conditions, notably the rights of minorities, for statehood. Not only could Russia claim the higher moral ground but it was also asserting an independent course—against the wishes of Milošević, Greece, and also the United States and EC/EU, neither of which had given its blessing to the new state. In Bosnia, Russia sided with a series of UN resolutions, starting with UNSC 757 introducing sanctions against rump Yugoslavia (see Figure 2 below). Russia committed troops to the UNPROFOR peacekeeping operation, originally established in February 1992 to oversee the ceasefire in Croatia.

In working with the West, Kozyrev saw Russia's role as one of a bridge to Belgrade and the Bosnian Serbs. Answering his detractors at home, he observed that "it [was] not a coincidence that our Western partners appeal[ed] to Russia as a privileged interlocutor to Belgrade," adding that his diplomatic team did "everything so that the lawful interests of Serbs and Serbia [were] fulfilled."[27] The problem was that on the other side of the line were Milošević and

UN Security Council resolutions		
UNSC 757	30 May 1992	Sanctions against FRY (Serbia and Montenegro)
UNSC 816	31 March 1993	No-fly zone over Bosnia and Herzegovina
UNSC 819	16 April 1993	'Safe area' around the city of Srebrenica
UNSC 824	6 May 1993	Sarajevo, Tuzla, Žepa, Goražde, Bihać proclaimed safe areas.
UNSC 827	25 May 1993	Fully establishing the International Criminal Tribunal for former Yugoslavia (ICTY), following UNSC 808 (February 22, 1993)
UNSC 836	4 June 1993	UNPROFOR, UN peace mission, authorized to use force in defence of safe areas

Figure 2 Key UN Security Council resolutions endorsed by Russia

Karadžić, rather than "the Serbs," a fair number of whom opposed the war. Wisely enough, Kozyrev and Yeltsin sought to draw a distinction between the FRY and the RS leadership. Yet they, along with the bulk of Russian democrats and reformers, failed to develop ties of any significance with Serbia's opposition, let alone with liberals and anti-nationalists elsewhere in former Yugoslavia.[28]

Russia's position on Bosnia rested on three assumptions. First, the Serbs were not the only guilty party ("it is impossible to determine who is right and who is wrong"). Kozyrev assured his domestic critics that UNSC resolutions were directed against all belligerents, including the Bosniaks and the Croats. Second, the use of military power was unacceptable and there could only be a diplomatic solution. NATO could enforce the no-fly zone— presumably against Serb forces as no one else had air-power capabilities. It could also support UNPROFOR in case "safe areas" were under attack. Yet Russia reserved the right to veto, thanks to the so-called "dual key" arrangement requiring the alliance to seek prior authorization from the UN Secretary General. Third, Moscow was an indispensable partner and no resolution was feasible without its sanction.

In effect, Russia was using Yugoslavia to stake its vision of the post-Cold War order. The statist consensus pictured a consortium of powers, a flashback to the nineteenth-century Concert of Europe, whereby the Russian Federation would partake on an equal footing with the United States and prominent Western European states. The same vision was at play in Moscow's disapproval of NATO enlargement and its insistence that the Organization for Security and Co-operation in Europe (OSCE) be put in charge of security "from Vancouver to Vladivostok." Russia shared, in principle, the Western objective of halting bloodshed in Bosnia. Its preferred scenario foresaw a condominium in former Yugoslavia recognizing its special title.

At least initially, the chosen strategy paid off. In February 1994, Deputy Foreign Minister Vitalii Churkin (who would make a name later as ambassador to the UN) negotiated a deal with Bosnian Serbs to withdraw heavy weapons away from the outskirts of Sarajevo. The last-ditch intervention, coming to the utter surprise of many Western governments, averted a NATO strike after RS forces shelled the Markale market in the Bosnian capital and refused to comply with an ultimatum to pull out. Russia negotiated the insertion of two battalions serving under UNPROFOR between the Bosniaks and the RS army (*Vojska Republike Srpske*, or VRS). To Kozyrev, the Sarajevo crisis proved that "Russia could not and should not be excluded from the common efforts to regulate the conflict in the Balkans, a region where Russia has long-term interests and influence."[29]

The Sarajevo crisis presaged the April 1994 formation of the Contact Group for former Yugoslavia, involving Russia and the United States as members together with France, Britain, and Germany. Its formation felt like a proper achievement. The Contact Group both enhanced Russia's status and placed NATO under additional restraint. Moreover, it presented an opportunity to play off Western states and exploit differences amongst them. Britain and France, in particular, were skeptical about NATO air strikes, fearful that they could put their own Blue Helmets (UN peacekeepers) in harm's way. The French government saw the danger of NATO assuming too great a responsibility, to the detriment of the EU's budding Common Foreign and Security Policy (CFSP). British and French reticence regarding the Atlantic Alliance, and by extension closer American involvement, allowed more room for Russia's diplomatic initiatives. And if a solution to the Bosnian conflict through the Contact Group appeared within reach, Moscow's arguments in favor of a pan-European security architecture based on the OSCE, or another non-NATO institution, acquired more weight.

By the time the Contact Group kicked off work, Russia's strategy was already in trouble. On 28 February 1994, NATO downed several Bosnian Serb aircraft violating the no-fly zone. The alliance had used force for the first time in its history and Russia could do little about it. Despite the violation, Iulii Vorontsov, Moscow's ambassador to the UN, did not take the effort to convoke the United Nations Security Council.

Even worse, the Bosnian Serbs tried to trick and use Russia for their own interests. In April, Churkin attempted to broker a deal on the safe area of Goražde, repeating his earlier achievement from Sarajevo. General Ratko Mladić was holding hostage 150 UN peacekeepers after NATO had bombarded his troops, which had shelled the besieged city. Churkin thought he had clinched a deal with the speaker of the RS parliament, Momčilo Krajšnik, for a withdrawal and the release of the Blue Helmets. The Serbs' U-turn was nothing short of a humiliation. Kozyrev, supported by Yeltsin, broke ties with the RS, declaring that Milošević was the only legitimate negotiator. Russia's actual influence was put to the test once more in August 1994 when a RS referendum rejected a peace plan devised by the Contact Group.[30] Moscow resumed contacts with the Bosnian Serbs after the United States did so in December.

The intransigence of the Bosnian Serbs softened Russia's resolve to claim the role of their international patron. The prevalent mood was one of anger and frustration. "The tail should not wag the dog. It is really quite simple," Churkin burst out in an interview following the Goražde flop, "we have our own interests and our own positions too." The Russian media agreed. "The Bosnian Serbs must understand that

in Russia they are dealing with a great power, not a banana republic,"
argued a renowned columnist.[31]

But the downturn in relations with Pale (the capital of Republika
Srpska in the hills above Sarajevo) made Russia even more reliant
on Milošević. Moscow tried to link the tightening of sanctions
against the Bosnian Serbs with the relaxation of those targeted at
the Federal Republic of Yugoslavia. In September 1994, Russia won
UN Security Council approval for eased restrictions with international civilian flights to Serbia and Montenegro. This allowed for a
100-day probationary period, and Yugoslav sports teams were
allowed to perform in competitions abroad.[32] The Federal Republic
of Yugoslavia, in return, agreed to close the border with Bosnia. The
Russian attempt at persuading the Serbian leader to recognize
Croatia and Bosnia and Herzegovina led nowhere.[33]

The tail could wag the dog also because domestically Yeltsin and
Kozyrev had less and less room for maneuver. The Duma reas-
serted itself while the Kremlin switched to a conciliatory mode.
Yeltsin toned down his statements on former Yugoslavia and, in
December 1994, he vetoed a draft UNSC resolution against the
Croatian Serbs.[34] As the U.S. Congress pushed to remove the arms
embargo against the Bosniaks, the Duma responded with resolutions calling for lifting sanctions on the Federal Republic of
Yugoslavia. Milošević's amiable ties with the opposition were no
secret and he was making the most of them. Acting in co-ordina-
tion, Yeltsin and President Bill Clinton applied vetoes to curtail
rebellious legislatures. "I know that members of Congress share my
goals of reducing the violence in Bosnia and working to end the
war," said Clinton as a recourse to the veto in August 1995. "But
their vote to unilaterally lift the arms embargo is the wrong step at
the wrong time."[35] At the very same moment, as Operation Storm
was underway (see below), the Duma convened in an extraordinary session—in the middle of the summer break—to pass two acts
("On Russia's Exit from the Sanctions Regime against Yugoslavia"
and "On the Measures to Prevent Genocide against the Serb
Population in the Krajina"). Yeltsin wasted no time striking them
both down.

Endgame in Bosnia

As 1994 drew to a close, Russia found itself in a bind. The brinkman-ship of the Bosnian Serbs risked provoking NATO while Milošević was denying responsibility. The only way to cut the Gordian knot that was Bosnia entailed more robust American involvement. The United States had already brokered a power-sharing deal ending the war between Bosniaks and Croats. The VRS attacks against the UN safe areas in the summer of 1995, the fall of Žepa and Srebrenica (followed by genocide), and the second massacre at Sarajevo's Markale market, propelled NATO into action. At this point, Moscow was left with no option but to go along.[36] Casting aside "dual key," Operation Deliberate Force (August–September 1995) delivered heavy blows to the VRS, in conjunction with a Croatian–Bosniak offensive.[37] Shortly thereafter, in November, Presidents Milošević, Tuđman, and Izetbegović gathered at the American air force base in Dayton, Ohio, to sign a peace settlement for Bosnia.

Dayton and the lead-up to it exposed Russia's weakness. Hoping to be the bridge between the West and the Serbs, Moscow had wound up being ignored by both. In the process, NATO had emerged as a guarantor of security in Europe, the very outcome Russia had worked to forestall. Publicly, Yeltsin called the alliance's operation "inadmissible". Still, while the Duma spoke in fury of "barbaric actions" and "mass extermination of Serbs,"[38] the president admitted the latter "[had gotten] what they deserved."[39] The challenge for Moscow was to get the best possible deal in post-war Bosnia. It therefore presented the settlement as a collective achievement of the international community and not an American triumph.[40] Russia bargained to be the co-leader of the peacekeeping operation behind the Implementation Force (IFOR) but it had to accept NATO's primacy.[41] As a compromise, the 1,600-strong Russian contingent was to be deployed near the strategic enclave of Brčko, reporting to an American general and not the NATO command. Russian commentators swiftly dubbed the deal "Operation Fig Leaf".

That was a rather harsh judgment. Russia had made real diplo-matic gains. Besides its seat in the Contact Group, it won a place in the steering board of the Peace Implementation Council (PIC)—the international body overseeing the Dayton settlement and the work of the UN-appointed High Representative.[42] Russia was one of the guarantors of peace in Bosnia, together with the Western powers, Turkey, and Japan. The United States and its European allies seemed to view the outcome in a similar light. In the words of Strobe Talbott, Deputy Secretary of State, "what (Russia) wanted most was to restore a sense, however symbolic, that they still mattered in the world. Behind our efforts to include Russia in the Bosnian negotiating process lay a fundamental belief—that it was essential to find the proper place for Russia in Europe's security structure, something it had not been part of since 1914."[43]

After the War

Russia remained engaged in post-Dayton Bosnia, though its ambitions were scaled down. Multiple contradictions riddled its policy. On the one hand, Moscow did go along with the Western efforts at rooting out Karadžić's influence within Republika Srpska. On the other, it objected strongly whenever the Stabilization Force (SFOR) and Western powers, the United States first and foremost, applied force to impose their will. Thus, the Russians did not do much to oppose America when it weighed in on the side of RS President Biljana Plavšić as she clashed with Momčilo Krajšnik, the Serb member of the tripartite collective presidency of Bosnia and a prominent ally of Karadžić. What they did instead was to keep Plavšić at arm's length and deny her a meeting with Yeltsin, despite her wishes.[44] Furthermore, Russia threw its weight behind the High Representative Carlos Westendorp as he pressed the Bosnian government on issues such as common citizenship of the state and the appointment of ambassadors, threating a boycott by the international community. Russia did not obstruct the introduction of the so-called Bonn Powers in December 1997, allowing the High Representative to pass extraordinary legislation as well as remove elected officials. The Russian Ministry of Foreign Affairs (MFA) became more vocal only when British commandos, part of the

SFOR, launched an operation to arrest a Serb official charged in July 1997 by the International Criminal Tribunal for the Former Yugoslavia (ICTY). In Moscow's reading, these actions had gone well beyond the peacekeepers' mandate to police the peace deal and facilitate economic reconstruction. The suggestion that the peace-keepers should go after Karadžić himself was anathema as well. The Russians argued that this could rupture the fragile settlement. Generally, officials in Moscow were in two minds about The Hague tribunal. As a matter of principle, Russia supported it, having voted in favor of the original UNSC resolution to establish an interna-tional body to prosecute war crimes. However, it viewed the ICTY as something of a leftover from the "internationalist phase" under Andrei Kozyrev. When the ICTY acquired teeth after Dayton, including arrests and trials, the media in Moscow were quick to dismiss the tribunal as victors' justice as well as a prime example of the double standards underlying American foreign policy.[45]

The end of the Bosnian war spelled opportunities as well. It was possible for Russia to reinvigorate political and economic links with the Federal Republic of Yugoslavia, its principal ally in former Yugoslavia, and play the role of facilitating its reintegration into international society. Moscow spearheaded the effort to have the sanctions against Belgrade removed at the earliest possible moment. It criticized the United States over hints that the restrictions, which the UN Security Council agreed were to expire after Bosnia held its first elections (September 1996), could be extended and linked to the FRY's commitment to domestic democratization. At the UN, Russia solicited support from Britain and France for its campaign to bring Serbia and Montenegro back from the cold. Bilateral ties grew stronger and deeper. After a visit to Belgrade by the newly appointed Foreign Minister Evgenii Primakov in May 1996 (more about him below), the Russian government lent the FRY $150 million—allowing the latter to repay outstanding debts to Gazprom. The two defense ministries signed a co-operation protocol as well. However, the Russian leadership was fully aware that placing all bets on Milošević, who had proven to be unreliable on more than one occasion, was an ill-advised choice. Starting in 1998, it identified the Montenegrin President Milo Đukanović (aged just thirty-six at the time), who was veering away from Milošević and towards the West, as a partner who could be trusted.

The other benefit of Dayton, from a Russian perspective, is that it presented a test case of working with NATO. General Leontii Shevtsov served as deputy supreme commander of the SFOR, together with General George Joulwan, the U.S. Supreme Allied Commander Europe (SACEUR), under the elaborate command-and-control mechanism that allowed Russia to be fully integrated but still separate.[46] Although Moscow's relations with the Atlantic Alliance were far from perfect, because the latter was on the verge of expanding eastwards, its diplomats, notably Foreign Minister Primakov and Vitalii Churkin, believed a *modus vivendi* was possible and desirable. Analysts concurred. The military's attitude was more hostile. There were certainly those influenced by the experience of co-operating with NATO troops on the ground in Bosnia. However, even they continued viewing the alliance through a zero-sum lens.[47] It is hardly coincidental that the commander of Russia's Airborne Brigade stationed in the town of Ugljevik (northeastern Bosnia), Colonel Nikolai Ignatov, and Lieutenant General Nikolai Stas'kov, commander of the Airborne Troops (*Vozdushno-desantnye voiska*, or VDV), played a central part in the so-called dash to Prishtina in June 1999 (more below). Although NATO typically hailed the IFOR/SFOR as a success story of military-to-military co-operation with Russia, some in its ranks took a dim view. General Wesley Clark (SACEUR, 1997–2000) put it bluntly: "I had closely observed the double standard the Russians had in the Bosnia mission. They took care of the Serbs, passing them information, tipping them off to any of our operations ... while keeping up the pretense of full co-operation with us."[48]

The Kosovo Debacle

The 1998–99 Kosovo crisis put Russia's policy in former Yugoslavia to another rigorous test. The outcome was even more frustration at the West. Yet again Moscow had to face up to its diminished status and stomach another American-led intervention. Russian decision makers confronted an already painfully familiar dilemma. Their ties to Slobodan Milošević provided them with leverage and bolstered Moscow's international standing. But the wily and unscrupulous Serb leader could be a liability just as well, threatening to put Russia on a collision course with the United States and its allies. With NATO's air strikes against Serbia, Operation Allied Force (OAF), Moscow had to choose between two bad options—providing military assistance to embattled Serbia or bowing to the West. Either way, its national interests were bound to suffer.

Kosovo bruised Russia's ambition to reinvent itself as an independent center of power in a multipolar world. It found an ardent advocate in Kozyrev's successor at the Foreign Ministry, Evgenii Primakov. The former head of the Foreign Intelligence Service (SVR, *Sluzhba vneshnei razvedki*) saw alignment with countries like Iran, Iraq or indeed the Federal Republic of Yugoslavia, ostracized though they were by the West, as an asset for Russia as it strove to interact with the United States as an equal. Appealing to nationalists and the security establishment, Primakov was nonetheless a pragmatist—like most of his fellow *gosudarstvenniki*. With the May 1997 Russia–NATO Founding Act, he traded Russia's acquiescence with the alliance's expansion for guarantees that no external military forces or nuclear weapons were to be stationed in new member states. Primakov's was a simple logic. Russia could do little to stop enlargement so it might as well sell its reluctant endorsement dearly. According to Strobe Talbott, Clinton's man on Russia, the essence of Primakov's strategy was "to play a weak hand well."[49] It is an irony that an accomplished *Realpolitiker* like him would end up in a situation as intractable and risky as Kosovo.

Part of the reason was that the crisis caught Moscow off-guard. Following Dayton, the Balkans went down Yeltsin's list of priorities. The watershed presidential election in June–July 1996, the conflict in Chechnya, and the 1998 financial meltdown kept the Kremlin busy. But, in fairness, the rest of the Contact Group was not prepared either. The United States had taken the deliberate decision to keep Kosovo off the table in Dayton. Milošević had transformed, literally

overnight, from problem maker to partner. It was only the emergence of the Kosovo Liberation Army (KLA) in 1997–98 that
changed the equation. Even so, the Russian leadership's disinterest
stood out. Oleg Levitin, second secretary at the embassy in Belgrade
in the 1990s, reminisces:

> I attended most meetings between Kozyrev and Milošević in
> the mid-1990s. To the best of my knowledge, the Russian side
> never initiated any serious discussion of Kosovo at that time.
> On those occasions when the topic did arise, Kozyrev limited
> himself to listening to Milošević's version, which was far indeed
> from reality. At such moments, I felt like a time-traveller over-
> hearing the *Conversations with Stalin*, recorded so famously by
> [Yugoslav politician and dissident writer] Milovan Djilas: Stalin
> asking the Yugoslav delegation in the mid-1940s to explain
> something about these mysterious Albanians, but contenting
> himself with meager explanations and concluding that Moscow
> had no need to take an interest in Albanian matters.[50]

Such indifference is all the more striking given the centrality of
Kosovo in Russian discourse on international politics since 1999
and, arguably, in the popular psyche too (e.g. Russian football fans
chanting "Kosovo is Serbia" at international fixtures).[51] But it does
underscore the point that mental maps evolve and conceptions of
history evolve and change over time.

To be sure, Primakov was an exception, in that he took an interest
in Kosovo. Levitin testifies that the new foreign minister surprised
Yugoslavs in having dwelled on the issue unexpectedly long at his
first meeting with Milošević in May 1996. That made only marginal
difference. Up to 1997, Moscow vetoed the inclusion of Kosovo in
the Contact Group's deliberations, concerned about the link to
Chechnya. If the West was putting Milošević to the test over a separatist movement in a volatile corner of Serbia, what would stop it
doing the same with regard to Russia's own restive province in the
North Caucasus? The connection between Yugoslavia and the threat
of further disintegration in Russia and the wider post-Soviet space,

which had come to the fore in the early 1990s, was very much alive in the mind of Moscow's foreign-policy elites.

When fights between the KLA and Belgrade security forces escalated in 1998, Moscow tried to forge a position whose tenets were that military action by NATO was unacceptable, and no settlement was permissible without Russia. As in the past, the overarching priority appears to have been Russia's standing in European security affairs. However, Moscow was short on substantive ideas as to how to resolve the conflict and engineer compromise between Belgrade and the Kosovar Albanian leaders. It was late establishing links with the moderate wing around President Ibrahim Rugova and never accepted the KLA, sniping at its leaders' presence in the Rambouillet negotiations in the spring of 1999.

In the initial stages of the conflict, Russia seemed to have a strong hand. Primakov, promoted to prime minister in September 1998, assumed the role of intermediary between Belgrade and the West. His efforts bore fruit. Talks between Yeltsin and Milošević in June of that year resulted in a ceasefire and the deployment of a fifty-strong observer mission, including Western diplomats and military personnel. Even more important, Russia helped avert NATO strikes in September and October. First, it threw its weight behind UNSC Resolution 1199 (23 September) demanding a ceasefire, a withdrawal of Serb forces, and the return of refugees. When NATO handed an ultimatum to Belgrade, Russia negotiated a new verification mission, this time under the auspices of the OSCE. It looked as if Russia was having, yet again, its Sarajevo 1994 moment.

Yet, just like in Bosnia, Serbian intransigence wrong-footed Russian policy. Milošević was not willing to call off the anti-KLA operations. Refugee flows out of Kosovo intensified. The massacre of forty-five Kosovars at Račak in January 1999 pushed NATO to the brink once more. The end result was the alliance's air campaign against former Yugoslavia. Not only did it bring about the worst crisis between Russia and the West but it also exposed Moscow's weakness. Russia maneuvered itself into a situation where it faced a stark binary choice: fight NATO head-on together with Milošević or retreat and accept the *fait accompli* created by the United States and its allies. Moscow opted for the latter, suffering a humiliating setback.

Initially, the Russian leadership, still basking in the glory of their achievement from October 1998, responded to the uptick of violence in Kosovo by posturing and upping the ante. Moscow's rhetoric toughened. Yeltsin went on record that he would not allow war against the Federal Republic of Yugoslavia. Together with Primakov, he clearly underestimated NATO's resolve to act, the dangers of a potential escalation for Russia, and the extent of his leverage in relation to the United States and the EU.[52] The Rambouillet conference (February–March 1999) was a missed opportunity. Instead of pressuring Milošević to accept a compromise and then use his consent to secure better terms from the West, Moscow backed Belgrade's rejection of the proposal for Kosovo's autonomy. The point of contention was the military annex, which the FRY delegation interpreted as conferring on NATO the right to occupy the country's entire territory, an argument that Russia bought. Having obstructed or delayed for months on end the Contact Group's efforts to come to a settlement, Moscow could not offer an alternative plan of its own either. It effect, its stiff resistance at Rambouillet signaled to Milošević that Russia would stay firmly on his side in the game of chicken he was about to embark upon.[53]

The ensuing NATO campaign against Serbia highlighted the mismatch between Russia's ambitions and capacity to shape events. Moscow could embarrass the Western coalition by scrapping co-operation with NATO and practically freezing ties with the United States. Primakov made history by ordering his airplane back, in the middle of the Atlantic, upon learning from his host, Vice President Al Gore, about the imminent air strikes against the Federal Republic of Yugoslavia. The turn-around stood out as a symbol of deteriorating relations between Russia and the West and pushed Primakov's popularity ratings at home through the roof (Vladimir Putin was still a largely unknown figure at that point). Russia furthermore did its best to expose Operation Allied Force as a severe violation of international law and the hallowed principle of state sovereignty. Its implied veto made it pointless for America, Britain, and France to solicit an enabling resolution from the UN

Security Council. Instead, the NATO allies justified the air campaign on extra-legal grounds, pointing to the humanitarian disaster, gross violations of human rights, and refugee exodus, all of which it aimed to reverse (later known as the doctrine of "humanitarian intervention"). Yet Russia could do little to stop the bombs. It was unwilling and unable to project military force into former Yugoslavia. Even if it was to do so, the Atlantic Alliance enjoyed "escalation dominance." In other words, it is doubtful whether Russia could muster and deploy conventional military force on a meaningful scale so as to push back against NATO, short of resorting to its nuclear capability.

The Russian leadership chose diplomacy over military force. It claimed the moral high ground, underscoring that their concern was not Serbia, much less Milošević whose implication in ethnic cleansing was beyond denial, but rather the integrity of international law. NATO's actions were an affront to rule-governed order, an undisputed common good. However, Russia failed to capitalize on its stance. The UN Security Council members opposed a draft denouncing the intervention against the Federal Republic of Yugoslavia, which the Russians introduced together with India. What was even more humiliating was the reluctance of most members of the Commonwealth of Independent States, apart from Belarus and Tajikistan, to support Moscow. Most former Soviet leaders elected to maintain a low profile with the United States.

The Kosovo war made the already emasculated Yeltsin vulnerable at home. His bellicose rhetoric was coming back to haunt him. Gennadii Seleznev, the communist speaker of the Duma, revealed that Russia's nuclear arsenal was taking aim at NATO members—a claim the Kremlin rushed to deny. Anti-Western mood was rampant. "It is Russia which is being attacked," clamored newspaper headlines, TV news, and mass demonstrations at the gates of the American Embassy and the NATO Information Office in Moscow. "NATO's Aggression is a continuation of Hitler's 1941 [invasion of USSR]," one placard read.[54] The Kremlin came under sustained pressure from the usual suspects in the Duma and the military high command. Short of direct military involvement, radical voices advocated sending arms to the Serbs to help them repel NATO's jets. Reports accumulated of groups recruiting volunteers to be sent to the Balkans, an echo of the Slavic Committees active in the Russian Empire during the 1876 Serbian–Ottoman War. Predictably, Vladimir Zhirinovskii, head of the Liberal Democratic Party, vented his anger, but the United States also drew opprobrium from liberals such as Grigorii Iavlinskii who nonetheless opposed military involvement. To them, the anti-Western turn undermined years of democratic and market reforms. In a show of solidarity, the leading reformist politicians Egor Gaidar, Boris Nemtsov, and Boris Fedorov flew to Belgrade. It appeared that the era of co-operation with the West ushered in by Gorbachev was coming to a close.

Yeltsin had a tough choice to make. As much as he abhorred the American decision to discount Russia and could not afford to stand by idly, he was conscious that further escalation might do even more damage. The president harbored a deep resentment against the Belgrade leadership. As he would later reflect in his memoirs:

> Milošević behaved in an absolutely unprincipled manner. In relations with Russia his main bet was the Russians' indignation at my foreign policy, discord in society, pushing us to political and military confrontation with the West.[55]

An application by the Federal Republic of Yugoslavia to join the Russia–Belarus State Union, which fell two votes short of approval in the Duma, stood out as a prime example of the Serbian strongman's last-minute scheming at the Kremlin's expense.[56]

As a NATO land invasion of Kosovo became imminent, Yeltsin opted for conciliation with the United States and its allies. On 14 April 1999, he appointed former Prime Minister Viktor Chernomyrdin, a pro-Western figure with extensive links to Gazprom, as mediator. Chernomyrdin's task was to make it clear to Milošević that Russia was not coming to the rescue and it was therefore time for him to sue for peace. On 6 May, foreign ministers from the G8 who were gathered in Petersberg near Bonn paired up Chernomyrdin with Martti Ahtisaari, the president of neutral Finland, to represent them in Belgrade. The

U-turn in Moscow was completed with the firing of Primakov and the designation of Sergei Stepashin as the new prime minister. Primakov had become a liability for Yeltsin. Beyond that, the former prime minister was not short of ambition, which caused consternation in the Kremlin. Indeed, with his approval ratings virtually going through the roof, Primakov would use his hard-line record on Kosovo to campaign for his new party, Fatherland–All Russia, posing a challenge to the Kremlin in the December 1999 legislative elections and laying the groundwork for a presidential bid. In a nutshell, the time was ripe for Russia to take a step back and seek a way out of the Kosovo quagmire that it had walked into.

Having lost the support of its last major ally, Serbia surrendered on 9 June 1999, six days after Ahtisaari and Chernomyrdin had held talks with Milošević. Russia voted in favor of UNSC Resolution 1244 (10 June), which placed Kosovo under the international administration of the United Nations Mission in Kosovo (UNMIK), and mandated a NATO peacekeeping operation (KFOR).[57] The face-saving formula helped relieve pressure on the Kremlin. Forced to accept the outcome of NATO's operation, Russia nonetheless obtained partial recognition of its guarantor. What is more, though NATO military action actually decoupled Kosovo from Serbia, Resolution 1244 still referred to the province as part of the Federal Republic of Yugoslavia. The resolution enshrined the international law principle of border inviolability that Moscow had advocated with great determination. Most importantly, the deal was an opportunity for Russia to re-establish its relations with the United States and the EU. That became clear after a meeting between Yeltsin and Clinton on the margins of the G8 Summit in Cologne (8–10 June). Russia joined the Stability Pact for Southeast Europe, a German initiative launched at the summit.

While it was horse-trading with the West, Russia scrambled to create facts on the ground and entrench its position. As NATO rolled in, a Russian paratrooper detachment from SFOR marched overnight on 11–12 June from Bosnia to Prishtina's Slatina airport. Most likely orchestrated by the General Staff or the Airborne Troops command, the gamble certainly bore Yeltsin's stamp of approval.[58] With Primakov gone, he was now calling the shots on Kosovo. The "dash to Prishtina" (*brosok na Prishtinu*) was aimed at securing a territorial sector for Russian peacekeepers, a prize that Moscow had been denied in Bosnia. But the pre-emptive move raised risks too. It was thanks to the British General Michael Jackson, commander of the NATO expeditionary corps, that a showdown was averted: "I'm not going to start Third World War for you," he said to General Wesley Clark, head of NATO forces in Europe. Heavily outgunned and cut off from supplies, Moscow's paratroopers found themselves in a tough spot. Ukraine, Romania, and Bulgaria had all declined access to their airspace, ruling out a Russian military build-up. In such circumstances, Russia was left with no choice but to seek a compromise and ultimately bring its paratrooper contingent within the KFOR peacekeeping operation.

Kosovo was nothing short of a bruising experience for the Russians. To them, it marked another peak of American unilateralism. Russia had been presented with a *fait accompli* as well as a dangerous precedent, which, in its view, could have ramifications in the post-Soviet space. The intervention also aggravated a festering wound, Moscow's dramatic loss of status since the collapse of the Soviet Union. At the time, many predicted a complete rift with the West and the return to a confrontation reminiscent of the Cold War. This, however, is not what happened. After coming to power in 2000, Vladimir Putin restored dialogue with the Atlantic Alliance. In an interview that year the new president said he was after a "more profound relationship" with the alliance and that he would not rule out Russia joining in, in case its "views [were] taken into account as an equal partner."[59] Less than three years after Kosovo, in May 2002, the NATO-Russia Council was launched at the Rome Summit, heir to the Permanent Joint Council of 1997. In the wake of the 9/11 attacks in 2001, both Putin and U.S. President George W. Bush felt Russia and the West were fighting on the same side. In short, the Kosovo episode, though never forgotten, was conveniently set aside. Russia shifted its attention elsewhere. It was not until the mid-2000s, during Putin's second presidential term, that Kosovo came back onto Moscow's agenda, amidst a new era of tensions with the West.

Conclusion

The Yugoslav wars of the 1990s highlighted the ambivalent relationship between Russia and Southeast Europe. On the one hand, links with the region empowered Moscow in its quest to strike a security bargain with the West, tailored to its needs and preferences. Despite setbacks in Bosnia and Kosovo, and the failed aspiration of a condominium over the Balkans on equal footing with the United States and EU, Russia gained a foothold as well as (partial) recognition of its status. On the other hand, the conflicts dragged Yeltsin and his team into a series of crises beyond their control and made them the target of scheming manipulators such as Milošević. The mythology of a Serbian–Russian camaraderie only served to advance that strongman's agenda, to the detriment of Russian strategic interests.

In Kosovo, Russia came near to the brink and suffered, in its own eyes, a demeaning loss. Once in power, Vladimir Putin would recast the defeat into part of a compelling narrative, blaming Russian weakness on the times of disorder and turmoil (*smutnoe vremia*) in the 1990s and pledging to recover his country's strength and international prestige. His message was to resonate powerfully in parts of the Balkans holding a grudge against the United States and its allies going back to the disintegration of Yugoslavia. Under Putin's watch, Russia was to embark on a policy towards Southeast Europe that was perhaps less ambitious but certainly more attuned to Primakov's dictum of the necessity to play a weak hand well.

The Balkan crises of the 1990s illustrated the limits of Russia's diplomatic strategy. So long as Moscow was not in a position to use military force to balance NATO, it would not be treated as a co-equal player by its Western interlocutors, or indeed the local powerbrokers. The constant fights between the Kremlin and the communist and nationalist hardliners in the Duma did not help either, even after Primakov's prime ministership that seemed to offer a pragmatic, middle-of-the-road approach to foreign policy acceptable to both Westernizers and hawks. Nor did Yeltsin advance the situation, for by the time of the Kosovo war he was behaving erratically, hampered by his heavy drinking and poor health. In a way the unsung hero of the 1990s was Chernomyrdin—who negotiated a way out of the crisis together with Ahtisaari but also, as prime minister between 1993 and 1998, was in charge of the gas trade with Serbia and its neighbours. As we shall see in the next chapter, Putin's key accomplishment—beyond centralizing decision-making—was to turn energy into a formidable foreign-policy asset. It made a profound difference in former Yugoslavia. In the 2000s, Serbia, Montenegro, Bosnia, and the remainder of former Yugoslavia became gradually integrated into the West. Russia, whose economy was similarly more and more intertwined with the vast EU marketplace, went along with the flow. Yet, by doing so, it carved out its niche of influence in the former Yugoslav lands.

CHAPTER 2

MEDDLING IN EUROPE'S BACKYARD
Russia and the Western Balkans

The withdrawal of our troops from Kosovo was a correct move, and I believe they must not return. We are defending not Serbia, but international law. The Serbs must defend themselves.
—Dmitrii Rogozin, Permanent Representative to NATO,
January 2008[1]

The disturbing fact is that there has been increasing talk in Montenegro about "dirty Russian money". I ask myself why there is no talk of "dirty American, English or Hungarian money". Is "Russian money dirty" because Russia is a large state? The good relations between Russia and Montenegro no longer need to be mentioned. There is no other country in Europe closer to us than Serbia-Montenegro and its peoples. We have had good co-operation with Montenegro since Peter I.
—Vladimir Vaniev, Russian Ambassador to Serbia Montenegro,
2 October 2005[2]

Never mind the pouring rain, the military parade, the first one Belgrade had seen in decades, was nothing short of a personal triumph for Vladimir Putin. In a rebuff to Western sanctions, Serbia heartily welcomed the Russian president as the guest of honor at the festivities marking the seventieth anniversary of Belgrade's liberation in the Second World War. The hosts had gone out of their way to accommodate Putin's heavy travel schedule; the parade had been moved to 16 October 2014, several days ahead of the actual date the Wehrmacht left in 1944 and Yugoslav partisans and the Red Army's Third Ukrainian Front moved in.

It was an occasion to remember. Under the rain a 20,000-strong crowd greeted the Kremlin's master as Soviet-made MiGs dashed overhead and tanks rolled down the city's boulevards adorned in the two countries' red, blue, and white flags. The pomp and circumstance brought back memories of Putin's last visit, as prime minister in March 2011. Then, tens of thousands of Serbian fans had cheered him during the FC Red Star game against his native St Petersburg's Zenit in *Mala Marakana* (Little Maracanã) stadium. Moreover, the Serbian Patriarch had decorated him with the Church's most prestigious order, in St Sava Cathedral—another Belgrade landmark.

But this time around, Serbia's leadership was also keen to show that the love story had a pragmatic side as well. In the presence of Putin, Prime Minister Aleksandar Vučić and President Tomislav Nikolić jubilantly announced to journalists that the Fiat cars, assembled at the old Zastava plant in Kragujevac, would be sold freely across the Russian Federation—as would Serbian cheese too. Russian countermeasures targeting EU's agricultural imports could well be a blessing for brotherly Serbia. Amidst the cheerful mood, few took notice of reports, several weeks after the visit, that Gazprom was poised to cut deliveries to Serbia by 28 percent in 2015 over unpaid debts of some $224 million.[3] Tough love that was indeed.

Serbia occupies a special place for Moscow. Having signed a Strategic Partnership declaration (24 May 2013) with Russia, the country is an observer in the Moscow-led Collective Security Treaty Organization (CSTO) and nurtures links with the Eurasian Economic Union (EEU). But Serbia's flirtation with Russia is hardly unique. Others in former Yugoslavia do precisely the same. Led by Prime Minister Nikola Gruevski, Macedonia has refused to join the EU sanctions against Russia. Republika Srpska's (RS) President Milorad Dodik, another guest at the 2014 Belgrade parade, ensured

Bosnia stayed out as well. Even NATO and EU members Croatia and Slovenia have turned to Moscow for economic opportunities. By default or by design, Russia has assembled a friendly bloc across the so-called Western Balkans and, more broadly, in former Yugoslavia. Politicians in Belgrade, Skopje, and Banja Luka look towards Moscow for investment, trade, financial assistance, and diplomatic support. Pundits extoll the benefits of multibillion dollar projects such as the South Stream pipeline. Why sacrifice national interests for the sake of the West, which has so often victimized or ignored their countries, they contend. EU membership is desirable but, admittedly, it is a long way off. And besides, being part of "Europe" had not done neighbouring Bulgaria and Romania that much good, not to mention the deprivations Greece has gone through courtesy of its eurozone membership.

What Serbia, Macedonia, and even Republika Srpska opt for is the time-tested Titoist policy of balancing between West and East. But even pro-Western countries such as Croatia and, especially, Montenegro, already included within NATO and the EU or edging closer to membership, have been fond of ties with Moscow. Only the Ukraine crisis made them take sides—reluctantly so. In fairness, the attitude of Balkan elites has differed little from that of many of their Western colleagues, with German Chancellor Gerhard Schröder and Italy's Silvio Berlusconi setting an example as to how the blend of business and politics shapes views of Russia.

What follows is the story of how Russia and former Yugoslav states reinvented their relations in the 2000s. The military withdrawal from Kosovo and Bosnia in June–July 2003 ushered in a new phase of Russian engagement.[4] "We are coming to the Balkans in a different form," argued Sergei Razov, deputy foreign minister, stressing the promotion of economic interconnectedness as the strategy of choice.[5] Compared to the 1990s, Russia was using its energy assets and diplomatic clout more effectively to broaden its footprint and assert its interests. As the Western Balkans integrated ever more deeply into the EU, they opened the door wide for Russia. The "rain parade" in Belgrade in October 2014 was anything but a surprise.

Someone Else's Concern

In the 2000s, the former Yugoslav states commenced their belated "return to Europe", as did neighboring Albania. (Slovenia joined the EU with the first wave in 2004.) The death of Franjo Tuđman on 10 December 1999 and the downfall of Slobodan Milošević on 5 October 2000 gave the starting signal for the westward journey. The EU took over responsibility for the "Western Balkans" from the United States, promising the region membership at the Thessaloniki Summit in June 2003 in exchange for political and economic reforms and efforts at reconciliation. Croatia joined the EU in 2013, with Serbia and Montenegro further back in the queue. NATO expanded as well, taking in Croatia and Albania in 2009 and Montenegro in 2017.

Former Yugoslavia's turn to the West left little room for Russia. Busy with consolidating power at home, Vladimir Putin downscaled foreign commitments and focused on improving ties with both the EU and the United States. The memory of Kosovo was as painful as before, but other issues had come to the foreground. The Kremlin forged common cause with President George W. Bush in the post-9/11 "war on terror". Co-operation with NATO resumed, after the freeze caused by the 1999 intervention against the Federal Republic of Yugoslavia (FRY). The Balkans, on the other hand, had ceased to be a top Russian concern. When an armed conflict broke out in Macedonia in early 2001, pitting the government against the ethnic Albanian National Liberation Army, a seasoned Russian political commentator remarked:

> It is the EU and then the US who bear responsibility for Macedonia now. Let it be their headache, let them look for an exit from the dead-end into which they led the situation through their excessive leniency toward Albanian separatism (now in Macedonia, yesterday in Kosovo). Russia will limit its contribution to "moral solidarity" with the Macedonian authority and a "soft diplomatic support" when the UN Security Council will convene to adopt some resolution on the situation in the republic.[6]

Strained relations with the United States after the invasion of Iraq in 2003 and the "color revolutions" in Georgia and Ukraine did little to change Moscow's attitude to the Western Balkans. An enlarged EU driven by Brussels institutions hardly challenged Russia's vital security interests. The Kremlin had its eyes focused elsewhere, indeed much closer to home. In the words of the respected analyst Dmitri Trenin "[w]hen in 2003 Russia redeployed forces from the Balkans and 'conceded' the Baltics—under Putin, unlike in the Yeltsin period, there was no vociferous campaign protesting their membership, just clenched teeth— this regrouping was done to better consolidate Russia's few assets where it mattered most: in the CIS."[7]

Rekindling Friendship

Russia's withdrawal proved short-lived. Negotiations concerning Kosovo's status as a political entity, set in motion in 2004, effectively pulled Moscow back. The prospect of Serbia's former province transformed from a UN protectorate into an independent state rekindled the Moscow–Belgrade connection. Converging interests brought the two countries together after a period of disengagement and neglect following Milošević's ouster. Russia chose to push back against the West and assert the principle of territorial integrity; Serbia, for its part, rediscovered a growingly powerful ally to aid its cause. However, this has not grown into a patron-client relationship. Successive governments in Belgrade have pursued a policy of balance between Russia and the West in order to clench the best deal either might offer.

History, or a careful reading of it, may partly explain Serbia's choice. Since its emergence as a semi-independent entity in the nineteenth century, Serbia had maneuvered between the Ottoman Empire and Europe's great powers, including Russia—recognized as its protector after routing the Ottomans in 1828–29—and the neighboring Habsburg Monarchy whose influence was strongly felt in economic, social, and cultural life.[8] "Serbia and Russia are very far apart and we are in friendship with the Turks," was the message from Prince Adam Czartoryski, the Polish-born foreign minister, to a Serb delegation petitioning St Petersburg for support in 1805.[9] In the decades that followed, Serbia was governed by passionate Russophiles such as Nikola Pašić, prime minister from 1912 to 1918, but also by leaders lukewarm (at best) to the Tsarist state, like Ilija Garašanin[10] and Prince Mihailo Obrenović, an autocratic Westernizer. The founder of modern Serbia, Karadjordje (Karađorđe) Petrović, for one, had a notoriously bad relationship with St Petersburg's envoy, Konstantin Rodofinkin. Serbs welcomed Russian support but were also taken aback by the patronizing tone of pan-Slavists berating the "European poison" trickling into the Balkans.[11] Serbia's rivalry with Bulgaria, another Slavic Orthodox land and occasional client of Russia's, complicated matters further. Yet it was the Bolshevik revolution that opened up a real chasm. The Kingdom of Yugoslavia, dominated by Serbs, was more than a friend to the White Russians, who settled there in the thousands, but not to the Soviets.[12] In a nutshell, the Titoist policy of juggling ties with both Moscow and the West, one continued under Milošević throughout the 1990s, had an illustrious pedigree.

There was no love lost between Russia and the Serbian politicians who came after Milošević. Having neglected the opposition in the 1990s, Moscow was tainted by its association with the former regime. It was, moreover, the place of exile of the deposed leader's closest family, including his elder brother Borislav, Milošević's son Marko and, after February 2003, his wife Mira Marković, who escaped criminal investigation. Prime Minister Zoran Đinđić, leader of the Democratic Party (*Demokratska stranka*, DS), held markedly pro-Western views. Educated in West Germany, he had studied under the philosopher Jürgen Habermas and then returned to Yugoslavia in 1989 to become one of the most popular faces of the anti-Milošević opposition. All the way until his assassination in March 2003, Đinđić's main goal was to restore ties with the West and end Serbia's predicament of a pariah state in Europe. Much later, in March 2008, right after Kosovo proclaimed independence, the Russian TV channel Rossiia caused a stir after the journalist Konstantin Semin remarked that the "Western marionette" Đinđić "deserved the bullet", referring to his assassination. Officially, Russia had made an ally of President Boris Tadić, Đinđić's heir at the helm of the DS. But a Kremlin mouthpiece had no regrets to offer concerning the slain prime minister and his political legacy.

It was not just the personal factor at play, however. Relations with Moscow were also held hostage to the constant bickering between Serbia and Montenegro in the common state that barely held together all the way to 2006. It was not until January 2004 that one Milan Roćen, a Montenegrin, was designated ambassador to Moscow, a post long occupied by Borislav Milošević.[13]

The one friend Russia had in Belgrade, other than ultranationalists such as Vojislav Šešelj who were tainted by their association with Milošević's misrule, was Vojislav Koštunica, the incoming president of the Federal Republic of Yugoslavia.[14] He made his maiden journey to Moscow on 27–28 October 2000, the first time Vladimir Putin welcomed a Balkan leader (Milošević was never granted an official visit). Putin returned the compliment in June 2001, fresh from his landmark summit in Bled, Slovenia, with President George W. Bush (who said of Putin, "I looked the man in the eye. I found him very straightforward and trustworthy"). The last time a Moscow leader had set foot in Belgrade was Mikhail Gorbachev in 1988.[15] What drew Koštunica close to the Russians was his unabashed nationalism. Unlike his rival Đinđić, who saw the way forward in working with the West on the breakaway province's final status and extracting the best deal for Serbia, Koštunica was intent on fighting till the bitter end. As prime minister (2004–8), he was also hopeful that the Kremlin connection might give him an edge against domestic political competitors. To his chagrin, Putin was anything but forthcoming and avoided commitments. During a meeting in Sochi in June 2004 he declined to extend support for Dragan Maršićanin, Koštunica's preferred candidate in the imminent presidential election in Serbia.

Putin's Russia was certainly in no mood to do Serbia any political favors. Unpaid debt to the tune of $400 million resulted in a cut-off of the gas supply in June 2000. As *Kommersant* opined, "such a tough framing of the issue corresponds fully with Russia's new foreign

policy concept, which prescribes thinking first and foremost
about its national interests."[16] Gazprom would not agree to settle
the bill against old Soviet debts owed to former Yugoslavia. A deal
was struck only in November 2003 when Belgrade agreed to repay
$306 million, in part by commissioning Russian firms to modernize
the Đerdap hydropower plant on the Danube and in part by direct
export of goods.[17] During an earlier visit to Moscow in February
2001, Đinđić had already won another key concession—eliminating
the intermediary company Progresgas Trading linked to the former
prime minister, Mirko Marjanović, a prominent member of
Milošević's entourage.[18] For its part, Serbia opened its doors to
Russia's Lukoil, which purchased a controlling stake in Beopetrol.
Ten years thereafter, the transaction sparked off a huge scandal
when the Anti-Corruption Council (*Savet za borbu protiv korup-
cije*), a state watchdog, accused Lukoil and the Privatization Agency
of defrauding taxpayers of €105 million by issuing themselves a loan
out of Beopetrol funds.[19] Russia's penetration of the Serbian
economy was anything but problem-free.

The New Battle of Kosovo

The Kosovo "status process" breathed new life into the Russo-
Serbian affair. Starting in 2004, the pursuit of a final settlement
restarted the Contact Group and inserted Russia into Balkan politics once again. Moscow had both a stake and the leverage. But its
comeback reflected the fact that Belgrade made a conscious choice
to seek Russian support and resist the West. It was a team effort of
sorts whereby the entire Serbian leadership—Koštunica, President
Boris Tadić (who succeeded Đinđić at the top of the DS), foreign
ministers Vuk Drašković (2004–7) and Vuk Jeremić (2007–12)—all
played a role at least as significant as that of the Russian Ministry of
Foreign Affairs (MFA) or the Kremlin.

   In hindsight, it is striking how few people thought, at the outset,
that Russia would mount a tough challenge to the United States and
powerful EU member states over Kosovo. Putin no doubt harbored
bitter feelings about 1998–99. Yet he, so the argument went, also

epitomized the rational leader who put good ties with the West first. The general expectation was that Russia would, begrudgingly, stomach Western decisions, having scaled back its presence in the Balkans. Independence or "disguised independence" seemed attainable; the only thing missing was the *quid pro quo* that would facilitate the consent of all parties. There were rumors that the Kremlin was prepared to trade in its approval for concessions in other areas.[20]

To be sure, all members of the Contact Group had converged on several points, even before negotiations started in Vienna in early 2006.[21] First, there could be no return to the pre-1999 status quo. Second, Kosovo's borders were to remain unchanged, irrespective of whether the outcome would be a state or an autonomous entity within Serbia. Third, Kosovo was to be denied the right to merge with neighboring countries, a thinly veiled reference to Albania. Everyone agreed that human rights and the principle of multiethnicity had to be respected and that Prishtina was to be granted a "European perspective."[22] Moscow was happy with the mediator appointed by the UN Secretary General Kofi Annan as well. Martti Ahtisaari, the former president of neutral Finland, was known for his dovish views of Russia. Together with Viktor Chernomyrdin he had negotiated the terms of surrender during NATO's campaign in 1999, providing for Yeltsin a way out of the Kosovo quagmire (see Chapter 1). Moreover, Russia invested more trust in Ahtisaari than did Serbia. Throughout 2006, the Russians ignored the Serbs' complaints that the Finnish mediator was biased in favor of granting independence to Kosovo.

No sooner had the talks started than profound differences started surfacing. The West and Kosovar Albanians saw independence as the only viable option and thought the negotiations had to smoothen the way. This was Ahtisaari's view too. Russia, by contrast, joined Serbia in insisting that the "status process" be open-ended. Sure enough, the talks could resolve certain technical or economic matters. But any outcome beyond broad autonomy was out of question. That left no scope for compromise. Belgrade would not accept Ahtisaari's plan for independence in exchange for self-rule for the Kosovan Serbs. For their part, Kosovars and Western leaders rejected any idea of partitioning Kosovo, which would leave Serb-majority municipalities north of the Ibar River under Belgrade's sovereignty. On paper, Serbia was against such a trade-off as well.

Putin hedged his bets right from the start. In the event that Kosovo remained part of Serbia, Russia would score a diplomatic victory. But should the West refuse to back down, Moscow was ready to harness the precedent and make the most of it. The Russian president asserted early on that the final decision on Kosovo would have universal implications and would not be a one-off event as the West maintained.[23] Abkhazia, South Ossetia, Transnistria or other separatist entities across the former Soviet Union aligned with Russia could well profit from the precedent. Putin made explicit the linkage between Kosovo and the Commonwealth of Independent States (CIS)—having ignored the Balkans during his first presidential term. At stake also was Russia's role on the world stage. It had the best of both worlds: donning the mantle of champion of international law without tying its own hands or foregoing opportunities to enhance its position. This is exactly what happened in the aftermath of the 2008 war with Georgia, when Russia recognized Abkhazia and South Ossetia's independence, and in 2014 with the annexation of Crimea.

To play the game, Russia focused on process, rather than substance. Rather than get their hands dirty with minutiae to do with territorial governance and constitutional rights of ethnic communities, Putin, Foreign Minister Sergei Lavrov, and UN Ambassador Vitalii Churkin (an old Balkan hand) insisted that no solution could be imposed from outside. Belgrade and Prishtina had to work it out themselves.[24] The West had no right whatsoever to twist Serbia's arm on issues of sovereignty. No one phrased Russia's position better than Putin himself. At the 2007 Munich Security Conference, where he famously blamed the United States for undermining global security, he responded to a journalist's question on Kosovo in the following way:

> What will happen with Kosovo and with Serbia? Only Kosovars and Serbs can know. And let's not tell them how they should live

their lives. There is no need to play God and resolve all of these peoples' problems. Together we can only create certain necessary conditions and help people resolve their own problems. Create the necessary conditions and act as the guarantors of certain agreements. But we should not impose these agreements. Otherwise, we shall simply put the situation into a dead end. And if one of the participants in this difficult process feels offended or humiliated, then the problem will last for centuries. We will only create a dead end.[25]

At the tactical level, Russia opposed the notion that the Vienna talks were pegged to a strict deadline, the end of 2006. It fought hard on this point, creating breathing space for Serbia. The fact that the status process continued into 2007 constituted a minor diplomatic victory for the Russians.

Of course, the extended timetable made little difference in the end. Serbia rebuffed the Athisaari proposal for independence under international supervision and powers devolved to Serb municipalities. Russia took its side and made it abundantly clear it would veto the plan at the UN Security Council. Its stringent opposition ushered in a new round of talks in August 2007, this time led by the senior German diplomat Wolfgang Ischinger (EU), Aleksandr Botsan-Kharchenko (Russia), and Frank Wisner (United States). That marked another diplomatic coup for Moscow and Belgrade as it effectively shelved the Ahtisaari Plan. But as negotiations predictably ended in a cul-de-sac, America and the EU great powers were left with no other option but to go for a unilateral solution bypassing the UN.[26] Against the objections of Belgrade, Moscow, and five EU member states,[27] the Kosovar parliament declared independence on 17 February 2008.

The enduring legacy of the "status process" has been the realignment of views on Russia in Serbia. In the 1990s, it was the ultranationalist Serbian Radical Party that lobbied for an alliance with Moscow. Milošević's approach was instrumental, turning to the Russians when convenient and then tilting to the West. In the mid-2000s, it was the turn of the pro-Western spectrum in Serbian

politics, personified by Boris Tadić and his cohort, to embrace
Moscow. "It was the West which pushed us to Russia then," pointed
out a Serbian diplomat and high-ranking member of DS as he
reflected on the impact of Kosovo's declaration of independence in
2008.[28] To him, Western powers treated Milošević better than the
democratic opposition of the 1990s, in that UNSC Resolution 1244
left Kosovo as part of the then Federal Republic of Yugoslavia. Russia,
by contrast, could be relied upon to wield its veto and aid Serbia.

The consensus in favor of working with Russia was reflected in
the declaration on neutrality voted by the Serbian parliament on
26 December 2007—a year after joining NATO's Partnership for
Peace. The post-Đinđić DS, Koštunica's Democratic Party of Serbia
(*Demokratska stranka Srbije*, DSS),[29] the Radicals, and the post-
Milošević Socialist Party of Serbia (*Socijalistička partija Srbije*,
SPS), all backed the motion. The only outliers were the Liberal
Democratic Party (LDP) and the League of Social Democrats of
Vojvodina. Public opinion was highly supportive. "Russia's prestige
is very high and President Putin's rating is over nearly any politician
in Serbia," mused Finance Minister Božidar Đelić of DS on a visit to
Moscow in the autumn of 2007.[30] Serbia's neutrality cemented the
alliance with Russia and paved the way for numerous joint initiatives in the areas of security and defense (see Chapter 6).

Serbia firmly believed that Russia's assistance would seriously
change the odds in the campaign to fight back against Kosovo's
declaration of independence. President Tadić, narrowly re-elected
in January 2008, and Foreign Minister Vuk Jeremić, were leading
the charge. They approached the UN General Assembly, which
voted on 8 October 2008 to refer the Prishtina parliament's declaration to the International Court of Justice (ICJ). At the UN, Russia
rallied its friends and CIS allies.[31] Moreover, it lent Serbia full
support during the ICJ proceedings, submitting a long statement to
argue that Kosovo's declaration breached international law.[32] Tadić
and Jeremić were hopeful that a favorable ruling would bring the
Kosovars back to the negotiating table. In contrast to 2006–7, now
they hinted at partition as a last resort.[33] That is why Serbia needed
Russia and why its pro-Western politicians, telling Brussels and

Washington their hold on power was under constant threat from nationalists on their right, had no qualms in reaching out to Moscow and pursuing EU membership at the same time.

But by that point Russia was weighing in on the side of secessionism. In an op-ed published by *The Financial Times* right after the Georgian war, President Dmitry Medvedev reasoned as follows:

> [I]gnoring Russia's warnings, Western countries rushed to recognise Kosovo's illegal declaration of independence from Serbia. We argued consistently that it would be impossible, after that, to tell the Abkhazians and Ossetians (and dozens of other groups around the world) that what was good for the Kosovo Albanians was not good for them. In international relations, you cannot have one rule for some and another rule for others.[34]

Putin was to go one step further: in an interview for a German TV channel, he evoked the memory of the Srebrenica genocide in Bosnia (July 1995) and the Western doctrine of humanitarian intervention in justifying Russia's use of force against Georgia.[35] In a remarkable turnaround, Russia shifted from defending the Serbs to implicitly sympathizing with the plight of Kosovar Albanians and Bosniaks.

The alliance with Russia failed Serbia's expectations. The Jeremić–Tadić game plan backfired massively when the International Court of Justice found, by ten votes to four, that Kosovo's declaration did not breach general international law, UNSC Resolution 1244, or the Constitutional Framework adopted under the United Nations Mission in Kosovo (UNMIK).[36] The Advisory Opinion transferred the dispute from the UN to the EU, limiting Russia's role. Starting in March 2011, direct talks under the auspices of Catherine Ashton, High Representative for Foreign and Security Policy, linked Kosovo to the EU's enlargement into the Western Balkans. As shown by the Brussels Agreement (19 April 2013), the prospect of membership has been an incentive for both Prishtina and Belgrade to normalize relations, establish a *modus vivendi*, and perhaps work out a formula for settling the dispute.

As Serbia agreed to entrust the EU with the Kosovo issue, Russia moved to the sidelines. The country's tilt to the East was followed by a tilt to the West. Ironically, it was self-avowed pro-Western politicians such as Tadić who oversaw the resumption of relations with Moscow. And it was Aleksandar Vučić, a one-time prominent member of Šešelj's Radicals, who, first as deputy prime minister between 2012–14 and then as premier, would advocate rapprochement with the Kosovars as an entry ticket to the EU.

The Money Factor

Serbia had been banking on hopes that the Russian connection would yield profit in the economy, first and foremost in the field of energy. Up until the mid-2000s, energy had been a sore point in the relationship. Public-sector entities such as NIS and Srbijagas (established in August 2005 as a separate company) owed the Russians hundreds of millions in unpaid bills. The first Ukraine gas crisis in 2006 had taken its toll on Serbia, which was overwhelmingly dependent on Gazprom deliveries through Hungary. But now it looked as if Belgrade could capitalize on Moscow's interest in bypassing Ukraine, and turn from a consumer to a transit channel for Russian gas.

Vojislav Koštunica was particularly keen to develop energy ties, accommodating Moscow's demands. In late 2005 he and his energy minister, Radomir Naumov, oversaw the insertion of YugoRosGaz as an intermediary—as Progresgas Trading was in Milošević's day. Gazprom was furthermore allowed to increase its stake from 50 to 75 percent via an offshore branch—at a discount price. Critics saw that decision as entrenching Russia's dominance and inflating the rates charged to consumers.[37]

On 23 January 2008, just weeks before Kosovo proclaimed independence, Koštunica and Tadić signed a framework agreement in Moscow on co-operation in energy. It contained a package deal. Gazprom Neft was to purchase a 51 percent stake in NIS, one of Serbia's largest companies. Gazprom, for its part, would take over the underground gas storage facility at Banatski Dvor and invest in upgrading it. In return, Russia made an informal commitment that Serbia would be included in the South Stream gas pipeline. Less than a week beforehand, on 18 January, Putin had signed an agreement on the pipeline's extension through Bulgaria.

The Moscow framework agreement was like a gift from heaven to Tadić as it fell in between the two rounds of the presidential election. Already supported by the EU, he could pose as a patriot and a friend of Russia in the uphill struggle against Tomislav Nikolić, leading the ultranationalist Radical Party, who was ahead in the first round. The deal spurred criticism too. The Economy and Regional Development Minister Mlađan Dinkić, leader of the pro-market G17+ party, argued that the NIS sale had to wait till after the parliamentary polls (11 May 2008). Dinkić objected to the price that NIS was sold for: €400 million amounted to a fraction of the company's value, he believed.[38] He demanded firm guarantees that South Stream would pass through Serbia, rather than Romania, an increase of annual capacity from 10–15 or even 18 billion cubic meters (bcm), and a deferral of the transfer of 26 percent from NIS until the final deal on the pipeline was sealed. "If it is a gift to the Russians, we should say it openly," Dinkić challenged his coalition partners. Čedomir "Čeda" Jovanović, leader of the pro-Western LDP and one-time rising star within the DS, went a step further: Russia, in his view, was turning Serbia into its colony. However, Tadić was simultaneously facing pressure from the Russian ambassador, Aleksandr Konuzin, and the opposition comprising Koštunica and the Radicals. The Serbian parliament ratified the framework agreement on 9 September 2008. Outgunned in the team negotiating the commercial terms with Gazprom Neft, Dinkić stepped down as its head two months later.[39]

Ultimately, Serbia managed to obtain a better bargain from the Russians. NIS's privatization contract was signed by Presidents Tadić and Medvedev in Moscow. Gazprom Neft promised to invest an additional €550 million.[40] Yet Serbia had to make reciprocal concessions. It conceded to Gazprom 51 percent in the joint-stock company operating South Stream's section on its territory. All other countries involved in the project had a 50–50 arrangement with the

Russian side. In effect, Gazprom won control over the transit infrastructure to be built in Serbia, together with the Banatski Dvor
facility. Construction services related to South Stream formed a
major part of the package as well. The Serbian stretch of the pipeline was estimated at €1.4 billion in 2008 but the cost had soared to
€2.1 billion in July 2014.[41]

In the longer run, the 2008 deal left a bad taste for both Moscow
and Belgrade. When Putin called off South Stream in December
2014, blaming Brussels and the EU member state Bulgaria, the
Serbian government could not help but think that the family silver
had been sold on the cheap. NIS held a monopoly on imports of
crude oil and oil derivatives (lifted only in January 2011). Gazprom
Neft retorted that Serbia had got a good deal. NIS was heavily in debt,
employed far too many people, had close to five million citizens as
minority shareholders, and a number of its assets in Serbia and across
former Yugoslavia were subject to legal disputes.[42] Gazprom had put
up money to overhaul antiquated facilities, including the refinery at
Pančevo degraded by the NATO airstrikes of 1999. However, all these
improvements were a far cry from the ambitions to turn Serbia into
a transit corridor for Russian gas and reap a bonanza. South Stream
had paid off only in part. Srbijagas, overseen since October 2008 by
the deputy chairman of the *Socijalistička partija Srbije*, Dušan
Bajatović, had spent €30 million on assorted contracts.[43]

Energy links helped Russia make further inroads into the Serbian
economy. In 2012–13, two major Russian lenders, Vneshtorgbank
(VTB) and Sberbank, started operating in Serbia.[44] Occupying
respectively the eleventh and twenty-fifth position in the rankings
of Serbian banks in terms of the size of assets, the subsidiaries in
question are not big players on the local market. Yet they do benefit
from political connections. In 2012, shortly after entering Serbia,
VTB administered the sale of government eurobonds worth
$750 million.[45] However, the presence of two financial institutions
targeted by the Western sanctions has given Serbia additional reason
for refusing to align with the EU. Serbia benefits from a free-trade
agreement (FTA) with Russia dating back to August 2000, when
Milošević was still in power. Yet it excludes key export items, such as

cars—manufactured at the Kragujevac factory acquired by Fiat in 2008—and certain agricultural products.[46] Although Serbia's exports picked up as a result of the counter-sanctions imposed by Moscow on the EU, trade remains unbalanced because of the large-scale imports of Russian oil and gas. Serbia's deficit in 2013 had risen to €610 million.

Since the inception of the global economic crisis, successive Serbian cabinets have courted Russia for financial assistance too. During his visit to Belgrade in October 2009, President Medvedev offered budgetary aid and investment to the tune of €1 billion. Yet all Russia could disburse in 2013 was €344 million in the form of a loan. Still, Moscow manages to get the maximum bang for its buck. A poll in June 2014, commissioned by the Serbian government, found that 47 percent of people believed Russia was ahead of all other donors, where in fact it trails behind the EU, the United States, and even Japan.[47]

The push to attract further Russian investment, very prominent under the Serbian Progressive Party (*Srpska Napredna Stranka*, SNS) that came to power in 2012, has not been particularly successful either. Gazprom has refused to swap debt for shares that Srbijagas holds in Petrohemija (Pančevo), where NIS/Gazprom Neft holds 12.7 percent of the shares. Large Russian firms like Vimpelcom and Aeroflot decided not to bid for strategic assets such as Telekom Srbija and the national air carrier JAT (rebranded Air Serbia after its purchase by the Abu Dhabi-based Etihad). Contrary to speculation, Moscow money has not come to the rescue of loss-making state-owned enterprises such as the utility company EPS (*Elektroprivreda Srbije*) and Serbian Railways. The October 2015 dismissal of the head of Russian Railways, Vladimir Iakunin, one-time confidant of Putin's and frequent visitor to Belgrade, has slashed hopes for the overhaul of Serbian Railways with help from Moscow. As much as Prime Minister Aleksandar Vučić has struggled to cash in on good political ties, Russia has not been particularly forthcoming. Buffeted by international sanctions and plummeting gas prices, Moscow has not demonstrated a particular appetite to pour money into Serbia in recognition of its geopolitical significance.

A Friend Lost?

There is hardly any other place in former Yugoslavia where pro-Russian sentiments are as deeply rooted as Montenegro. "There are 300 million of us together with the Russians" (*"Nas i Rusa trista miliona"*) goes a familiar saying in the minuscule republic whose actual population is only a notch over 600,000. From St Petersburg's subsidies to the Prince-Bishops of the Black Mountain, to princesses marrying into the Romanovs, to Montenegrin communists remaining loyal to Stalin and opposing Tito in 1948, links between Montenegro and Russia have spanned decades and even centuries.[48]

These legacies mattered little in the 1990s when Moscow ignored Podgorica and channeled relations exclusively through Belgrade—dealing with the leader of Montenegrin extraction, Slobodan Milošević, nonetheless. It all changed right before the Kosovo war. President Milo Đukanović had already taken a turn towards the West, distancing himself from Milošević. This brought Đukanović onto Russia's radar. He was in Moscow in May 1998, days before defeating Belgrade's ally Momir Bulatović in the parliamentary elections, and held talks with Primakov. Following NATO's intervention, in August 1999, the Montenegrin president was welcomed by Prime Minister Sergei Stepashin and Foreign Minister Igor Ivanov.[49] "Moscow's bet on Đukanović is entirely justified," observed *Kommersant*'s Balkan correspondent Gennadii Sysoev. "Not only because he is a democrat and reformer, as the Russian political elite counts itself. Having been for many years Russia's main partner in the Balkans, Milošević behaves with growing insincerity towards Moscow. Đukanović is not pledging Moscow eternal love but offering mutually beneficial projects."[50]

Ties blossomed during the 2000s. In January 2001, Russia opened a General Consulate in Podgorica. Đukanović saw Putin during a private visit to Moscow in 2004, and Russia was quick to recognize Montenegro's independence after the referendum on 21 May 2006. In a sense, politics had a hard time catching up with already thriving economic ties. Montenegro became early on a favorite holiday destination for Russians. Following the lifting of the visa regime in 2008, the share of visitors from the Russian Federation reached 20–30 percent of the total.[51] Russians were said to take the lion's share of foreign-owned commercial and residential properties, especially in trendy coastal spots such as Budva or Herceg Novi.[52] Investors included prominent personalities such as (then) Moscow's mayor Iurii Luzhkov, a friend of Đukanović's, who has been linked to a "Russian Village," a vacation community above the Adriatic town of Sveti Stefan.[53] The Russian Embassy estimated the number of Russians holding permanent residency in Montenegro at 7,000.[54] Suspicions of money laundering through the real-estate sector have always been rife. Putin's statement from 2006 that Russians had invested €2 billion was in contrast with the 135 million reported by the Central Bank of Montenegro.

Montenegro attracted Russian investment in the industrial sector too. In 2005, the tycoon Oleg Deripaska purchased a controlling stake in Kombinat Aluminijuma Podgorica (KAP), an aluminium smelter. Considered Russia's richest man and a protégé of the Kremlin, the billionaire negotiated directly with Đukanović, at that point serving as prime minister. No formal state body took part in the deal that had been discussed during Đukanović's visit to the Kremlin in 2004. Built in the 1970s, KAP accounted for 20 percent of Montenegro's GDP and a full 80 percent of its exports. The *Dan* newspaper remarked that Russia could well end up owning half of the Montenegrin economy if Deripaska's business empire would pass into state ownership like Mikhail Khodorkovsky's Yukos.[55] Such statements were to be taken with a grain of salt. Even with KAP, Russia came seventh in the list of investors, with Slovenia topping the list. The KAP deal was, in fact, dwarfed by the sale of the national telecommunication company to Norway's Telenor in 2004 and of Jugopetrol to Hellenic Oil.

Subsequent developments strained relations between the tycoon and Montenegrin authorities. The 2008 economic crisis resulted in a rapid decline in aluminium prices. KAP became dependent on rescue funds from the government.[56] Deripaska was forced to leave when the company went bankrupt in 2013. He ended up filing a €100 million lawsuit against the state of Montenegro.[57]

The KAP imbroglio drove down Russia's stock in Podgorica at a moment when the country had made decisive steps towards not only the EU but also NATO. Accession negotiations with the EU kicked off in the summer of 2012. In December 2015, Montenegro received an invitation to join NATO (having been implementing a membership action plan since 2009). Despite polarized public opinion, Đukanović made a choice in favor of the West. In 2013, Montenegro shunned Russian requests to use the port of Bar as a logistics center for its navy in the Mediterranean.[58] In the spring of 2014, the country sided with the Western sanctions against Russia, in clear contrast with Serbia. "My mother is Montenegro, not Russia as with [Serbian President Tomislav] Nikolić." These words of President Filip Vujanović reflect the effort of the Podgorica governing elite to rebrand their country from a Russian enclave to an outpost of Western influence. In April 2015, Montenegro changed its legislation making the acquisition of temporary residence more difficult for real-estate buyers.

Montenegro became a battleground in the tug of war between Moscow and the West. In late October 2015, mass protests against Montenegro's entry into NATO and corruption in high places swept through Podgorica. Đukanović linked the demonstrations to "nationalist circles in Serbia and Russia" meddling in the country's internal affairs. He implied the protest's leaders, such as Andrija Mandić (of the New Serb Democracy Party), were on the Kremlin's payroll. Although denied by both Moscow and the protestors, such allegations are not widely off the mark. In June 2016, Mandić signed a co-operation agreement with Putin's United Russia, along with other leaders of pro-Russian parties from around the Balkans. After NATO invited Montenegro to join in December 2015, he called for a referendum on membership, a position advocated by the Russian Ministry of Foreign Affairs.[59] In actual fact, polarization has benefited Đukanović. By pointing at Russia, Montenegro's undisputed master since 1998, he has been able to deflect attention away from allegations to do with the abuse of power and links to organized crime.

Passions boiled over in October 2016 when the Montenegrin authorities accused Russia of taking part in a conspiracy to stage a military coup spearheaded by a retired general who was formerly the head of the Serbian gendarmerie. According to reports, Serbia expelled several Russian citizens, which made Nikolai Patrushev, head of the Russian Security Council, rush to Belgrade to limit the damage caused by the scandal. In the meantime, Đukanović declared he would step down as prime minister, explaining his decision with pressure from Moscow. In Belgrade, Prime Minister Vučić, who initially talked down the whole story as a propaganda stunt by the Montenegrins, admitted "foreign services, both from the West and from the East" were plotting to assassinate both Đukanović and himself. In February 2017, Special Prosecutor Milivoje Katnić accused the Russian government, as opposed to simply "Russian nationalist structures," of orchestrating the alleged coup attempt. Investigative journalists have pointed in the direction of Konstantin Malofeev, a Russian tycoon who sponsored the separatists in eastern Ukraine at the outset of the war.[60] Whether this murky affair was a case of a botched Russian-backed conspiracy, a plot by rogue security operatives intent on selling it to Moscow, or indeed a false-flag operation, it did highlight the extent to which Russia had become a critical player in the domestic politics of both Balkan countries.[61]

"Republika Srpska is a state, and Russia is its ally"[62]

In the Western Balkans, it is Republika Srpska that comes closest to being a Russian client. Economic and political relations have boomed since Milorad Dodik assumed power in the entity within Bosnia and Herzegovina, first as prime minister (2006–10) and then as president. Moscow's seat at the Steering Board of the Peace Implementation Council (PIC) overseeing the Dayton Accords has provided ample opportunities for Russia to balance the West. It has been an indispensable ally for Dodik in resisting one push after the other by the EU or the United States to centralize authority in Bosnia.

In the early days, Russia's relationship with the West was not adversarial, though it was far from easy. As already mentioned, Moscow went along with the introduction of the so-called Bonn powers in December 1997. The PIC invested the Office of the High

Representative (OHR) with the right to sack and override decisions of elected officials, in the interest of peace and stability. Ironically, the first time the extra prerogatives were used by Carlos Westendorp was when he reappointed Dodik, then a favorite of the West, as prime minister of RS in 1999. He was certainly preferable to the affiliates of Radovan Karadžić's Serbian Democratic Party. It was only a decade later that Moscow argued that the use of the Bonn Powers was unjustified and represented part of the problem, rather than the solution, to Bosnia's constitutional conundrum.[63] Last but not least, Russia endorsed Bosnia's ambitions to join the EU. As late as 2008, the Russian Ministry of Foreign Affairs maintained that was the best way forward for the country following the war.[64]

The confrontational turn in Russian–Western relations during Putin's second term had a direct impact on Bosnia. By 2007, Moscow was heavily criticizing the broad use of the Bonn Powers by the OHR that was justified by the need to break the institutional deadlock and advance EU integration. Russia was in favor of handing more power to Bosnian politicians and replacing the OHR with a EU special representative with a narrower mandate.[65] However, in February 2008, the PIC resolved to extend the OHR's term indefinitely, listing comprehensive constitutional reform as the key precondition for winding up the position. Russia went along with the decision yet it has been maintaining ever since that the time is ripe for the Western viceroy to pack his bags and leave.[66]

Russia has aligned itself with the RS leadership's effort to shore up the autonomy of the Serb-dominated part of Bosnia. Moscow acts as a spoiler, providing Dodik with political cover as he resists the West. It kept a low profile in the spring of 2011 when he tried to hold a referendum on the secession of RS from Bosnia, the worst crisis since the one the Dayton Accords defused through the intervention of the EU foreign policy chief Catherine Ashton. But in 2014–15, at the height of the Ukraine conflict, Russia took a series of defiant steps. In November 2014, it abstained in the UN Security Council vote to prolong the mandate of EUFOR Althea. The message was not difficult to decipher: the Russians could have blocked the EU peacekeeping mission had they wanted. Then, on 8 July 2015, Russia vetoed another resolution to mark the anniversary of Srebrenica by disputing the use of the term "genocide".

More to the point, Russia intervened on Dodik's behalf in RS's domestic politics. In September 2014, Putin received him at the Kremlin, a direct sign of support in the run-up to the legislative and presidential elections in Republika Srpska. Dodik was reconfirmed in office, several thousand votes ahead of his competitor, Ognjen Tadić. He used the visit to Moscow to restate support for South Stream, at that point a merely symbolic act given the project's imminent cancellation. "Our support for Russia is unwavering," Dodik declared. "We are a small community but our voice is heard loudly." On election day, 12 October, Dodik was spotted in Banja Luka with the notorious Russian businessman Konstantin Malofeev (see above), "the Orthodox Oligarch," patron of the activists and paramilitaries spearheading the "Russian Spring" in the Donbas, a prominent presence on the West's list of sanctions and well known to Moscow's military intelligence, GRU.

Moscow backed Dodik in his conflict with Sarajevo and the international community. In November 2015, for instance, he threatened a plebiscite on the OHR's power to pass legislation and on the authority of Bosnia's Constitutional Court. Ambassador Petr Ivantsov refused to join the rest of the PIC in issuing a tough statement or threatening sanctions. While even Serbia spared no criticism of Dodik's brinkmanship, Russia did not change tack, allowing him to stick to his guns for long enough. Still, Moscow did not treat the Crimea referendum ("legitimate and legal," according to Dodik) as a precedent for RS secession. Foreign Minister Lavrov insisted that the revision of Dayton represented a "red line."

Push came to shove on 25 September 2016, when RS voted overwhelmingly in a referendum on "the state holiday" (9 January, or St Stephen's Day, the date Bosnian Serbs proclaimed their "state" in 1992) in defiance of a ruling by the Constitutional Court as well as of Serbia. On the occasion, Russia stood by Dodik who went all the way to Moscow to see Putin three days ahead of the plebiscite. Although the Russian leader said nothing of RS's secession aspirations, Dodik had enough wind in his sails. The "rally behind the flag" effect helped him win the local elections (2 October), deflecting the widespread allegations of corruption harnessed by his opponents.

Dodik's alliance with Russia has a strong economic dimension too. In February 2007, the Russian state-owned oil company Zarubezhneft paid €121.1 million for Bosnia's sole refinery at Bosanski Brod, the motor-oil plant and filling stations' operator Petrol. They were sold directly rather than through an open tender. Dodik advocated this decision along with the new owners' commitment to keep jobs and pay overdue salaries in the heavily indebted firms.[67] The next stage was RS's inclusion within the South Stream project when Gazprom accepted, in September 2012, to build an offshoot pipeline from Serbia along with two gas-fired power stations. When Vladimir Putin called off the pipeline in December 2014, Dodik lashed out at the EU for depriving RS of €2 billion in investment.[68] At this point, Russia appeared as a guarantor of RS's financial stability. In 2014, the Serb entity received €72 million in direct budgetary support from Moscow, having been unable to fall back on the IMF.[69]

It is the same familiar story. Expending minimal resources, Russia has carved out a niche of influence right in the middle of a country whose stability continues to be underwritten by the EU and the United States. The alliance with RS gives the Kremlin a valuable pressure point against the West. Banja Luka blocks Bosnia's accession to NATO, demanding it be approved by a referendum.[70] Having frustrated Russia on so many occasions in the 1990s, the Bosnian Serbs have emerged as its most trustworthy partners in the Western Balkans, ahead of neighboring Serbia or Montenegro. As far as Russia is concerned, by applying low-intensity spoiler tactics, it has time and again put a spanner in the works of the West, stopping short of triggering a major crisis. What is more, it has framed the RS referendum as consistent with the spirit and letter of the Dayton Accords, rather than a challenge. So, at least on paper, the Russians remain committed to the political status quo.

Moscow's actions have been followed with concern by the Bosniak community. "Russia has been supporting for some time everything that comes from RS," lamented Bakir Izetbegović, the

Bosniak member of the common state's tripartite presidency. "The support of a political gamble which puts into question all institutions created by the Dayton Peace Agreement will harm everyone—Bosnia and Herzegovina, the RS, the region, and finally Russia."[71] By contrast, the Bosnian Croat leadership has maintained good relations with the Russian Embassy—very much in accordance with the policy of playing off Serbs and Bosniaks in order to extract concessions. In February 2017, Dragan Čović, the Croat member of the presidency, spoke of the need to nurture ties with the Russians and, together with Ambassador Ivantsov, called for the equality of all communities.[72] Čović's conciliatory tone contrasts with the concerns over Russia's moves in Zagreb (see below).

Russian policy in Bosnia has been followed closely in key Western capitals. In November 2014, Britain and Germany launched a diplomatic initiative to speed up accession to the EU. Bosnia's Stabilization and Association Agreement would come into force even without the passing of constitutional amendments required by Brussels.[73] That in turn made it possible for the Bosnian government to apply for membership in February 2016. To show her support, Chancellor Angela Merkel made a stopover in Sarajevo during a Balkan tour in July 2015. The visit came the day after Russia vetoed the Srebrenica resolution (proposed by the UK) at the UN Security Council. In February 2013, the EU ambassadors decided to cut ties with Dodik to sanction him for his disruptive actions. The RS president had previously been denied a U.S. visa. Placed under formal sanctions in January 2017 over the referendum he had convoked, Dodik was prevented from attending the inauguration of President Donald Trump. In short, relations between Russia and the West regarding Bosnia are at one of their lowest points since the 1990s—if not *the* lowest.

Luring the Rest

Russia has managed to cultivate ties with Croatia, Macedonia, and Albania, traditionally seen as forming a pro-Western bloc within the region. It did not object to Zagreb and Tirana's accession to

NATO in April 2009, a foregone conclusion at that point. Similarly, Russia responded with indifference to the EU's expansion. Unlike the countries of the "near abroad" and even Montenegro, whose entry into the Atlantic Alliance did cause a stir, Croatia and Albania did not come into the spotlight as far as Russia's tenuous relations with the West were concerned. One factor was certainly the timing of NATO's Balkan enlargement. It coincided with the policy of reset enunciated by the Obama administration and the thaw between the United States and Russia. Russia's ties to Slovenia, which is formally not a part of the Western Balkans but certainly is a cornerstone of the "Yugosphere", are nothing short of cordial.

Croatia's interest in Russia grew exponentially in the 2000s, all the way up to the Ukrainian crisis of 2013–14. Although President Franjo Tuđman oversaw the conclusion of a friendship and co-operation agreement during a 1998 visit to Moscow, it was his successor, Stjepan "Stipe" Mesić (in office 2000–10), who invested heavily in the expansion of economic contacts with the Russians. From his first trip to Russia in April 2002 onwards, Mesić lobbied for assorted investment and trade deals—starting with the sale of the ironworks in the town of Sisak to Mechel, a conglomerate based in the industrial city of Cheliabinsk. A decade and more later, as an ex-head of state, Mesić was still a frequent visitor to Moscow, arguing for continued contacts, even as the EU sanctions took their toll on bilateral trade. Back in the days when he was president, the veteran politician, whose career dated back to the Yugoslavia of the 1960s, sought to position Croatia in Russia's energy schemes covering Southeast Europe. Mesić welcomed Putin as the guest of honor at a summit in June 2007 where Gazprom unveiled the South Stream gas pipeline. The Russian president used the Zagreb energy forum to pour praise on his hosts by stating "it's a confirmation of Croatia's international authority." Croatia officially joined the project in March 2010 in Moscow when Prime Minister Jadranka Kosor, of the center-right Croatian Democratic Union (*Hrvatska Demokratska Zajednica*, HDZ), initialled a state-to-state agreement with Putin, then also prime minister.[74] Another venture for which Mesić lobbied was the intended physical interconnection of the Druzhba oil pipeline with Adria, a pipeline that has been in operation since 1989. Known initially as *Jugoslavenski Naftovod* (Yugoslav Pipeline or JANAF), the Adria pipeline links the port of Omišalj (on the island of Krk) all the way to the refinery at Pančevo, Serbia. Once connected to the Druzhba pipeline, it could reverse the flow and start shipping Russian oil to the Adriatic. In December 2002, Croatia signed an agreement with Russia, Belarus, Ukraine, Slovakia, and Hungary, which however failed to win parliamentary endorsement in Zagreb.

Even if ultimately neither the South Stream offshoot through Croatia nor the Druzhba–Adria project made significant headway, they paved the way for a cross-party consensus that it was important to work with the Russians. When Kosor was running against Mesić in the 2005 presidential election, she campaigned against Druzhba–Adria on the grounds that the limited financial returns from the project failed to offset the environmental risks. But during her 2010 visit to Moscow, she had converted into a proponent—despite the negative environmental impact assessment and the vocal opposition by groups such as the Croatian chapter of the secular Franciscan Order. A new round of talks took place in 2012, involving the Russian firm Zarubezhneft, which showed an interest in buying a stake in the Adria pipeline.[75] Kosor's U-turn suggested that as Croatia entered the EU as its twenty-eighth member (July 2013), it effectively joined the club of those within the Union who viewed Russia as a source of opportunities, not a hostile power. In that sense, it was no different from Central European nations such as neighboring Hungary, the Czech Republic, and Slovakia. Or indeed Serbia, which was widely perceived as Russia's main ally in former Yugoslavia. The oil and gas diplomacy pursued by Moscow in the 2000s delivered a partnership with Croatia, thereby diversifying Russian connections in the region.[76]

Russian money made inroads into the domestic economy. Lukoil, already established in other parts of Southeast Europe, entered the country's market in 2008 and had developed a network of fifty-two filling stations by the following decade. When the Croatian government fell out with the Hungarian company MOL, which held 49.1 percent in the national oil company INA after a controversial privatization deal finalized in 2009, Rosneft or Gazprom Neft were rumoured as a possible replacement.[77] As recently as 2016, Russia's ambassador to Croatia, Anvar Azimov, maintained that the offer was still on the table. He intimated Russian investors could also bid for 25 percent of Croatia's national electricity company, *Hrvatska elektroprivreda*, which was up for sale.[78] Rosneft and Gazprom Neft took part in the tender for offshore exploration licences in the Adriatic, though they had no success.

Denser economic links have had political ramifications. In the summer of 2016, *Nacional* broke the story that the HDZ, a senior partner in the governing coalition, had received a donation of €350,000 from a murky Russian foundation.[79] The investigation, triggering the downfall of HDZ chairman Tomislav Karamarko, was nothing short of an embarrassment. The scandal gave extra reasons to President Kolinda Grabar-Kitarović (HDZ), a former foreign minister and ambassador to NATO with strong links to the United States, to take a hawkish line on Russia. In November 2016, she accused Russia of waging "hybrid warfare" in former Yugoslavia, singling out the recent referendum in Republika Srpska as a case in point. Yet there were other prominent players in Croatian politics and the economy eager to continue searching for opportunities. The colorful mayor of Zagreb, Milan Bandić, touted his links to his Moscow colleague, Sergei Sobianin. And one of Croatia's foremost business people, Ivica Todorić—CEO of Agrokor, the largest private firm in the country—took loans from Sberbank (operating in Croatia since 2013) and Vneshtorgbank totaling €1.3 billion by early 2017. As Agrokor faced financial difficulties and Sberbank injected an additional €300 million in March, rumors sprang up that the Russian creditors might take over the struggling company.[80] While the Western sanctions halved bilateral trade turnover (about €1.8 billion, heavily skewed in favor of hydrocarbon exports from Russia), links at the level of political and business elites seem to be strong.

Croatia's overall pragmatic perspective on relations with Russia is more than matched by neighboring Slovenia, a member of the EU and NATO since 2004. The richest successor state of former

Yugoslavia has put extensive efforts into developing business links with Moscow. In March 2011, it officially joined the South Stream pipeline project during a visit by Putin (then still serving as prime minister) to Ljubljana. Russia is Slovenia's most important non-EU trading partner and, unlike other countries in Central and Eastern Europe, Slovenia runs a surplus. In the first ten months of 2016, it exported goods (pharmaceuticals, machinery, etcetera) and services worth €586 million, while imports (mostly energy) were worth €191 million.[81] From the time of the 2001 Bled Summit between Putin and George W. Bush, Slovene leaders have tried to position their country as an intermediary between Russia and the West. In July 2016, Slovenia welcomed Putin—nominally on a visit to consecrate a monument commemorating the tragic death of 100 Russian POWs held in Austro-Hungarian captivity in 1916. Speaking at the Russian chapel some 1,600 meters up in the Julian Alps, Putin praised the Slovene people's "caring attitude to … shared history," while the Sputnik Agency did not miss an opportunity to extol the common Slavic heritage binding the two nations. "Not every Eastern European nation has been infected with the virus of Russophobia," stated Aleksei Pushkov, chairman of the Duma's Foreign Affairs Committee. "Monuments to Russian soldiers have been destroyed in Poland. Slovenia has just erected one."[82] Naturally, the Slovenes had more down-to-earth motives in courting Russia. In February 2017, President Borut Pahor signed two co-operation agreements in Moscow, saying eleven business deals were in the pipeline as well. Pahor came under fire from Janez Janša, leader of the center-right Slovenian Democratic Party. But, to be fair, when Janša served as prime minister (2004–8; 2012–13), he himself had worked to strengthen economic ties with Russia and paid visits to Putin.

Similar to its former Yugoslav partners, Macedonia has scrambled to get a piece of the action too. In July 2013, Prime Minister Nikola Gruevski negotiated a branch away from the main trunk of the pipeline to his country, with Russia agreeing to accept Soviet-era debt (€42 million) as Skopje's contribution to the joint stock company that Macedonia and Gazprom were planning to set up. Gruevski trumpeted the deal as a shining success. A Greek veto had prevented

Macedonia's accession to NATO and membership talks with the EU, but now Macedonia had discovered a new partner in Moscow. Fresh money would be pouring into the economy, in the footsteps of energy firms like Lukoil and Sintez already present.[83] Last but not least, cultural links have been on the rise. In 2014, the Moscow State University delivered an honorary doctorate to President Gjorge Ivanov. The Skopje government has been harboring hopes that the Russian Orthodox Church might facilitate the recognition of its Macedonian opposite number, however slim the prospects. All in all, Gruevski and company have pursued a policy that differed little, whether in form or substance, from the course taken by neighboring Serbia.

Russia's relations with Albania have lagged behind. That is not only because of the country's accession to NATO, its staunchly pro-Western orientation, or indeed the dispute over Kosovo's independence, but also due to the fact that economic ties are underdeveloped. Albania does not import gas, indeed it consumes low volumes. Still, there have been some developments. President Alfred Moisiu (in office 2002–7), a Soviet graduate from the 1950s, was a guest of honor at the anniversary Victory Day parade in Red Square on 9 May 2005. Russian commentators did not miss the fact that Moisiu belonged to the Orthodox Christian community in Albania. In 2011, Tirana for its part hosted a Russian cultural festival. However, the crisis in Russia's relations with the West after 2014 effectively put an end to this momentum. The Albanian government used the Russian threat, directed at the broader region rather than the country per se, to boost its pro-Western credentials. "There are third-party players who can benefit from gaps within the [European] Union. I'm talking about Russia and about radical Islam," opined Prime Minister Edi Rama in an interview for the *Frankfurter Allgemeiner Zeitung* in November 2016.[84]

Ukraine Hits the Balkans

The Ukraine crisis put on display the leverage that Moscow had built in the Western Balkans over a decade. Serbia, Macedonia, and Bosnia and Herzegovina refused to support the EU. Some pro-government media in Belgrade, Skopje, and Banja Luka echoed

Moscow's line on events in Kyiv, Crimea, and the Donbas ("fascist takeover," "Banderovites," "U.S.-directed putsch," etcetera). Reports spread of Serbian volunteers in the breakaway Donetsk and Luhansk People's Republics, as well as of Croats fighting on Kyiv's side. Commentators berated the cancellation of South Stream and the billions lost as a result of the geopolitical contest between Russia and the West. Looking for compensation, governments lined up to join TurkStream, the new pipeline project announced by Putin. Moscow could demonstrate to the West that Serbia and Macedonia still counted on its friendship, similar to EU member states critical of the policy of isolating Russia such as Greece or Hungary.

The Western Balkans proved a fertile ground for Russian "strategic communications." The Kremlin-friendly media painted anti-government protests erupting in Macedonia in the spring of 2015, prompted by revelations of corruption and election rigging, as yet another "color revolution" instigated by the West.[85] Conspiracy theorists linked demonstrations to a plot to derail TurkStream. As in Ukraine, the false fighters for democracy were causing chaos, instability, and state collapse. After the armed clashes between the country's security forces and Albanian radicals in the city of Kumanovo (May 2015), Foreign Minister Lavrov accused NATO members Albania and Bulgaria of plotting to partition Macedonia.[86] Speaking from Belgrade, Lavrov blamed the EU for condoning separatism and the push towards Greater Albania.[87] The Albanians in turn blamed Russia. In November, Hashim Thaçi, deputy prime minister of Kosovo and sometime face of the Kosovo Liberation Army, identified Russia as one of the three great threats to the Balkans, on a par with Islamic radicalism and the refugee crisis.

The protracted Macedonian crisis showcased Russia's capacity to insert itself in the troubled spots of the Western Balkan. By July 2015, all major parties had made a commitment to hold early elections, an achievement for the EU Enlargement Commissioner Johannes Hahn who stepped in as mediator. Yet Moscow continued to snipe from the sidelines. The Ministry of Foreign Affairs, together with government-controlled media such as the TV news channel RT (formerly known as Russia Today) and Sputnik, continued following the deepening political crisis in Macedonia in 2016–17. When anti-corruption protesters poured into the streets of Skopje in April–July 2016, they took the side of the governing center-right party VMRO-DPMNE and Prime Minister Gruevski. They latter portrayed Macedonia's "Colorful Revolution" (*Šarena revolucija*), a wave of street protests between April and July 2016, as a blatant case of Western interference. Twice postponed, the early elections finally took place on 11 December 2016 but resulted in a stalemate. Gruevski failed to put together a coalition, unable as he was to find a compromise with Albanian parties. In March 2017, when President Gjeorge Ivanov declined to hand the opposition Social Democrats a mandate to form a cabinet (in violation of the constitution), Russia again ratcheted up its rhetoric. A press spokesman from the Ministry of Foreign Affairs deplored "[the] attempts, which are actively supported by EU and NATO leaders ... to make Macedonians accept the 'Albanian platform'" (a set of demands Albanians put forward as a price for supporting the Social Democrats).[88] The statement signaled support for Gruevski, who rallied his own supporters, ostensibly to defend the nation that was facing yet another existential threat. As in Bosnia, Russia was weighing in on the side of forces ready to push back against the West—in this case the European Commission, the High Representative for Foreign and Security Policy Federica Mogherini, and the American Embassy in Skopje. In addition, it was magnifying the ethnic dimension of the crisis, which was triggered originally by the release of tapes indicating the abuse of power and corruption by Gruevski and his entourage.

Macedonia was therefore a classic case study of Moscow's disruptive tactics in former Yugoslavia: taking advantage of indigenous problems to score points against the Europeans and Americans and thwart their efforts to steer events on the ground. Yet, one should not lose perspective. After all, it was not Lavrov, let alone someone higher up the chain of command in Moscow, who addressed the tussle in Macedonia. For all the hype around Russian interference amongst Balkan watchers, the former Yugoslav republic did not feature prominently in the Kremlin's list of external priorities. Lastly, Russia could do little to prevent the opposition coming to power in May 2017.

The rupture between Moscow and the West complicated Serbia's balancing act. President Nikolić took a staunchly pro-Russian line and was the only European leader from outside the Commonwealth of Independent States to attend the Victory Day parade in Red Square on 9 May 2015. In the meantime, Foreign Minister Ivica Dačić, presiding over the Organization for Security and Co-operation in Europe, planned to travel to Kyiv, together with a Serbian military band, canceling the trip at the very last moment. Prime Minister Vučić cultivated connections with the United States, meeting with Vice President Joe Biden in September 2015.[89] "Serbia is neither a 'little Russia' nor a little America. It makes its own decisions," declared Vučić.[90] Belgrade proceeded with its defense co-operation with Moscow, while upgrading, often under the radar, relations with NATO. Vučić's policies came under fire domestically. In the run-up to the parliamentary elections in Serbia (26 April 2016), a wave of mass demonstrations called for a referendum on NATO membership. Hard-line parties, supporting canceling EU accession and aligning fully with Moscow, received a boost at the polls.[91] Vučić and SNS were given a first-rate opportunity to play the part of "moderates," "pro-Europeans," and "reformers." The tactic of using the threat posed by Russia to rally support in the West has been widespread across the Balkans. In a more subtle and non-confrontational way, Vučić has been following the example of his fellow politicians elsewhere in the Balkans, notably Milo Đukanović, Edi Rama in Albania, Hashim Thaçi (who, in early 2017, accused Serbia of hatching a "Crimean scenario" in Northern Kosovo), the Croatian President Kolinda Grabar-Kitarović, and others.

In the following episode, Vučić claimed the nomination as his party's candidate in the presidential elections (2 April 2017). The staunchly pro-Russian incumbent Tomislav Nikolić, the founder of SNS, was sidelined. Having toyed with the idea of running a separate bid, Nikolić resolved to step down. Vučić's triumph in the intra-party power struggle suggests that the moderate, "neo-Titoist" line in Belgrade is set to prevail over the hardcore pro-Moscow position championed by Nikolić and the ultranationalists to the right of SNS.

Conclusion

Following a brief absence, Russia has succeeded in inserting itself in the Western Balkans: by co-opting governments, forging alliances with political leaders, appealing to domestic populations, spreading its story about the wars in Ukraine and Syria far and wide. For a good part of the 2000s, Moscow did not use its clout to balance the EU and the United States, accepting that former Yugoslavia lay squarely within their sphere of influence. Ukraine changed that. Now the Kremlin's message is: if you interfere in our backyard (Ukraine, Moldova, Georgia, etcetera), then we can and will most certainly do the same in yours. With the abrupt end of the South Stream project, Russia may have lost its most potent trump card. However, it has become increasingly adroit in penetrating domestic politics and wielding its soft power (discussed at some length in Chapter 8).

The post-Yugoslav states and their leaders are far from passive objects of Russian policies, much less Moscow's pliant instruments. The record shows they have been hedging their options, never putting all their eggs in one basket. EU membership remains the ultimate destination, yet this does not rule out engagement with Russia driven by the pursuit of political gains and economic profits. Putin's standoff with the West certainly made fence-sitting more difficult and costly. Yet Serbia continues to practice it as before, as does Macedonia. By contrast, other countries—Albania, Montenegro (or rather its government), and Kosovo have gone in the opposite direction—amplifying the Russian threat to reconfirm their links to the EU and NATO and make political mileage. The most serious concern, therefore, is that the soaring competition between Russia and the West may reinforce the alarming trend towards democratic backsliding: by increasing the wiggle room of political elites, providing a handy excuse for ignoring corruption and the lack of rule of law, and ultimately weakening external pressures for domestic change in a vulnerable European region.

Russian activism has put Western policymakers on alert. The story of the failed coup in Montenegro (October 2016) in particular made headlines on both sides of the Atlantic. Whether it was a genuine attempt by the Russian state to intervene robustly in the politics of the region or a locally hatched plot, involving Russian citizens, it clearly raised the stakes and put former Yugoslavia in the spotlight. Moscow's meddling in Bosnia, and particularly its backing of Dodik's referendum, fueled even more tensions. One should not be surprised that the specter of yet another Balkan war was quick to reemerge in the Western media. "Putin is planning his revenge over Bosnia and Kosovo," argued a piece in *The Observer* in January 2017.[92] In all likelihood, such fears are overblown. The chances of a return to the 1990s are slim, mostly because Balkan politicians lack the means to wage war and are able to obtain all the benefits—rallying their populations behind the flag and stirring nationalist sentiments—without going past the brink. Yet, the frailty of the region's democratic regimes, the weakening pull of the West in the age of Brexit and Trump, and the raw wounds of the past, all provide Russia with ample opportunities to assert itself in an area as fragile as the Western Balkans.

CHAPTER 3

ACROSS THE BLACK SEA
Bulgaria and Romania

This administration has shown that equally good ties could be maintained with the U.S., with Europe and with the Soviet Union—with Russia, I beg your pardon. There is no trade-off whatsoever.

—Solomon Passy, Bulgarian foreign minister, 2004[1]

Russia treats the Black Sea as a Russian lake.
—Traian Băsescu, Romanian president, to Romanian students at Stanford University, September 2005[2]

"I would like to congratulate all Orthodox Slavs around the world on winning the Third Crimean War and remind them that the Balkans come next." Nikolay Malinov, member of the Bulgarian Socialist Party (BSP) leadership, publisher of its unofficial mouth-piece *Duma*, and chairman of the National Movement of Russophiles, was both jubilant and unapologetic. It was beside the point that Russia's seizure of Crimea in 2014 fell short of a war or that most Ukrainians qualified as "Orthodox Slavs." Malinov's ruminations, aired on the public broadcaster BNT, came as a rebuke of the BSP-dominated cabinet's decision to endorse the EU sanctions against Moscow.[3] The party chairman, Sergei Stanishev—born in the city of Kherson in southeast Ukraine—was mildly supportive. "With Europe but never against Russia" was the line he took.[4] But Malinov claimed to speak on behalf of the staunchly pro-Putin grassroots cheering at Russia's resurgence and brimming with resentment against the West.

On the opposite bank of the Danube, in neighboring Romania, more hawkish views prevailed. The center-right President Traian Băsescu and Prime Minister Victor Ponta of the post-communist Social Democratic Party (*Partidul Social Democrat*, PSD), otherwise fierce political enemies, converged. "I think this is the greatest security risk for Romania and for the region since 1989," contended Ponta, calling for a robust response by NATO.[5] Băsescu warned of a Crimean scenario unfolding in Transnistria, a secessionist region in the Republic of Moldova. Both Romania and Bulgaria welcomed the upgrade of NATO's eastern flank heralded at the Wales Summit (September 2014) as well as the U.S. government's European Reassurance Initiative. But Romania also pushed forcefully for an allied naval presence in the Black Sea to contain Russia. Still, at the Warsaw Summit (July 2016), Sofia—this time represented by a center-right government with foreign and defense ministers skeptical of Russia—said "no" to Bucharest's proposal for a joint NATO flotilla.

Romanians and Bulgarians tend to see Russia differently. The German Marshall Fund's Transatlantic Trends survey found in 2012 that 78 percent of those polled in Bulgaria held favorable views, with a similar percentage supportive of the EU. That compared to 44 percent of Romanians.[6] Whereas Romanian politicians see Russia as a threat, the bulk of their Bulgarian colleagues think in terms of opportunities. Russia treats the two in a dissimilar manner too. Vladimir Putin has been to Sofia three times (2003, 2008, 2010) and only once to Bucharest (attending the NATO Summit in April 2008). On the flipside, the Russians expect more from Bulgaria too. Putin lashed out at Sofia in 2014 over the cancellation of South Stream. He had kept his end of the deal, offering all manner of monetary incentives to decision makers and their business cronies. But Bulgarian politicians ended up telling him that they could do little to change EU rules and make sure the pipeline would go through.

Clichés and stereotypes often mislead by simplifying and obscuring the richness of nuance. This is certainly the case for Bulgaria and Romania's dealings with Russia. The present chapter shows how, starting from 1989, Bulgaria has not been a selfless friend of the Russians and nor has Romania acted as a foresworn adversary. Relations have fluctuated depending on the changing cycles in domestic politics and in EU-Russia relations. There are hawks in Sofia as there are a fair number of pragmatists in Bucharest happy to do business with Moscow. The rhetorical veneer that typically covers state-to-state relations obscures rather unsentimental realities. It is, in a nutshell, a tale of interests, whether overlapping or diverging. Overall, both Bulgaria and Romania, before but also after joining NATO and the EU, have faced the dilemma of how to strike a productive balance between engaging with and hedging against Russia. The calculation has been particularly difficult for Bulgarian decision makers, on account of the considerable Russian leverage in the country's internal affairs.

The Shadow of the Past

"Russia in the Balkans" evokes, in most people's minds, former Yugoslavia. But, in fairness, Russia is much more intimately connected to the eastern parts of the peninsula. Bulgaria and Romania were part of the Soviet camp, unlike non-aligned Yugoslavia and isolationist Albania after 1961. Bulgaria even came to be known as "the Sixteenth Soviet republic," thanks to its unswerving loyalty to Moscow. Romania pursued a very different course: it refused to join the Warsaw Pact in the suppression of the Prague Spring, becoming the first communist country to welcome an American president in 1966 and entering the Global Agreement on Tariffs and Trade (GATT) and the IMF.[7] The neo-Stalinist regime that Nicolae Ceauşescu built up starting in the early 1970s continued to be out of favor with Moscow till the end.

But the story goes much further back than the Cold War. Romanian encounters with the Tsarist Empire began in the early eighteenth century. Russia occupied the Principalities of Wallachia and Moldova, vassals to the Ottomans, on multiple occasions (1739, 1769–74, 1806–12, 1828–34, 1848–51, and 1853–56). By 1774, a Russian army commanded by General Aleksandr Suvorov had made a foray into present-day northeastern Bulgaria, routing the Ottoman army and paving the way to the Treaty of Küçük Kaynarca, which established Russia as a Balkan power. Under General Hans Karl von Diebitsch (nicknamed Diebitsch Zabalkanskii, literally "the One who Crossed the Balkan Mountain Range"), the Tsar's troops reached the city of Adrianople (today's Edirne, across the border with Bulgaria) in 1828–29, having captured the ports of Varna and Burgas. Thousands of Bulgarians, Gagauz, Greeks, and others followed the Russians back to settle Bessarabia after the conclusion of the peace treaty. A Bulgarian community lives in Ukraine and Moldova to this day, which has given the old country two prime ministers, intellectuals, and military leaders. The Russo-Ottoman War of 1877–78 (in alliance with Romania, Serbia, and Montenegro) led to the emergence of modern Bulgaria. This is the reason why the Bulgarian national narrative celebrates Russia, in stark contrast with Romanian history books that cast it as an oppressor. The annexation of Bessarabia, formerly part of the Principality of Moldova,[8] over-shadows positive contributions made by the Russians, such as the *Regulamentul Organic*, the principalities' first constitutional document drafted by the then military governor, Pavel Kiselev (Kiseleff). Russia's defeat in the Crimean War in 1856 paved the way to Romania's reunification and its reorientation toward France, its venerated *sœur latine*.[9] Romanians remember the Molotov-Ribbentrop Pact of 1939 and the Soviet annexation of Bessarabia and northern Bukovina in 1940.[10] The alliance with Russia in the First World War does not figure prominently in the public memory.

Bulgaria's part of the story is equally tangled. Officials from St Petersburg were instrumental in building the state. Bulgarian cities boast streets named after Russian generals, diplomats, and intellectuals, whereas Bucharest has only a boulevard honoring Kiseleff. An equestrian statue of Emperor Alexander II ("The Liberator Tsar") stands proudly opposite the National Assembly in Sofia. However, Bulgarian elites would rebel against Russian tutelage, especially after the assassinated Alexander II was succeeded by the reactionary Alexander III in 1881. The two states severed diplomatic relations in the mid-1880s, amidst feuds between Russia's partisans and liberal nationalists attracted to Austria-Hungary and Germany. Stefan Stambolov, the most eminent figure amongst the latter group, would distinguish between the debt of gratitude to "the good-natured Russian people" and Russia as a great power whose policies he resented. Subsequently, Bulgaria won back favor and even became an ally of sorts in the Balkan League, considered at the time of its creation in 1912 as a triumph of Russian diplomacy.[11] Yet, in 1915 the discordant and volatile politics of the Balkans made it turn, once again, into an enemy of Russia. Despite the presence of a solid bloc of Russophile parties in its public life, Sofia entered the First World War on the side of the Central Powers. Having fought against the Tsarist armies on the battlefields of Dobrudja and Macedonia, both considered parts of the nation's irredenta, Sofia was a signatory of the Brest Litovsk peace agreement concluded by the Bolsheviks in March 1918. In the Second World War, Bulgaria was once again on the opposite side, aligned with Nazi Germany. But unlike the Romanians who actually fought against the Red Army, all the way to Stalingrad, Sofia refrained from declaring war on the Soviets. Once the Third Ukrainian Front marched into Bulgaria, in early September 1944, it did not suffer a single casualty.

This brief historical excursus reiterates just how complex is the baggage that Romania and Bulgaria carry. Romania, a majority Eastern Orthodox country, evolved from a protectorate of Russia to self-professed bulwark of the West against Eastern barbarism and then, during communism, to a reluctant ally. Bulgaria's degree of cultural connections with Russia is unparalleled in Southeast Europe, including former Yugoslavia. "*Kuritsa ne ptitsa, Bolgariia ne zagranitsa*" ("The hen is not a bird, Bulgaria is not abroad," according to the popular Russian phrase). Closeness manifests itself in multiple ways—for example, the Cyrillic alphabet used by both Bulgarians and Russians, which diverges from the Serbian version reformed in the mid-nineteenth century. Yet Bulgaria's political relationship with Russia has witnessed many turnarounds, certainly

many more than any other country in the Balkans: from a protectorate to a pariah, an untrustworthy partner, a battlefield adversary,
a loyal satellite, and so on. The past is riddled with conflicting and
dissonant memories. Needless to say, they resonate strongly in the
debates and struggles of today as attitudes to Russia mark a dividing
line in Bulgarian domestic politics, in contrast to Romania where a
negative view is much more uniform.

Partying with the Soviets

The Soviet Union played a central role in the dramatic events in
Romania and Bulgaria at the end of 1989. Of the two, Bulgaria was
doubtless more susceptible to the winds of change blowing from
Moscow. Mikhail Gorbachev's reforms were frowned upon by
Ceaușescu as "right-wing revisionism," but in Sofia, Todor Zhivkov,
having survived several Soviet leaders since 1954, paid lip service to
perestroika and *glasnost'*. The Bulgarian intelligentsia's proficiency
in Russian exposed them to the iconoclastic journalism of
Literaturnaia gazeta, *Ogonek* or the TV programme *Vzgliad*. In an
odd twist, the imperial center was fueling dissent and destabilizing
the communist regime. When a palace coup deposed Zhivkov on 10
November 1989, the chief plotters were in close contact with the
Soviet ambassador, Viktor Sharapov, a KGB Major General and one-
time deputy to Iurii Andropov, General Secretary of the Communist
Party of the Soviet Union. Foreign Minister Petâr Mladenov and
Andrey Lukanov, the Moscow-born deputy prime minister, posed as
pro-Gorbachev reformers.

Moscow's involvement in the revolution (or choreographed
coup, depending on one's perspective), which put a bloody end to
Ceaușescu's reign, was more limited. Romania was barely mentioned
in the conversation between Gorbachev and U.S. President George
H. W. Bush in Malta on 2–3 December 1989.[12] Yet, the day after, the
Soviet leader clearly conveyed to the Romanian strongman that his
time was up. As popular revolts broke out in Timișoara and then
Bucharest, the American Secretary of State James Baker signaled to
the Soviets that the United States would not object to a military

intervention.[13] Although Moscow stayed out, in conformity with the so-called Sinatra Doctrine of non-interference in Eastern Europe, the revolution's outcome suited Gorbachev. Power passed to the National Salvation Front (*Frontul Salvării Naționale*, FSN) presided over by Ion Iliescu, a Moscow-educated member of the *nomenklatura* who had fallen out of grace in the early 1970s. Iliescu and Prime Minister Petre Roman were in the *perestroika* mould. The revolution had aimed at toppling Ceaușescu, not dismantling socialism, as Silviu Brucan, another FSN grandee, argued at the time.

Moscow's friends rooted in the former regime won in the first competitive elections in 1990 in both Romania and Bulgaria, in contrast to Poland, Hungary or Czechoslovakia where the pro-Western opposition gained the upper hand. Neither the Bulgarian Socialist Party[14] nor the FSN favor a radical split from the Soviet Union. Iliescu even entertained the idea of strengthening security ties with Moscow. Shunned by the West after the violent suppression of opposition protests by pro-government miners in June 1990 (dubbed "the Mineriad", the first one amongst several), he looked to the East for alternatives. Romania was the last member to sign off the disbandment of the Warsaw Treaty Organisation in February 1991. Soon thereafter, on 5 April, Iliescu and Foreign Minister Adrian Năstase signed a friendship and co-operation treaty with the USSR. It committed each of the parties not to join military alliances directed against the other. In other words, Romania would stay out of NATO. However, the Soviet Union's demise at the end of the year invalidated the treaty.[15]

In Bulgaria, it was not only the former communists but also the opposition that looked to Moscow. To its embarrassment, the BSP failed to condemn the anti-Gorbachev putsch in August 1991. President Zhelyu Zhelev, however, did not wait to see which way the wind was blowing. An affiliate of the opposition Union of Democratic Forces (UDF), he sided resolutely with Boris Yeltsin, which gave rise to a close relationship between the two.[16] In October 1991, Zhelev paid an official visit to Yeltsin, a de facto recognition of the Russian Federation's independence while the Soviet Union was, formally, still in existence. The Bulgarian president believed the new state was heading in a pro-Western direction. Bulgaria became the third former member of the former Eastern bloc, after Czechoslovakia and Poland, to sign a friendship and co-operation treaty with Russia in 1993. All in all, democratic changes seemed to bode well for relations with Moscow.

Between Russia and NATO

While both Bulgaria and Romania initially hoped to preserve special ties with Russia, NATO enlargement in the mid-1990s saw their positions drifting apart. Moscow's hostility to the eastwards expansion was clear and unconditional. Would Bucharest and Sofia take on board the Russian objections or push for membership regardless, just like Poland, the Czech Republic or the Baltic states? Which of the two scenarios posed the greater risk: antagonizing Russia or lagging even further behind Central Europe in a geopolitical grey zone?

As early as 1993, Romania chose NATO. Iliescu, re-elected in 1992, and the post-communist Social Democratic Party of Romania (*Partidul Democrației Sociale din România*, PDSR),[17] sensed that the enfeebled Russia of the 1990s was not in a position to offer similar security guarantees as the superpower that was the USSR, even in its twilight days. Developments in the Republic of Moldova bore on Bucharest's change of perspective too. The lapsed friendship treaty of 1991 promised Romania the right to spread its cultural influence across the Prut River. The conflict in Transnistria pitting the Soviet (later Russian) 14th Guards Army against newly independent Moldova, partly armed by Romania, changed the perspective. In January 1994, Romania became the first state in Eastern Europe to join NATO's Partnership for Peace. Still, Iliescu went on insisting that Bucharest pursue *both* membership in the alliance and security partnership with Russia—exemplified by a military co-operation accord signed by the two states.

In contrast to Romania, the Bulgarian political scene was deeply split. The BSP, in power between 1994 and 1997, was fearful of alienating Moscow. Joining the EU was uncontroversial, but becoming part of a military pact divided the former communists. Some endorsed deepening ties with NATO, others rooted for neutrality. To make things worse, the government was embroiled in a tangled commercial dispute with Gazprom. Prime Minister Jean Videnov, a graduate of the Moscow State Institute of International Affairs (*Moskovskii gosudarstvnnyi institut mezhdunarondnykh otnoshenii*, MGIMO), opposed the transfer of an ownership stake in the Bulgarian grid to Russia. He clashed with Lukanov, who acted as Gazprom's semi-official representative within the country—up until he was assassinated in the autumn of 1996 (see below). To placate the party base and tone down conflicts, Videnov fudged the NATO issue. The center-right UDF and President Zhelev, on the other hand, pushed for membership, insisting it was part of the same package as the EU.

Bulgaria's posture changed only after a hyper-inflationary crisis, mass protests, and early elections installed the UDF in power. On 8 May 1997, the National Assembly voted to apply for NATO membership. Relations with Russia became even more fractious as a result. In October 1997, the pro-Western Bulgarian cabinet refused to invite the Russian Defense Minister Igor Sergeev to a Balkan ministerial meeting attended by the United States and Turkey. As far as Sofia was concerned, security co-operation in the region was the business of NATO's Partnership for Peace and only members or aspiring members of the alliance were welcome in the club. Little wonder the Russians did not appreciate Bulgaria's volte-face.[18]

Romania went through a very similar shift after Emil Constantinescu, of the center-right Democratic Convention (*Conventia Democrată Română*, CDR) coalition, defeated Iliescu in the November 1996 presidential election. A native of Bender/Bendery in Transnistria, Constantinescu was adamant that the friendship and co-operation treaty under negotiation with Russia had to include a condemnation of the Molotov–Ribbentrop Pact. Another sore spot was the demand for restitution of the ninety-four tons of gold transferred for safekeeping to the Tsarist Empire in December 1916. In opposition, the CDR had torpedoed Iliescu's search for a compromise. Embarrassingly, the Russian Foreign Minister, Evgenii Primakov, returned empty-handed from

Bucharest when the Romanians, to his unpleasant surprise, refused to sign the initialed treaty.[19] Irked by this mishap, Primakov swore not to yield an inch to Romanian demands. (The USSR's legislature had condemned the Molotov–Ribbentrop Pact back in 1989, and there was no documentary proof regarding the gold, diplomats argued.) Facing elections, Yeltsin was not inclined to compromise either. Moscow ratcheted up the conversation, insisting on the insertion of the non-alignment clause from 1991 into the new treaty. In consequence, relations between Romania and Russia were practically frozen, all the way until late 1999.

The absence of a deal with Russia presented an obstacle to Romania's accession to NATO. As a condition of its entry, the alliance demanded that Bucharest resolve outstanding issues concerning minorities and borders with its neighbors. Sure enough, for NATO, fundamental treaties with Hungary (signed 9 September 1986) and Ukraine (2 June 1997) took precedence. But without Moldova and Russia on the list, Romania could not be invited to join NATO at the Madrid Summit of July 1997, unlike Hungary, Poland, or the Czech Republic. This failure bred a sense of insecurity. Romanian elites feared their country could undergo a Yugoslav scenario or prove vulnerable to Russian meddling. Commentators detected Moscow's hand when striking Jiu valley miners marched, yet again on Bucharest, in January 1999 ("the Fifth Mineriad").[20]

Moscow's involvement in former Yugoslavia served to reinforce the perception that Romania and Bulgaria found themselves in the middle of a resurfacing fault line between Russia and the West. Both countries seized the opportunity to showcase their pro-Western credentials, for example opening their airspace to NATO military jets during the war in Kosovo. In June 1999, they refused to allow Russia a transit corridor through their airspace to reinforce paratroopers in Prishtina airport. Public opinion was skeptical of NATO's actions, looking to Serbia as a historic ally. In Bulgaria, the BSP voted against the Operation Allied Force. Romania, Iliescu, and the PDSR abstained in the parliamentary vote on the OAF, but a poll showed that only 1 percent of citizens supported the NATO air campaign.[21] The choice paid off. In December, EU leaders invited the two countries to start membership negotiations, despite the European Commission's misgivings about the progress of economic and institutional reforms. On that occasion, saying "no" to Russia advanced Bulgaria and Romania's interests.

"Boy, I will either bypass you or roll over you"

The early 1990s was a time when Bulgaria and Romania's economic ties with Russia and the rest of the Commonwealth of Independent States (CIS) declined sharply, whereas those with the EU surged dramatically. The demise of COMECON (the Council for Mutual Economic Assistance) in June 1991 brought down the system of preferential tariffs and financial arrangements operating between the Soviets and their former satellites. In 1992–93, Bulgaria and Romania signed Association Agreements with the EU, removing duties on industrial goods and facilitating the trade of agricultural products and services. Russia itself was reorienting to Western Europe. By 1993, only 12.9 percent of imports into the country came from former COMECON countries, compared to 56.3 percent in 1989. The same process was taking place on the other side too.[22] In 1994, Russia accounted for 4.2 percent of Romanian exports but 13.8 percent of imports. The corresponding shares for Bulgaria (in 1996) were 12.32 percent of exports and 26.2 percent of imports (Russia was still the lead importer!).[23] The gap in trade flows reflected the continued dependence on Russian oil and gas, particularly in Bulgaria. Moscow was reluctant to address the issue; it classified both Romania and Bulgaria as "developed nations," refused them special treatment, and insisted on reciprocal concessions—which would have raised complications with the EU.

To make matters worse, Soviet disintegration ended the barter arrangements signed in 1985–86 whereby Eastern European states would build the energy infrastructure in Russia, to be repaid with gas.[24] As early as August 1989, Viktor Chernomyrdin, the future prime minister, directed the transformation of the Ministry of Gas Industry into State Gas Concern Gazprom (*Gosudarstvennyi gazodobyvaiuschii kontsern "Gazprom"*), a business entity combining state and private ownership. The former Soviet grid was soon to be partitioned amongst the successor republics. The inherited trading model became obsolete virtually overnight.

In the early 1990s, a patchwork of intergovernmental memoranda of understanding (MoUs) and agreements came to complement and replace the former barter accords. Gas continued to flow westwards but a legal mess had set in. The Russian Federation owed money to both Bulgaria and Romania related to the construction services, but calculating the exact amount was a matter of dispute. Moscow, moreover, raised objections that the Soviet Union had invested handsomely in the two countries over the decades, building heavy industries from scratch.[25] Even when the sums were worked out, Russia was not prepared to repay its dues through gas shipments. In 2002, the Deputy Prime Minister Aleksei Kudrin put it rather bluntly to the Bulgarians: "[this is] not a question for the state but for Gazprom's shareholders."[26] Sofia had to settle for a cut from $132 million to $88.5 million, to be repaid by nuclear fuel and spare parts for MiG fighter jets. Romania has meanwhile so far failed to recover its $200 million.

Russia could dictate the terms of gas commerce. Gazprom would sell through intermediary companies, rather than directly to Bulgaria's national utilities Romgaz and Bulgargaz. That raised a host of legal and political issues. Topenergy, the Bulgarian intermediary set up in May 1995, started as a 50–50 partnership but later on, in January 1996, Bulgargaz's share dropped to 25.1 percent. Companies linked to Multigroup, a highly influential corporate empire with links to the criminal underworld, moved in.[27] One of those companies, Overgaz, was a joint venture between Multigroup and Gazprom. The prevailing view at the time, including within Bulgaria's Socialist government, posited Topenergy as a slush fund whose goal was to take control of Bulgaria's transit infrastructure. Gazprom lobbied for a concession, promising to expand and upgrade the Bulgarian grid and pay back more in transit fees to the national budget from shipments to Turkey and Greece. The former Prime Minister Andrey Lukanov, head of Topenergy, spoke of Bulgaria as a future "gas hub" in the Balkans. Gazprom carried a stick too: in case Sofia turned down the offer, it faced the risk of higher prices, which would worsen its already precarious financial position. There were other possible routes to Turkey too. "Boy, I will either bypass you or roll over you," the Gazprom CEO, Rem Viakhirev, reportedly told the youthful Prime Minister Videnov, who held out to pressure.

Lukanov's departure from Topenergy, his subsequent assassination, and the collapse of the Videnov cabinet ended this murky chapter in Russo-Bulgarian relations. In a coda, the incoming UDF government managed to turf out Multigroup and pass Topenergy into Gazprom's sole ownership. However, the new twelve-year contract signed in May 1998 contained concessions to the Russian giant: advance payments, a "take-or-pay" clause, and lower transit fees.[28] Gazprom decided to negotiate directly with Turkey the construction of a new infrastructure to meet rising demand, initiating the Blue Stream pipeline going under the Black Sea (see Chapter 5).

Romania's relationship with Gazprom turned out to be much less problem-ridden, as the country could cover most of its energy needs from domestic sources. In the late 1990s, Romgaz was importing 1.5 billion cubic meters (bcm), half of the gas volume taken by Bulgaria, and extracting ten times that domestically (mostly from fields in Transylvania). Positive energy ties were in stark contrast with the freeze at the political level.[29]

Large-scale privatization in the late 1990s opened the door to the Russian oil business. Lukoil acquired 51 percent of Petrotel, Romania's biggest refinery near Ploeşti, in February 1998, and 58 percent of Neftochim Burgas, on the Bulgarian Black Sea coast, in October 1999. Neftochim is Bulgaria's only refinery and one of the largest in Southeast Europe as well as the largest taxpayer in the country.[30] It enabled the Russian giant to expand its retail business across the region, including in former Yugoslavia.[31] Petrotel came with about one-fifth of the Romanian market. While the political implications of Lukoil's acquisition were considerable, it was not part of a grand strategic design hammered out officially in Moscow. Both refineries were sold by Western-leaning, center-right governments that were not in Russia's good books at the time. Yet Lukoil had an advantage over other bidders. Petrotel and Neftochim operated with

Soviet hardware and technology,[32] using crude oil from Russia and the CIS and employing staff trained in former days. At the time, the Western powers had little interest in loss-making facilities saddled with debt. Lukoil's arrival solidified the Russian foothold in the energy sector of both Romania and Bulgaria, but especially the latter. A cable from the American Embassy in 2006 called Valentin Zlatev, the head of Lukoil in Bulgaria, "[a] vastly influential kingmaker."[33]

Marching Westwards, Looking East

Just as Russia entered the Putin era, Bulgaria and Romania took decisive steps in joining the West. Accession talks with the EU proceeded. The two countries entered NATO in 2004 and moved closer to the United States, contributing to the International Security Assistance Force (ISAF) in Afghanistan and backing George W. Bush's war in Iraq. Scolding "New Europe," the French President Jacques Chirac singled out the two countries: "Romania and Bulgaria were particularly irresponsible. If they wanted to diminish their chances of joining Europe they could not have found a better way."[34] Russia clearly shared Chirac's analysis. Yet it did not view Sofia and Bucharest's pro-American turn as quite so dramatic. First, because Putin himself had worked to improve ties with the United States and the EU. Second, because stable relations with Moscow were a prerequisite for membership of NATO. A more confident Russia took every opportunity to broaden contacts with both Romania and Bulgaria.

Vladimir Putin found a partner in Ion Iliescu who, upon returning to the presidency, restarted negotiations on a Basic Treaty in 2001. Two years later, in July 2003, Russia and Romania signed an agreement based on compromise.[35] With the *Partidul Social Democrat* back in office, bilateral ties grew stronger. Foreign Minister Mircea Geoana was on particularly good terms with Igor Ivanov, his Russian opposite number. As chairman of the Organization for Security and Co-operation in Europe (OSCE) in 2001, Geoana took extra care to avoid friction with Moscow. Romania and Russia collaborated on the Black Sea Naval Force (BLACKSEAFOR), a security initiative proposed by Turkey in 2001, with Bulgaria, Ukraine, and Georgia also taking part.

Bulgaria was even more amenable to Russian overtures. The former king Simeon Saxe-Cobourg-Gotha, elected prime minister in 2001, balanced the strong push for joining the EU and NATO with cozying up to Russia. In 2002, his government revived the project for a second nuclear power plant at Belene, which had been dropped after 1989.[36] With the BSP leader Georgi Pârvanov becoming president, Russia won another friend in Sofia. On 3 March 2003, the national holiday in honor of the 1878 Treaty of San Stefano, Pârvanov welcomed Putin at a historically charged commemoration on Mount Shipka, the site of a major battle in the Russo-Ottoman War of 1877–78, fought by the Russians along-side Bulgarian volunteers. Memories of brotherhood and war camaraderie provided the backdrop for a reinvigorated political partnership. The "year of Russia in Bulgaria," 2008, saw the conclusion of a package of energy agreements, including the Belene nuclear facility assigned to Rosatom, South Stream, and the Burgas–Alexandroupolis oil pipeline. Having made it into the EU in 2007, Sofia seemed to be back within the Kremlin's orbit, as in the good old days.

Bulgaria and Romania's views started diverging only in the mid-2000s. In December 2004, Traian Băsescu defeated Adrian Năstase, Iliescu's appointed successor, in the presidential race. The former Bucharest mayor embarked on a more assertive course towards former Soviet neighbors, just as Putin was pushing back against the "color revolutions" and the spread of Western influence in its "near abroad." Băsescu believed Romania could spearhead NATO and the EU's expansion into the Black Sea area, spoke of a "Bucharest–London–Washington" axis, and likened his victory over the PSD to the Orange Revolution in Kyiv. He fraternized with Mikheil Saakashvili of Georgia and Ukraine's President Viktor Yushchenko, who both attended the Black Sea Forum hosted in Bucharest (July 2006). Romania was amongst the initiators of the short-lived Community of Democratic Choice, a pro-Western alternative to the CIS. Contacts with Moscow were reduced to a minimum. Băsescu used Russia to fight domestic rivals. In the 2009 presidential campaign he accused the PSD's candidate Mircea Geoana of having visited Moscow. Romania and Russia saw eye to eye on only one issue: their shared rejection of Kosovo's independence. That, though, was very much the exception confirming the rule.

Bulgaria took a different path. It sought to profit from Western expansion of the EU without picking fights with Moscow. In August 2004, Foreign Minister Solomon Passy made Bulgaria a NATO liaison country for Georgia. Bulgarians were selling weapons to Tbilisi as well. Together with Bucharest, Sofia championed "Black Sea Synergy" (2007), an EU outreach initiative. At the same time, business ties with the Russians were on the rebound. The BSP returned to power in 2005 under yet another Moscow-educated prime minister, Sergei Stanishev, who, on top of that, had held Russian citizenship until the mid-1990s.

In fairness, Russia had little reason to fear Romanian or Bulgarian encroachments. In April 2008, NATO's summit in Bucharest—more than a nod to Romania's growing contribution to the alliance—declined to give membership action plans (MAPs) to both Georgia and Ukraine. Russia's war with Georgia four months later ruled out any expansion of NATO. Attention shifted to Romania and Bulgaria's decision to station American troops on their territory. Moscow argued that deployments breached the 1997 Russia–NATO Founding Act. Romania's decision in February 2010 to host elements of the NATO missile shield also provoked a harsh reaction in Moscow.[37] Still, the U.S.–Russia reset piloted by Presidents Barack Obama and Dmitry Medvedev was in full swing. Tensions would be kept under a lid, as much as conceivably possible.

Seen from Moscow, Romania continued to pose a challenge in the Republic of Moldova. Bucharest viewed itself as both an elder brother and gateway to the West for Moldovans, but their sympathies were divided between Russia and the EU. The pro-European group tended to identify with Romania as well.[38] Between 2001 and 2009, the country's communist President Vladimir Voronin veered between Russia and the EU. Voronin turned down Băsescu's proposal for a state merger (April 2009) as a fast track to Europe and he slammed Romanian imperialism.[39] He resisted Russian pressure to federalize Moldova by reincorporating Transnistria. Since the communists lost power in July 2009, a succession of Moldovan governments advanced along the EU path. The number of Romanian citizens in Moldova grew, reaching up to 800,000 according to some estimates.

In a nutshell, Russia's relationship with Bulgaria and Romania in the 2000s was characterized by pragmatism. Moscow was neither willing nor able to prevent the two countries from veering towards the West. They, in turn, could do little to harm core Russian interests in the Black Sea area. At worst, Russia could live with the outcome of the EU and NATO's expansion to encompass its erstwhile satellites. At best, it could actually benefit from it. "You are our Trojan horse in the EU, in the good sense," said Vladimir Chizhov, Russia's ambassador to Brussels, to Bulgarian journalists on the eve of the country's accession to the EU.[40]

The Grand Energy Slam

In the late 2000s, Bulgaria became a lynchpin of Russia's strategy to build a gas corridor across Southeast Europe and bypass Ukraine. The South Stream pipeline, with a capacity of 63 bcm, was flanked by two further projects of considerable scale, the Belene nuclear power plant and the oil pipeline linking Burgas to the Greek port of Alexandroupolis. The "grand energy slam" (*golyam energien shlem*), as President Pârvanov styled it, reflected Russia's growing clout in Bulgarian politics. It was to become the subject of fervent debates concerning high-level corruption and state capture.

Burgas–Alexandroupolis

Plans for an oil pipeline bypassing the clogged Turkish Straits were first floated in 1992. Despite much talk, the Burgas–Alexandroupolis project did not make headway until 2007, mainly because Bulgaria and Greece would accede to the Russian demand for a 90 percent share in the venture. Finally, Athens managed to broker a three-way deal reserving a majority package to Russia's Transneft, Gazprom Neft, and Rosneft.

Burgas–Alexandroupolis courted controversy. First, there were no firm guarantees regarding the throughput. Second, the parties set transit fees too low to make the pipeline competitive for tanker shipments through the Straits. Third, local authorities along the Bulgarian Black Sea coast, a major tourist destination, opposed it. Upon coming to power in 2009, the center-right Citizens for European Development of Bulgaria (*Grazhdani za evropeysko razvitie na Bâlgaria*, GERB) started backtracking. Prime Minister Boyko Borisov used the pretext of local referenda in the cities of Burgas and Pomorie to walk away from the project in May 2011. The decision came as a bad surprise for Greece, which had leveraged Burgas–Alexandroupolis to buy Moscow's acquiescence for a branch of the South Stream gas pipeline (see Chapter 4). Russia, by contrast, could put a brave face on it: it touted an alternative oil connection traversing Turkey from Samsun to Ceyhan, agreed with Turkey (Çalık Enerji) and Italy (ENI) in October 2009.

Map 1 The Burgas–Alexandroupolis oil pipeline and the Belene nuclear power plant

The Belene Nuclear Power Plant

The stakes were much higher concerning the second piece of the package deal, the Belene nuclear power plant. Both the Saxe-Coburg-Gotha cabinet (2001–5) and the BSP-dominated administration that replaced it (2005–9) were strong proponents. "Does Bulgaria really need yet another vastly expensive white elephant?" critics objected. Even after the closure of four units at the Kozloduy nuclear facility, the country produced far more electricity than it consumed. Demand from neighbors was in decline, so prospects for export were not encouraging either. To break even, the second nuclear plant had to charge prices three times higher than Kozloduy's remaining units.

The choice of contractor was at least as controversial. In February 2006, months before the government announced the outcome of the public tender, Energy Minister Rumen Ovcharov of the BSP noted, right after a visit to Moscow, that "[w]ithout Russian participation, building the Belene nuclear power plant would be exceptionally difficult from the technical standpoint, and doubtful from the legal standpoint."[41] Given that one of the bidders was Rosatom, a Russian state-owned company, and the other Škoda Alliance, in which Russia's OMZ held 50 percent, Ovcharov (a graduate of Moscow's Institute of Energy) was clearly not far off the mark. From the 1980s, the project had inherited Soviet-made equipment and a site suited for reactors and technology supplied by Russia. Predictably, the consortium led by a Rosatom subsidiary, Atomexportstroy (AES), won the contract.[42] Years later, in 2013, Milko Kovachev, the energy expert who had overseen the restart of the Belene nuclear facility while serving as minister, would land a job at Rosatom. The people who took and executed the decision to build the plant were clearly in cahoots with the Russian side.

The Bulgarian government's choice in favor of a second nuclear power plant carried important political consequences. Belene would be the first nuclear facility built by the Russian Federation on EU territory. It would give a boost to Moscow's reputation as an exporter of high-end technology, rather than a source of raw materials. Inside Bulgaria, advocates eulogized the nuclear plant as a step towards reindustrialization, reversing a decade or more of economic decline. As in the good old days, Russia was lending a helping hand as well as securing cheap electricity for the benefit of impoverished Bulgarian households.

The GERB government, and particularly its energy minister Traicho Traikov, were not convinced of Belene's merits. The prospects of the nuclear power plant moving on without the provision of state funding were thin. That was a tough proposition in good times, let alone during an economic slowdown and recession. Germany's energy company RWE, which had joined in, decided to quit in October 2009.[43] Sofia declined a €2 billion loan offered by Prime Minister Putin in exchange for 80 percent of the venture. In the meantime, costs had soared from €4 billion (agreed in November 2006) to €6.3 billion, not counting the €2 billion already spent on preparing the site. Negotiations led to a stalemate and Prime Minister Borisov called off the project in March 2012.[44]

The decision to abandon the Belene nuclear facility gave Russia additional leverage over Bulgaria's government, including on South Stream. AES filed an arbitration suit and in June 2016 won an award of €500 million (half of the sum it claimed). The nuclear saga caused domestic commotion as well. On 27 January 2013, Bulgarians voted in a referendum on whether a second nuclear power plant was needed—initiated by BSP, the party to which the so-called "nuclear energy lobby" (businessmen, experts, opinion makers, and so on) traditionally gravitated. While low turnout invalidated the plebiscite, it illustrated Russia's ability to penetrate domestic politics. But again, the main mover and shaker was not Moscow but the Socialists who seized on the Belene facility to drum up electoral support. The question of who pocketed the €2 billion spent on Belene remains pertinent to this day.[45]

South Stream

South Stream was no doubt the crown jewel amongst Russia's three ventures. It promised substantial investment, extra income from transit fees, and, not least, a reduction of the tariffs that Gazprom charged Bulgaria. The GERB government was positive overall, as the Socialists had been before them. As ever, it was the small print that mattered. Russia had to settle for a 50–50 partnership to build the pipeline extension through Bulgaria (as opposed to a 51–49 formula endorsed for the respective joint venture in Serbia). In addition, the project was not to use the existing grid but lay new pipes. In 2009, Energy Minister Traikov demanded an increase to the transit fees. Gazprom responded by overtures to both Turkey and Romania (President Băsescu blocked talks). Haggling ended only in November 2012 when Gazprom settled for a 20 percent discount and reduction of the "take-or-pay" quota in Bulgaria's new ten-year contract.

The question was how much South Stream Bulgaria would cost and who was to cover Sofia's contribution. As in the case of the Belene nuclear facility, the figure kept rising: from €1 billion in January 2008, to €3.3 billion in November 2012, to €3.5 billion in November 2014 (or €4.1 billion, including VAT). Experts explained the increase with the tacit agreement between Moscow and Sofia that politically connected Bulgarian subcontractors were to be brought in. Who the lead contractor was became clear early on. In August 2013, even before the public tender was activated, the Moscow daily *Kommersant* released the name of the winner— Stroytransgaz owned by Gennadii Timchenko, a personal friend of Vladimir Putin.[46] The list of Bulgarian subcontractors featured firms linked to all major political parties, including GERB which had moved to opposition in June 2013.[47] To foot the soaring bill, the Bulgarian government decided, in 2012, to draw a €450 mliion loan from Gazprom to be repaid with transit fees over fifteen years. Later on, the sum was revised up to €620 million (repaid over twenty-two years), but Sofia and Gazprom kept confidential the negotiated amount of transit fees.[48]

Murky politics aside, South Stream would have moved on had it not been for the Ukraine crisis. It ruined the chances for the European Commission and Gazprom to reach a compromise regarding the application of EU rules on third-party access to

South Stream. The oligarch Timchenko ended up on the Western sanctions' list. Brussels threatened Bulgaria with an infringement procedure for breaching EU's public procurement legislation and went as far as blocking part of its funding.[49] The prime minister, Plamen Oresharski, declared Sofia was halting its work on South Stream, pending a deal between Russia and the European Commission. What followed was a political crisis. In June 2014, the governing coalition, led by the BSP, split and early elections in the autumn brought back to power Boyko Borisov's GERB.

Apart from bringing down the government, South Stream led to the demise of Corporate Commercial Bank (KTB), Bulgaria's fourth largest lender. This was no ordinary financial institution but a business empire controlling assets in key sectors such as energy, tobacco, telecoms (the largest national company Vivacom), media—and benefiting from public funds in the form of deposits from state-owned enterprises and access to government contracts. KTB financed the New Bulgaria Media Group, a leading market player, whose outlets provided media comfort for successive governments. Russian capital was involved as well: Vneshtorgbank (VTB) held 9.6 percent of the shares. KTB (Bulgarsovinvest) was originally established in 1988 as a Bulgarian–Soviet joint venture, with Vneshekonombank, VTB's predecessor, as a partner. Critics would point to KTB as nothing short of a state-capture scheme on a grand scale. With South Stream off the table, the bank clashed with its principal partner, the tycoon Delyan Peevski who had borrowed money against future construction contracts related to the pipeline.[50] KTB faced a bank run and closure. VTB declined to come to the rescue. Still, the tycoon Konstantin Malofeev, a prominent sponsor of the pro-Russian separatists in Ukraine and target of Western sanctions, stepped into the fray with a bid to acquire KTB's telecom business and its TV channel.[51]

Putin, who pronounced South Stream dead in December 2014, was furious with the Bulgarians. Together with Gazprom, he had gone out of his way to accommodate their demands over the years. Russia had given them discounts and had allowed their companies to dip in. And now they were withdrawing from South Stream, without doing their job and lobbying Brussels on the project's behalf. Bulgaria acted as a vassal of the West, forfeiting its own interest:

> It is well known that the EU and Bulgaria torpedoed South Stream and did not allow us to carry through this project. Although it is, no doubt, fully in line with the interests of Bulgaria as well as of the entire southern Europe. Countries that gave up taking part in its constructions are left with counting their missed profits.[52]

At a closer reading however, the end of South Stream has not been a game-changer. Bulgaria continues being dependent on Russia for gas. Unlike neighboring Romania it has no domestic resources, while poor infrastructure connectivity makes it difficult, though certainly not impossible, to import gas from alternative suppliers.

Responses to Ukraine

The conflict in Ukraine closed the ranks in Romania's famously fractious political scene. Even the *Partidul Social Democrat*, traditionally well-disposed towards Moscow, called for a tough response. Băsescu's successor, Klaus Iohannis, redoubled the effort to anchor NATO in the Black Sea. The Warsaw Summit gave a green light to the deployment of a multinational brigade at the Mihail Kogălniceanu airbase near the city of Constanța, including troops from Poland, Bulgaria, and other allies. Casting aside past problems, Romania strengthened its ties with Ukraine too, becoming the first EU member to ratify Kyiv's Association Agreement in July 2014 and signing a military co-operation deal.

In Bulgaria, opinions were split. In 2014–15, the BSP and former president Georgi Pârvanov, who had split from his former colleagues, supported conciliation with the Kremlin. The xenophobic Ataka party rallied against the West, echoing the Kremlin's talking points about the decadent EU and the perils of American imperialism. "It was not the EU but Russia that liberated us from the Turkish yoke," read a slogan at their rally on Bulgaria's national day, 3 March 2015. The ultranationalists despatched observers during the Crimea referendum and exploited the issue of a Bulgarian minority in Ukraine, presumably a victim of the post-Yanukovych regime. The center-right diverged. President Rosen Plevneliev along with the ministers of foreign affairs and defense voiced their strong support for Western sanctions and for an upgrade to the NATO presence in Eastern Europe. "For us, Crimea is Ukraine and Ukraine is Europe," Plevneliev declared before the European Parliament in June 2016.[53]

Prime Minister Borisov, however, spoke of the need to relaunch energy co-operation with Russia—in compliance, of course, with EU rules. In his view, Bulgaria had lost money on South Stream and paid the full price of acting as a good European citizen. It was therefore entitled to compensation. The country could host a gas hub fed by an updated version of South Stream and volumes from Azerbaijan and other suppliers.[54] Instead of being torn apart between the EU and Russia, Bulgaria could benefit from both, the prime minister assured his constituents.

In another twist to the story, in November 2016, Bulgarian voters elected as president a candidate who campaigned for restoring ties with Russia. Backed by the opposition BSP, General Rumen Radev, formerly head of the air force, took a markedly different position from his predecessor, Plevneliev. "We need to look at realities. Of course, there is an infringement of international law [regarding Crimea's annexation]. This is a fact. But it is also a fact that at this moment there is a Russian flag waving over Crimea," the general argued in a televised debate.[55] Radev also lambasted the Western sanctions as counterproductive. "Pro-Russia Candidate Wins in Bulgaria" was the headline in the international media, drawing a parallel to the election of Igor Dodon as president of Moldova, another politician rooting for a turn to Moscow. Such views were overblown. At the very least, Radev was a NATO general schooled at the Air War College in Montgomery, Alabama. Even if his narrow circle included personalities known for their admiration of Putin's Russia, it was too much to expect that he would preside over a radical turn in Bulgaria's policy of risk aversion as laid out by Borisov and others.[56] As the early elections at the end of March 2017 approached, the BSP, GERB, and President Radev sparred over whose position was the least confrontational vis-à-vis Russia.[57]

Romania went through its own moment of change. In December 2016, elections brought to power a coalition between the *Partidul Social Democrat* and the *Alianța Liberalilor și Democraților* (ALDE, the Alliance of Liberals and Democrats), a centrist party.[58] Sorin Grindeanu's cabinet introduced no changes to Romanian foreign policy, whether in terms of rhetoric or substance. Unlike Bulgaria, relations with Russia did not come under the spotlight. The government had plenty of other concerns; it faced a massive wave of protests over its changes to anti-corruption legislation. The foreign minister, Teodor Meleșcanu, had already served as first diplomat in 1992–96, the period during which Romania had made its maiden steps into NATO and the EU. However, having the PSD in charge raised questions whether Bucharest would soften its tone towards Moscow by a notch or two. Meleșcanu's early meeting with Ambassador Valerii Kuzmin reportedly brought up the issue of resuming co-operation.[59] However, Romania persisted lobbying for an enhanced NATO presence in the Black Sea. Although in the run-up to the alliance's Warsaw Summit it failed to enlist Bulgaria's support for an initiative supporting a permanent naval task force, a meeting of defense officials in February 2017 resolved to boost military deployments.

Conclusion

Bulgaria and Romania have come a long way since 1989: from integral parts of the Soviets' outer empire to membership in NATO and the EU. However, ties to Russia as well as the wider post-Soviet space have proven durable, courtesy of the two countries' geographic location and recent history. Connections are certainly stronger compared to those between Russia and the Western Balkans.

Moscow and Bucharest have been direct competitors in the Republic of Moldova. Economic, human, and cultural links bring Bulgaria into Russia's orbit. Following the collapse of the USSR, relations with Moscow have remained a focal point in both Bulgarian and Romanian foreign policy. Russia, for its part, has a great deal of leverage. It is capable of shaping Bulgarian politics from within thanks to a plethora of allies in the governing party, business, culture, and so on. That is manifestly not the case in Romania. Still, Moscow is in a position of influence even there, owing to the fallout from its actions in Moldova.

For all their differences, Romania and Bulgaria followed a common pattern in relations with Russia up to 2005. Senior officials following the collapse of communism advocated engagement, while the center-right took a hawkish view. The gap between the two Black Sea countries grew wider under Presidents Băsescu and Pârvanov, who were at the opposite ends of the spectrum when it came to Russia. The Ukrainian crisis has brought the two neighbors closer together, even though a succession of Bulgarian governments have aired diverse, at times contradictory, messages. At the end of the day, Sofia has gone along with the NATO policy of containment, despite the rhetoric of positive-sum economic links and avoidance of confrontation. Differing perspectives on Russia have not overruled the fundamental fact that the principal anchor of both Romanian and Bulgarian politics has been the West. Even in Bulgaria, where pro-Russian sentiments traditionally run strong, membership in NATO and especially the EU has not come under serious questioning, even at a time in which the West appears to be in retreat.

Russia's policy vis-à-vis Romania and Bulgaria has delivered mixed results. Surely, Moscow wields the power to thwart Romanian ambitions for exporting EU and NATO integration to the Black Sea littoral, starting with Moldova. Moscow no doubt has a strong lobby in Bulgaria, controls key chunks of the economy, and enjoys unqualified sympathies in some electoral segments of the population. On the flip side, Russia has failed to fully co-opt the Bulgarian political elite and enact a "Trojan horse" scenario.

The ill-fated "grand slam" demonstrates the limits of using corruption as a lever of power. Forced to make a choice between the EU and Moscow, Bulgaria opted, however begrudgingly, for the former.

CHAPTER 4

FRIENDS WITH BENEFITS
Greece and Cyprus

We value the centuries-old traditions of friendship between our peoples. Our co-operation [with Greece] rests on a rock-solid base of common civilizational values, the Orthodox culture and a genuine mutual affection.

—Vladimir Putin, 26 May 2016[1]

It felt like a pilgrimage, not a routine state visit. Mere months after coming to power in Athens, Alexis Tsipras, the poster boy of Europe's radical left, was to meet Putin at the Kremlin. While Yanis Varoufakis, the maverick economics professor turned minister of finance, was battling his eurozone colleagues over yet another bailout package, the Greek premier turned up in Moscow, on 3 April 2015, to petition help for his country's faltering finances. The creditors were ganging up on Athens and Grexit, the dreaded expulsion from the EU's single-currency area, loomed large once more. It was not inconceivable that Greece would bring back the drachma, wiping out the already thinning deposits in its shaky banks. But perhaps Russia could come to the rescue at this critical moment. Having already hosted Prime Minister Matteo Renzi of Italy, Putin relished the opportunity to show that Western sanctions along with the strategy to isolate Russia was doomed. He and Tsipras talked at length about TurkStream. Extending the pipeline

into Greece was fine—with just one proviso. At the press conference after meeting Putin, Tsipras let journalists know that the
extension would be known as "Greek Stream." The bad news was
that Moscow would not provide financial aid nor was it going to
make an exception for Greece with regards to the restrictions
slapped on EU food imports.

Tsipras's visit, followed by another one to St Petersburg two
months later, fueled suspicions that crisis-ridden Greece had come
fully under Russian sway. Many had warned about the pro-Kremlin
sympathies of Syriza (*Syanspismós Rizospastikēs Aristerás*, Coalition
of the Radical Left), even before it emerged victorious at the early
elections in January 2015. Throughout 2014, the anti-austerity party
had poured scorn on the "fascist Kiev junta," lamented the "genocide
in Ukraine's East," and spoken favourably of the secession referendum
in Crimea. Its members in the European Parliament typically voted
"no" on all initiatives linked with the EU's Eastern Partnership and
Ukraine, including its Association Agreement that triggered the crisis
with Russia.[2] Comments made by Foreign Minister Nikos Kotzias, a
former politics professor, raised fears that the incoming government
might attempt to obstruct the renewal of EU sanctions against
Moscow. Syriza's junior partner, the Independent Greeks (*Anexártētoi
Éllēnes*, ANEL), was equally suspect. The right-wing nationalists'
leader Panagiotis "Panos" Kammenos, in charge of defense, had been
spotted at a gathering of conservative and far-right politicians
convened by the oligarch Konstantin Malofeev, a self-proclaimed
torchbearer of (Orthodox) Christian values and notorious sponsor of
the separatists in eastern Ukraine.[3] Kammenos called on the EU and
NATO "to do everything possible to lift the embargo," which he
decried as a "disaster both for Russia and the EU."[4] The love of Russia
united radical leftists and conservative nationalists as much as resentment against Germany, the reviled Troika, and the fiscal restrictions
they dictated.

Russia is universally popular in Greece. Sympathies span the
political spectrum and resonate with public opinion. A Gallup poll
conducted between May and June 2015 found that 62 percent of
citizens opposed Western sanctions and only 11 percent were in

favour.[5] Back in 2007, a "power audit" prepared by the European Council on Foreign Relations (ECFR) had depicted Greece as one of Russia's closest friends in the EU. It had gone as far as calling the country "a Trojan horse," a label originally applied to Bulgaria.[6] Contrary to the memorable phrase in Virgil's *Aeneid*, the Greeks are not exactly bearing gifts. However, europundits warns us we should beware all the same.

What is true of Greece is even more pertinent for Cyprus. In 2008, the presidential election was won by Dimitrios Christofias from the left-leaning AKEL (*Anorthōtikó Kómma Ergazoménou Laoú*, Progressive Party of the Working People). An outgrowth of the underground communist movement that battled against British colonial rule in the 1930s and 1940s, AKEL collaborated closely with the USSR. Christofias himself had spent five years as a history student at the Soviet Academy of Sciences, similar to many other of his compatriots schooled across the Eastern bloc. A fluent speaker of Russian, he managed to negotiate a loan from Moscow once the Greek crisis hit the shores of Cyprus in 2011. But, in fairness, Christofias's policies differed little from those of his nationalist forerunner Tassos Papadopoulos. Or indeed of his successor, Nikos Anastasiades from the conservative DISY (*Dēmokratikós Synagermós*, Democratic Rally). In February 2015, Anastasiades and Putin struck a deal whereby Russia restructured the 2011 loan and was granted access to Cypriot naval facilities in return.

As in the case of Serbia or Bulgaria, it is tempting to explain Greece and Cyprus's attachment to Russia via religion and the bonds of shared past. Yet in both of those countries Western influences throughout modern history have been more consequential. With the partial exception of the Cypriot left, Russophilia is a skin-deep phenomenon. The flirtation with Moscow, this chapter shows, is a legacy of the late Cold War and its immediate aftermath in the 1990s. It has always been shaped, first and foremost, by strategic and commercial interests. Emotions and historical sentiments come second, both for Russia and for Greece and Cyprus. And contrary to the entrenched stereotype, the two countries have not been pawns in Russia's game but self-interested players wedded to their own, oftentimes parochial, goals. Yet, as we will find out, high expectations on both sides have often been at variance with political reality.

A History of Encounters

It is true that modern Greece and Russia share rich historical links, which go back to the baptism of Kievan Rus in 988 sealed through the marriage of Grand Prince Vladimir to Anna Porphyrogenita, the sister of Basil II Bulgaroktonos (the Bulgar-Slayer). That said, the original encounter was hardly a happy one. In June 860, a fleet of Rus vessels descended on Constantinople and pillaged several of its suburbs, passing into the Sea of Marmara.[7] This episode has long been erased from public memory. The enormous cultural debt that Slavs owe to the Eastern Roman Empire (known anachronistically as Byzantium) is beyond doubt. The Cyrillic script, essentially a modified version of the Greek alphabet making its way to Kiev Rus from the ninth-century Balkans, stands as a compelling visual proof of the bond.[8] Prior to the fall of the empire to the Ottoman Turks in 1453, the "Byzantine Commonwealth," studied by the Russian émigré scholar Dimitri Obolensky, spread far north of Constantinople's outposts in Crimea. Visitors to Muscovite churches marvel at masterly frescoes that elaborate on models derived from Byzantium. Back in those days, cultural influences traveled from the south to the north. Much later, in the eighteenth and especially nineteenth century, the flow would be reversed and it would be Russia's turn to leave its imprint on Balkan societies and cultures.

The emergence of modern Greece is perhaps a more appropriate starting point in our story. Greeks were amongst the first in the Balkans to witness the growing might of the Romanov Empire. Since the eighteenth century, Greek-speaking intellectuals (such as Evgenios Voulgaris, who served as librarian at the court of Catherine the Great and archbishop of Kherson in today's Ukraine) and merchants across Ottoman lands and Europe had followed with admiration the rise of Russian power north of the Black Sea, had found refuge in the empire and enlisted in its bureaucracy.

St Petersburg emissaries were behind a major rising in 1770, while a flotilla commanded by Catherine the Great's favorite Count Aleksei Orlov reached the shores of the Peloponnesus spurring a local revolt (still remembered as *Ta Orlofiká*, literally "the Orlov events"). A generation later, Greek traders in Odessa formed the secretive Society of Friends (*Filikē Etairía*), which in 1821 started the War of Independence—with an incursion into Ottoman-held Bessarabia. Russia, together with Britain and France, defeated the Ottoman–Egyptian fleet at Navarino in 1827, paving the way to independence two years later. Greece's first head of state was none other than Count Ioannis Kapodistrias. Known as Ioann Antonovich Capodistria in St Petersburg, this Greco-Venetian aristocrat had served as Russian foreign minister in 1816–22. For seven years the Russian Empire had run his native Corfu as a protectorate, together with the rest of the Ionian Islands, something of a Greek embryo state. Vladimir Putin evoked Kapodistrias and Russia's role in the liberation war in a column he contributed to the center-right daily *Kathimerini* on the eve of his visit to the Hellenic Republic in May 2016.

Yet Russia was not to become the Hellenic kingdom's patron. Neither Kapodistrias nor Theodoros Kolokotronis, the celebrated war commander who founded the so-called "Russian party," tied their country's fortunes to the northern empire. Tsarist influence waned as Greece espoused constitutional government in 1843 and Russia suffered a humiliating defeat in the Crimean War in 1856.[9] Russia's support for the Bulgarian Church's secession from the Constantinople Patriarchate and especially for the short-lived Greater Bulgaria in 1878 drove a wedge between Moscow and Athens. In Catherine the Great's time, St Petersburg entertained plans of restoring the Byzantine Empire. One hundred years later, it favored the South Slavs and therefore obstructed the Hellenic state's "Great Idea" to recreate the empire by uniting all of the Sultan's Orthodox subjects and by conquering Constantinople. Greece gravitated to the maritime powers of Great Britain and France and joined with them in the First World War, when Prime Minister Eleftherios Venizelos challenged the pro-German King Constantine I.[10]

As elsewhere in Europe, Russia won sympathies thanks to the universalist appeal of Bolshevism and revolution.[11] Interwar authoritarian rulers such as General Ioannis Metaxas failed to stamp out the Communist Party of Greece (*Kommounistikó kómma tēs Elládas*, KKE). Communists picked up strength during the armed resistance against occupation by Nazi Germany and its allies. Once the Wehrmacht withdrew in 1944, it seemed plausible that the communist-dominated National Popular Liberation Army (*Ethnikós Laïkós Apelefterōtikós Stratós*, ELAS) would establish a Soviet regime, like the partisans in Yugoslavia and Albania. Anti-communists prevailed only after Britain and then the United States intervened. The KKE suffered defeat in part because it remained loyal to Stalin after the 1948 split with the Yugoslavs.[12]

The devastating experience of wars, military coups, authoritarian rule (most recently, the Colonels' junta of 1967–74), occupation, and internecine conflicts has left deep scars in the Greek psyche. They account for the deeply ingrained anti-American and anti-Western sentiments across large swathes of society. They mesh with what the political sociologist Nikiforos Diamandouros has notably called "the Greek underdog culture," the historical traumas breeding introspection and a suspicion of foreigners, from the United States in the Cold War to Angela Merkel's Germany.[13] It is this phenomenon that explains Russia's popularity, particularly with the Greek left, which was on the losing side for most of the post-Second World War period, but later on with other political strands as well, including the extreme right. Greece's complicated and occasionally adversarial relationship with the West bridged the distance between Athens and Moscow, both before and after the collapse of the Soviet Union.

The Origins of the Russo-Greek Affair

If there is one politician to be credited with the blossoming of links with Moscow in the 1980s and 1990s, that person is certainly Andreas Papandreou. Papandreou's career epitomized the complexity of recent Greek history and politics. Arrested by the Metaxas regime in 1939 as a Trotskyist, he went on to earn a PhD in economics from Harvard University and teach at a number of top American universities. But Papandreou, who led the All-Greek Socialist Movement (*Panellēnikó Sosialistikó Kínēma*, PASOK) to power in 1981, tapped deep into the Greek feelings of victimhood at the hands of the West, which had increased with Turkey's invasion of Cyprus in 1974. He promised to cancel Greece's membership of NATO and the European Community (EC)—only to wrest concessions from both once he was elected prime minister.[14] At the height of the "Second Cold War," Papandreou pushed for closer ties with the Soviet Union and its clients, from Muammar Gaddafi's Libya and the PLO to martial-law Poland and communist Bulgaria. The prime minister praised the USSR as "a factor that restricts the expansion of capitalism and its imperialistic aims."[15] He advocated the establishment of a nuclear-free zone in the Balkans, a proposition the Soviets welcomed in contrast to the Greek allies in NATO. The revision of Greece's defense doctrine in 1984 removed Moscow from the list of threats and included Ankara instead. Papandreou's independent foreign-policy line caused a headache across the Atlantic, so much so that, according to reports, the United States fretted about Greece leaking military technology to the Soviets.[16]

Starting in the 1980s, diplomatic rapprochement with Russia went hand in hand with co-operation in the energy field. During an unprecedented visit by the Soviet Prime Minister Nikolai Tikhonov in February 1982, the PASOK government agreed to purchase two million tons of Soviet oil annually—more than 20 percent of national consumption. In October 1987, it followed this up with a deal for the delivery of 1 billion cubic meters (bcm) of gas each year—pending the construction of a physical link to the Soviet grid.[17] By 1985, imports of electricity from Bulgaria reached 700 GWh. A $450 million aluminum plant, equipped by the USSR and partly financed by the Soviet Bank for External Trade, would help Greece exploit its large bauxite reserves, access technology, and boost exports—thanks to the commitment by Moscow to buy its produce at a premium price.[18] The Soviets helped build a lignite-fired power plant as well.[19] Committed to the West, Greece was nonetheless happy to explore and reap opportunities in the East.

Cyprus followed a similar trajectory. The left blamed Western powers for the division of the island following a failed military coup and the invasion by the NATO member Turkey in 1974.[20] It was therefore amenable to co-operation with the Soviets, as also were the centrists. Cyprus's president, Archbishop Makarios (known as "the Fidel Castro of the Mediterranean" to officials in the Nixon administration), certainly viewed the Soviet Union as a friend, not a geopolitical or an ideological menace.[21] For its part, Moscow seized every opportunity to build influence in the non-aligned republic, located next to the strategically important Levant. It supplied tanks and other military equipment to the Greek Cypriots from 1965 onwards. To strike a balance, the Soviets were also keen to foster good ties with Turkey in that period and had opposed the island's unification (*enōsis*) with Greece since the early 1960s. It endorsed the UN resolutions calling for complete withdrawal of foreign troops (including those of Britain, ensconced in the sovereign bases of Dhekelía and Akrotiri). However, it was only after Mikhail Gorbachev came to power in 1985, as General Secretary of the Communist Party of the Soviet Union, that Moscow became more outspoken on the Cyprus issue. The USSR called for an international conference at which it would attend as an arbiter of equal standing to the West. Soviet diplomats considered such a formula far superior to a scenario of double *enōsis*, with the south and the north annexed by its respective kindred state and incorporated into NATO.

Game of Arches

The Cold War's abrupt end, the fall of communist regimes, and the USSR's subsequent disintegration was not a cause of celebration in Athens. Just like Russia, Greece felt it was on the losing side. The whole edifice of informal alliances built by Papandreou was coming apart and threats seemed to multiply. Yugoslavia's violent collapse raised trouble north of Greece's borders in the Balkans. Newly independent Macedonia pushed its claims on the legacy of Alexander the Great, stitched the star of Vergina on its flag, and mapped areas of northern Greece as an unredeemed part of the homeland. Greece's traditional ally Serbia came under international sanctions because of its role in the wars in Croatia and Bosnia and Herzegovina. Last but not least, next door, Albania was going through tumultuous times, with thousands upon thousands of illegal migrants crossing south into Greece. Policymakers and talking heads in Athens interpreted all these developments as strengthening the hand of arch-rival Turkey. Ankara wooed post-communist Balkan countries as a gate-opener to NATO and the United States, developing diplomatic and defense links with the Republic of Macedonia and Albania, pushing for military intervention against Bosnian Serbs. A section of Greek opinion makers, of a nationalist bent, concluded that an "Islamic arch" (*Islamikó Tóxo*) was taking shape, threatening to smother Greece with the connivance of the Americans.

While those fears certainly verged on paranoia, Greece did face a challenge in the Aegean. The disputes with Turkey on thorny issues such as sovereignty rights over the continental shelf, territorial waters, and air space, grew more acrimonious and heated in the 1990s. In 1994, Turkey's Prime Minister Tansu Çiller had the Grand National Assembly pass a resolution stipulating that any unilateral decision by Greece to extend territorial waters up to twelve nautical miles as foreseen under the 1982 Law of the Sea convention would constitute a *casus belli*. The two states narrowly avoided a military showdown two years later over Imia/Kardak, an uninhabited rock in the Dodecanese. To the consternation of the United States and other NATO members, a war within the alliance did not seem to be out of the question.

To offset the challenge from Turkey, Greece had two strategies at its disposal. First, it would use its leverage within Western institutions and strengthen its hand diplomatically. Athens wielded its veto in the EU to pressure Ankara as well as to bring Cyprus into the Union (it threatened to block the accession of Eastern European countries if the island was excluded). Second, it would attempt to encircle Turkey through an alliance with Russia, Syria, Armenia, and other countries.[22] Russia represented a central piece of the puzzle. True, by the time President Boris Yeltsin visited Athens in July 1993, the superpower might of the Soviet Union was all but a fading memory. Yet the Russian Federation still retained a seat at the UN Security Council, exported arms on a large scale, and retained connections across the Balkans and the Eastern Mediterranean. Furthermore, it was watching with unease Turkey's push into the post-Soviet Caucasus and Central Asia. In short, Moscow could be an ally in containing Ankara—or, at the very least, in tipping the scales in Greece's favor.

In a more positive mode, Greece also sought to facilitate Russia's integration into the West. It was at the EU summit in Corfu (July 1994) that President Boris Yeltsin signed a Partnership and Co-operation Agreement (PCA) to institutionalize and advance political and economic ties with the twelve-member bloc.[23] (Greece and Russia had already concluded a treaty of friendship and co-operation the previous year.) In the words of Andreas Papandreou, having his last spell as prime minister at the time, the PCA "confirm[ed] the EU's support for the on-going process of democratisation in Russia" and contributed to "stability and security in Europe."[24] For a change, Greece had a chance to be a constructive player within the EU, not the perpetual naysayer blocking Turkey and twisting the arm of the (former Yugoslav) Republic of Macedonia with a trade embargo.

Greece engaged Russia in the Balkans as well. Regional institutions furnished extra means to counterbalance Turkey, which had its own platform of choice—Black Sea Economic Co-operation (BSEC), counting both Russia and Greece as members. In June 1993, the Greek premier Konstantinos Mitsotakis invited Yeltsin to Athens, where they signed the Friendship and Co-operation Treaty and devised plans for a "Balkan Helsinki", naturally with officials representing rump Yugoslavia present. Both Moscow and Athens favored the inclusion of FRY, which was subject to international sanctions at the time. Russian diplomats attended as observers of Balkan summits that took following the end of the Bosnian war in 1995, on the joint initiative of the PASOK cabinet in Athens and their Socialist allies governing Bulgaria.[25] Defense Minister Akis Tsochatzopoulos even proposed a "Balkan Security Council" having Russia as a full member and not as a guest. There were few takers, however, and Bulgaria, where the Socialists were replaced by a center-right administration in the spring of 1997, was not one of them. By 1998, military co-operation in Southeast Europe was attached to NATO, with the United States as an observer and Russia not invited. The Kosovo war closed the discussion for good.

Importantly, Greece's outreach to Moscow in the 1990s attracted more interest than just from the usual suspects on the left. The center-right New Democracy (ND), otherwise a vocal proponent of the EU and NATO, shared PASOK's positive outlook on closer links to Moscow. The party's founder, Konstantinos (Constantine) Karamanlis, had adopted a wide-ranging approach to foreign policy, traveling to the USSR and its Eastern bloc satellites as a prime minister in the late 1970s.[26] And it was Mitsotakis, Karamanlis's successor at the helm of ND, who as premier had welcomed Yeltsin to Athens to sign their common treaty in 1993.

Conservatives in Greece and Russia could bank on religious and cultural similarities. Having shed the Soviet regime, the Russian Federation now counted as a fellow Orthodox country, not a beacon of world communism. This was precisely the message that Patriarch Aleksii II conveyed during his visit to the Hellenic Republic in June 1992. The First Diplomat of All Russia (*Diplomat Moskovskii i Vseia Rusi*),[27] as *Kommersant* called him, half-jokingly, would bless Foreign Ministers Igor Ivanov and George Papandreou (a liberal Socialist and son of Andreas Papandreou) before a meeting between the two in 2000. "Greece is," Papandreou pointed out, "the sole Eastern Orthodox country in the EU and NATO and therefore is a bridge between Orthodox and Non-Orthodox Europe."[28] Religion proved an indispensable foreign-policy asset—even an atheist like Tsipras, who resolutely refused to take his prime ministerial oath on the Bible, was to pay his respects to the Russian Patriarch Kirill in 2015.

Immigration from across the former USSR reinforced human bonds too. If the 1980s saw the repatriation of civil war exiles scattered across the Warsaw Pact countries, the post-Cold War decade witnessed the arrival in Greece of thousands of people from Russia, Georgia, Ukraine, and so on, claiming ethnic Greek ancestry. By the mid-1990s Russian was commonly being heard in Athens, Thessaloniki, and other large urban centers.[29]

Moscow's Balancing Act

No doubt, Greece had good reasons to court Russia. But was Russia itself willing to cast its lot with the Greeks? To a certain degree, yes. By late 1994, Moscow was clearly losing ground in former Yugoslavia, with NATO and the United States assuming the lead in Bosnia. Reinforced ties with Greece as well as with Bulgaria, where the December 1994 elections put in power a Russia-friendly Socialist government with good links to Athens, could make up for the setbacks. "Despite its membership in the EU and NATO, [Greece's] view on the settlement of the Bosnian conflict is, perhaps, closest to that of Russia," observed *Kommersant*, highlighting the shared belief that bringing Belgrade back in from the cold was essential.[30] A defense agreement was in the works, since Yeltsin's visit to Athens the year before. Meanwhile, Prime Minister Viktor Chernomyrdin lobbied for a three-way energy partnership, including Bulgaria (more below).

Russia was much less keen to intervene in the delicate web of Greek–Turkish disputes in the Aegean. The long-standing Soviet policy of non-involvement in those disputes carried through into the post-1991 period. As noted by Monteagle Sterns, "exploiting [Greek–Turkish problems] ha[d] been as far beyond the reach of Soviet policy as solving them ha[d] been beyond the reach of U.S. policy."[31] The weakened Russia of the 1990s was at an even greater disadvantage. Moscow's naval presence south of the Turkish Straits, in decline since its peak around the Yom Kippur War (1973), was scaled back even further after the Soviet disintegration. While the Aegean and the Eastern Mediterranean remained a vital route for Russia's commercial traffic, it was not until the mid-2000s that the Black Sea fleet would establish a firm presence, with help from its long-time ally Syria.

The preference for non-involvement was not unqualified. The Russian government and the state-owned monopoly trader, *Rosvooruzhenie*, were eager to reap arms contracts—especially in a NATO member state such as Greece with a substantial defense budget. Soviet-made tanks from Eastern Germany had made their way into the Greek and Turkish militaries, generating demand for spare parts and additional equipment from Russia.[32] Moscow delivered weapons to Cyprus under a new military-technical agreement initialed with Cyprus (March 1996). Already an attractive offshore zone for the Russian capital, the island was turning into a focal point of Moscow's military ties with Greece. Athens and Nicosia adopted a unified defense doctrine in 1994 while Greek Prime Minister Costas Simitis threatened war in case Turkish troops rolled south of the green line in Nicosia dividing Cyprus. Formally, Russia's Ministry of Foreign Affairs advocated the demilitarization of the island. In practice, however, Moscow faced the risk of being dragged into a tangled conflict from which it could gain little.

Russia's exposure to the turbulent politics in the Aegean became apparent in January 1997. Nicosia-based media leaked a story about a contracted sale of two batteries of advanced surface-to-air missiles (S–300 PMU1s) along with radar and other equipment. President Glafcos Clerides weighed in strongly in support of the deal worth $660 million. Once deployed, the anti-aircraft systems with a range of 150 kilometers would tip the balance in favor of the Greeks and even cover a portion of Turkey. Ankara's response, emanating from the Foreign Ministry rather than the Islamist Prime Minister Necmettin Erbakan, was predictably bellicose. Turkey threatened military action against the missile sites, approached Israel for how to neutralize S–300s, and probed the United States with respect to a potential unilateral strike (the answer was negative). Athens and Nicosia maintained that their intentions were purely defensive.[33] Although Turkey's threats were not directed at the transport vessels, Russia did find itself in a delicate position. Still, it stuck to its guns and even toyed with the prospect of deriving geopolitical dividends. "The contract can be cancelled only for one reason—if the whole territory of Cyprus is demilitarized," insisted Foreign Minister Evgenii Primakov on a visit to Athens in February 1998.[34]

The maximalist goal was certainly far beyond its reach, but Russia managed to benefit from the crisis all the same. Clerides backed down in December 1998, under pressure from the United States and the EU, agreeing to redeploy the missiles to the Greek island of Crete. Although Cyprus formally retained ownership of the S–300s, Greece, a NATO member, was taking onboard advanced Russian systems. Moreover, Athens gave to Nicosia shorter-range TOR-M1 and Buk-M1 mobile complexes made in Russia. By 2000, *Rosvooruzhenie* had supplied $1 billion in military hardware to Greece, Cyprus, as well as Turkey. Although that accounted for a fraction of the $10 billion rearmament program implemented by Athens, Russia was no more a bystander in the security affairs of Greece and its volatile region. The story continued into the 2000s. In December 2007, Prime Minister Costas Karamanlis signed in Moscow a deal to pay €1.2 billion for 420 BMP–3M personnel carriers.

Pipelines and Pipedreams

What has brought Greece and Russia together since the early 2000s is energy, rather than defense links or indeed the Turkish threat. The liberal turn in Greek foreign policy after 1999 made the alliance with Russia less relevant. Simitis and especially his foreign minister, George Papandreou, reinvented Greece from being an egotistic veto player to a far-sighted promoter of EU enlargement. The hallmarks of the new course were the conciliation with Turkey after the summer of 1999 and the 2003 Thessaloniki Summit giving the green light to EU expansion into the Western Balkans. Papandreou hoped to "Europeanize" fractious relations with Greece's neighbors and use the appeal of EU membership and its democratizing effects on countries such as Turkey to resolve outstanding conflicts. Greece had therefore now become the outpost of the EU in Southeast Europe, not a besieged fortress in need of Russia's support.

Energy links continued on an upward trajectory throughout the 1990s and 2000s. As of November 1996, Greece started importing gas from Russia under the 1987 contract, upon completing the link to Bulgaria at Kulata-Promahon. As Per Hogselius observes, Greece was similar to other parts of Western Europe—for example, Austria, Finland, Northern Italy, and Bavaria—in that it linked up with the Soviet (subsequently Russian) grid *before* it could obtain access to gas supplies from other sources.[35] By the 2000s, Greece was receiving in excess of 70 percent of its gas from Russia—as well as 40 percent of its oil.[36] Greeks welcomed Russia's rise as an energy superpower under Putin. Finally, the time was ripe to capitalize on time-tested connections. When Putin came to Athens in early December 2001 to sign a package of agreements, the Development Undersecretary Alexandros Kalafatis summarized the prevailing mood in Athens in an interview for the state-run NET radio: "Business alliances are being made . . . that will help Greece fulfil its aim of become the energy hub of the region."[37]

To be sure, security co-operation continued unabated. Having opposed the Iraq War, Greece and Cyprus refused to recognize the independence of Kosovo after February 2008, a position shared with Russia. Athens and Nicosia refused to support Moscow on Abkhazia and South Ossetia. But they argued strongly for a speedy normalization of EU–Russia relations after the August 2008 war with Georgia. Reportedly, the Hellenic Republic was amenable to opening liaison offices in the two breakaway republics too (just like the ones Athens and Moscow both operated in Kosovo).

But what truly fueled links between Moscow and Athens were two multi-billion projects: the Burgas–Alexandroupolis oil pipeline and South Stream, a gas venture. This time around it was ND, defeating PASOK in the 2004 elections, that championed the Moscow connection. Prime Minister Costas Karamanlis brokered a compromise deal with Russia and Bulgaria on the distribution of the shares in Burgas–Alexandroupolis, reviving the scheme that had lingered on since 1994.[38] Under the three-way agreement that Putin and Bulgarian Prime Minister Sergei Stanishev signed in Athens on 15 March 2007, the $1.13 billion pipeline would ship up to thirty-five million tons of Russian and Kazakh oil each year from the Black Sea to the Aegean. That corresponded to about a third of the annual traffic through the Turkish Straits. Russia would be in a position to safeguard the port of Novorossiisk's role in crude exports, despite tightening regulations concerning the passage through the congested Bosphorus. Greece, in turn, would pocket $80 million a year in transit fees but, more importantly, boost the development of the far-flung province of Evros at the frontier with Turkey and Bulgaria.[39] The project appeared to be a boon for Greek big business too. Hellenic Petroleum and Thraki, co-owned by the Latsis Group, and Prometheus Gas linked to the magnate Dimitrios Kopelouzos and Gazprom, would take Greece's 24.5 percent in the joint company.[40]

Right from the start, a political linkage was in place connecting Burgas–Alexandroupolis to the branch of South Stream projected to go through Greece. Politicians, diplomats, and pundits alike viewed South Stream as a matter of fundamental national interest for Greece: it would be transformed from a consumer to a transit country, the security of gas shipments would be guaranteed, Gazprom would lower its prices. Concerns about dependency on Russia were countered by arguments that the alternative was leaning on Turkey.[41] Putin had a more direct, no-nonsense message. South Stream was economically profitable. After the conclusion of the inter-governmental agreement with Karamanlis, on 29 April 2008, he observed:

> If Greece needed some ordinary goods—watches, underpants or a tie—they could buy them wherever they wanted. You could buy them in China, Switzerland . . . or in Italy, for example. But you can count on a single hand the countries that are able to be the primary supplier of energy at the necessary volumes and at competitive prices for Europe.[42]

Greek politicians hardly needed convincing. Both ND and the opposition PASOK voted to ratify the deal on 28 August, less than a fortnight after hostilities in Georgia ended. Greece was thus amongst the first in the EU to go back to "business as usual" with Russia, a choice laden with symbolism.

Contrary to high expectations, both Burgas–Alexandroupolis and South Stream turned out to be dead ends. No sooner had ink on the signatures dried than the former scheme came under fire from several directions. In the run-up to the general election in October 2009, PASOK's leader George Papandreou slammed ND for overlooking the environmental cost of the oil pipeline abutting territories covered by the EU's NATURA 2000 program. There were serious political concerns as well. Russian state-owned companies were to obtain a piece of strategic infrastructure within the EU. The economics of the pipeline raised even more serious doubt. Russia would provide no guarantees set in stone that Transneft would be able to secure sufficient volumes of crude to make the venture profitable. That was understandable: tanker transit through the Bosphorus remained a cheaper option. The large quantities of Kazakh crude to be extracted from the Kashagan ("cash all gone," pundits quipped) field and shipped via Novorossiisk did not materialize. Despite that, Greece clung on to Burgas–Alexandroupolis until the bitter end. It hoped that Bulgaria would reverse the decision it took in 2011 to quit the project (see Chapter 3). Once the government changed in Sofia, in May 2013, Deputy Foreign Minister Dimitris Kourkoulas declared to ITAR-TASS that Athens was ready to restart the pipeline.[43] However, no relaunch was in the offing.

South Stream failed to bear fruit as well. The story came to an end in November 2012 when Gazprom decided to cancel the leg through Greece and press ahead with the main branch bound for Central Europe and northern Italy. The company argued that projections of demand did not justify the investment in new infrastructure, particularly the underwater stretch between Igoumenitsa and Otranto. Greece, where gas consumption was shrinking too as a result of the acute economic crisis, could be supplied through the existing pipeline connection with Bulgaria. The cancellation of Burgas–Alexandroupolis offered one more reason why Russia had now lost interest in Greece.

The end of the South Stream and Burgas–Alexandroupolis projects in 2011–12 shifted Greece's attention away from Russia.

The Trans-Adriatic Pipeline (TAP), a 10-bcm project to ship Azeri gas to Italy, became a priority. Having won endorsement from the Shah Deniz consortium in June 2013, construction work kicked off on 17 May 2016, with an inaugural ceremony in Thessaloniki. Gazprom still counted as a strategic partner, but in 2013 the Russians unexpectedly withdrew their bid for the Public Gas Corporation (*Dēmósia Epiheírēsē Parohēs Aeríou*, DEPA), sold as part of the conditions of the EU and IMF bailout from May 2010.[44] The Russians were also unhappy about being denied the opportunity to purchase the grid operator DESFA, formally owned by DEPA, but tendered separately and sold to Azerbaijan's SOCAR as part of the TAP project favored by Brussels.[45] Gazprom's withdrawal undercut the government's program of fiscal consolidation. Having already secured an 11 percent discount and a reduction of the take-or-pay volume under the long-term contract, Prime Minister Antonis Samaras was hoping to obtain further concessions, narrow the 30 percent price differential with Western Europe, and reduce Greece's energy bill.[46]

Russia came back on the agenda only after Putin announced in December 2014 that South Stream would be replaced by TurkStream, with Greece taking Bulgaria's place as a transit route. The Tsipras government, inaugurated after snap polls in January 2015, jumped onboard. The Economy Minister Panagiotis Lafazanis signed a Memorandum of Understanding on a joint company at the St Petersburg Economic Forum in June, with Russia's Vneshtorgbank (VTB) promising to finance DEPA's 50 percent share. To Lafazanis, TurkStream/GreekStream was "a pipeline for peace, stability in the whole region."[47] However, in reality, the prospects of an extension into Greece remain nebulous to this day, despite the agreement reached by Turkey and Russia in October 2016. At a minimum, Gazprom and the European Commission need to reach common ground on the contentious issue of "third-party access."[48] To cut a very long story short, the much-touted energy partnership between Greece and Russia has yet to materialize and deliver the benefits.

The Coveted Island

Cyprus has long been well ahead of Greece in building an economic relationship with Russia. Right from the early 1990s, the Mediterranean island had become a preferred offshore destination for Russians, whether business people, second-home owners or tourists. While the 2011 census registered a little more than 8,000 Russian citizens living in the Republic of Cyprus (out of a population of roughly 838,000), the actual number could be five times larger.[49] In terms of inward investment, Russia is in the same league with major partners such as Greece and the United Kingdom. Moody's has estimated that the deposits held by Russian firms and individuals, around $31 billion (more or less equal to the country's GDP), account for between one-third and one-half of all money in Cypriot banks.[50] To quote one prominent example, in September 2010, Dmitrii Rybolovlev, a Russian tycoon and sometime owner of the Uralkali fertilizer conglomerate, acquired a 9.7 percent stake in the Bank of Cyprus. He became the largest shareholder in the island's main lender, accounting for about a third of the deposits and 40 percent of loans. Another eminent investor in the bank has been Viktor Veksel'berg, the billionaire owner of the telecom company Vimpelcom whom President Dmitry Medvedev appointed as director of the Skolkovo Innovation Park—the project Russia branded as its answer to Silicon Valley. Major Russian companies such as Rosneft, Lukoil, and VTB operate subsidiaries in Cyprus.

Alongside Russia's oligarchs, there are many middle-class Russians residing or running businesses on Aphrodite's island. Thanks to the favorable taxation regime dating back to a treaty signed with the USSR at the end of 1998,[51] Cyprus emerged as an investment gateway to and from Russia. Home to around 40,000 Russian-owned companies, the island ranked as the third most significant investor in the Russian Federation's economy. Clearly, this "achievement" had much to do with capital originating from Russia and "recycled" through the island's banking system. According to some estimates, up to 90 percent of transactions on the Moscow Stock Exchange are channeled through Cypriot offshore companies.

Russia's economic footprint, expanding to an unprecedented scale in the golden years between Putin's ascent to power in 1999–2000 and the onset of the global crisis in 2008, has been matched with its long-standing involvement in Cypriot politics. Its seat in the UN Security Council gives it a great say in the international efforts to manage and resolve the division of the island dating back to 1974. Moscow has not refrained from intervening in the island's politics. The first time Russia used its UN veto since the collapse of the Soviet Union, in May 1993, it did so with regard to the United Nations Peacekeeping Force in Cyprus (UNFICYP).[52] Moscow asserted itself once again in April 2004, ahead of a referendum where both Greek and Turkish Cypriots were about to vote on a reunification plan designed by UN Secretary General Kofi Annan. Ambassador Gennadii Gatilov vetoed a resolution on security arrangements in a unified Cyprus, prepared by the United States and the United Kingdom together with Annan. The decision came in the wake of a visit to Moscow by the Cypriot foreign minister, Georgios Iacovou. Russia argued that the draft resolution was premature as it was coming before the plebiscite and therefore prejudging the outcome. In effect, the veto move bolstered President Tassos Papadopoulos and the "No" campaign that won the day in the Greek part of Cyprus. The government was thankful. UN Ambassador Andreas Mavroyiannis greeted Moscow's decision, lamenting that the "Americans and British care[d] only about the interests of the Turks."[53] The veto came as an early example of Russia's ability to play "hard ball" with the United States and its allies.

The Cypriot government repaid the favor whenever it was in a position to do so. In September 2009, Cyprus rejected a proposed EU common position in support of a UN General Assembly Resolution on the "Status of Internally Displaced Persons and Refugees from Abkhazia and South Ossetia and the Tskhinvali Region/South Ossetia, Georgia." Symptomatically, Greece sided with the resolution, despite the Russians' criticism. Although, in principle, Nicosia supports Georgia's territorial integrity—drawing an analogy with the case of the 1974 division and the Turkish occupation of the north—it takes extra care to avoid antagonizing Russia. But Cypriot diplomats insist that the Trojan Horse label is exaggerated and unfair. In the words of one of them: "[w] have our national interests, our issues, so we try to help Russia as much as possible, but not doing it in a way that might be interpreted or misinterpreted by our partners."[54]

Parallel to political and economic co-operation, Cyprus and Russia have developed strong defense ties. In addition to tanks, armored vehicles, and anti-aircraft systems, Nicosia purchased a batch of Mi–35 attack helicopters in the early 2000s. In December 2013, while Cyprus was in the throes of a banking crisis, the governments signed a deal with *Rosoboroneksport* to service the helicopter fleet.[55] Russia saw a major advantage in co-operation with a neutral country with a strategic location. Ahead of President Nikos Anastasiades's visit to Moscow in late February 2015, there was a frenzy of speculation that Cyprus was preparing to give Russia rights to bases at the port of Limassol as well as the Andreas Papandreou airbase near Paphos. Anastasiades renewed the defense agreement from 1996 and concluded another document allowing Russian warships access to Limassol (which they had enjoyed since 2013). The message of the visit, a fortnight after the Minsk II agreement on Ukraine, was unmistakable. Cyprus was not to jettison its vital security relationship to Russia. Still, Anastasiades and his foreign minister, Ioannis Kassoulides, downplayed the practical implications of the agreements.[56] But even if Cyprus was not to become a springboard for Russian naval expansion in the Mediterranean, it counted as one of Moscow's most reliable allies in the EU. On 7 July 2016, the parliament voted, thirty-three in favor and with seventeen abstentions, a resolution to lift sanctions against Russia.[57]

Times of Crisis

Although Russia never suffered from a lack of popularity in Greece, the wholesale financial and economic disaster that befell Greeks from 2010 onwards pushed Moscow's stocks through the roof. In some quarters, Russia appeared as an alternative to the loathed diktat by the eurozone creditors and the Troika of financial institutions. Assuming office in January 2015, Prime Minister Alexis Tsipras never openly advocated the option, but he was clearly willing to probe the Russians. "If it is submitted we will consider it," was how the Russian finance minister, Anton Siluanov, viewed the suggestion of Moscow offering Athens a loan.[58] In all seriousness, it was unreasonable to expect Russia to come to Greece's rescue at a moment when its own economy was going downhill, burdened by sanctions and plummeting oil prices.

Tsipras decided to play the Russian card regardless, in the hope of achieving leverage vis-à-vis the creditors. He was unsuccessful. Heavy on symbolism though it was, his visit to Moscow in April 2015 failed to yield any substantive result. The Kremlin did not lift the import restrictions on foodstuffs coming into Greece. Instead, Putin simply restated the Russian interest in privatizing the Greek railways and the port of Thessaloniki, Greece's second largest.[59] Months later, on 19 July, the daily *To Vima* (leaning to PASOK) ran a story that at the meeting Tsipras made a request for a $10 billion loan to facilitate a return to the drachma, with Varoufakis, Kammenos (defense), and other key cabinet members being aware of the plan.[60] The Greek prime minister committed to follow Russia's line on Ukraine, including the support for a pro-independence referendum in the Donbas. According to *To Vima*, Putin considered the idea seriously but balked and left Tsipras empty handed, except for a vague promise to transfer a $5 billion pre-payment for TurkStream (which, conceivably, would have landed Greece in trouble with the European Commission, since the pipeline would have not have been in compliance with the "third-party access" rules). The story was partially corroborated by the French president, François Hollande, in 2016.[61] Yet the Kremlin spokesman Dmitrii Peskov denied it, arguing that the Russian National Wealth Fund (*Fond natsional'nogo blagosostoiania Rossii*) could not have raised $10 billion on such short notice, to start with.[62]

Whatever the truth of the matter, at the end of the day, bailing out Athens and buying into its financial problems was a step too far for the Russians. Ultimately, it was for the EU not Russia to shoulder the responsibility. The Kremlin was doing its share by plugging Greece into the TurkStream project. "If the EU wants Greece to pay its debt then it should be interested in the Greek economy growing," Putin remarked in June 2015. "The EU should be applauding us. What's bad about creating new jobs in Greece?"[63] It was hard to argue with the president—although, in actual fact, the sector where Russia bolstered employment was tourism. Arrivals from Russia surged by a fifth in 2016 as holidaymakers chose Greece over traditional destinations such as Egypt or Turkey.

Unable and unwilling to rescue Greece financially, Russia made mileage out of the drama that unfolded in the summer of 2015. The referendum on the Troika bailout initiated by the Syriza–ANEL government pushed Greece to the brink, threatening the cohesion of the eurozone. Having turned against Russia, the EU was facing an existential crisis of its own. Tsipras's defiant rhetoric and the resolute "No" (OXI) winning in the referendum (5 July 2015) brought up the memories of the resistance against Nazi Germany and its allies. In was in tune with the Kremlin's constant evocations of the Second World War in connection to Ukraine. In a piece entitled "Lessons of History Forgotten by Europe," Sergei Naryshkin, the Duma spokesman, promised "a chain of new and deep shocks."[64] Ironically, his commentary appeared on the same day Tsipras that made a 180-degree turn (known as "*kolotoumba*" or somersault in Greek) and accepted the creditors' conditions.

Before trying to play off Russia against the EU, Tsipras should have known better. After all, Cyprus had faced a similar situation not that long before. As the island's banking sector was staring at the abyss in the spring of 2013, collateral damage from the crisis in Greece, it had turned to Russia for help. Back in December 2011, President Dimitrios Christophias had secured a loan of €2.5 billion (a little under 10 percent of GDP) to prop up the banking sector and protect Russian deposits. Two years later, however, Russia refused to disburse a second loan. In March 2013, the finance minister, Michael Sarris, returned empty-handed from Moscow, having tried to convince the likes of Sberbank and Gazprombank to buy the struggling Laïki ("Popular") Bank of Cyprus.[65] The Russian government did not do anything beyond extending the 2011 loan and lowering the interest rate. According to reports, Gazprom offered to recapitalize struggling banks in exchange for exploration rights in the Aphrodite gas field in Cyprus's Exclusive Economic Zone. President Anastasiades turned down the proposition.

Without Russia on its side Cyprus settled on the bailout package proposed by the EU and IMF in March 2013. The terms of the deal affected Russia in a negative way. The €10 billion grant was conditional upon Nicosia's ability to raise another €5.8 billion from a "haircut" on deposits above €100,000 at the Bank of Cyprus and Laïki Bank. The bail-in clause hurt Russian depositors disproportionately. It dampened the Kremlin's appetite to intervene in the eurozone crisis, in ways other than purely rhetorical. That has been the case in Greece where Russia is less exposed compared to Cyprus. Cypriots, for their part, complained that they had been unfairly singled out as a safe haven for "dirty Russian money," a common problem across EU member states, and had been punished with the "haircut" of conditionality.[66]

The banking crisis did have a devastating effect, but on the plus side it pushed the Greek leadership back to the negotiating table with the leaders of the Turkish Cypriots. In May 2015, Anastasiades kicked off a new round of the UN-sponsored reunification talks together with Mustafa Akıncı, a leftist politician elected president of the unrecognized Turkish Republic of Northern Cyprus the previous year. The prospect of a joint exploitation of newly discovered offshore gas and oil deposits clearly prompted leaders on both sides, amongst several other factors. When it came to Russia's view of the talks, many Cyprus watchers could not help but wonder whether Moscow would not try to be the spoiler. Stanislav Osadchii, the Russian ambassador, spoke critically of Anastasiades and attended a meeting of parties opposing a deal with the Turks. That inevitably led to concerns that Russia might use its influence to stir nationalists and the Orthodox Church to block a settlement.[67] Keeping the island divided would perpetuate Russia's influence, keep NATO's at an arm's length, and even block the Atlantic Alliance's co-operation with the EU, according to this line of reasoning.[68] But as of early 2017, a repeat of the 2004 referendum scenario, and a Greek "No" to reunification, remained not as great as it seemed at the outset because the Anastasiades-Akıncı talks were losing momentum.

Conclusion

Greece and Cyprus became Russia's friends and allies because they found the partnership advantageous, as back in the Soviet days. Historical, cultural, and religious bonds, important as they are, provide the rhetorical packaging but do not account, in their own right, for policy choices. For all its modern existence, Greece has been anchored in the West, a connection that has always been ridden with tensions—from Britain's gunboat diplomacy in the 1850s, to the American intervention in the civil war and collusion with the colonels' regime in the 1960s and early 1970s, to the agony of the eurozone crisis. The cleavage between the country's cosmo-politan, pro-Western business and political establishment, and the underdog mentality reigning supreme in parts of society, has been a recurrent theme in Greek history and public life. Yet, neither the Westernizers and the liberals nor the conservatives and nationalists, be it on the left or on the right, have had any qualms about reaching out to Russia. Since the collapse of the Soviet Union, all factions and strands have favored intense co-operation with Moscow, seeing it, in most cases, not as an alternative but as a useful add-on to Greece's primary relationship with the EU and NATO. The same is even truer of Cyprus, whose non-aligned status, offshore banking sector, as well as the continued division between the Turkish-dominated north and the Greek south, have advanced links with the Russians.

The question is to what degree cordial ties have worked to the gain of Greece and Cyprus. At times the choice for Russia has paid off, at other times it manifestly hasn't. Overall, the high expectations that Russia could balance Turkey, make Greece a privileged partner on energy, or underwrite financial stability, have failed to deliver, leaving frustration in their wake. Moscow did lend a helping hand to the Cypriots in the early stages of the eurozone crisis, but when the going got tough in 2013 it stopped short of bailing out the island's struggling banks, contending it was the EU's job. Even if the evidence of direct meddling to prevent Cypriot reunification is scant, it is beyond doubt that Russia is not interested in a final settlement.

Russia has made the most from the special relationship with Greece and Cyprus. It has added to the Kremlin's influence inside the EU and enlarged the Russian footprint in the Balkans and the Eastern Mediterranean. Most recently, Moscow exploited to the fullest the Greek crisis in its war of words with the West, avoiding far-reaching commitments. The image of Greece victimized by its creditors and threatened by hundreds of thousands of refugees and asylum seekers storming in from neighboring Turkey has been a gift for pro-Kremlin media exposing the utter bankruptcy of the EU. Greece has been unreservedly supportive of Russia's energy projects, though, of course, developing contacts with competing suppliers of gas such as Azerbaijan and investing in schemes to diversify supplies. The bruising experience of the 2013 banking meltdown and the EU's rescue package did not derail co-operation between Moscow and Nicosia, though it certainly contributed to lower expectations on the Cypriot side. Whatever the weather, Greece and Cyprus are likely to remain at the core of the pro-Russian camp within the EU.

CHAPTER 5

THE RUSSIAN–TURKISH MARRIAGE OF CONVENIENCE

Until this moment Russia has wanted to reach the Mediterranean's warm waters through Turkey. But this time with the help of Russian tourists.

—Mikhail Gorbachev[1]

Moscow respects Ankara's independent stance vis-à-vis the United States, as a NATO ally that can say "no" to Washington. Neither does the moderate Islamism of the AK Party government evoke much concern in the Kremlin. Turkey's ascendance and independence fit well into the general Moscow concept of a multipolar world in which U.S dominance is reduced.

—Dmitri Trenin[2]

The United States is our ally. But Russia is our strategic neighbor. We buy two-thirds of the energy we need from Russia. That country is Turkey's number one partner in trade ... No one must expect us to ignore all that. Our allies must adopt an understanding approach.

—Recep Tayyip Erdoğan[3]

"A stab in the back perpetrated by accomplices of terrorists": Vladimir Putin could barely contain his anger. On 24 November

2015 a Turkish F–16 had shot down one of Russia's attack aircraft on the border with Syria. The Sukhoi Su-24M had been pounding Turkmen villages controlled by militiamen allied with Ankara. "We considered Turkey not just a neighbor, but a friendly state, almost an ally. And everything is being destroyed in such a brusque and thoughtless manner. Such a pity," lamented the Russian leader, clenching his fists. Less than a year before, in December 2014, Putin's visit to Ankara had taken everyone by surprise with the news of an ambitious project for a gas pipeline to Turkey. TurkStream amounted to nothing less than a joint rebuke of the EU by Putin and President Recep Tayyip Erdoğan. The European Commission had blocked South Stream but there was friendly Turkey offering Putin a way out of the limbo. A NATO stalwart and longstanding American ally, it refused to abandon its relationship with Moscow—and was even prepared to swallow the Russian annexation of Crimea and the resultant shift of the strategic balance in the Black Sea.

Fast forward twelve months and Syria was straining and pushing bilateral relations to the brink. The Russian military was virtually on Turkey's doorstep, waging war on rebel groups aided by Ankara, and turning the tide of the conflict in favor of President Bashar al-Assad. The Su-24M incident unleashed a vicious war of words between Putin and Erdoğan. As New Year 2016 set in, Russian authorities introduced sanctions, which were to take their toll on Turkish tourism, agriculture, and the construction industry. The worldwide commentariat indulged in speculations of an imminent showdown between the Tsar and the Sultan." Would the Russian–Turkish rivalry, reminiscent of the era when the Romanovs and Ottomans reigned, spark off proxy wars across the Balkans and the Caucasus? At a stroke, the positive record of more than two decades of co-operation appeared consigned to the past and therefore irrelevant.

The pundits and their forecasts were soon to be proven hopelessly wrong. In a dazzling reversal, Erdoğan and Putin managed to mend ties in the summer of 2016. Turkey offered a carefully worded apology for the downed jet, while Russia's president gave strong backing to Erdoğan's side after a failed military coup attempt on 15 July. Just as Western criticism of the mass purges of magistrates, officials, journalists, academics, and military officers in response to the putsch turned louder and louder, the Kremlin unequivocally took the Turkish government's side. A summit between Erdoğan and Putin on 9 August heralded the end of the Russian sanctions and a restart of strategic co-operation in energy, including TurkStream and the Akkuyu nuclear power plant.[4] Turkey and Russia would be working side by side yet again. Remarkably, Moscow gave its stamp of approval to Euphrates Shield (*Fırat Kalkanı*), a cross-border operation by the Turkish military and allied rebel forces in northern Syria, ostensibly to push out the self-styled Islamic State but in reality targeting Kurdish fighters as well.

This chapter tells the story of how post-Soviet Russia and Turkey have developed a highly complex and ambivalent relationship since the 1990s, blending co-operation and competition. Rising interdependence along with the shared love-hate attitude towards the West have brought the two historical adversaries together. But clashing interests on a range of issues—from security in the Balkans to the transit of Caspian hydrocarbons to Europe, and from regime change in the Middle East to conflicts in the Southern Caucasus—have put them at odds. Overtime, Russia and Turkey have learned to deal with such contradictions. And their bilateral dynamic leaves a deep imprint on the politics of Southeast Europe as a whole.

Foes, Friends—or Something in Between?

For better or worse, history has made Turkey *part* of Southeast Europe. Although its territory is mostly in Anatolia, Turkey shares strong demographic, cultural, political, and economic links with its erstwhile provinces in Rumeli (literally, "the land of the Romans"), which once formed the very core of the empire. In that sense, it differs from Russia—enmeshed in the politics of Southeast Europe but certainly not of the region. A staggering percentage of the people who built the modern Republic of Turkey, notably Mustafa Kemal Atatürk, had Balkan roots.[5] Istanbul is by far the largest urban center in Southeast Europe, even without the quarters located on the Asian side. But Turkey, heir to an empire spanning three continents, has deep-running links to the Caucasus, the northern shores of the Black Sea, and the Middle East. Therefore, it encounters Russia in several regional settings, not just in what cartographers of the nineteenth century labeled "Turkey-in-Europe."

When one thinks of the historical legacies permeating the Russian–Turkish relations of today, it is impossible to avoid associations of relentless struggles for territory and dominance, feuds, and incessant bloodshed. Between the reign of Ivan the Terrible (1530–84) and the Brest Litovsk Peace of March 1918, the two empires fought full twelve wars for dominance in the Balkans, the Caucasus, and the northern Black Sea. Muscovy's push to the south, starting with the conquest of the Khanate of Astrakhan, brought it into a direct collision with the Ottomans or their Tatar vassals in Crimea. Over the eighteenth and nineteenth centuries, the Tsarist Empire dislodged its Muslim adversary from today's southern Ukraine and Moldova, large swathes of the Caucasus and Southeast Europe. As a result, Serbia, Greece, and Bulgaria attained statehood while the semi-autonomous Danubian Principalities and Montenegro became independent. To survive this onslaught, the "Sick Man of Europe" needed the protection of the great powers of the day—first France and Britain and then the Kaiser's Germany.

However, the two empires on the edge of Europe occasionally found their interests converging and struck a common cause. They teamed up against Napoleon—Admiral Fedor Ushakov commanded a joint Russo-Ottoman fleet that captured the island of Corfu from the French in 1799.[6] Ever the exponent of dynastic legitimism, Emperor Nicholas I single-handedly rescued the Ottomans in 1831 when his troops landed in Üsküdar/Scutari and deterred Egypt's invading army into a retreat.[7] In the 1830s and 1840s, Russia enjoyed the status of an external patron to the Porte. Count Nicholas Ignatieff (Nikolai Ignat'ev), ambassador in Constantinople between 1864 and 1877, had no doubts as to where St Petersburg's strategic goal lay: "Russia cannot do otherwise than be a master either by assuming an exclusive influence over the sovereign and existing authorities at Constantinople or by annexing this place."[8] Annexation, desirable though it was, raised the danger of other European powers intervening. The humiliating defeat at the hands of Great Britain and France in the Crimean War (1853–56) proved the point. By overreaching, Russia brought an end to its virtual protectorate over the Ottoman Empire, forfeited its right to maintain a naval force in the Black Sea, and lost influence and prestige across the Near East. As a consequence, Russian policy became much more risk-averse—and Russia chose war only as a last resort.[9]

The Russian Empire and the Ottoman Empire shared a range of similarities. As Dominic Lieven points out, they both grew on the periphery of other power centers and cultures that they came to dominate later on. Just as Moscow was a periphery of Kievan Rus, itself a distant outpost of the Byzantine world, so were the Ottoman Turks descendants of tribesmen from Central Asia who were originally at the margins of the Islamic civilization. The two empires developed in the shadow of, and in reaction to, the Mongol expansion across Eurasia. Lieven underscores the centrality of the cavalry subordinate to the ruler, as the principal agent of state-building too.[10] And of course, not to forget the ambivalent relationship that both polities had with Europe: it was both an ideal to be emulated and followed, as was the case in Russia since Peter the Great and with the Tanzimat reforms in the late Ottoman Empire, and a formidable challenge and even a threat to the state's very survival.

In times when Western powers put in jeopardy Russia and Turkey, the two could join forces to push back. What scholars and current affairs analysts often forget is how Russia and Turkey stood side by side in the earlier decades of the twentieth century. The Bolshevik regime rendered critical assistance to Mustafa Kemal during the War of Independence (1919–22) and remained an ally or even a role model for the fledging Turkish Republic until the very end of the 1930s. The Republic Monument on Taksim Square in central Istanbul features a statue of Semen (Semyon) Aralov, Soviet Russia's first envoy to Ankara and one of the founders of the Red Army's intelligence service (*Glavnoe razvedyvatel'noe upravlenie* or GRU), right by Atatürk's side.[11] For their part, Lenin and his comrades viewed the future Atatürk and the nationalist movement he spearheaded as allies in the fight against imperialism. But the Bolsheviks and the Kemalists could also co-operate against enemies other than the Western powers. In late 1920, the Red Army and the Turkish General Kâzım Karabekir crushed the so-called First Armenian Republic, an independent state that had risen from the ashes of the Tsarist Empire. Armenians view this episode, the Turkish–Armenian War of 1920 in particular, as part of the genocide commencing in 1915.[12] In 2015, Putin's appearance at the centennial commemoration of the *Medz Yeghern* ("great calamity") ruffled feathers in Turkey. But the issue of Soviet complicity is rarely mentioned. Going back to the interwar period, the Kemalist regime's embrace of Bolshevik Russia continued well into the 1930s. Only Stalin's pact with Hitler in August 1939 compelled Ankara to quietly drop the non-aggression treaty it had signed with Moscow in 1925, though it kept the Straits closed to the Wehrmacht after the German invasion of the Soviet Union in 1941.[13]

The Cold War turned Moscow and Ankara into adversaries, but even then they found a *modus vivendi*. In the early stages, Turks had perfectly legitimate reasons to fear Soviet expansionism. Following Turkey's first multi-party elections of 1946, Stalin demanded a revision of the Soviet–Turkish borders as well as rights to bases in the Straits.[14] Turks sought security in allying with the United States (the 1947 Truman Doctrine identified Turkey as vulnerable to communist aggression) and ultimately joining NATO and the Central Treaty Organization in the 1950s.[15] In the 1960s, however, the superpower détente along with cracks in the Turkish–American relationship over Cyprus enabled a pragmatic reengagement with the USSR.[16] By the end of the decade, Turkey became the most significant recipient of Soviet foreign assistance in the Third World. The arms embargo imposed by the U.S. Congress in the wake of the 1974 invasion of Cyprus encouraged Moscow to ramp up financial aid (totalling $650 million by 1979). The list of common projects carried out as a result of that included an oil refinery, an aluminum smelter, and a steel mill. In gratitude, Ankara allowed the free passage of Soviet aircraft carriers in 1974 and 1979—an apparent violation of the terms of the Montreux Convention. The danger of

Turkey tilting to the Soviets made the administration of President Jimmy Carter lift the arms embargo in September 1978.

Another significant Cold War legacy is the tremendous cultural influence that the Soviet Union had over leftist intelligentsia whose ranks swelled in the 1960s. Their idol, the iconoclast poet Nâzım Hikmet (another native of the Balkans), had spent the last years of his life as an exile in Moscow in the 1950s and 1960s. His poems were the staple of *Bizim Radyo* (*Our Radio*) broadcasts from Leipzig, fondly remembered to this very day. However, Turkish authorities appreciated the fact that Moscow kept itself at arm's length from leftist militants in the 1970s, many of whom leaned towards Maoism anyhow.

Russian–Turkish co-operation in energy, which blossomed in the 2000s, dates back to the Cold War era as well. Formally, the Soviet Union was the arch-enemy. The military coup of September 1980 resulted in a sweeping crackdown against the left. Communist subversion of social and cultural life was a paramount concern for the generals who took the state's reins. In practice, once Turkey reverted to civilian rule in 1983, links with the Soviets rebounded. Liberal economic reforms championed by Prime Minister Turgut Özal brought in its wake an open invitation to all neighbors. A visit by the Soviet Prime Minister Nikolai Tikhonov in 1984 produced an energy agreement, followed by a twenty-five-year commercial deal for the import of natural gas two years later. The first volumes arrived in 1987, via Romania and Bulgaria.[17] Between 1986 and 1989, the value of trade tripled to $1.2 billion, and grew further to $1.9 billion by 1990. Like COMECON members, Turkey benefited from a clause allowing it to cover its gas exploitation with the provision of construction services inside the USSR. Divided by politics, Moscow and Ankara quickly learned how to do mutually profitable business—a recurrent theme, as we shall see.[18]

The Scramble for Eurasia

As the Soviet Union unraveled, few would have ventured to predict that Russia and Turkey would coexist happily. Taken together, the memories of past conflicts and the Hobbesian quality of post-1991

Eurasian politics bode ill for their bilateral relationship. With Russia in retreat, Turkey could exploit the political vacuum and take the lead in the Caucasus and Central Asia. "One nation, two states" (*bir Millet, iki Devlet*), enthused many Turks, as Ankara recognized independent Azerbaijan in November 1991. Adepts of pan-Turkism, especially on the far fight, savored the vision of older brother (*agabey*) Turkey uniting Turkic nations ranging from the Danube to China's Xinjiang province. A champion of opening up to neighbors since the 1980s, President Özal embraced the cause. From the unprecedented visit to (then Soviet) Azerbaijan and Kazakhstan in March 1991 all the way to his untimely death in April 1993, Özal passionately made the case for focusing on the Caucasus and Central Asia. "The twenty-first century will be the century of the Turks," he was fond of saying.[19] Overall, the West was favorably disposed too. Beyond doubt, Özal's fusion of market capitalism, democratic politics, and moderate Islam was preferable to the alternative of theocratic Iran next door.

To no one's surprise, Russia was hardly in thrall to the vision of a Turkey-led Eurasia. True, Özal was more acceptable than Ayatollah Khomeini, yet few in Moscow took a liking to the notion of a Russian "vacuum" in the region. Quite the opposite, broad agreement stipulated that the Russian Federation had legitimate interests in the post-Soviet southern tier. In addition, Turkish activism appeared threatening as it could, policymakers believed, encourage Turkic and Muslim separatists within Russia to solicit Ankara's support. To quote one example, the autonomous Republic of Tatarstan, holding about a quarter of Russia's oil reserves, voted for independence in March 1992. It took two years to craft a compromise and for Tatarstan to recognize Moscow's sovereignty. And then there was Chechnya, whose bid for secession elicited sympathy and support across Turkish society, particularly amongst the millions of citizens who could trace their ancestry to the waves of migrants from the Caucasus who had been flocking into Anatolia since the mid-nineteenth century.[20]

Russia and Turkey became enmeshed on opposing sides in a series of violent conflicts. In Bosnia, Moscow backed the Serbs while Ankara sided with the Muslim Bosniaks, considered as a kin community. In Nagorno-Karabakh, Turkey was fully aligned with the Azeris whereas Russia leaned towards the Armenians. Proxy conflicts stoked fears amidst politicians and military chiefs in Ankara that Turkey was being encircled by an informal pact including Russia as well as newly independent Armenia, Greece, former Yugoslavia, and Syria. The (perceived) alliance also involved the Kurdistan Workers' Party (*Partiya Karkerên Kurdistanê*, PKK) whose campaign against the Turkish state in the southeastern provinces, ongoing since 1984, peaked in the mid-1990s.[21]

Russia and Turkey were at odds with respect to as vital and strategic an issue as the transit of Caspian oil and gas. Successive governments in Ankara worked hard to relieve producer countries such as Azerbaijan, Kazakhstan, and Turkmenistan from dependence on export routes through the Russian Federation. As Süleyman Demirel (president, 1993–2000) put it in August 1995, "[f]or the sake of good relations [with Russia], these [Turkic] countries should not give away concessions from their independence. Our brother countries must have direct access to world markets without obstacles."[22] The Baku–Tbilisi–Ceyhan (BTC) oil pipeline project linking the Caspian and the Mediterranean became the centerpiece of Turkish foreign policy. By contrast, Russia wished to safeguard the route from the Black Sea port of Novorossiisk and the Black Sea fed by a pipeline crossing war-torn Chechnya. It viewed with suspicion the Turkish Grand National Assembly's unilateral decision in July 1994 to tighten regulations for tankers transiting through the Bosphorus as a hostile ploy and did not go along with the environmental concerns cited by the opposite side. Russia threatened to pursue a claim before the International Maritime Organization. Turkey, for its part, calculated that Russia would not risk opening the question on the status of the Straits. A revision of the 1936 Montreux Convention could put Moscow at a disadvantage, insofar as existing rules limited the access by navies of non-littoral nations—essentially, the United States and its NATO allies—to the Black Sea. To diversify its options, Russia launched the Burgas–Alexandroupolis project (discussed in Chapters 3 and 4).[23]

Dogs that did not Bark

Given all those tensions and points of friction, why and how did Russia and Turkey manage to avoid a full-frontal clash? There are several reasons—Ankara's realization of its own limits, the steps undertaken to cushion conflict, and, of course, the domestic problems besetting both countries. By the end of the 1990s, Russia and Turkey had learned to live with their differences.

The dream of a Turkic commonwealth with Turkey at the helm was divorced from realities on the ground. Post-Soviet leaders responded lukewarmly to Ankara's daring plans for a single market, an investment bank, and oil and gas pipelines. It did not take long before it became patently obvious that Russia's economic weight far outstripped that of the rest of the former Soviet Union. While turnover in the Southern Caucasus and Central Asia jumped from just $145 million in 1992 to $5.6 billion in 1999, the volume with Russia was twice as large. Moreover, Turkey was no match for Russia when it came to cultural attraction or the provision of security to local regimes. Russian preserved its status as the lingua franca across Central Asia. Over time, local elites built direct political ties to the United States, without needing Turkey as a go-between. Moreover, China emerged as an economic center of gravity. By 1995, the notion of Turkey as the leader of an imaginary Turkic World was all but dead.[24]

Turkey carved out a niche in the Southern Caucasus but even there its influence was checked. In June 1993, its closest ally, President Abulfaz Elchibey of Azerbaijan, fell from power after a putsch backed by the Russians and Heydar Aliyev took his place. The republic's last Soviet-period boss and former head of the local KGB branch mastered the art of balancing between Russia, Turkey, and the United States. Turkey was unable to intervene effectively in Nagorno-Karabakh. In May 1992, Demirel (then prime minister) promised President Yeltsin in Moscow that he would not respond to an ongoing Armenian offensive.[25] Marshal Evgenii Shaposhnikov, commander of the joint forces of the Commonwealth of Independent States, had issued a blunt warning that a putative Turkish intrusion would trigger no less than a Third World War. Russian troops were stationed in Armenia—and they remain there until this day. Moscow became the arbiter in Georgia too, after President Eduard Shevernadze deferentially brought the country into the CIS, following a brief civil war in 1993. Russian peacekeepers deployed in the breakaway provinces of Abkhazia and South Ossetia, in addition to troops in Adjara region (next to Turkey) and the town of Akhalaki. Turkey's defense cooperation with Georgia and Azerbaijan posed no substantial challenge to Russian military preeminence in the region.

There was no head-on collision in the Balkans either. As Bosnia went ablaze in 1992, Turkey, the home of up to four million people of Bosnian descent, witnessed a wave of solidarity for fellow Muslims. Ultranationalists and Islamists called for armed intervention. Özal delivered a rousing speech to a vast crowd gathered at Istanbul's Taksim Square, promising that "Bosnia would not become a new Andalusia" and that its Muslim heritage and populations would not be destroyed. While Russia played the role of international spokesman for Republika Srpska, Turkey pushed for lifting the arms embargo on the Sarajevo government, lobbying the Organization of the Islamic Conference (OIC), Azerbaijan, and the Central Asian republics for this cause. However, despite its pro-interventionist attitude—which unnerved its Western European allies—Turkey trod with caution. It favored collective action through NATO over unilateral moves, contributing to the alliance's Deliberate Force operation policing the no-fly zone over Bosnia. The Turkish foreign minister from 1991 to 1994, Hikmet Çetin, for one, shared a broader understanding of the conflict. In his view, at stake were universal humanitarian principles, rather than the survival of Balkan Islam per se. Çetin established a good working relationship with his Russian counterpart, Andrei Kozyrev, who prioritized co-operation with the West in former Yugoslavia.

Still, Turkey anxiously followed Russian moves in Bosnia. It was taken aback when Russia was invited to join the UN Protection Force (UNPROFOR) in Bosnia and Herzegovina in February 1994, part of the deal to defuse the crisis over Sarajevo. The decision set aside the informal rule that states with historical links to the region were not eligible to take up peacekeeping duties, and, as a result, the

Turks demanded compensation. In March, 1,467 Turkish Blue Helmets were deployed around the town of Zenica to separate the local Bosniaks and Croats. Turkey repaid Croatia's acquiescence by helping Zagreb join NATO's Partnership for Peace (PfP). Positive ties with both the Bosniaks and the Croats contrasted with Russia's exclusive focus on the Serbs, adding to Turkey's international credentials.

Throughout the 1990s, Turkey paid special attention to the Southern Balkans. It courted Albania, Macedonia, and Bulgaria in a bid to outmaneuver Greece, which in turn nurtured an alliance with former Yugoslavia, Bulgaria, and Russia in order to balance Turkey. Albania and Macedonia, as well as Bulgaria after 1997, looked to Turkey as a facilitator in their bid to move closer to the United States and NATO. Officials in Ankara portrayed Greece as the region's mischief-maker, the odd one out in the Western alliance, whose behavior was in stark contrast with Turkey's constructive approach. The Greek policy of engaging Russia in the Balkans spelled trouble as it dovetailed with Athens's embrace of Slobodan Milošević and Serb nationalism. In all seriousness, however, these frictions lacked the potential to provoke an all-out Russian–Turkish collision.

Avoiding a clash during the Cyprus Missile Crisis of 1997–98 was another achievement. To prevent the delivery of two batteries of S–300 Russian surface-to-air systems, the Turkish navy and coastguard started intercepting and searching vessels flying the Russian flag in September 1997. Turkey announced that the deployment of the missiles would be a declaration of war. Russia's ambassador to Athens, Georgii Muradov, responded that Russia would not stand idly by should Cyprus come under attack.[26] The Greek media speculated that the Russian navy would escort the S–300s in order to deter the Turks. Turkey pursued a two-track approach: talking tough to Nicosia and Athens, while seeking a deal with Moscow. In May 1998, the commander of the Turkish Armed Forces, General İsmail Hakkı Karadayı, spent five days in Moscow along with his deputy to defuse tensions. Both countries were relieved when the United States stepped in to broker a compromise.

Russia and Turkey were able to mitigate conflict by shifting attention to non-contentious issues, which would become a tactic of choice in the years to come. Ankara invited Moscow into the Black Sea Economic Co-operation (BSEC), a multilateral initiative it had formulated.[27] Boris Yeltsin came to Istanbul to take part in the inaugural summit in June 1992 hosted by President Özal. The BSEC aimed to diversify Turkey's economic and political ties at a moment when its prospects of entering the EC/EU were becoming bleaker. By having Greece onboard as a EU member, as well as the EU hopefuls Romania and Bulgaria, the BSEC signaled it was fully compatible with the policies of Brussels institutions. Russian–Turkish relations were therefore part of a pan-European trend towards functional integration through trade and the development of cross-border infrastructures.

Turkey and Russia cultivated a productive relationship at the bilateral level. During his trip to Moscow in May 1992, Prime Minister Demirel signed a friendship and co-operation treaty. Yeltsin praised the document as opening "a new page" between the two countries. The Turks talked up the prospect of increasing purchases of Russian gas and buying arms to the tune of $300 million. Between 1992 and 1996, Demirel and Tansu Çiller— his successor as prime minister and head of the True Path Party (*Doğru Yol Partisi*, DYP)—visited Moscow four more times. The visits yielded fifteen agreements covering areas from culture and education to defense and the fight against terrorism.[28] In a goodwill gesture, Turkey agreed to reschedule Soviet-era debts in 1994–95. Clearly, there was a sustained effort to keep economic ties separate from issues where Moscow and Ankara's interests were at variance (Chechnya, the war in Bosnia, Caspian oil, and so on).

Entrepreneurs and society at large were a key part of the story, always several steps ahead of their political leaders. The 1990s were a period when Turkey's economic achievements became visible to ordinary Russians, keen on low-cost consumer goods, from textiles to chewing gum and washing powder. Trade nearly quadrupled in the 1990s, thanks to gas as well as the fact that Russia granted Turkey the preferential "developing nation" status and cut tariffs by a quarter. Informal or "suitcase" trade shot up too. In the 1990s, it employed more than two million Russian Federation citizens and had an estimated annual turnover of around $8 billion.[29] Russian became widely spoken in Istanbul districts such as Laleli and Aksaray. Traditionally viewed as backward and conservative, Turkey acquired an image of vibrant and dynamic capitalism that had its appeal in Russia and elsewhere in the post-Soviet space. Tourists visited in ever greater numbers, from 587,000 in 1995 to 1,258,000 in 2003.[30] By 1997, Russians came second only to Germans in annual tourism statistics.

The last reason explaining why competition between Russia and Turkey did not get out of hand had to do with the enormous problems that both countries were facing at home. Russia's turbulent 1990s were more than matched by the disarray that took root in Turkey following Özal's untimely demise in 1993. Between that year and 1999, inconclusive elections produced a succession of six governments led by the Motherland Party (*Anavatan Partisi*, ANAP), the DYP, and the Islamist Welfare Party (*Refah Partisi*). The economy went through a never-ending cycle of boom and bust. The combination of resurgent political Islam and Kurdish militancy posed a radical challenge to the established order, at least from the point of view of Kemalist elites. In 1997, Turkey became the scene of a bloodless coup when the military forced Necmettin Erbakan, leader of the Welfare Party, to tender his resignation as prime minister. Twice, the country came to the very brink of war—against Greece in June 1996 and Syria in October 1998. The overconfidence of the Özal era gave way to a pervasive sense of vulnerability, not a far cry from how Russia felt at that very moment. In many respects, the 1990s were a lost decade for Turkey—just like the Putin regime claimed they were for Russia.

From Détente to Entente?

The late 1990s marked the moment when Turkey and Russia found common ground on a host of divisive and sensitive issues. Domestic political shifts were at play once again. When the Kemalist establishment toppled Erbakan in 1997, Ankara lost a fervent partisan of the Chechen cause.[31] Hard-line secularists regarded the Chechens with suspicion because of their association with political Islam. Ankara's response to the Second Chechen War in 1999 differed dramatically from its attitude to the conflict in 1994–96. On the eve of the Russian assault on Grozny (November 1999), Prime Minister Bülent Ecevit, head of the coalition government that replaced *Refah Partisi*, paid a widely publicized visit to Moscow resulting in a joint declaration against terrorism co-signed with Vladimir Putin, the newly appointed premier who led the war. Interviewed by the public broadcaster TRT, the veteran Turkish center-left politician bluntly stated that Chechnya was Russia's internal business, triggering an irate response by Erbakan. Even though Moscow continued complaining that Turkey harbored Chechens, Ankara clamped down on émigré networks in line with the bilateral anti-terror protocol from 1995.[32] Attacks within Turkey carried out by radicals from Chechnya and other parts of the Caucasus, such as a 2001 hostage drama at Istanbul's exclusive Swissôtel, swung public opinion in a negative direction too.[33] An assault on the tourist industry at a time of a severe economic slump did not wash well with ordinary Turks. The negative stereotype became entrenched when it transpired that the 2003 bomb attacks against synagogues and an HSBC branch in Istanbul had been perpetrated by al-Qaeda affiliates with connections to Chechnya.

Moscow reciprocated Turkey's accommodating moves by downscaling support for the PKK, originally a Soviet-inspired Marxist–Leninist movement. "Russia never supported, and will not support in the future, terrorism against Turkey," pledged Putin to Ecevit during their summit.[34] The Russians had already built a positive track record in the eyes of Ankara. In late 1998, Moscow stayed neutral as the Turkish military strong-armed its ally Syria into evicting the PKK's founding leader Abdullah Öcalan. Prime Minister Evgenii Primakov and President Boris Yeltsin averted a crisis by vetoing the Duma's decision to grant "Sarok Apo" (Leader Apo, as Öcalan is known to his supporters) asylum once he turned up in the Russian capital.[35] Russia subsequently closed down several

PKK-run facilities, including a hospital used to treat wounded militants. However, it stopped short of listing the guerrilla movement as a terrorist organization, as Turkey would have preferred. Nevertheless, Ankara did appreciate the signal all the same.

Russians and Turks could find common ground even where they held divergent views. In Kosovo, for instance, Turkey backed the NATO intervention and even offered access to its airbases but showed a degree of empathy with the Russian position. It initially opposed military action and insisted on the sacrosanct principle of state sovereignty. Turkish diplomats drew a distinction with Bosnia where, in their view, one independent and internationally recognized state had come under attack by another. The Kurdish issue conditioned a negative view of self-determination, manifest in Turkey's refusal to acknowledge Tatarstan, Chechnya, or even Moldova's Gagauz province as independent entities.

Turkey's fractious relations with NATO presented an additional inducement to mend ties with the Russians. As the First Chechen War broke out in 1994, the alliance accepted troop deployments in the Caucasus going over the limits set by the Conventional Armed Forces in Europe (CFE) agreement. Turkey's objections were overruled in May 1996 when NATO negotiated modifications to the CFE, linking its assent to Russia's acceptance of enlargement to Central and Eastern Europe. As a result, Ankara pursued a bilateral arrangement with Moscow. The deal struck in January 1999 foresaw a withdrawal of Russian forces from Moldova and Georgia.

The rapprochement was not just a matter of ideological affinities or overlapping security interests but also economic interdependence. Prime Minister Viktor Chernomyrdin's visit to Ankara in December 1997 unveiled a bold plan for Blue Stream, a pipeline under the Black Sea with an annual capacity reaching a maximum of 16 bcm in 2007. Since the 1980s, Russia had supplied Turkey with gas through the Balkans. Now it could deliver from the east as well, feeding the capital city of Ankara. The dependency on fickle transit routes such as through Ukraine, Romania, and Bulgaria would diminish. Gazprom, which would control the pipeline, relished the prospect of tapping into a rapidly growing market. Electricity consumption in Turkey had soared by a massive 150 percent between 1980 and 1996—compared to a 40 percent growth in the population.[36] To give Blue Stream a go-ahead, the state-owned energy company BOTAŞ signed a twenty-five-year contract inclusive of a "take-or-pay" clause.[37]

Blue Stream was anything but a run-of-the-mill transaction. In league with Turkey, Gazprom had in effect developed the blueprint for future bypass pipelines of the 2000s, such as North Stream and South Stream. Blue Stream moreover preempted the advance of competing schemes, notably the proposed Trans-Caspian Pipeline, which would channel gas from Turkmenistan, Kazakhstan, and Azerbaijan to Turkey and the EU. The venture cemented a three-way co-operation between Russia, Turkey, and Italy, as *Ente Nazionale Idrocarburi* (ENI) took a stake. ENI's know-how was crucial for completing the 385-kilometer undersea stretch from Beregovaia in Russia's Krasnodar region to the port of Samsun.[38]

Blue Stream facilitated the completion of the BTC. Prime Minister Ecevit's visit to Moscow and President Bill Clinton's partic-ipation in the OSCE Summit in Istanbul, both in November 1999, sealed everyone's final agreement. In 2005–6, Caspian oil reached international markets, strengthening Azerbaijan's hand with the help of Turkey and the United States.[39] Ankara could finally live up to its ambitions to act as the advance guard of Western influence in the former Soviet Union. Russia decided to go along (though Lukoil, which was interested in the project, decided not to buy a stake). In a quid pro quo, Turkey adopted new, more advantageous regulations on commercial traffic through the Straits.

Turkey viewed burgeoning security and energy ties to the Russians as a useful counterweight to the West. Chernomyrdin's visit took place right after the EU's Council at Luxembourg on 12–13 December 1997 refused to proclaim Turkey as a potential candidate for the EU. In his fury, Prime Minister Mesut Yılmaz threatened to freeze links with the Union. "Turkey has very close relations with the Turkic republics of the Caucasus and Central Asia, and very good relations with Balkan countries except Greece," he argued, underscoring that the EU was not the only option at hand.[40] Russia was clearly part of the very same equation. In the words of Philip Robins, "Turkey's gas relationship with Russia, which had never in any case since Özal's day been exclusively a function of commerce, moved firmly into the realm of high politics."[41]

At the turn of the millennium, Turkey and Russia had come close to transforming their mutual relationship. In November 2001, at the margins of the UN General Assembly, Foreign Ministers Igor Ivanov, of Armenian descent, and Ismail Cem signed an action plan for "multidimensional co-operation in Eurasia." However, it was too premature to speak of an alignment. In the words of Duygu Bazoğlu Sezer, a Turkish professor of international relations, Russia and Turkey had entered a virtual alliance where

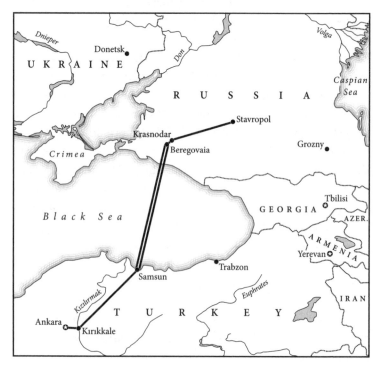

Map 2 Blue Stream

public manifestations of state-level adversity and hostility [had] nearly completely disappeared; the importance of co-operation in a range of fields for furthering respective national interests [was] mutually perceived and publicly articulated; governments desist[ed] from using inflammatory rhetoric so as not to arouse public hostility; and officials [kept] the lines of communication open in order to safeguard relations against the impact of sudden crisis. On the other hand, a hard kernel of mutual fear, mistrust, and suspicion remain[ed] in the minds of the decision-makers and political elites.[42]

The Putin–Erdoğan Double Act

Although the groundwork for rapprochement was laid in the 1990s, it was with the rise of Vladimir Putin and Tayyip Erdoğan that Russian–Turkish relations blossomed. Rooted in (partly) convergent interests, ties became highly personalized: "I gave my word to the Prime Minister," Putin said in September 2010, "I am certain the [Samsun–Ceyhan oil] pipeline will be built."[43] Observers would come to see the two strong-willed leaders as political twins: men of the people, straight-talking, tough on opponents, never shrinking from a punch-up with the West in the name of their nations' honor. "Our countries deserve respect," the two leaders appeared to be saying with the one voice, "they should be treated as equals, not as a second-class appendage to Europe."

Ironically or not, Putin and Erdoğan assumed power in a period when Russia and Turkey were forging better relations with the EU. Turkey seemed to be edging closer to membership, opening accession talks with the Union in 2005 as a reward for political and economic reforms. Russia meanwhile had deepened its energy ties with the EU and co-operated with the United States on security post-9/11. But by the latter part of the decade, resentment for being kept at arm's length or, in Russia's case, for Western meddling in the privileged sphere of influence, prevailed. Putin and Erdoğan had more than one reason to invest in their mutual relationship. Fiona Hill and Ömer Taşpınar, analysts at the Brookings Institution, called it "the Axis of the Excluded."[44] Ten years down the line, many consider Putin and Erdoğan to be part of an authoritarian wave contesting the Western liberal model rooted in the rule of law, accountable government, free media, and pluralist civil society.

At closer inspection, Putin and Erdoğan make an unlikely couple. Boris Yeltsin's handpicked heir with a background in the KGB, propelled from obscurity into political stardom thanks to a TV promotion campaign orchestrated by top Kremlin brass as well as to a war, had less in common with the streetwise politico working his way up from the back alleys of a conservative, lower-middle-class Istanbul neighborhood to the apex of power. Styling himself as an underdog, Erdoğan had built a career by confronting the so-called "deep state" (*derin devlet*) embedded in the military, the security establishment, and high bureaucracy, in alliance with the EU and the liberal intelligentsia. He served time in prison after Erbakan's downfall in 1997. Putin, by contrast, felt very much like Russia's deep state. He was ensconced in power by reining in the media, crushing the Chechens, re-establishing state control of the oil sector, and selling the story that the chaotic 1990s had been replaced by rule with the firm hand.

In Turkey itself, Russia and Putin originally captivated Erdoğan's detractors, including hard-core Kemalists resentful of Western interventionism and EU influence. ("A Kemalist in the Kremlin" is how *The Moscow Times* described Putin in a piece dated 4 April 2005.) In early 2002, General Tuncer Kılınç, secretary general of the all-powerful National Security Council, dropped a bombshell by openly advocating an alliance with Russia and Iran.[45] Some figures hailing from the left went so far as to embrace Aleksandr Dugin's Eurasianist doctrine. They considered it a potential cornerstone for a new political identity, distinctive from both political Islam and radical Europhilia which, in their minds, threatened to erode Turkey's foundations as a nation state and turn it into a Western colony.[46] The prospective alliance with Russia therefore presented an alternative to the pro-EU course charted by Turkey's Justice and Development Party (*Adalet ve Kalkınma Partisi*, AKP), especially early in its tenure. In 2013, Doğu Perinçek, the most prominent personality amongst the Duginists, was sentenced under the landmark Ergenekon case on charges of conspiring against the government. Later on, in a fascinating turnaround, the Eurasianists were to side with Erdoğan in his struggle against the pious movement—which they invariably portrayed as the epitome of evil metastasizing within the Turkish body politic.[47]

It was not until late 2004 that Putin and Erdoğan had a chance to meet face to face. From that point onwards, the two leaders presided over a leap in bilateral relations. Putin's Ankara visit of December 2004 yielded six agreements covering energy, finance, and security. That was the first time a Russian leader had come on a bilateral visit to Turkey in more than three decades.[48] Boris Yeltsin had been twice in Istanbul, in 1992 and 1999, but both occasions involved multilateral summits (the BSEC and OSCE). Erdoğan returned the compliment and visited Moscow in January 2005, and then had a meeting with Putin in Sochi in July.[49] The "multidimensional partnership" about which diplomats rhapsodized was finally taking shape. On 17 November 2005, media across the world posted pictures of the two presidents inaugurating the Blue Stream Pipeline in Samsun, in the company of Italy's Silvio Berlusconi (an acknowledgement of ENI's contribution). While Putin and Erdoğan largely inherited the Russian–Turkish rapprochement from the late 1990s—as testified by the case of Blue Stream—they did raise it to new heights.

"Our strategic neighbor"

What conditioned the Russian–Turkish alignment, unprecedented since the interwar years, were ultimately shifts in the area of security. The Iraq War (2003–11) was a case in point. In a surprising move, Turkey decided not to join the American-led coalition of the willing and open a second front against Saddam Hussein from the north, as in the 1991 Gulf War. The drive for greater autonomy in foreign policy encouraged Moscow to look to Ankara as a potential ally to offset American unilateralism. It clearly had Turkish public opinion on its side. A majority opposed the war and viewed with suspicion George W. Bush's post-9/11 war on terror. Fears of the knock-on effects of Iraqi Kurdistan's advancement to full independence pervaded large swathes of society. The Turkish government, on the other hand, weighed up its options. The Turkish prime minister, Abdullah Gül,[50] haggled hard with the United States, demanding monetary compensation and/or guarantees for Turkey's presence in post-Saddam Iraq. Many expected Turkey, begrudgingly, to jump on the American bandwagon. Yet a group of AKP parliamentarians rebelled and, on 1 March 2003, defeated by a narrow margin the motion for joining the U.S.-led coalition. In other words, Turkey and Russia ended up on the same side of the barricade thanks to a contingency. But that did not alter the fact that there was a confluence of views in Moscow and Ankara. What mattered were the consequences. The state with the second largest military in NATO had stood up to the all-powerful United States. The Putin–Erdoğan summitry, kicking off not long after the invasion of Iraq, was a reflection rather than the cause of the rapprochement.

The Turks and Russians agreed that they could manage their common frontier. In early 2001, Moscow had joined the Black Sea Force (BLACKSEAFOR) delegated to take charge of naval security—discharging tasks such as search-and-rescue and maritime policing. Touted as a contribution to the global war on terror, BLACKSEAFOR kept its distance from NATO and excluded the United States. More than that, Turkey opposed the extension of the Atlantic Alliance's Operation Active Endeavor from the Mediterranean to the Black Sea. As an alternative, in the spring of 2004, Moscow and Ankara launched a BLACKSEAFOR operation, Black Sea Harmony, tasked with intercepting terrorists and traffickers of arms and drugs. The Black Sea area would be a Russian–Turkish shared responsibility—or even a condominium. Yet Turkey had to strike a delicate balance. Its diplomats worked hard to convince the Americans that Black Sea Harmony was an incremental step, and not an impediment, to NATO's involvement.[51] When America applied to become an observer in the BSEC, the economic leg of Black Sea regionalism, Turkey abstained and Russia's response was a resounding "*nyet*."[52]

The 2008 war in Georgia showed how deeply entrenched Russian–Turkish security co-operation had become. Georgia was no ordinary neighbor. In the early 1990s, when Turkey was at logger-heads with most countries around its borders, amicable links with Tbilisi were a welcome exception. Georgia served as a bridge to the Azeris and the Caspian Sea and was key to the BTC while Turkey topped the list of its trading partners. Militaries co-operated and, at least in principle, Turkey pushed for Georgia's integration into NATO.[53] President Mikheil Saakashvili's radically pro-Western orientation therefore suited Ankara's priorities. Yet his row with Moscow, escalating into a fully fledged war in August 2008, put the Turks in a delicate position. The prompt defeat of the Georgian forces, Abkhazia and South Ossetia's declaration of independence, and the ramped-up Russian military presence close to the Turkish border, were not good news. However, any direct confrontation with Russia would contradict Turkey's interests. Here is how Prime Minister Erdoğan himself put it, in an interview for *Milliyet*:

It would not be right for Turkey to be pushed toward any side. Certain circles want to push Turkey into a corner either with the United States or Russia after the Georgian incident. One of the sides is our closest ally, the United States. The other side is Russia, with which we have an important trade volume. We would act in line with what Turkey's national interests require.[54]

Turkey weighed its options. At the outset of hostilities, on 8 August, Erdoğan called Saakashvili to assure him of his support. Soon enough, however, as the Russian army pushed back, he changed tack. On 12 August, the Turkish prime minister travelled to Moscow to pitch the so-called Caucasus Stability and Co-operation Pact, which was little more than a statement of neutrality.[55] To accom-modate Moscow, Turkey was adamant that American military ships delivering humanitarian aid to the Georgians had to abide by a special provision of the 1936 Montreux Convention, in effect barring two large American hospital vessels, USNS *Comfort* and *Mercy*.[56] Turkey's Ministry of Foreign Affairs assured Moscow that the smaller ships the United States had to despatch instead would depart before the expiry of the treaty-mandated twenty-one-day period. This tilt towards Moscow did not go unnoticed in Washington. Turkey was excluded from Vice President Dick Cheney's tour of regional allies, which included stopovers in Tbilisi, Baku, and Kyiv. At the same time, Foreign Minister Sergei Lavrov came to Istanbul, on 2 September 2008. Back in 2005, the American diplomat Richard Holbrooke had written about "a little noticed charm offensive to woo our all-important (but deeply alienated) ally Turkey into a new special relationship that would extend Russia's influence."[57] The war in Georgia made everyone notice.

The West's speedy return to "business as usual" with Russia soon after the war in Georgia confirmed to the Turkish leadership that they had made the right choice in August–September 2008. President Barack Obama's "reset" unveiled in the summer of 2009 placed a bet on Dmitry Medvedev, Putin's successor as president. With the exception of the United Kingdom, the major EU powers were similarly in engagement mode, with Germany investing heavily in a "Partnership for Modernization" with Russia. As the 2000s came to a close, Turkey's conciliatory approach, based on the premise that economic interdependence was the key to resolving political conflicts, seemed hardly exceptional.

It was only right and proper that Russia should become a highlight of Turkey's "policy of zero problems (*sıfır sorun politikası*) with neighbors," a doctrine articulated by Ahmet Davutoğlu, an academic who became foreign minister on 1 May 2009. Earlier editions of the policy, essentially a blueprint for strengthening economic and political links with countries and regions abutting Turkey, had contributed to a warming of relations with Moscow, especially under President Özal in the 1980s and during Ismail Cem's tenure as foreign minister (1997–2002). This time around Russia could be of help on some tangled issues. It supported President Gül's overtures to Armenia, in 2009. Although Putin subsequently spoke out against Turkey's demand for substantive concessions in Nagorno-Karabakh as a precondition for full normalization of ties with Armenia, it was obvious that he did not see Ankara's new activism as a threat.[58] The Russians and Turks were no longer bitter competitors in the Southern Caucasus, irrespective of the fact that their interests were not exactly in accord either. Even more remarkably, the Kremlin was relaxed about Turkey's connections to the Muslim communities within the Russian Federation. In February 2009, President Gül, the first Turkish head of state ever to visit Russia, included Tatarstan's capital of Kazan in his itinerary.[59] Several years later, in September 2015, Putin and Erdoğan would stand side by side in Moscow at the inauguration of the renovated Cathedral Mosque, one of Europe's largest. Who would have foreseen that in the 1990s?

At the strategic level, Russia had a perfectly good reason to be cheerful. Turkey's zero-problems policy with its neighbors distanced Ankara from the United States. The Turks were engaged with all of Moscow's friends and partners in the Middle East, including Iran, Syria, and Libya. In its quest for a wide-ranging international policy, Turkey had no trouble dealing with regimes shunned by the West. The rupture in Turkish–Israeli relations in 2010 following the *Mavi Marmara* incident[60] widened the gap between Ankara and its allies. An anti-Western mood surged within Turkey. A survey from 2012 found that more than two-thirds of Turks viewed the United States as the main threat to their country, while Israel was feared by another 52 percent. The previous year, another poll registered 70 percent support for increased political relations with Russia and 76 percent for stronger economic ties.[61] Moscow was clearly the beneficiary of a crisis it had little to do with.

A Hundred-Billion-Dollar Vision

Thriving Russian–Turkish ties rest on solid economic bedrock. In the 2000s, hydrocarbon imports into Turkey made Russia its top trading partner, surpassing Germany (yet still behind the EU taken as a bloc). Commercial links grew at a rapid pace after the Turkish economy recovered from the effects of the 2001 financial meltdown and Blue Stream came online in February 2003. Starting from about $10 billion in the early 2000s, turnover peaked at $38 billion in 2008, on the eve of the global crisis. "[E]conomic and commercial relations between our countries are similar to a locomotive leading the diverse, good neighborly and friendly cars of a train," Evgenii Primakov once observed, in a near-poetic bout.[62] Putin and Erdoğan talked of hitting the $100 billion mark by the centennial of the Turkish Republic in 2023. The recession in 2008–9, slower growth rates, and the effects of the Su-24 crisis and its aftermath in 2015–16 have made the achievement of that goal unlikely. But the two countries have remained committed. Erdoğan's visit to Moscow in August 2009 saw the establishment of a High-Level Coooperation Council, a format uniting the two governments, co-chaired by Deputy Prime Minister Igor Sechin, one of Putin's closest associates.[63]

There has always been a snag about the two countries' economic links, however. At an average of $6 billion, Turkish exports of goods and services are five times lower than imports from Russia. Put differently, dependence on Russian gas puts Turkey in a strategic position similar to post-communist Eastern Europe. The resultant trade deficit has been a sore spot in Moscow–Ankara relations since the 1990s. Back then, Russian authorities argued that Turkey balanced the books thanks to the unreported suitcase trade (trade in small quantities of cheap goods purchased during shopping trips) and the export of construction services.[64] They lamented the exclusion of Russian contractors from the heavily guarded Turkish market.[65] There is an element of truth in this, to be sure. Russia has provided lucrative opportunities for major Turkish contractors such as ENKA, Rönesans, Esta, Alarko, and others. In Moscow alone, their portfolio includes landmark buildings such as the headquarters of Gazprom and the mayor's office, along with a chain of Ramstor supermarkets owned by the Koç Group. A Turkish firm repaired the White House, the seat of the Russian Federation government, heavily damaged after President Yeltsin's forces stormed it in October 1993. By 2009, the overall value to Turkey of completed projects in Russia had reached $30 billion.[66]

Russia has been a hugely important player in the Turkish tourism market. The number of Russians visiting Turkey soared from 587,000 in 1995 to 1.25 million in 2003 and 2.8 million in

2008.[67] By 2002–3, Russia had overtaken the United Kingdom in terms of tourist arrivals and had started contesting first place with Germany. Russian was commonly spoken in popular holiday spots such as Antalya in Turkey—attracting around 70 percent of tourists and holiday-home owners. Russia marked 2007 as "a year of Turkish culture," and Turkey reciprocated in 2008, investing $10 million in a campaign to promote itself in the race against competitors such as Egypt. In 2010, Moscow and Ankara abolished visas (prior to that, Russians could acquire entry permits directly at the border). A true tourist and travel boom ensued. A staggering 4.1 million Russians, for the most part tourists, visited Turkey in the first nine months of 2014, an increase of 300,000 compared to the same period in 2013.[68]

The record levels of economic exchange and interdependence have clearly done a lot of good to both Russia and Turkey, enabling stability in their complex political relationship. But, as we shall see below, dense trading links have also spelled vulnerability. Following the Su-24M incident in November 2015, Moscow has proved capable of inflicting considerable damage on several sectors of the Turkish economy and of changing President Erdoğan's strategic calculations in its favor.

Haggling over Energy

Since the late 1980s, energy has been the umbilical cord connecting Russia and Turkey. Turkey is the second most important market for Gazprom after Germany. By the late 2000s, imports reached 27 bcm, accounting for around 55–60 percent of Turkish consumption. By comparison, the second-largest supplier to Turkey, namely Iran, exports 10 bcm a year.[69] Ankara's long-term objective is to diminish dependence on Gazprom by diversifying supplies. It has also pushed hard to bring down prices and improve the terms of trade. At the end of 2011, BOTAŞ declined to renew the 1986 contract on gas delivered through the Trans-Balkan Pipeline.[70] Since 2014, Turkey has been driving a hard bargain on the TurkStream project as well, hoping to use its geographic location to secure a larger discount from the Russian side (more below).

Turkey has always been a critical component of Russian plans to reduce the dependence on imports. The so-called Southern Gas Corridor passes, for much of the way, through Turkish territory. The corridor started taking shape in 2006 with the inauguration of the South Caucasus Pipeline (SCP), which runs parallel to the BTC from Baku to the eastern Turkish city of Erzurum.[71] On 13 July 2009, Ankara hosted the signing of a deal on Nabucco, an extension of the SCP endorsed by the European Commission and the American government. The Commission head, José Manuel Barroso, and Andris Piebalgs, the Energy Commissioner, were both in attendance. Co-piloted by two energy companies, Austria's OMV and BOTAŞ, the project enlisted Bulgargaz, Transgaz (Romania), and MOL (Hungary) as partners. It aimed at creating a physical pipeline connection between Anatolia and Central Europe.

Yet Turkey has been hedging its bets, much like other downstream countries in Southeast Europe. While it seeks alternatives, it continues to play along with the Russians. That is not difficult to understand. Common projects carried out with Moscow have enhanced Turkish energy security. Direct connectivity to the Russian grid, via Blue Stream, largely spared Turkey from the midwinter energy cut-offs in 2006 and 2009. In addition, Ankara was prepared to help Gazprom bypass Ukraine. In December 2011, after talks with Vladimir Putin, Energy Minister Taner Yıldız gave the South Stream consortium the green light to lay pipes in Turkey's Exclusive Economic Zone (EEZ). Russia had previously, in 2009, entertained the idea of routing the pipeline through Turkey—a bargaining tactic to put pressure on Bulgaria as it dragged its feet.[72]

Doing favors to Russia, Turkey expected a handsome payback in return. For instance, it conditioned the access to its EEZ in the Black Sea on the possible extension of Blue Stream towards the Middle East.[73] That was a long shot. Nevertheless, as part of the 2011 deal on South Stream, Gazprom agreed to scrap the "take-or-pay" clauses in the 1997 contract linked to Blue Stream. This decision resolved a simmering conflict between the Russians and Turks that went largely unnoticed. BOTAŞ never met its commitment to purchase 16 bcm through Blue Stream and pressured

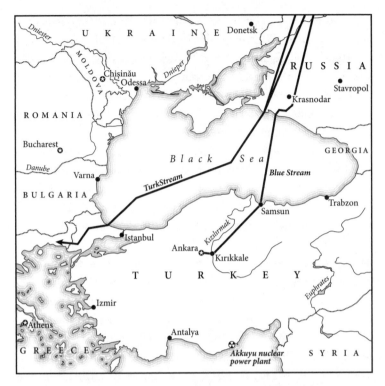

Map 3 Blue Stream, TurkStream and the Akkuyu nuclear power plant

Gazprom to revise the terms of the agreement in order to avoid being overcharged.[74] Energy relations between Moscow and Ankara have never been problem-free.

History was to repeat itself with TurkStream. Putin's pitch in December 2014 caught Erdoğan and the Turkish government off-guard. They signed a Memorandum of Understanding with the CEO of Gazprom, Aleksei Miller, but left substantive negotiations for later on. There was no meeting of minds; Turkey demanded a much higher discount on the long-term contract than the 6 percent offered by the Russians. Ankara insisted on a longer pipeline route, all the way to Kıyıköy on the European side, nearly 900 kilometers west of Samsun—also preferred by Moscow. Gazprom had to halve the projected capacity of the pipeline to 31.5 bcm. The Turks frowned at the Russian negotiations with Athens for a terminal across the Greek–Turkish border. In October 2015, BOTAŞ filed an arbitration suit against Gazprom. TurkStream received a boost a year later, when Putin came to Istanbul to oversee the signature of an intergovernmental agreement (IGA). Energy co-operation is now back on track, but whether TurkStream has a chance to extend beyond Turkey's borders with the EU remains an open question.

As we have seen, Turkey traditionally balances between the EU and Russia. It is a critical player in the much-debated Southern Gas Corridor. In December 2011, Azerbaijan and Turkey unveiled the Trans-Anatolian Pipeline (TANAP) running from Erzurum west-wards to the EU border.[75] Although the deal undermined the chances of the Brussels-favored Nabucco (and then Nabucco West) getting off the ground, it opened the prospect of Caspian gas reaching Europe by the end of the current decade.

Russia targeted other sectors of the Turkish economy in addi-tion to gas. Ankara agreed to purchase electricity from Inter RAO UES in November 2008, and imports (via Georgia) started in March 2010. However, the partnership became strategic when Turkey and Russia focused on nuclear energy. In August 2009, the Turkish Atomic Energy Authority (*Türkiye Atom Enerjisi Kurumu*) signed two agreements with Rosatom for the construction of a nuclear power plant in Turkey, followed up by a state-to-state deal initialed by Presidents Gül and Medvedev (May 2010). Under the terms of the deal, Rosatom would build, own, and operate the $20 billion facility featuring four reactors with a combined capacity of 4,800 megawatts.[76] Turkey would pay up to 20 percent of the bill and its companies were to acquire 49 percent of the venture. The Turkish Electricity Trade and Contract Corporation (*Türkiye Elektrik Ticaret ve Taahhüt A.Ş.*) committed to buy the electricity at set prices.

At least on paper, the Akkuyu project was supposed to be a win-win situation. With Russia's assistance, Turkey could fulfill a long-standing aspiration. Nuclear energy could meet the country's soaring demand and bring in valuable know-how. Once more, as in the 1960s and 1970s, Moscow was instrumental in developing a whole

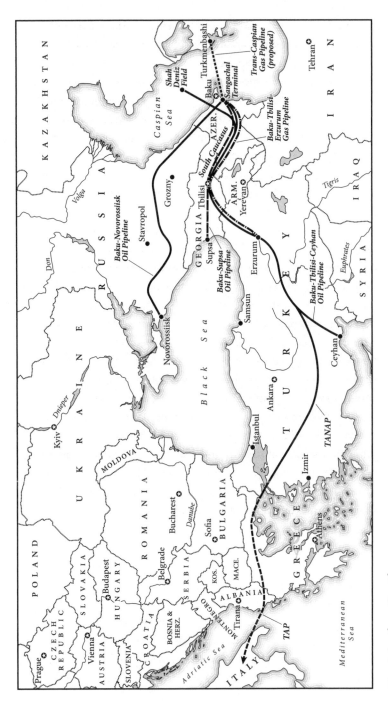

Map 4 Southern Corridor

new sector of the Turkish economy. In its turn, Russia obtained access to a growing market for one of the few high-tech exports it had. The energy minister, Sergei Shmatko, estimated the income from uranium-fuel exports to Turkey at $60 billion over fifteen years. Russia could showcase the Akkuyu nuclear power plant to attract customers elsewhere in the emerging world. Vladimir Putin praised the deal, as well as the virtues of Russia's nuclear industry: "this range of services [storage, repossessing, financing] allows us to charge reasonable rates, well below what our competitors demand."[77] Russia was charging half as much as America, insisted Putin during a visit to Ankara in 2009.[78]

With regard to Akkuyu, Turkey made a concession to the Russians. It dropped its original demand to take ownership control of the nuclear facility. But the AKP had to face criticism that it was deepening the dependency on Russia. That is why the government refused Rosatom the commission to construct a second nuclear power plant at Sinop. There have been plenty of other outstanding issues, even before the Su-24M crisis triggered rumors that Akkuyu might be abandoned altogether. According to analysts, "the AKP's rush to develop nuclear power as quickly and cheaply as possible could pose a number of safety and security risks. The 'build-operate-own' model has never been used for a nuclear power reactor. With the plants being operated by foreign companies, Turkish officials will have to find a way to ensure that suppliers do not cut corners to keep costs low."[79] Dogged by financial problems, Rosatom has been on the lookout to sell 49 percent in the Akkuyu project to an external investor—thus far without much success.[80]

A Syrian Test

In hindsight, it is hardly remarkable that the war in Syria has caused the gravest crisis in Russian–Turkish relations since the end of the Cold War. Russia's military intervention in Syria in the autumn of 2015 saved the Assad regime from collapse and dealt a heavy blow to Ankara's ambitions. Moscow appeared to be renewing its alliance with the PKK, which was once more fighting the Turkish government. Tensions were on the rise, both before and after the shooting down of the Su-24M. "An attack on Turkey means an attack on NATO," Erdoğan warned Russia in October 2016. Moscow's ambassador had already been summoned three times over airspace incursions.[81] The Turks were prepared to take action, in all likelihood underestimating Putin's resolve to strike back. Even though Moscow and Ankara desisted from a direct military confrontation in the wake of the downing of the Russian jet, the ensuing political spat was serious enough.

Russia's response took a heavy toll on the Turkish economy. In 2016, Russian authorities introduced sanctions targeting agricultural imports from Turkey, prohibited tour operators from selling holidays, abolished the visa-free regime, and severely tightened residence regulations for business people and students. Turkish construction companies in Russia were also reportedly feeling the heat. The Turkish tourist industry announced the biggest drop in visitors in twenty-five years, with close to 90 percent fewer Russians visiting the country in the first six months of 2016 compared to the previous year. Together with the Western visitors deterred by the series of terrorist attacks by the self-proclaimed Islamic State, the overall slump for Turkey reached 40 percent. Deputy Prime Minister Mehmet Şimşek estimated the potential loss at $9 billion, or 0.3–0.4 percent of Turkish GDP.[82] Turkey was in a much less advantageous position than Russia. It could not switch off overnight gas imports from Russia, despite Prime Minister Ahmet Davutoğlu's tour of Qatar, Azerbaijan, and Turkmenistan in early 2016 to explore opportunities for alternative supplies in the event of a cut-off. Nor could Turkey simply cancel the Akkuyu project without having to pay a hefty indemnity to Rosatom.

The row changed the pattern of relations between Russia and Turkey. From August 2011, when Turkey made a U-turn and cut (the hitherto close) links to the Assad regime in Damascus, up to late 2015, Putin and Erdoğan had agreed to disagree about Syria and carry on with bilateral business as usual. Tensions were not allowed to spin out of control.[83] In the meantime, economic ties were flourishing. From $23 billion in 2011, trade turnover climbed to about $33 billion in 2012, and then came down to $30 billion in 2013 and 2014.[84] Turkish Airlines' business in the Russian Federation was booming, while Turkish contractors completed projects to the tune of $1.6 billion during the 2014 Sochi Winter Olympics. Erdoğan attended the opening ceremony, ignoring protests by Turks of Circassian descent whose ancestors were uprooted from the region by the Tsarist authorities in the 1860s.

In order to avoid conflict with Russia, Turkey kept a low profile during the takeover of Crimea in 2014. It showed plenty of sympathy to the Tatars, a kindred community that, for historical reasons, stood on Ukraine's side in the dispute. President Gül even gave a state award to Tatar leader Mustafa Dzhemilev (Mustafa Abdülcemil Kırımoğlu) in April 2014. Right after the Crimean referendum, Davutoğlu held a joint press conference with Dzhemilev to declare that Turkey would never recognize the legitimacy of the vote. Yet Ankara refused to side with the Western sanctions, pledging to protect the rights of Tatars with "determined diplomacy."[85] Similarly, Turkey had a muted reaction to the war in the Donbas. "The U.S. has itself to blame," a Turkish diplomat remarked, "it gave Russia a carte blanche by not intervening in Syria."[86] But behind the scenes the AKP government was changing its position. First, it joined NATO's missile-defense program, hosting a radar in the Kürecik base in the southeast of Turkey. Second, Russia's militarization of Crimea made Ankara accept, in incremental steps, that the alliance could play a larger role in Black Sea naval security, a reversal of its traditional stance.

The aftershocks of the Russian–Turkish collision were felt across Southeast Europe. In December 2015 the Movement for Rights and Freedoms (MRF), a Bulgarian party drawing votes from the country's Turks and Muslims, ousted its leader Lütfi Mestan who had taken sides with Ankara. The MRF founder Ahmed Doğan led the charge, accusing Mestan of pitching Bulgaria into the crossfire between Turkey and Russia ("its rise is an irreversible process," he claimed). The Greek prime minister, Alexis Tsipras, underscored Turkish violations of Greek airspace in the Aegean, prompting an angry exchange on Twitter with his opposite number, Ahmet Davutoğlu. But, all things considered, such repercussions amounted to little more than a storm in a teacup. Contrary to all the doom and gloom, there was no spiral of proxy conflicts across the region. "We would like that all problems between Russia and Turkey are solved the best possible way," commented Serbia's prime minister, Aleksandar Vučić, after hosting Davutoğlu in Belgrade at the end of December 2015.[87] "Bosnia is not taking sides," commented the foreign minister, Igor Crnadak.[88]

It is hardly surprising that Turkey and Russia worked to find a way out of the crisis and turn the clock back to the time before November 2015. The stand-off served no one's interest, once the Kremlin painted Erdoğan as the arch-villain of the Middle East to deflect domestic attention away from diplomatic efforts to strike a deal with the United States on Syria. What is truly remarkable is that Erdoğan and Putin managed to make a 180-degree turn so quickly.[89] Events in June–July 2016 developed at breakneck speed. On 5 May, Prime Minister Davutoğlu, classified as a hardliner on Russia, tendered his resignation following rumors of a rift between him and his erstwhile patron, Erdoğan. Foreign policy effectively moved to the president, who demonstrated a degree of flexibility. On 14 June, celebrated as a national day in Russia, Erdoğan sent a conciliatory letter to Putin. Then, on 27 June, he expressed "sympathy and condolences" for the death of Oleg Peshkov, the Su-24M pilot. Describing Moscow as a "friend and a strategic partner," Erdoğan added, "We never had a desire or a deliberate intention to down an aircraft belonging to Russia."[90] But the critical point came with the failed military coup d'état in Turkey on 15 July. Two days later, Putin called the Turkish president to express support. While the West criticized the heavy-handed clampdown in the wake of the putsch, the Kremlin clearly aligned itself with Erdoğan. Putin made a point of condemning "anti-constitutional acts and violence," a subtle reference to Moscow's portrayal of Ukraine's Maidan uprising and "color revolution."[91] The Putin–Erdoğan summits on 9 August and 10 October put rapprochement on a solid footing. As Russia accepted Operation Euphrates Shield launched by the Turkish army in northern Syria, along with allied factions of the Free Syrian Army, to fight Islamic State but more importantly the Kurdish Democratic Union Party (*Partiya Yekîtiya*

Demokrat, PYD) and its armed forces, the YPG (*Yekîneyên Parastina Gel*, People's Protection Units). Ankara facilitated the withdrawal of rebel factions from eastern Aleppo and the handover to Assad and the Russians in late December. Even the shocking assassination of the ambassador, Andrei Karlov, by a disgruntled Turkish police officer on 19 December 2016, at the height of the campaign by Russia and Assad against the besieged city, could not derail newly reignited co-operation between Putin and Erdoğan. A ceasefire between the regime and the moderate militias, again brokered by Russia and Turkey, went into effect. In January 2017, Russian and Turkish jets bombed Islamic State targets at al-Bab. In return, Turkey acquiesced in the fall of eastern Aleppo to the Syrian regime backed by Russia and Iran in mid-December 2016, and softened its rhetoric regarding Bashar al-Assad's future in power. In the following episode, Turkey, Iran, and Russia sponsored several rounds of peace talks in Kazakhstan's capital Astana, with the United States joining in at the last minute as an observer. Although inconclusive, the meeting gave the start to a diplomatic process led by Russia in which Turkey agreed to play a supportive role. But Ankara and Moscow remained divided on a handful of issues— including the ultimate fate of Bashar al-Assad and, even more important, whether Syrian Kurds should be granted an autonomous region as part of a future power-sharing arrangement. To the Turks' regret, Russia was reluctant to downgrade ties with the PYD/YPG, which was considered a branch of the PKK.

Despite the rapid rapprochement, in all likelihood Russia and Turkey were heading towards the time-tested mode of bilateral relations—one characterized by a blend of competition and co-operation. Turks and Russians continue to disagree on a number of issues in Syria, notably the autonomy status that Moscow offered the Kurdish community in a draft constitution and, less vocally, Assad's future role. At a NATO ministerial meeting held in February 2017, Turkey endorsed enhancing the alliance's naval and air-force presence in the Black Sea. For all the talk of Putin and Erdoğan turning into bosom buddies in the aftermath of the 15 July coup attempt, Turkey's long-standing policy of soft balancing appears to remain intact.

Conclusion

Russia's relationship with Turkey is so rich in history, ambivalent, multifaceted, and rich in nuance that it merits a whole book on its own. The disadvantage is that it is also a relationship that does not lend itself easily to labels and generalizations. Whatever one says or writes is bound to be true only up to a point. That was as much the case in the classical era of empires prior to the First World War as it is at present, nearly thirty years since the Cold War ended. Periods of strife and war have followed moments of mutual accommodation and coexistence. The same pattern took hold after the collapse of the Soviet Union, and by the 2000s Russia and Turkey could boast a thriving economic relationship based on growing levels of economic interdependence, a partial overlap of strategic interests, and a shared love-hate relationship with Europe and the West. It is doubtful whether Moscow and Ankara could ever become true friends or allies, but clearly they have proven, time and again, their willingness and capacity to do business together. From the Russian blitzkrieg against Georgia to the roller-coaster ride over Syria in 2015–16, the Putin–Erdoğan double act has posed more than one challenge to decision makers on both sides of the Atlantic.

Built in stages since the mid-1990s, the "virtual alliance" between Russia and Turkey has suited both parties. Moscow has taken advantage of the estrangement between Ankara and its Western allies to outmaneuver both the United States and the EU. Russia's energy firms have furthermore found a lucrative and ever-expanding market. In turn, economic interdependence gives the Kremlin a powerful instrument to bind Turkey and enlist its support on a range of political issues. As far as Turkey is concerned, multiple governments in Ankara, long before the AKP and Erdoğan appeared on the scene, have worked with Russia to manage potential conflicts in regions sandwiched in between the two neighboring powers and capitalize on economic opportunities. But, as illustrated by ambivalent relations around energy and security issues—in the Balkans, the Caucasus, and more recently in the Middle East—what exists between Ankara and Moscow is fundamentally a marriage of convenience, not an affair of the heart. For instance, Russia has not phased out all the economic sanctions slapped on Turkey at the end of 2015. Still, the bond has been tested and has proven resilient. Winning over Turkey probably remains one of the most significant achievements of Russia's policy in Southeast Europe over the past three decades.

PART II

AREAS OF RUSSIAN INFLUENCE

CHAPTER 6

FROM A MILITARY STANDOFF
TO HYBRID WARFARE

Today we see an aggressive and nationalistic Russia, which pursues a policy of restoring its influence. [It is] creeping towards the Balkans.
　　　　　　—Bulgarian President Rosen Plevneliev, 9 May 2014[1]

The presence of a strong state—which is a military ally of Serbia—will calm any aggressor down.
　　—Russian Deputy Prime Minister Dmitrii Rogozin, Belgrade,
　　　　　　　　　　　　　　　　　　　　　11 January 2016[2]

If there is one timeless truth about Russia's view of international politics, it is its unflinching belief in hard power. "While the waging of major wars is far less conceivable in a nuclear age, military strength remains central to Russian conceptions of great power-ness (*derzhavnost'*)," asserts Bobo Lo, a seasoned observer of Moscow's foreign policy.[3] The "neo-Hobbesian" outlook boils down to Lenin's classical question of "*kto kogo?*" ("Who will get whom?") The conflicts in Georgia and Ukraine put on display Russia's willingness and capacity to project military force beyond its borders. Yet intervention in the Syrian civil war, in turn, highlights the fact that the Kremlin is prepared to send its troops farther afield from the immediate sphere of influence it lays a claim to in the former Soviet Union.

Military power plays a significant part in Russia's dealings with Southeast Europe. The fact that the Warsaw Pact is long gone and Russian peacekeepers left former Yugoslavia more than a decade ago does not make Moscow's hard power irrelevant. First, the Russian military build-up in the Black Sea, especially after the annexation of Crimea in 2014, affects the strategic calculations of three southeastern littoral countries within NATO: Turkey, Romania, and Bulgaria. Second, Russia has forged strong security and defense ties with Serbia and has stiffened its opposition to NATO's expansion in the Western Balkans. Foreign Minister Sergei Lavrov has called the alliance's prospective expansion to include former Yugoslav countries such as Macedonia or Bosnia and Herzegovina "a wrong policy or even a provocation."[4] Third, the war in Syria has scaled up the presence of the Russian Black Sea Fleet in the Aegean and the Eastern Mediterranean. In sum, Russian force is more visible now than at any point since the end of the Cold War.

Russia is also relevant to security in Southeast Europe because it wields non-conventional capabilities, which have the potential to disrupt critical infrastructure, from government websites and email servers all the way to electric power grids, and interfere in the domestic politics of foreign countries (for example, by strategic information leaks). Starting with the cyberattacks against Estonia in the spring of 2007, suspicions have been rife that Russia has targeted its adversaries and critics, assisted by groups of "hacktivists." Although the attribution of such attacks is a thorny issue, foreign security services have more than once pointed a finger in Moscow's direction. The American intelligence community, for instance, has "high confidence" that Russia was behind the theft of emails and documents from the Democratic National Committee released in July 2016 on WikiLeaks.[5] The controversy of whether Russia "hacked" the U.S. presidential election in November leading to the victory of Donald Trump over Hilary Clinton shows no signs of abating. The West has long focused on the internet as a source of vulnerability playing into the hands of challengers such as Russia but also China. At the 2014 Wales Summit, NATO, which dealt with the implications of the Ukrainian crisis, listed cyber defense as part of its core mission enshrined in Article 5. Cyberspace is now a "domain of operations" on a par with air, land, and sea.

Last but certainly not least, Russia's security services are present on the ground across the region. Beyond routine intelligence gathering, they have the capacity to mount "active measures" (*aktivnye meropriiatia*), a term with an illustrious pedigree going back well into the Soviet past, often in co-operation with a vast array of local assets—former communist-era officials and security operatives, businesses, the media, civilian groups, and political parties. Links with the criminal underworld have come into play as well. This whole range of coercive instruments defines Russia's impact on the security landscape of the region located on the geographic edge of the EU and NATO.

The Making and Unmaking of Security Order in Southeast Europe

The defining characteristic of security order in Southeast Europe is the pivotal role of the West, a difference from either the former Soviet space or the Middle East. The end of the Cold War and the Yugoslav Wars of the 1990s have all brought the region firmly into the ambit of the EU and NATO. In the Balkans, the EU is clearly in the driver's seat: states are either members or candidates for accession. The European Union Rule of Law Mission in Kosovo (EULEX Kosovo) remains the most ambitious Common Security and Defence Policy (CSDP) operation to date, and EUFOR Althea is deployed in Bosnia. The promise of EU membership has brought to the negotiating table Serbia and Kosovo.

NATO has established a solid foothold as well. The alliance provides the firmest institutional link between the West and Turkey, alienated from the EU. In former Yugoslavia the alliance still carries the main responsibility for policing peace.[6] NATO continues to enlarge towards the area, having accepted Montenegro as member in June 2017. It maintains the strategic defense infrastructure: the naval base in Souda Bay and on the island of Crete (Greece); the airfields at Incirlik and Izmir (Turkey);[7] elements of the missile defense system (Romania, Turkey). A number of local states benefit from robust military ties with the United States. For instance, since 2006, the Pentagon operates joint facilities in Romania and Bulgaria.

The Western-centric order, however, is far from complete or consolidated. The institutions and rules that define it are under constant strain. In part this has to do with the economic and political challenges dragging down and hollowing out the EU as well as with the American disengagement over the course of the 2000s. In part, it is also down to problems specific to the region. In any event, dysfunctionalities are easy to spot. From the severe financial crisis in Greece to the democratic decline in Turkey to state capture and corruption in former Yugoslavia, the political realities of today are at odds with the bold transformative vision projected by the EU and NATO in the late 1990s and early 2000s. Indicators of democratization, media freedom, transparency, and fairness of institutions or quality of governance tell a story of stagnation and, in some cases, backslide. Turkey's negotiations with the EU have ground to a halt, while relations with the United States are marred by tensions and suspicions, especially after the failed coup attempt of 15 July 2016. As we have seen in Chapter 5, Ankara has opted for an autonomous foreign and security policy, drifting apart from its allies. In former Yugoslavia, there are countries stuck halfway on their path towards joining the EU and NATO. Macedonia, once a frontrunner, is hostage to the so-called "name dispute" with Greece. Bosnia's fragmented internal politics have stymied progress towards Western clubs, perpetuating the international protectorate inaugurated in Dayton, Ohio, in 1995.

EU enlargement cuts both ways: integrating the region into common policies and institutions but also confining it to the outer circle of an increasingly differentiated political structure. The flood of immigrants through Turkey and the so-called Western Balkan route in 2015–16 highlights this predicament. Southeast Europe has morphed into a buffer zone between the conflict-ridden Middle East and "core Europe."

In the meantime, the severe economic crisis sweeping through Europe has sapped military capabilities and stalled reforms in the security sector. In 2000, before they entered NATO, Bulgaria and Romania were spending on defense respectively 2.7 and 2.5 percent of GDP. By 2015, the percentage had gone down to 1.4 percent. Greece, a country with a traditionally high defense budget, saw a slump from 3.6 to 2.6 percent over the same span. Serbia's defense allocation went down from 4.5 percent in 2001 to 2.3 percent in 2012, and Croatia down from 2.7 to 1.7 percent. Amongst NATO members in the region, only Greece meets the defense target of 2 percent of GDP.[8] Turkey fell below the threshold after 2015. For better or worse, the demilitarization of Europe deplored by experts across the Atlantic is a fact. It is visible even in the once volatile Balkans.

Such an environment presents opportunities for Russia in its contest with the West. As Part I of the book demonstrated in some detail, it has not shied away from using its influence to gain advantage. Following Ukraine, Moscow seeks to balance NATO militarily, upgrade security alliances, ramp up pressure on adversaries, and, to some extent, dilute EU enlargement. The sections that follow take a closer look at Russia's strategy and its applications in Southeast Europe.

The Black Sea Challenge

The Black Sea is the arena where the competition between Russia and the West is at its toughest. Three southeastern littoral states within NATO—Turkey, Romania, and Bulgaria—are confronted by a steep rise in Russian military power. The figures speak for themselves. In 2015, the Russian Federation spent about $65.6 billion on its armed forces, equivalent to slightly over 4 percent of its GDP and one-fifth of all public expenses. Russia is well ahead of Turkey, the leading military power in Southeast Europe, with a defense budget of $22.6 billion corresponding to 2.2 percent of GDP (down from 3.7 percent in 2000!).[9] Since 2008, Moscow has pursued the so-called State Armament Program (*Gosudarstvennaia programma perevooruzheniia*) whose goal is to modernize conventional forces. Even if reforms, initiated by Defense Minister Anatolii Serdiukov and now carried through by his successor Sergei Shoigu, have not closed the qualitative gap with leading militaries in the West, Russia wields an overwhelming superiority over its immediate neighbors and can use that to its benefit.

The 2014 annexation of Crimea tipped the balance in the Black Sea in Russia's favor. Moscow established full control over Sevastopol, home to its Black Sea Fleet.[10] The possession of the port yields enormous geographical advantage. Sevastopol is located roughly in the middle of the sea, with the most strategic points along the western and southern littoral within easy reach. Istanbul, Samsun, Constanța, and Varna are all less than 550 kilometers away. With appropriate capabilities, Moscow can easily project power across the Black Sea or even establish outright dominance. The base in Sevastopol is therefore essential for achieving what military planners call "anti-access/area denial" (A2/AD).

Such plans are already underway. "We turned Crimea into a fortress," boasted Vladimir Putin in a documentary aired by the Rossiia 1 TV channel on the first anniversary of the annexation. Before 2014, Russia had possessed only one surface ship capable of operating out of the area for extended time periods, the cruiser *Moskva* (launched in 1979). It lacked cruise missiles and strategic aviation capability. After the takeover, the Russian military deployed S–300 surface-to-air missiles with a range of 300 kilometers and a Bastion coastal battery. More importantly, Moscow unveiled ambitious plans for the build-up of the Black Sea Fleet. The reinforcements included six new frigates, two missile corvettes, six improved Kilo-class submarines, Su-30SM interceptors, Su-34 tactical bombers, and Tu-22M3 nuclear-enabled long-range bombers (NATO designation: "Blackfire").[11] Military planners envisage an addition to the Black Sea Fleet of fifteen to eighteen new vessels by 2020, bringing the total number of ships to 206. This is in addition to the fifty-seven warships seized from Ukraine but never handed back despite the deal struck in 2014.

NATO has been on alert. No less an authority than General Philip Breedlove, Supreme Allied Commander Europe (SACEUR, 2013–16), has acknowledged that the alliance is lagging behind. "Russia has developed a very strong A2/AD capability in the Black

Sea," he commented in a 2015 lecture at the German Marshall Fund. "Essentially their [anti-ship] cruise missiles range the entire Black Sea, and their air defense missiles range about 40 to 50 per cent of the Black Sea."[12] The general's remarks are spot on. To take one example, the 3M–14 (Kalibr) cruise missiles carried by the Black Sea Fleet's new corvettes and submarines could attack land targets at a range of 2,500 kilometers. They are also equipped with an advanced anti-ship system, the 3M–54 Klub cruise missiles. In October 2015, the Russian navy launched Kalibrs from the Caspian Sea to hit forces fighting President Assad in Syria, sending a strong signal to NATO about its newly acquired capabilities. Since August 2016, Crimea hosts S–400 missiles, Russia's most advanced anti-aircraft system with a range of 400 kilometers. An additional battery was deployed in January 2017.[13]

The ongoing build-up has terminated the hitherto Russian–Turkish duopoly in Black Sea naval security. Prior to the annexation of Crimea, Turkey had the edge with a combined tonnage of military vessels of 97,000 as against Russia's 63,000. Although spread between the Black Sea and the Aegean/Eastern Mediterranean, the Turkish navy had fourteen submarines and thirty-five first-class battleships, compared to just one and twelve respectively for Russia.[14] Ankara's advantage is being eroded. The only area where Turkey retains unrivalled superiority is in amphibious capabilities, especially since France cancelled a highly controversial deal in August 2015 to supply Russia with two Mistral-class helicopter carrier/assault ships.[15]

Unlike Turkey, Romania and Bulgaria are nowhere near Russia's capabilities. The modernization of their armed forces, urgent as it is, has run into difficulties, not least because of tight finances. Romania, which aims to meet NATO's 2 percent of GDP spending target in 2017 but may well fail to do so, is ahead in terms of upgrading its air force and navy. Yet even it lacks the advanced capabilities to counter Russia's submarines, cruise missiles, and state-of-the-art anti-aircraft systems. Bulgaria, expected to reach 2 percent of GDP spending in the 2020s, lags behind further than Romania—the two frigates acquired second-hand from Belgium are in need of an upgrade while the air force still consists of Soviet-era MiG fighters whose time is running out.[16] At the same time, both countries are vulnerable—they cannot protect adequately their Exclusive Economic Zones (EEZs), territorial waters, or even coastlines. Securing their airspace is at issue as well.

For the likes of Romania and Bulgaria, NATO offers the only avenue to set the balance with Russia right. Over the course of 2015, Turkey temporarily relaxed its long-standing opposition to giving the alliance a larger role in Black Sea affairs (it fell back on its traditional stance after the rapprochement with Russia in 2016).[17] Having conducted joint exercises with the Ukrainian navy in March–April 2016, Turkey threw its weight behind a Romanian initiative to establish a permanent NATO naval task force in the Black Sea. The proposal of the defense minister, Mihnea Ioan Motoc, came on the heels of a major surge in allied activities, part of NATO's Atlantic Resolve operation. In 2014 alone, American warships spent a total of 207 days in the Black Sea, compared to two short visits in 2013. Romania's plans did not come to fruition because of opposition from the Bulgarian prime minister, Boyko Borisov, who was fearful both of a harsh Russian reaction and a domestic backlash against putting Bulgarian warships under Turkish command, as part of a rotational arrangement. However, Sofia has supported all other NATO "forward presence" schemes and agreed to contribute troops to a multinational brigade stationed at the Mihail Kogălniceanu base near Constanta. The Obama administration's European Reassurance Initiative (ERI) covers the deployment of hardware and personnel at bases in Romania and Bulgaria ("front-line states") as well as joint training activities (see Appendix 3).[18] NATO continues to rotate warships in the Black Sea, even within the limitations established by the Montreux Convention.[19] At a NATO ministerial meeting in February 2017, Bulgaria supported the decision to enhance further the allied naval presence.

Russian entrenchment in Crimea and the sweeping build-up of the Black Sea Fleet have delivered strategic gains. Moscow has tightened its grip over the annexed peninsula and ramped up its capacity to project naval power beyond its immediate vicinity and into the Mediterranean. Yet it has unnerved neighbors and prompted a relatively robust response from the Atlantic Alliance. Naval co-operation through BLACKSEAFOR is practically frozen, the United States has "boots on the ground," while NATO is more closely involved and anchored in the Black Sea than ever, though certainly not on the same scale as in the Baltic States and Poland. Although that level of "forward presence" might not be sufficient to contain Russia, it makes outright aggression or the threat to use military force as a diplomatic lever less likely.

Quasi-Allies

Moscow's security influence extends far beyond the Black Sea littoral. States in Southeast Europe, which do not share a frontier with Russia and are geographically removed from Crimea, Ukraine, and "frozen conflicts" such as Transnistria, have a very different perception of threat compared to Romania, Turkey, and even Bulgaria. Serbia, in particular, maintains close defense ties with Moscow. The relationship rests on several pillars: the joint Humanitarian Emergency Situations' Center in the Serbian city of Niš, the military agreement from November 2013, as well as Serbia's observer status in the Collective Security Treaty Organization (CSTO).

The Niš Center has been the subject of controversy from the moment it started operations in April 2012.[20] Officially, its main task is to provide assistance in disaster relief operations—such as the devastating floods in Serbia, Republika Srpska, and Croatia in May 2014. But it has also fueled speculation, including from pro-government media in Belgrade, that the end objective is a fully fledged Russian military base. The city of Niš is located in southeast Serbia, close to the border with Kosovo and NATO member Bulgaria. Moreover, the Russian Ministry for Civil Defense, Emergency Situations, and the Elimination of Consequences of Natural Disasters (*Ministerstvo po delam grazhdanskoi oborony, chrezvychainym situatsiiam i likvidatsii posledstvii stikhiinykh bedstvii*), in co-founding the Niš Center, has a semi-militarized structure. Furthermore, Sergei Shoigu, who signed the original agreement with Serbia in 2011, became minister of defense the following year. Yet both Russian and Serbian authorities have consistently denied such plans or the use of Niš as an intelligence outpost, a view sometimes heard both in Serbia and Washington.[21] "When someone sends spies somewhere, he sends them where there is something to spy," observed Foreign Minister Ivica Dačić on national television in April 2016. "[The Center] does not function based on bloc division and bloc mentality," according to Maria Zakharova, the spokesperson of Russia's Ministry of Foreign Affairs.[22] However, Moscow has demanded that its personnel be granted diplomatic immunity, as extended to NATO staff under the agreement signed with Serbia in February 2016. Put differently, Russia treats the Niš Center as an equivalent to Belgrade's ties to the Atlantic Alliance—or indeed to the policy of "creeping NATO-ization" of Serbia, castigated by hard-line Russophiles who have been rallying for a referendum on neutrality.

Serbia and Russia have developed extensive military-to-military links under the defense agreement of November 2013 (Shoigu being the Russian signatory again). Serbian and Russian armies have trained together on several exercises. In SREM–2014 (November 2014), 207 Russian paratroopers from the 106th Guards Air Assault Division based in Tula rehearsed an anti-terrorist operation near the northern Serbian city of Ruma, just seventy kilometers from the border with NATO member Croatia. The following September, Serbian paratroopers joined the Slavic Brotherhood (*Slavianskoe bratstvo*) drill near Novorossiisk, together with the Russian army and Belarusian special forces. According to Colonel General Vladimir Shamanov, commander-in-chief of the Russian Airborne Troops, the scenario played out involved "anti-government elements to destabilize the political situation in a fictional state, including via the use of terrorist attacks." The Russian information agency Sputnik spoke outright of a Euromaidan-style "color revolution."[23] The Slavic Brotherhood 2016 drill took place again in Serbia, just as NATO carried out "Montenegro 2016" across the border (Serbia participated in that drill too!).

The litmus test for the depth of security co-operation is the question of whether Moscow is prepared to invest in Serbia's military and struggling defense industry. Since Vladimir Putin visited Belgrade as prime minister in March 2011, there have been speculations that Russia has been lending money for the upgrade of Serbian forces.[24] Yet there have been no major weapons transfers thus far, the most significant purchase being two second-hand transport helicopters (Mi–8MTs) bought for $25 million. In the meantime, pro-government media in Belgrade have touted prospects for acquiring S–300 missiles, up to sixteen Pantsir ground-based air-defense systems, combat helicopters, and MiG–29s.[25] The upgrade was intended to offset the addition of sixteen multiple-rocket launch systems to Croatia's army, following a donation from the United States. But the Serbian prime minister, Aleksandar Vučić, came away empty-handed from Moscow in October 2015 after lobbying for a discount or line of credit.[26] "This is only a [S–300] mockup copy. That's too expensive for us," he responded to a journalist when asked whether the government was to accept the offer of the Russian deputy prime minister, Dmitrii Rogozin, to sell the advanced anti-aircraft system.[27] Still, the prime minister's attempts to cut a deal with the Russians ended in success. In late December 2016, Shoigu agreed to donate to Serbia six surplus MiG–29 "Fulcrum" fighter aircraft, thirty T–72 tanks, and thirty BRDM–2 armored reconnaissance vehicles. The MiGs were expected to be in service at least until 2030, boosting Serbia's declining air-policing capabilities.[28]

Although Russia has helped Serbia to build up its military, it has a taken a skeptical view of suggestions that the two can work together on arms exports. In the words of Nikita Bondarev, head of the Balkan program at the Russian Institute for Strategic Studies (RISI), an outfit affiliated with the Kremlin:

> The root of the problem is the former SFR Yugoslavia. All military industries were organized in such a way that nothing was manufactured in a single place. A plant in Kragujevac would source components from Slovenia, from Bosnia; a plant in Bosnia would source parts from, say, Serbia and Macedonia. Serbia's defense industry today is part of a jigsaw puzzle which cannot be developed without the other parts: Slovenian, Croatian, Bosnian

... Russia, just like China, takes a cautious view of Serbia's military industry. If we could put together a group of producers, which would include defense products across the republics of former Yugoslavia, then the answer would be positive.[29]

The Russians have another legitimate reason to be circumspect. Having signed an Individual Partnership Action Plan (IPAP) with NATO in January 2015, the Serbian government has been pursuing extensive co-operation with both the alliance and the United States. In 2016 alone, Belgrade planned 127 joint activities with the American military.[30] IPAP, technically, is an equivalent of the Membership Action Plans (MAPs) adopted by countries queuing up to join the alliance. Although committed to neutrality since 2007, Serbia is doing its best to profit from military co-operation with both the West and Russia. Russia, in turn, has gained an allied enclave of sorts within NATO's territory, but without overcommitting its resources.

Non-aligned Cyprus is Moscow's other quasi-ally in Southeast Europe. Not only has the island republic supported Russia at the EU level and solicited its favors in relation to the unresolved North-South division, but it is also a profitable market for Russian defense exports, paying in hard cash. Between 1996 and 2011, Nicosia purchased €430.5 million worth of military hardware—tanks, combat and transport helicopters, surface-to-air missiles (SAMs), Grad multi-racket launchers, etcetera. That is in addition to the S–300s deployed in Crete, which were in Cypriot ownership between 1998 and 2007.[31]

The war in Syria has increased the strategic importance of Cyprus, just a stone's throw away from the Levantine coast. The deal to allow Russian ships and aircraft access to the port of Limassol and the Andreas Papandreou airbase near Paphos, initialed by President Anastasiades in February 2015, has been viewed with suspicion by the West. General Chuck Wald, deputy head at the U.S. European Command, has qualified the agreement as "part of the bigger picture of regaining the old spheres of influence." Moscow disbanded its Fifth Squadron operating in the Mediterranean at the end of 1992. It resumed its presence only in

December 2012. However, the naval facility in Tartus, Syria, cannot support an entire squadron. The Mediterranean group, headlined by the missile cruiser *Moskva*, operates from Sevastopol. That certainly increases the importance of Cyprus. In addition, experts claim that Russian intelligence has beefed up its presence on the island. Limassol and Paphos are close to the British sovereign bases at Akrotiri and Dhekelia, instrumental in the allied air campaign against the self-styled Islamic State.[32] Even if security and defense co-operation with Cyprus has a more limited scope, as the government in Nicosia asserts, Russia has cashed in with significant strategic benefits.

The Specter of Hybrid Warfare

Russia's coercive capabilities neither start nor end with brute military power. In the context of Ukraine, much ink has been spilled on the concept and practice of "hybrid war." Roughly, it is a blend of local insurgencies—like the so-called Russian Spring in the Donetsk and Luhansk *oblast'* as well as in other parts of eastern and southern Ukraine in 2014, political subversion and infiltration of government institutions, economic pressure, *dezinformatsiia* and outright propaganda (or "weaponization of information" or even "information warfare"), and cyberattacks against critical infrastructure. "Hybrid war(fare)" has spurred vigorous debates amongst scholars and experts: is it a new phenomenon or, on the contrary, an aspect of statecraft that has been with us for a long time? Does the term do a good job, or are other labels such as "non-linear war," "compound war," and so on more appropriate?[33] One thing is for certain: the challenge of responding to hybrid war has come to the foreground of Western thinking on security. NATO's summits in Wales (September 2014) and Warsaw (July 2016) laid out initiatives to respond to threats posed by "a wide range of covert military, paramilitary, and civilian measures ... employed in a highly integrated design." The EU's Foreign Affairs Council, the High Representative for Foreign Affairs and Security Policy, and the External Action Service have also contributed an array of ideas—from strengthening "strategic communications" to bolstering the security of critical energy and transport infrastructure.

Russia's hybrid toolbox has been mostly a concern of the Baltic countries where governments draw direct parallels with the Ukrainian crisis as well as the 2008 war in Georgia. However, the discussion has trickled down to Southeast Europe as well, particularly in the "front-line states" of Bulgaria and Romania. In an interview for *The Independent* in November 2015, President Rosen Plevneliev of Bulgaria stated that "[t]he very efficient and secure way for Russia to destabilize Europe is through the Balkans, so that is what Mr Putin is focusing on." He also thought that through the region Moscow was waging a "hybrid warfare campaign aimed at destabilizing the whole of Europe." The evidence he pointed to included cyberattacks against Bulgarian institutions just one month previously (more below).[34]

At a certain level such perceptions of threat appear overblown. There are key ingredients missing for a fully fledged "hybrid" scenario to unfold beyond the boundaries of the former Soviet Union. In contrast to Ukraine or indeed Estonia and Latvia, the likes of Romania or Bulgaria contain no substantial Russian(-speaking) minorities who can enact a scenario along the lines of Crimea or the Donbas. Middle-class home-owners along the Bulgarian Black Sea coast seem an unlikely constituency for a breakaway movement, while a "People's Republic of Burgas" remains a remote prospect.[35] That is even truer of Romania whose region of Northern Dobrogea (Dobrudja), home to a historical minority of Russian Old Believers (*Lipovans*), numbers fewer than 40,000 inhabitants. This is why Bucharest politicians, who are certainly not dovish about Russia, have been using "hybrid warfare" almost exclusively in reference to eastern Ukraine.

The other reason to be skeptical is that, overall, Russian policy towards the countries of Southeast Europe relies, in most of the cases and for most of the time, on co-optation rather than coercion. As detailed in Part I of this book, governments, political leaders, parties, and other actors have struck deals with Moscow to advance their own interests, while Moscow has brought into play a range of economic and financial incentives to win partners and cultivate profitable relationships. It is the carrot, rather than the stick, that has done the bulk of the work.

Yet "hybrid warfare" or at least elements thereof are part of the Russian carrot-and-stick strategies. The recourse to softer coercive instruments, removed several notches down from military force, makes more sense in dealing with states protected by the NATO deterrent. Softer instruments are less risky (no danger of uncontrolled escalation) and more efficient at the same time. The menu of choice includes classical Soviet-era "active measures," infiltration of state institutions, security services, domestic politics and economic structures, disinformation, and cyberattacks.

Is there sufficient empirical evidence to back up such claims or suspicions? It all depends on which dimension one examines. Disinformation is probably the most clear-cut case. Russia's capacity to shape the media landscape and plant and cultivate narratives pandering to local resentment of the United States and the EU, as well as fear of Islam, is beyond doubt. What is much more difficult to verify and measure is the Kremlin's ability to use local proxies to force its hand through domestic politics. Over recent years, observers have alleged that Russia colludes with and sponsors two types of actors mobilizing in sufficient numbers to advance causes aligned with Moscow's interests: (1) protest movements, social activists, environmentalists—for example, those rallying against "hydraulic fracturing" (fracking) in Romania and Bulgaria in 2012; and (2) ultranationalist and extreme right-wing parties and civic organizations opposed to NATO and the EU in Serbia, Montenegro, Greece, and Bulgaria. While the evidence implicating the former is at best inconclusive, the latter have been on the whole open regarding their links to Russia. We shall return to that subject in the closing chapter of the book.

Other forms of covert and deniable action are also highly relevant. Although the evidence is patchy and mostly anecdotal, Russia is widely suspected of employing covert action of various sorts to disrupt and gain advantage. Two types are worth highlighting: (1) cyberattacks; and (2) operations by Russia's secret services.

Targeted cyberattacks have picked up since 2014. The most remarkable incident occurred in Ukraine itself. On 23 December 2015, the country's power grid became a target of an attack, the first of its kind. Scores of regional substations went offline and more than 200,000 consumers were left, literally, in the dark. Kyiv authorities pointed a finger at Russia. But two months beforehand, Bulgaria had been hit as well. On 25 October, just after polling stations closed after the country's local elections and referendum, the Central Electoral Commission's sites came under "distributed denial-of-service" (DDoS) attack—essentially, blocking a server through an overwhelming volume of traffic. The Interior Ministry, the State Agency for National Security (DANS), the parliament, and the president's office were also affected. A subsequent DANS report laid the blame at Russia's door.[36] Sofia's neighbors have been on alert. The Romanian Intelligence Service's (SRI) National CyberINT Center has identified "state-sponsored attacks" as a foremost threat. It reported 250,000 cyber security "events" in 2015, with Russia and China as the main source countries.[37] On 18 December 2015, in the wake of the Su-24 incident, Turkey's National Response Center for Cyber Events closed down five servers after at least 400,000 websites experienced a DDoS attack. It is, therefore, not coincidental that defense against cyberattacks has steadily climbed up the ladder of priorities for the Western alliance.

Russian intelligence services have not remained idle. Old ties in the security sector have become more valuable since the expansion of NATO to former communist countries. Newly adopted legislation to comply with the alliance's security of information requirements has only partly dealt with the threat of leaks of classified documents and data to Moscow. In the words of a Russian security expert, "[g]etting into the Czech Republic or Bulgaria is a lot easier than Britain or Belgium." Still, there have not been high-profile scandals in either Bulgaria or Romania, in contrast to the Czech Republic or Estonia.[38] But that does not rule out suspicions, especially with regard to Bulgaria whose communist-era services were notoriously subservient to Moscow. A former head of the National Security Service (NSS), General Brigo Asparuhov, was forced to step down as advisor to the prime minister in

October 2003, after having been denied access to NATO's classified information. An American Embassy cable profiling Bulgarian Interior Minister Rumen Petkov (in office 2005–8) observed: "[he] has also long been publicly associated with Russians who are either directly or indirectly affiliated with Russian intelligence."[39]

Concerns about Russian infiltration have cast a shadow over Montenegro's accession to NATO. In June 2014, an unnamed source from the Alliance HQ in Brussels estimated that between twenty-five and fifty personnel at the ANB, the Montenegrin National Security Agency, could be double agents.[40] Seven years beforehand, Sergei Lebedev, director of Russia's Foreign Intelligence Service (*Sluzhba vneshnei razvedki*, SVR), had paid a secret visit to Montenegro, then more closely aligned with Moscow.[41] To meet NATO entry conditions, the Montenegrin parliament amended the law on ANB in February 2015 to improve vetting and recruitment. The Adriatic republic is potentially vulnerable to Russian-supported networks involving Serbian security officers, whether in active duty or retired. In October 2016, police arrested General Bratislav Dikić, former head of Serbia's gendarmerie, on suspicion of hatching a military coup to derail Montenegro's accession to NATO. The media speculated that the conspiracy threatened not only the life of Prime Minister Milo Đukanović (who blamed Russia for the alleged plot) but also that of his Serbian counterpart, Aleksandar Vučić. However, as already discussed in Chapter 2, there are many unanswered questions regarding this story, and the exact nature of the link to Moscow is yet to be verified, possibly during the trial against the suspected organizers of the coup.

The extent of Russian influence over the Serbian Security and Information Agency (*Bezbednosno-informativna agencija*, BIA) is just as debatable. BIA and Russia's Federal Security Service (*Federal'naia sluzhba bezopasnosti*, FSB) were, allegedly, at odds in the hunt for General Ratko Mladić, indicted by the International Criminal Tribunal for Former Yugoslavia (ICTY). According to the British journalist Julian Borger:

> The BIA operatives tracking the Mladić support network found themselves increasingly playing spy versus spy with the FSB.

"Every time we got close to getting one of the people in his circle to co-operate, they would go for a long session at the Russian embassy and come out of it with cold feet about talking to us," recalled Miodrag Rakić, the man entrusted with leading the manhunt during the Tadić presidency. He suspected that Russia was making regular payments to the Mladić family and entourage to relieve the financial pressure on them to give away the general's whereabouts.[42]

The capacity of the Russian security services to execute complex operations, often by contracting intermediaries (e.g. criminal gangs), should not be in doubt. Since 2008, Turkey has witnessed the assassinations of scores of prominent Chechens. Following the most recent incident, in January 2015, Deputy Prime Minister Bülent Arınç explicitly blamed Russia. "We know that the hand of a well-known organisation in Russia has killed five Chechens in Istanbul by now," he said. "However, we have not been able to catch the criminals, because the crimes were carried out at a highly professional level. We have not been able to determine what kind of activities the slain people were engaged in."[43]

Conclusion

Russia's coercive capabilities, hard and soft, make it a critical player in Southeast Europe. Countries around the Black Sea have to reckon with its growing military strength, and its intelligence services have a solid presence on the ground, from Turkey all the way to Montenegro. While NATO's containment policy makes a difference, it does little to offset "softer" instruments that are often more effective politically—from defense co-operation to espionage to cyber warfare. It is not easy to measure and pin down Russia's non-conventional capabilities, yet the available evidence indicates that its significance is only likely to rise in the future. Although Russia is far from turning, any time soon, into a fully fledged competitor to the West in the realm of security and military affairs as far as Southeast Europe is concerned, it will doubtless continue using its wide-ranging powers to assert its interests. Moscow will exploit all opportunities to strengthen defense ties with neutral countries such as Serbia or Cyprus, guard its position in the region's arms markets, pressure governments, exploit all weaknesses within NATO, and try to gain strategic advantage over the United States and its local allies as part of the ongoing rivalry with the West.

Although Russia's military muscle stands out as a first-rate political lever, one should not be oblivious of the fact that it is, still, secondary in importance to Russian money. As elucidated by Part I, co-optation is a more effective mechanism to attain one's goals than either coercion or subversion. As Mark Galeotti, a perceptive observer of Moscow's foreign policy, notes, "the greatest security threat is not Russian tanks or Russian disinformation, it is our own corruption—and the ways Russia seeks to use it."[44] Galeotti's concern is clearly the United States under President Donald Trump, and the core of the EU. However, the countries of Southeast Europe appear even more vulnerable on that count. This is the subject of the next chapter as it focuses on the energy sector, the area where Russia's influence has traditionally been overwhelming.

CHAPTER 7

PLAYING THE ENERGY CARD

Russia aims to develop comprehensive pragmatic and equitable co-operation with Southeast European countries. The Balkan region is of great strategic importance to Russia, including its role as a major transportation and infrastructure hub used for supplying gas and oil to European countries.

—Concept of the Foreign Policy of the Russian Federation,
12 February 2013

Visitors to Belgrade, crossing the Sava River through the Gazela Bridge on their way to the city center, cannot fail but notice a flashy billboard. It sports the flags of Russia and Serbia—or rather a single flag twisted in the middle. That way, the Russian Federation's white, blue, and red turns into the Serbian red, blue, and white. The same colors were endorsed by the First Pan-Slavic Congress in Prague in 1848, gracing the flags of more than one East European country.[1] But here is that ancient Slav *tricolor* binding two nations in a fraternal embrace. "Partnership for the Future" ("Partnerstvo za Budućnost") reads the caption set against the backdrop of a blue sky. But take a closer look and you will see there's more at the bottom of the billboard: two company logos, those of Gazprom Neft and NIS, Serbia's national oil companies sold to the Russians in 2008. The parallelism conveys a crystal-clear message. The symbolic melding would not be complete without the flow of energy bringing Russia and Serbia into an unbreakable union. The future is bright and the sky is the limit.

Moscow's energy clout in Southeast Europe and beyond is hard to overstate. "Russia," Emperor Alexander III once remarked, "has only two allies: her army and her navy." These days, oil and gas no doubt deserve a special place in the same pantheon. Hydrocarbons lie at the heart of the Russian economy, politics, and public life, generating close to half of all budget revenues and accounting for about 30 percent of GDP. Proceeds from them are vital for public investment and welfare provision. Booming prices in the 2000s contributed to the growth of a new middle class and legitimized Vladimir Putin's grip on power. Early in his tenure, the Russian president put the industry under his thumb: he took Gazprom, previously a fiefdom of Viktor Chernomyrdin and its chairman Rem Viakhirev, under state control; he despatched the oligarch Mikhail Khodorkovsky to a penal colony in Krasnokamensk, next to Lake Baikal, to take over Yukos; he renationalized Sibneft and orchestrated the rise of Rosneft, led by his lieutenant, Igor Sechin. By the mid-2000s, Russia Inc. was already in existence, with Putin presiding over the board of the directors.

Oil and gas, and the cross-border connections they entail, are an essential source of Russia's power. In the words of Putin, hydrocarbons constitute "a powerful political and economic lever of influence over the rest of the world."[2] In the 2000s, the Russian Federation became the biggest producer of oil and second-biggest producer of natural gas after the United States. Home to one-fifth of the world's gas reserves, Russia leads on the European market. A network of pipelines, refineries, gas storage facilities, and petrol stations spanning the continent testifies to Moscow's clout as much as it underscores the unprecedented levels of energy interdependence with the EU.

Export markets are of immense importance to Russia itself. To quote a fascinating piece of statistics: although Gazprom sells more than two-thirds of its gas domestically, two-thirds of the proceeds come from abroad. Compared to within Russia, Gazprom's prices are 3.4 times higher in the EU and 1.7 times higher in the rest of the former Soviet republics. Although this differential reflects the higher delivery costs over long-distance pipelines, this is essentially a form of subsidy to domestic consumers.[3] This is one among several reasons why interdependence represents as much an asset as a source of vulnerability in Russia's dealings with the EU and the wider world. That has become painfully obvious with the global economic crisis and especially since the collapse of oil prices after mid-2014. Faced with stagnating demand in core export markets as well as tightening EU regulations, the once seemingly omnipotent petrostate has found it much harder to set the rules of the game with regard to natural gas.

All these structural features and dynamics have tremendous repercussions in Southeast Europe. At least since the mid-2000s, Moscow has been looking to Turkey and the Balkans as a potential corridor for its gas deliveries to the EU, a vision reflected in the 2013 foreign-policy concept. South Stream, a personal hobbyhorse of Putin's, became a lynchpin in Russia's grand strategy. "Gazprom is the flagship in our co-operation with Balkan countries," Putin told an energy security summit in Zagreb in June 2007 when he unveiled his plans for the gas pipeline.[4] The Russian president has been personally in charge of the diplomacy surrounding South Stream and other oil and gas projects in the Balkans and Turkey. That was the case even in 2008–12 when he moved, temporarily as it turned out, to the office of the prime minister.

The following chapter argues that while gas and oil have given Moscow a great deal of leverage in Southeast Europe, the picture is nuanced. The alliances Russia has forged are far from reliable and the outcomes of its energy diplomacy are a mixed bag, at best. Even the friendliest and most accommodating states of the region have been hedging their bets, exploring ways to reduce dependence on Russia. Infrastructure projects that the country spearheaded have ended in failure. The EU's responses to the 2006 and 2009 gas crises have narrowed Moscow's room for maneuver.

Southeast Europe in Russia's Strategy

Russian energy policy in Europe has pursued a consistent set of objectives: lock in demand in major markets; nurture strategic ties with large and influential states, notably Germany, France, and Italy; keep competition in check; and expand access to end consumers to maximize profits. That is very much true about gas but less so about a globally traded commodity such as oil.

The Balkans and Turkey are critical to this Russian strategy for both positive and negative reasons. On the positive side, they provide an alternative to Ukraine, the route for 20 percent of Gazprom's gas exports to Europe, whose transit agreement expires in 2019. What is more, Russia is a top player in local markets and therefore carries a lot of political weight (see Figure 3). Less positive for Moscow, Southeast Europe represents a physical bridge between producers in the Caspian and the Middle East and consumers in Europe. If and when the much-discussed Southern Corridor becomes a reality and Caspian gas reaches the West, Russian commercial and political interests would inevitably suffer. Russia's priority has been to block or at least slow down diversification of supplies and shore up its position in Europe.

Natural gas is a thoroughly political commodity, with govern-ments playing a leading role in cross-border trade. The effects are often benign: gas has linked Russia (and the Soviet Union before it) with Western Europe since 1967 and contributed to trust and co-operation. On the flipside, the "gas wars" with Ukraine have exposed Russia's use of (inter)dependence to force its writ on neighbors.

	Gas	Crude oil
Bosnia	100%	no data
Bulgaria	92%	84%
Croatia	0%	31%
Greece	75%	20%
Macedonia	100%	0%
Romania	25%	50%
Serbia	80%	70%
Turkey	67%	10%

Source: International Energy Agency, 2014

Figure 3 Import dependence on Russia (% of domestic consumption)

Politicization is, in the main, a function of the traditional business model whereby gas is traded through long-term contracts (LTCs) with national companies underwritten by agreements between governments. In essence, a supplier and a consumer state make a mutual commitment over a number of years. LTCs entail benefits for both parties: the consumer secures stable supplies while the exporter can count on a steady revenue stream needed to maintain costly cross-border infrastructure (pipelines, compressor stations, measuring units, etcetera) and turn a profit. But, of course, it is politics and the relative power of the two parties that dictate the terms of the contract.

Russia has a strong preference for the above traditional model, which goes a long way in cementing its market dominance in post-communist Europe and elsewhere. Moscow furthermore strongly favors the vertical integration model, exemplified by Gazprom but also, traditionally, by national energy champions across the EU. That is in stark contrast to the European Commission's preference for liberalization and "unbundling" the transit, distribution, and trading of gas to bolster competition and empower consumers. The contest between the two models picked up momentum after the 2009 gas crisis, which resulted in a series of legislative and policy initiatives by Brussels for the reinforcement of the EU's energy security through diversification of gas supplies and increased market flexibility.

Back in the 2000s, when European demand was high, Russia set the rules. Take-or-pay clauses committed consumers to a minimum volume per year, about 85 percent of the contracted gas. Other standard features within the contracts prohibited the re-export of the gas as well. In the meantime, prices stayed high thanks to the linkage to oil in the contracts, notably those signed with the East Europeans but also Greece and Turkey as well as the bulk of contracts with Western Europe. Crude oil hit an all-time high, trading at $145.29 a barrel on 3 July 2008, on the eve of the collapse of Lehman Brothers and the ensuing meltdown. Gazprom thrived through its golden era. It controlled between one-quarter and one-third of market share in Europe as a whole, 58 percent in post-communist countries, and a whopping 72 percent in the former Soviet Union.[5] The gigantic operation turned $30 billion in profits in 2008 and boasted plans to reach a market capitalization of $1 trillion in due course. Many feared that a powerful empire was emerging—all the way from Siberia to the British Isles.

This is not how Western European utilities perceived the issue. Russia was, to them, a reliable partner, Gazprom a business entity, not a latter-day reincarnation of the Red Army. Neither the USSR's disintegration nor the 1998 financial collapse in the Russian Federation had stemmed the flow of gas from western Siberia to industries and households thousands of kilometers to the west. The split of the Soviet grid caused a crisis of pan-European dimensions only in January 2009. Of course, this attitude did not prevent the West Europeans from blocking Russians attempts to enter their highly shielded energy markets. Gazprom was able to gain a foothold in Germany through Wingas, a joint venture with Wintershall.[6] But it had encountered opposition from governments and regulators when turning to Centrica, owner of British Gas, and Repsol in Spain or Fluxys in Belgium. In a parallel development, the European Commission in June 2011 blocked a Gazprom bid to buy a 50 percent stake in the Central European Gas Hub at Baumgarten, Austria.

Southeast Europe was, and still is, in a much less enviable position. Gazprom enjoys a monopoly thanks to the limited connectivity between countries and the hub-and-spoke configuration of the transit infrastructure inherited from the period before 1989. Gas flows from Russia to Southeast Europe through three parallel routes: (1) the Trans-Balkan Pipeline running through Romania and Bulgaria to Turkey, with offshoots to Greece and Macedonia; (2) via Hungary to Serbia and Bosnia; and (3) via Austria to Slovenia and Croatia. Turkey is also served by Blue Stream running directly to Russia. Links between the three subsystems and the capacity to shift gas from south to north started developing only recently.[7]

Despite being geographically close to Russia, historically the countries of the region have paid Gazprom a premium. According to the European Commission, they were charged 16 percent more in 2015 and a whole 20 percent more in 2014 in comparison to Western Europe. In previous years, the differentials over Germany, taken as a benchmark, had gone beyond 30 percent (see Figure 4).

High rates charged by Gazprom have exacerbated chronic problems in the energy sector. Combined with regulated domestic prices, the burden of loss-making state-owned enterprises, and internal subsidies, the high rates have made it difficult for local companies to balance their books and invest in infrastructure. National energy champions in Southeast Europe have had few other options apart from Gazprom—squeezed additionally by the limited degree of interconnectivity, the lack of storage capacity and access to alternative sources. What is more, the likes of Srbijagas, Bulgargaz, BOTAŞ or DEPA (Greece) have owed, at various times, substantial sums to Russia and therefore faced risks of reduced supplies. All those factors place severe constraints on projects aimed at diversifying gas flows and enhancing energy security.

Dependence on Russia has adversely affected not only the affordability but also the reliability of gas deliveries.

	2010	2011	2012	2013
Bosnia and Herzegovina	339	429	500	421
Bulgaria	311	356	435	394
Greece	359	414	475	469
Macedonia	381	462	558	493
Romania	325	390	424	387
Serbia	341	432	40	386
Turkey	326	381	416	382
Average	**340.2**	**409.1**	**466.1**	**432.8**
Germany	270	379	353	366

Source: Jonathan Stern, 'Russian Responses to Commercial Change in European Gas Markets', in James Henderson and Simon Pirani, *The Russian Gas Matrix: How the Markets are Driving Change.* Oxford: Oxford University Press, 2014.

Figure 4 Gazprom LTC prices ($/1000 cubic meters)

During the second Ukrainian gas crisis (6–20 January 2009), Bulgaria, Serbia, and especially Macedonia and Bosnia were amongst the worst-hit countries anywhere in Europe. District heating plants came to a standstill and steel mills and fertilizer factories shut down. Heating was subsequently restored thanks to a switch to heavy fuel oil, but the consumption of electricity went through the roof, upsetting the balance at the national and regional level. Greece and Turkey could fall back on liquefied natural gas (LNG) imports or increased volumes via Blue Stream. Croatia and Romania tapped into emergency stocks. But the rest of the region suffered. Poor cross-border connections and the lack of capacity and reserves in storage facilities exacerbated the problem.[8]

High prices of natural gas and vulnerability to cut-offs translate into a huge advantage for the Russian side. Moscow's strategy in the former Soviet Union was to sustain political and business clienteles through cheap energy exports and threaten pro-Western governments with price hikes. By contrast, in the Balkans and Turkey high tariffs and restrictive commercial clauses allow for an approach based on carrots rather than sticks. Russia is in a position to co-opt governments and national companies by offering better contractual conditions, price discounts, investment into infrastructure, and new transit routes, generating income by way of extra fees. This, in essence, is the story of South Stream.

The South Stream Saga

South Stream, running over 1,380 kilometers through the Black Sea and the Balkans to Italy and Austria, furnishes the perfect example of how Russian influence works. The plan to bypass Ukraine gathered pace with Blue Stream and Nord Stream (coming online in 2011). By the time it pitched the plan for a new pipeline with an annual capacity of 63 bcm, Gazprom already had a business partner in Italy's ENI, its associate in the underwater Blue Stream Pipeline. In 2010–11, the consortium embraced Electricité de France (EDF) and Wintershall, a daughter company of Germany's BASF.[9] This was a signal that the $35 billion project was

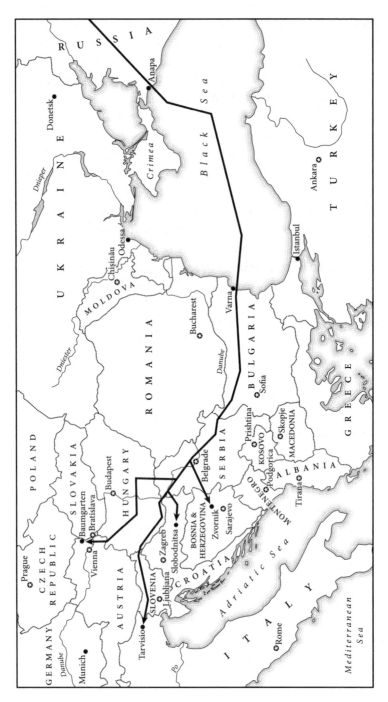

Map 5 South Stream

financially viable despite the slow-down in demand within Europe after 2008.

Despite the support of Europe's energy business, South Stream's geopolitical objectives seemingly trumped market reasoning. The pipeline was not going to channel new gas volumes but simply reroute existing ones away from Ukraine's transit system. Feeble demand in Southeast Europe could hardly justify the billions to be invested. True, there were savings to be made from transit fees owed to Kyiv, but that did not fully convince experts the venture would pay off.

Still, Putin, both as president and as prime minister (2008–12), made an extensive commitment to the project, taking the time to negotiate personally its terms with the leaders of all the downstream countries, from Bulgaria to Slovenia, Hungary and Croatia. Beyond neutralizing Ukraine, South Stream would reaffirm ties with Italy and Austria, two important friends located at the very core of the EU.[10] It also promised to delay or even make redundant the projects pushed by the European Commission, such as Nabucco—intended to unblock the Southern Corridor. Lastly, South Stream would amount to a triumph for Russia's vision of energy security, one that stressed the diversification of transit routes over that of supplies.

South Stream signaled the zenith of Russian influence in Southeast Europe. Having felt the consequences of the 2006 cut-off, all countries in Southeast Europe and beyond, from Greece to Slovenia and from Hungary to Bulgaria, signed Intergovernmental Agreements (IGAs) to endorse the project despite skepticism and misgivings in Brussels. "Transit risk will be practically zero," Gazprom's CEO Aleksei Miller assured them. In the wake of the 2009 crisis, the partners increased the pipeline capacity from 31 bcm to 63 bcm. The presence of large EU energy firms also gave the Russian project commercial respectability. By contrast, Nabucco appeared to be a political enterprise through and through. Last but not least, there had already been a precedent. If Germany and its mighty business conglomerates pushed Nord Stream, why wouldn't Balkan governments do the same on the southern flank? Local leaders such as Georgi Pârvanov or Boris Tadić, presidents of Bulgaria and Serbia respectively, could see themselves playing the very same role that Germany's Gerhard Schröder or Silvio Berlusconi had played in relation to earlier multi-billion ventures undertaken with Russia.

South Stream was not only a story of Russia co-opting states inside or on the margins of the EU in a one-way fashion. In truth, the project gave downstream countries strong bargaining chips vis-à-vis Russia. They all seized the opportunity to even the playing field, demanding lower prices, the abolition of punitive take-or-pay clauses, increased investment, and so on. Support for Russia's agenda did not come for free, though governments certainly differed in their ability to wrestle concessions from Moscow. Thus, Turkey was in a much better place compared with Serbia—relying on Russian support over Kosovo and saddled with debts to Gazprom. Still, in 2010, both Bulgaria and Serbia made an unsuccessful attempt to alter and extend the route of South Stream in order to increase the transit fees.

To reinforce their hand, governments hedged against Russia. Turkey, Bulgaria, and Hungary endorsed Nabucco (and Nabucco-West after 2012) as well as South Stream. Budapest and Sofia gave both projects priority status, a precondition for winning exemption from EU competition rules (see below).[11] Greece backed the Trans-Adriatic Pipeline (TAP) while Croatia pursued plans for a TAP extension via Albania and Montenegro, the Ionian–Adriatic Pipeline, as well as for a LNG terminal on the island of Krk.

Russia did not stand idly by either. It was doing its best to play off its partners in order to move the project forward. In February 2009, Gazprom's deputy CEO Aleksandr Medvedev was in Bucharest to discuss Romania's inclusion in South Stream. The move was in response to Bulgaria's attempt to bargain for higher transit fees. In case the Bulgarian government did not budge, Romania could provide an alternative route. Eight months later, Gazprom and Transgaz in Romania signed a Memorandum of Understanding. In addition, Russia reached out to Turkey—securing its permission to build South Stream through its exclusive economic zone (EEZ) in August 2009. Russia and Bulgaria reached a compromise only in November 2012. In return for a deal on South Stream, Sofia squeezed a 20 percent discount and a reduction of take-or-pay volumes from 90 to 80 percent of contracted gas. As Simeon Djankov (Dyankov), the Bulgarian finance minister, put it, "[Russians] can't bully us in the way they could before, and their weakness in the negotiations showed that. We got the sense they need us more than we need them, and we capitalized on that."[12] "The European Commission sued Gazprom for linking South Stream to discounts," one of Djankov's colleagues in the cabinet confided, "in truth, it was us twisting their arm."[13] In much the same way, at the end of 2011, Turkey refused to renew its twenty-five-year contract for deliveries over the Trans-Balkan Pipeline, eager to reduce the BOTAŞ bill for unused gas under the take-or-pay clause. Yet the two governments managed to work out a compromise deal, allowing Gazprom access to Turkey's domestic market.[14]

Why did South Stream fail, after all pieces of the puzzle had fallen into place? When Putin called the project off in December 2014, he blamed the cancellation on the EU's inflexibility. Indeed, Moscow and Brussels had profound differences about the legal regime to govern the pipeline's overland sections. Russia objected to the requirement, derived from the Third Energy Package (TEP), that half of the capacity should be offered to companies other than Gazprom. It argued that IGAs took precedence in that they came before the EU legislation and even that the TEP violated the Russia–EU partnership and co-operation agreement of 1997.[15] Gazprom was unwilling to apply for an exemption from the European Commission—as it had done for OPAL, Nord Stream's land extension endorsed by Brussels and the German regulator.[16] But as of the winter/early spring in 2014 there was the prospect that differences could be ironed out. According to the expert Jonathan Stern and his colleagues at the Oxford Institute for Energy Studies, "the Russian side appeared to believe either that the EU would be forced to agree a compromise (because of its need for the gas), or that once pipeline construction began it could be presented with a *fait accompli*."[17]

What delivered South Stream a *coup de grâce* was the annexation of Crimea in March 2014. Russia's move destroyed any goodwill in key EU capitals, narrowing the space for compromise as regards the legal and technical disputes surrounding the project. The working group set up by the European Commission and the Russian government, to deal with the regulatory aspects of the pipeline, disbanded; proceedings at the European Commission's Directorate-General for Competition were suspended. On top of that, the Commission had already initiated an infringement procedure against Bulgaria in June 2014, the issue being the choice of a construction company (Gennadii Timchenko's Stroytransgaz) in alleged violation of the EU's tendering rules. A deal on South Stream was not within reach, as it had been prior to the events in Crimea. Having already splashed out $4.7 billion on the pipeline, Gazprom had to back down. To save face, Putin unveiled TurkStream as an alternative during a visit to Ankara in December 2014. Russia's ambitions to establish a gas transit corridor have not evaporated, to be sure. The back and forth with Greece and Bulgaria has continued, yet moving forward without the approval of Brussels and compliance with EU rules does not seem to be on the cards. Despite this, Putin, assorted Russian officials, and the Gazprom management have been referring to South Stream as if the project has not been finally laid to rest. But there is a strong reason to suspect that such pronouncements amount to little more than a diplomatic tactic—for example, to put pressure on Ankara over the terms of TurkStream—rather than a signal that South Stream could be resuscitated and completed according to Moscow's conditions.

The Oil Dividend

Foreign-policy experts looking at Russia's influence abroad usually pay less attention to oil than gas. That is perfectly understandable given the lower level of politicization. There are no LTCs, intergovernmental deals; cross-border pipelines compete with tankers delivering crude oil directly to refineries; pricing reflects supply and demand. But in reality oil is highly political, not least in the Balkans where Russia has the upper hand in a number of markets. Russian crude-oil imports account for 84 percent (and maybe much higher than that) of the total consumption in Bulgaria and 70 percent in Serbia (see Figure 3). Lukoil Bulgaria is the biggest company in the country (corresponding to around 9 percent of GDP) and the third largest in Southeast Europe (excluding Greece and Turkey). Since 1999, it has controlled Neftochim refinery near the port of Burgas, one of the largest in the region (capacity 190,000 barrels/day). Gazprom Neft tops the list in Serbia, and by extension in the Western Balkans. In 2008, it acquired Naftna Industrija Srbije (NIS), a vertically integrated company whose assets include two refineries (150,000 barrels/day), a chain of filling stations, as well as minor wells and exploration sites. Since 2007, Zarubezhneft is in possession of two refining facilities in Bosnia's Republika Srpska (RS), while Rosneft was not long ago bidding for a 49 percent stake in INA, Croatia's largest oil company.[18] It is hard to overestimate the influence of these companies. They are both sizeable employers and leading contributors of excise duty and VAT to national budgets (for example, Zarubezhneft accounts for 25 percent of RS budget revenue). In addition, they are ensconced in the retail market: even competitors are dependent on the output of Lukoil or NIS refineries (see Figure 5).

The Russian government has strong links to all those entities. State-owned Rosneft's expansion in the 2000s owes a lot to Putin's patronage. Gazprom Neft, a subsidiary of Gazprom, emerged after the oligarch Roman Abramovich parted with Sibneft, the one-time market leader together with Yukos, in September 2005. The deal was the largest single acquisition in Russia's history. Zarubezhneft, again controlled by the state, dates to the Soviet period (1967) when it was established to develop oil facilities in friendly countries such as Vietnam, Cuba or Syria.

Lukoil, Russia's number 2 oil producer, is a slightly different case. The company dates back to the decentralization of the industry in the 1990s and remains largely in private hands. This of course does not mean that it is somehow insulated from the Russian state. Its Baku-born president and largest shareholder, Vagit Alekperov, deputy minister of energy in the final days of the Soviet Union, benefited from links to Prime Minister Viktor Chernomyrdin in the 1990s. Later on, Lukoil strove to cultivate the image of an

	Company	Assets	Market share
Bosnia and Herzegovina	Zarubezhneft (NeftegazInkor)	Brod (refinery)	100% (refining)
		Modriča (motor oil refinery)	60%
		Banjaluka Petrol (trade)	
	NIS/Gazprom Neft	Gazprom Petrol	
Bulgaria	Lukoil	Lukoil Neftochim (refinery, petrochemicals)	100% (refining)
		Lukoil Bulgaria (trade)	60–70% (wholesale), 25% (filling stations)
	Kirsan Iliumzhinov	Petrol Holding (trade)	15% (filling stations)
	Gazprom Neft	Gazprom Petrol (trade)	
Croatia	Lukoil	Lukoil Croatia (trade)	7% (filling stations)
Cyprus	Lukoil	Lukoil Cyprus (trade)	
Macedonia	Lukoil	Lukoil Macedonia (trade)	15% (filling stations)
Montenegro	Lukoil	Lukoil Montenegro (trade)	
Romania	Lukoil	Petrotel-Lukoil S.A. (refinery)	20% (refining and filling stations)
		Lukoil Romania (trade)	
Serbia	Gazprom Neft	Naftna Industrija Srbije (NIS) – refineries at Pančevo, Novi Sad, filling stations	100% (refining), 30% (filling stations)
	Lukoil	Lukoil Serbia (trade)	11% (filling stations)
Turkey	Lukoil	Lukoil Turkey (trade)	

Figure 5 Russian oil companies in Southeast Europe

independent corporation, at arm's length from politics.[19] Its main acquisitions in the Balkans, in Bulgaria and Romania, date to the late 1990s, before the Kremlin brought the industry into its fold. In 2014, Alekperov was not targeted by Western sanctions, unlike Putin's ally Igor Sechin at Rosneft. But, as an authority on Russian oil has pointed out, "he [Alekperov] never forgot who was ultimately the sovereign owner of Russia's oil and gas resources and pipelines, as well as the source of its foreign policy, in which energy has nevertheless ceased to play a major part."[20] The Russian state lent a helping hand. Serbia allowed Lukoil to expand its network of filling stations as part of the 2008 energy deal with Moscow. Alekperov serves on the board of the Gorchakov Public Diplomacy Fund, established by President Dmitry Medvedev in 2010 and active in the region.

The connection to the Russian state does not mean that Lukoil or Gazprom Neft are entirely beholden to Putin's foreign policy. As Bobo Lo has observed, "[i]n many instances, [Russian investors'] motivations are principally commercial. But it would be naïve to disregard the geopolitical dividend. While Russian companies are not mere instruments of the Kremlin, their participation in these often fragile economies can and does serve wider purposes."[21] There is no shortage of examples to that effect. In 2011, for instance, Lukoil Bulgaria's CEO Valentin Zlatev stepped in as a mediator in the negotiations over the Belene nuclear power plant, a venture strongly backed by the Russian Federation government.

Oil firms have furthermore contributed to Russia's public image in the region. The Pančevo and Novi Sad refineries in Serbia, part of NIS, had been damaged during the 1999 NATO bombing campaign. The ones in Republika Srpska, having lost the Yugoslav markets and having been degraded as a result of the war, were running up huge debts and had been shut down before Zarubezhneft made its entry. Russia has taken some credit for breathing new life into an industry in decline. Companies such as Gazprom Neft and Lukoil have been actively cultivating their corporate connections, for example by sponsoring popular sports teams like Crvena Zvezda (Red Star) Belgrade. One should not forget that in January

2009 fuel oil (*mazut*) sourced from Lukoil and NIS helped restart district heating plants in Serbia and Bulgaria, thereby cushioning the adverse effects of the gas cut-off.

Russia has failed to make good on plans to develop or acquire strategic infrastructure in Southeast Europe. The Burgas–Alexandroupolis Pipeline initiated in 2007 after more than a decade of discussions between Moscow, Athens, and Sofia was called off by the Bulgarian government in 2011. Similarly, repeated talks between Russia and Croatia for the potential sale of a stake in the Druzhba–Adria Pipeline connecting the port of Omišalj to refineries in Bosnia and Serbia did not bear fruit. Critics of Moscow's foreign policy have argued that such a deal would jeopardize energy security. Were Adria to ship crude oil from the east to the west, as opposed to offloading tankers and pumping their oil eastwards as happens at the moment, Russia would expand its control over the market in former Yugoslavia.

Both the Burgas–Alexandroupolis and Druzhba–Adria projects need to be put in perspective. On a broader level, the importance of the Black Sea and Southeast Europe as a transit route for Russian oil is in relative decline. The 2012 opening of the Ust–Luga terminal near St Petersburg and the completion of the Baku–Tbilissi–Ceyhan (BTC) Pipeline in 2006 diverted traffic away from the port of Novorossiisk. After the annexation of Crimea in 2014, the daily throughput of the oil terminal there fell to 620,000 barrels, the lowest level since 2008.[22] The prospects of a Russian energy corridor through the Balkans, with all its attendant geopolitical consequences, remain distant at best.

The Challenge of State Capture

What works in Russia's favor is not the development of strategic infrastructure but rather the pervasive state capture in the energy sector across Southeast Europe. It takes multiple forms—political appointees in state-owned companies, flawed public procurement, mismanagement of investment projects, lack of transparency and public scrutiny, etcetera. The slow pace of liberalization, justified on the grounds of social policy, has also been a contributing factor.

As a result, Russian companies have been able to act in tandem with local incumbents to extract and distribute rents. In the gas sector, for instance, opaque intermediaries—for example, Bulgaria's Overgaz and Topenergy (until 2003), and Progresgas Trading and later on YugoRosGaz in Serbia—have been suspected of being slush funds to buy political support and prolong Russia's market dominance.[23] Between 1992 and 2000, Progresgas Trading, established by Viktor Chernomyrdin and his friend Mirko Marjanović, later to become Serbian prime minister under Milošević, retained a commission of 1 percent. After 2000, gas trade with Russia was an exclusive domain of political parties involved in Serbia's coalition cabinets: first Vojislav Koštunica's Democratic Party of Serbia and then, as of 2008, Ivica Dačić's Socialist Party of Serbia—whose lieutenant Dušan Bajatović presides over Srbijagas.

Gigantic ventures such as South Stream have raised particular concerns. The price of the Bulgarian section rose fourfold between 2008 and 2014–15, owing to the inclusion of a host of politically connected construction companies. As examined in Chapter 3, on the Russian side, South Stream involved Stroytransgaz, a firm controlled by the billionaire Gennadii Timchenko, a close personal friend of Putin's. On the Bulgarian side, the project was to be implemented by a consortium involving entities with direct links to all major political parties. The inflated price together with the lack of transparency with regard to South Stream's stretch through Bulgaria made the pipeline a byword for wholesale corruption.[24] Of course, neither Russia nor Gazprom were the first to embark on state capture through the energy sector. Former communist countries such as Bulgaria or Serbia have never ceased to generate and reproduce corruption from within their own institutions, whether in the energy sector or elsewhere. What is certain, however, is that the deficit of good governance provides an enabling environment allowing Russia, whether the Kremlin or its energy firms, to get what they want.

Several Balkan governments have also enjoyed a cosy relationship with Russian oil. Thus, Bulgarian authorities revoked the Lukoil Neftochim licence in 2011 but allowed the refinery to continue operating. This monopolistic company has done well—maintaining wholesale prices up to 16 percent above market levels, even with the plummeting crude-oil price. There have been further allegations that Lukoil has consistently inflated its losses and engaged in a transfer-pricing scheme through a Swiss subsidiary in order to avoid paying corporate tax and VAT.[25] However, the suspicions that the Bulgarian petrol market is dominated by a cartel led by Lukoil, by far the main player, have not resulted in an investigation or state sanctions. By contrast, in 2016, Romania's Competition Council issued a hefty fine against a group of oil traders, including Lukoil but also OMV (Austria) and ENI (Italy), for running a cartel.[26] The previous year, top managers at Lukoil's Romanian subsidiary came under investigation over fraud and money laundering, with the authorities seizing company assets worth €230 million. It is highly unlikely that the business practices that have run foul of the law in Romania are wholly absent in either Bulgaria or the Western Balkans. On the contrary, tax avoidance and cartels usually prosper with the blessing of those in power. To use a Russian term, there is always a *krysha* ("roof"), that is, political protection when the stakes are this high.

In former Yugoslavia, the Russian oil business has fared much better. That might be a function of the cordial ties with Moscow or the laxer enforcement of laws and regulations—or indeed oa a combination of both. Yet even there, controversies and scandals abound. To this day the Serbian authorities face—and shrug off—complaints that *Naftna Industrija Srbije* (NIS), the national oil and gas champion, was sold under the market price in 2008 as an advance payment for South Stream, which was ultimately cancelled. Going further back in time, the 2003 purchase of Beopetrol by Lukoil has spurred a scandal in relation to kickbacks to state officials, including the future mayor of Belgrade, Siniša Mali.[27] By contrast, the over-the-counter sale of Bosanski Brod and Modriča refineries to Zarubezhneft, without a proper bidding process or tender, has not raised much objection in Bosnia and Herzegovina's Republika Srpska (RS). The 2007 deal was overseen by none other than Milorad Dodik, currently serving as RS president. There is every reason to believe that Russian oil and post-Yugoslav power holders have built a positive rapport.

As with the case of gas, it would be unfair to accuse Russian oil companies of being solely responsible for wholesale corruption in the Balkans. After all, the highest-profile case of bribery involving a major political figure was to do with an illegal payment to Ivo Sanader, Croatia's prime minister between 2003 and 2009, for selling a controlling stake of INA, the national oil firm, to Hungary's MOL.[28] Although MOL, whose major shareholder is the state of Hungary itself, has maintained close business ties with Russia and is partly owned by Surgutneftegaz, the INA affair proves, yet again, that Moscow has no monopoly over state capture and graft. But so long as the energy sector remains lacking in transparency and vulnerable to corruption, Russia is clearly at an advantage, which it exploits in the conduct of its foreign policy.

Beyond Dependence

Hydrocarbons do buy Russia influence in Southeast Europe. Moscow's negative leverage is substantial as well. Disruptions of the gas supply, should they occur, would still have a harmful effect—according to the European Commission and the association of EU transmission system operators.[29] However, there are clear limits to the political usefulness of the "energy weapon." Taken in conjunction, shifting market conditions and the EU push for liberalization and diversification of gas supplies have together been weakening Russia's hand.

First, the region does not consume large quantities of natural gas, nor does natural gas account for a substantial share of the energy mix—Romania and Turkey being the exceptions. It is overshadowed by coal, which corresponds to 40 percent of the consumption in the Western Balkans, Bulgaria, and Romania, two times higher than the EU average. Montenegro and Kosovo use no gas at all, while Albania has no distribution grid, having largely exhausted indigenous sources in the 1990s (Figure 6). Weak demand is a function of the low levels of households' gas connections in most parts of the region—a difference with Central Europe—which, in turn, is perpetuated by high, unaffordable prices. In countries such as

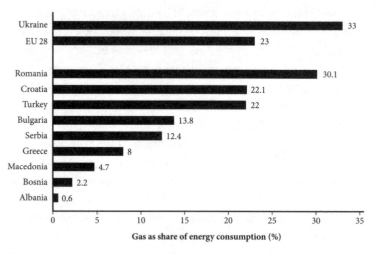

Figure 6 Gas as a percentage of primary energy consumption, 2013

Serbia, Bulgaria, Bosnia and Herzegovina, where Gazprom holds a near or complete monopoly, gas is used principally by municipal heating plants or industry.[30] Electricity generation relies primarily on coal (or lignite), hydropower (Albania, Bosnia and Herzegovina, Montenegro), and nuclear energy (Bulgaria and Romania).

Second, Gazprom has been losing market share. In Romania, for instance, gas imports have fallen from 25 percent of the total volume (16 bcm) in 2010 to under 10 percent at present. Croatia's utility Plinacro did not renew its contract with Gazprom in 2010, switching to ENI and EON Ruhrgas. Demand for gas has likewise shrunk in Greece and Serbia, with only Bulgaria registering a slight increase (see Figure 7).

Turkey, of course, is on an altogether different trajectory compared to its neighbors (see Figure 8). Demand remains robust and the share of Gazprom is more or less stable at about 27 bcm a year or two-thirds of local consumption, up from 18 bcm in the mid-2000s. Turkey absorbs a full 17 percent of Gazprom's exports to Europe, compared to 5 percent for the Balkans. However, as discussed in Chapter 5, Russia's dominance on the Turkish market is not set in stone. Turkish authorities prioritize diversification and

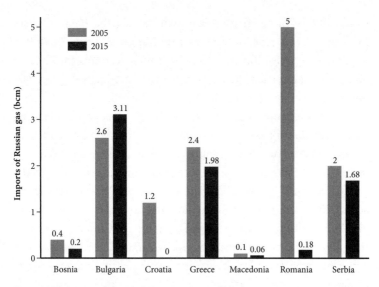

Figure 7 Imports of Russian gas, 2005/2015 (bcm)

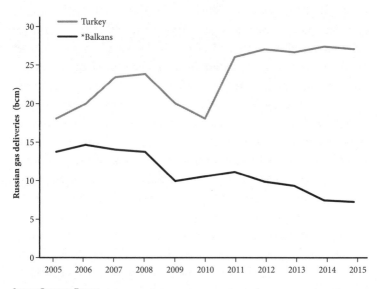

Source: Gazprom Export
*Bosnia, Bulgaria, Croatia, Greece, Macedonia, Romania, Serbia

Figure 8 Russian gas deliveries to Southeast Europe, (bcm)

would like to bring in more Caspian gas via the Baku–Tbilisi–
Erzurum (BTE) Pipeline and its extension, the Trans-Anatolian
Pipeline (TANAP). Russian gas, which now accounts for close to
50 percent of electricity generation, could be gradually displaced by
nuclear energy and renewables, as well as by coal.[31]

Third, Gazprom is operating in a much less accommodating
environment compared to the 2000s. EU policies and rules have
started to bite. Brussels is pushing candidate countries, members of
the so-called Energy Community, to harmonize legislation with the
TEP, "unbundle" national gas companies, and allow third-party
access. There are rules on prevention and contingency planning in
case of disruption to energy flows. The European Commission's anti-
trust case against Gazprom, opened in August 2015, has attacked
core clauses in the LTCs benefiting Russia, such as the re-export
prohibition. Brussels furthermore has taken issue with Gazprom's
linking of price discounts with concessions related to infrastructure,
for example the South Stream section through Bulgaria. According to
DG Competition, "such behaviour, if confirmed, impedes the cross-
border sale of gas within the Single Market thus lowering the liquidity
and efficiency of gas markets. It raises artificial barriers to trade
between Member States and results in higher gas prices."[32] After
South Stream, the Commission is demanding the right to examine
IGAs *ex ante* for conformity with EU law.[33] In March 2017, Gazprom
and Brussels concluded a preliminary agreement on the anti-trust
case. Under its terms, the Russian company agreed to lift the gas
resale ban in its LTCs and curtail the practice of linking discounts to
states' endorsement of its infrastructure projects. Despite a series of
caveats, the deal marked a tentative victory for Brussels in its quest to
liberalize and interconnect gas markets in post-communist Europe.

Lastly, and most importantly, markets have turned against
Gazprom, eroding Russia's monopolistic position. Europe's economic
troubles have sapped demand while the "fracking revolution" in the
United States led to a LNG boom and pushed down prices at gas hubs.
The share of gas traded on the spot market rose from 15 percent in
2008 to 64 percent in 2015, according to the energy consultancy
Platts. Of course, Southeast Europe is a laggard: only 5 percent of

prices are indexed to hub trading.[34] By comparison, half of the prices in Central Europe are now determined on a spot basis.[35] Gazprom's large customers in the EU sought rebates and the revision of LTCs, winning a series of arbitration cases. As a result, the price gap between spot and contract gas narrowed considerably: from 70 percent in 2009 to 5–6 percent in 2013.[36]

Officially, Russia continues to argue for oil indexation, marshaling support from the other members of the Gas Exporting Countries Forum (GECF). But Gazprom has tacitly gone along with the trend towards the decoupling of oil and gas prices.[37] As a consequence, Russia's bargaining power vis-à-vis consumer countries has declined. What works in its favour is, paradoxically, the precipitous fall of oil prices after 2014. They have further reduced prices under the LTCs and rendered the pursuit of alternative sources less urgent.

The paramount challenge facing Southeast Europe remains the upgrade of cross-border infrastructure needed to spur diversification and gas-to-gas competition. Even prior to the Ukrainian conflict, the EU was promoting the establishment of a corridor linking national grids from the Baltic to the Balkans. Improved connectivity, reverse-flow capacity, and access to pipeline gas through the Southern Corridor and to LNG are all steps on the roadmap charted in Brussels. Coming onstream around 2020–21, the TAP will mark the first stage. It could be extended towards Montenegro, Bosnia, and Croatia through the planned Ionian–Adriatic Pipeline (capacity 5 bcm). The EU-supported transmission systems' interconnectors linking Bulgaria with Greece and Romania will also enable flows from south to north. In the meantime, Croatia and Greece have developed plans for LNG terminals on their coasts (on the island of Krk and off Alexandroupolis not far from the borders with Bulgaria and Turkey) to supply their neighbors. The plans for a Western Balkan gas ring and a national-grid interconnector between Serbia and Bulgaria would complete the picture. Last but not least, if Russia terminates deliveries through Ukraine after 2019, the existing Trans-Balkan Pipeline could be reversed to pipe gas from Turkey and Greece northwards.

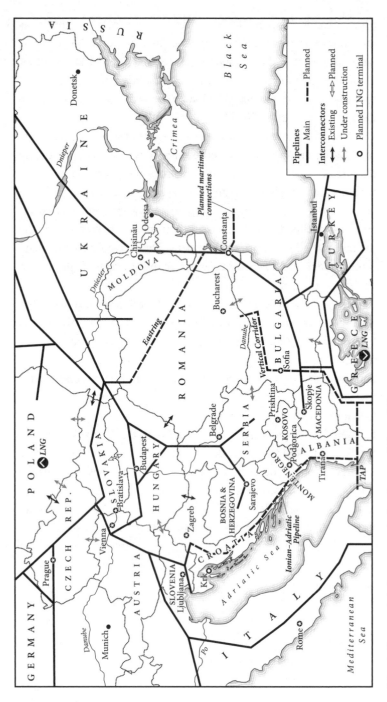

Map 6 Gas transit infrastructure in Southeast and Central Europe

All those ambitious schemes are popular with politicians but, except for the TAP, have failed to raise sufficient funds from the private sector or EU instruments such as the Connecting Europe Facility (CEF). In the age of low oil prices and depressed consumption, it is difficult to make the business case for costly infrastructure, be it pipelines or LNG facilities. Still, it is a safe bet to assume that interconnectivity, combined with gradual reforms to the energy sector, will make headway in the 2020s, thereby reducing Southeast Europe's dependency on Russia even further.

Conclusion

Although Russia's foothold in the energy sector of Southeast Europe is still extensive, its grip has weakened since its heyday in the 2000s. High hydrocarbon prices, generally co-operative relations with the EU, alliances with governments and national companies, used to be the planks of Moscow's power. That is less and less the case at present, when Russia is coming under pressure from various directions. The strategy to turn Southeast Europe into an outpost or a corridor for Russian gas and oil exports has not delivered. At the same time, Russia continues to play its energy card and leverage ties to governments and business to advance its political and economic goals. Turkey remains a significant customer for its gas. Plans for a route bypassing Ukraine, either a revamped version of South Stream or an extension of TurkStream, are not off the table. And, lest one forgets, the nosedive in oil prices makes Russian energy exports competitive against those of rival suppliers, whether actual or potential.

Although Russia may lose market share in the face of stiffer competition and a denser network of pipelines allowing the flow of gas from all directions, its sway will not decline precipitously. On the contrary, so long as national energy companies in countries such as Serbia, Bulgaria, and elsewhere serve as cash cows to those in power, there will be abundant opportunities for Gazprom to preserve its dominance. Vast infrastructure projects such as South Stream, TurkStream, and whatever the future brings may never materialize, but state capture in the energy sector is a formidable problem in Southeast Europe that cannot be resolved overnight, even if the political will was present (a heroic assumption, beyond doubt). It is a safe bet that dealings with Russia will continue to appeal to decision makers and business leaders as a second-to-none source of rent. And whatever headwinds they face, oil companies such as Gazprom Neft and Lukoil will be there to stay. They are not necessarily an extension of the Kremlin, of course. But it would be naive to believe that Russia's foreign policy functions in a parallel universe. Oil and gas are to remain key assets that Moscow will wield in Southeast Europe and beyond. That billboard in Belgrade is not going away anytime soon.

CHAPTER 8

THE ALLURE OF RUSSIA'S MIGHT

Putine, Srbine—Srbija je uz tebe (Putin, you Serb—Serbia is
with you)
—FC Red Star Belgrade's supporters chanting during the game
against FC Zenit St Petersburg, Belgrade, "Mala Marakana"
("Little Maracanã"), 22 March 2011

Football fans paying homage to the Kremlin's master, leather-clad
bikers waving the Russian flag, silver-haired pensioners adorned
with the orange-and-black ribbon of St George (the Russian military
symbol popularized with the patriotic upsurge around Crimea and
the war in the Donbas), Greek abbots rolling out the red carpet before
the latter-day Tsar, journalists applauding the Russian expeditionary
corps' exploits in Syria, displays of gratitude to Russia for the liberation from Ottoman rule, posters of Donald Trump and Putin side by
side as the apostles of a new, more just global order—Southeast
Europe has it all. Russia may not be as influential in the field of energy
as a decade ago and its military may not provide it with a great deal
of political mileage. Yet there is more than one domain where its
presence is unmistakably strong and resonant: the public sphere.

It is hard to deny that Russia and Putin command a tremendous
amount of support across countries with Eastern Orthodox
majorities (Serbia, Bulgaria, Greece, Republika Srpska in Bosnia,

Macedonia, and the Greek part of Cyprus). Polls show that up to
two-thirds of the population in these places view the Russian
Federation as a friendly power, not a menace. From Banja Luka to
Nicosia, party leaders and opinion makers make the case for co-oper-
ation or even full alignment with the Kremlin. The Western sanctions draw opprobrium. Putin's cult status appears uncontested; his
image adorns political rallies and souvenir stalls, business offices and
watering holes. Since about 2001, there have been tens of books in
Serbia alone glorifying Vladimir Vladimirovich's reign. Titles such as
Vladimir Putin and the Resurrection of Russia, *The Rise of Russia*, *The
West or Russia*, *A New Course for Russia* all speak for themselves.[1]
The media often take a pro-Russian line in covering events such as
the annexation of Crimea, the wars in the Donbas and Syria, the
downing of Malaysia Airlines MH17, American domestic politics
and foreign policy, and so on, taking cues from the Kremlin's mouth-
pieces such as Sputnik and RT. Outside the former Soviet Union,
Southeast Europe is where Russia wields the greatest influence.

This chapter looks at the workings of Russian "soft power," one of
the Kremlin's most potent weapons deployed in the Balkans. The
very choice of the term opens a quandary of sorts. The concept of
miagkaia sila, featured in the 2013 version of the Russian foreign-
policy strategy, differs from the one prevalent in the West and
familiar from the writings of influential international relations
scholars such as the Harvard professor Joseph Nye. He himself
stresses that soft power is a function of how attractive a given
country's economic and social model is, how great the appeal of its
popular culture, and so on. Nye has questioned whether Russia's
state-centric understanding qualifies as soft power. In his own
words, "[g]overnments can control and change foreign policies.
They can spend money on public diplomacy, broadcasting, and
exchange programs. They can promote, but not control popular
culture. In that sense, one of the key resources that produce soft
power is largely independent of government control."[2]

That is emphatically not the case of Russia. It is true that in the
former Soviet Union, as Fiona Hill notes, "a burgeoning popular
culture spread by satellite television, a growing film industry, rock

music, Russian popular novels, a revival of the crowning achievements of the Russian artistic tradition, and new jobs in the service
and other sectors have made Russia an increasingly attractive
country."[3] But in the wider world the narrative focuses primarily on
Russia as a great power and on Putin as a strong-willed leader. State-
centrism and the use of "soft power" by government actors to interfere in the domestic politics of other countries is the reason why
certain authors speak of "soft coercion."[4] The distinction between
state and society as the carrier of soft power may be of a less practical
significance from the point of view of day-to-day politics. As Tomila
Lankina and Kinga Niemczyk argue, "Putin has shown himself to be
a significantly more artful player in the 'smart power' game—in Nye's
conceptualisation, a strategy consisting of a combination of hard and
soft power—than Nye would give him credit for."[5] In other words,
what ultimately counts is the outcome, rather than the contents.

In the Kremlin's worldview, there is no substantial difference
between how Russia or the West deal with soft power. For all the
liberal talk, Russian authorities assert, self-seeking governments on
both sides of the Atlantic set the script for the media, NGOs, human-
rights advocates, donor bodies, and so forth. The notion of autonomy
is a sham. To take a prominent example, Dmitrii Kiselev, a popular
Russian TV host whom many consider the Kremlin's propagandist in
chief, casts George Soros's Open Society Fund as an extension of the
American quest for world dominance, rather than an independent
body pursuing its own agenda of promoting democracy. Media smear
campaigns have worked in tandem with legal restrictions. In July
2015, the Federation Council, the Russian legislature's upper chamber,
blacklisted as threats to national security the Soros Foundation along
with the MacArthur Foundation, Freedom House, the Charles
Stewart Mott Foundation, the National Endowment for Democracy,
the National Democratic Institute, and the International Republican
Institute. In much the same way, Russian pro-government media
lambast Western outlets for toeing their government's line.
"Isn't it curious then, that when a State Department email dump
revealed, in late October, that CNN actually co-ordinated their
coverage of a 2013 congressional hearing on Libya," as RT commented

in December 2015.[6] Media and civil society, therefore, constitute an arena of remorseless struggle and *kto kogo* ("who will get whom"). As argued by Peter Pomerantsev and Michael Weiss, Russia has "weaponized" ideas, culture, and information.[7] In Moscow's view, the contest over Ukraine has confirmed this zero-sum understanding. The sustained effort to mould public perceptions and narratives beyond Russian borders is part and parcel of what the Kremlin considers as the assertion of the national interest in a competitive environment.

Much ink has already been spilled on how Russia deploys narratives, manipulates the media to nudge public opinion, and recruits allies to spread its message—be it in the former Soviet Union or in the West. Putin's return to the Kremlin and the Ukraine crisis in particular have given rise to a rhetoric extolling conservative values and religion and berating the alleged moral decay of the West shackled by political correctness and obsession with minority rights ("Gayropa" is often singled out as a target of ridicule). What comes into play are also the memories of the Second World War and the fight against Nazism, in addition to vintage anti-Americanism and the fear of Islam. It has won Russia and Putin support across the political spectrum in Europe, from the far left all the way to the Front National in France or the Alternative für Deutschland (AfD).

The case of Southeast Europe stands out. Societies have been affected as well—less than those in the former Soviet Union, to be sure, but most likely more than in Western Europe. For Greeks begrudging EU-imposed austerity measures, Serbs praising Russian opposition to Kosovo's membership in international bodies such as UNESCO, or Bulgarians nostalgically reminiscing about life before 1989, Russia stands out as a full-blown alternative to the political and economic status quo and counterweight to the perfidious West. Similar to the former Soviet Union, Moscow is in position to draw on vast symbolic resources: shared history, religious bonds, cultural and linguistic affinities with the Southern Slavs, human contacts, emotions, and fears. That is why Russia's soft power offensive has been a success: if not in terms of co-opting each and every potential target state as an ally against the West, then in winning over large swathes of public opinion and broadening its political leverage.

Who Does Soft Power?

The Russian Federation is a novice when it comes to the use of soft power. It was only with the "color revolutions" in the 2000s that the Kremlin came to appreciate its value. As part of the pushback against regime change and the pro-Western shift in countries such as Georgia and Ukraine, Moscow set up its own associations, media, social movements, pressure groups, cultivated links to parties and leaders. Organizations such as Ukraine's Choice (*Ukrainskii Vybor*), an outfit established by the pro-Kremlin politician and tycoon Viktor Medvedchuk, were instrumental in the opposition against EU integration in the crucial months before the fateful Vilnius Summit of November 2013. Similar structures sprang up in other countries covered by the EU's Eastern Partnership.[8]

Russia has also built a tier of institutions overseeing public diplomacy as well as links with "compatriots" (*sootechestveniki*)—a broad and vague category potentially covering anyone born in the USSR but mostly focused on ethnic Russians and Russian speakers.[9] These institutions include the Federal Agency for the Commonwealth of Independent States, Compatriots Living Abroad, the International Humanitarian Co-operation (*Rossotrudnichestvo*), the *Russkii Mir* (Russian World) Foundation, and the Aleksandr Gorchakov Public Diplomacy Fund at the Ministry of Foreign Affairs. Russia touts these bodies as its own version of the British Council or the U.S. Agency for International Development (USAID). Critics of the Kremlin describe them as the outer layer of a complex machine working towards the re-establishment of the empire lost in 1991.

All these institutions have their branches across the Balkans. *Rossotrudnichestvo* inherited the erstwhile House of Soviet Science and Culture in the heart of Sofia. In Belgrade it operates from the so-called *Ruski Dom* (Russian House) established by White émigrés in 1933. *Russkii Mir* maintains centers at Belgrade University and Sofia's Municipal Library and supports youth camps on the Bulgarian Black Sea coast.[10] The Gorchakov Fund sponsors frequent conferences and round-table discussions. They are often run in partnership with the Russian Institute for Strategic Studies

(*Rossiiskii institut strategicheskikh issledovanii*, RISI) attached to the Russian presidency, which has an office in Belgrade. The RISI's former director, Lieutenant General (retired) Leonid Reshetnikov, who holds a history PhD from Sofia University, is a regular commentator on international affairs in the Serbian media.[11]

The Russian Orthodox Church (ROC) is also present in the field, acting in unison with state diplomacy and institutions. In March 2016, Patriarch Kirill of Moscow and All Russia presented Serbian President Tomislav Nikolić with an award for his "lifetime effort to uphold the virtue of Orthodoxy and the great friendship and brotherhood with Russia."[12] "We rely on God and on Russia," the Serbian Patriarch Irineus (Irinej) stated after meeting Putin in Moscow in the summer of 2013, thankful for the Kremlin's support to Serbs in Kosovo.[13] Two years beforehand, in March 2011, the patriarch awarded Putin with the Order of St Sava, in the landmark cathedral by the same name located in central Belgrade.[14] Orthodoxy has also made bridges with Greece. Not only was Putin honored at the monasteries of Mount Athos, but Prime Minister Alexis Tsipras, a radical leftist who in January 2015 refused to take his inaugural oath on a copy of the Bible, paid a visit to Patriarch Kirill. In short, religion can make relations between states deeper.

The ROC's sway is particularly strong in South Slav countries. The Bulgarian Patriarch Neophyte and several members of the Holy Synod have been educated in Moscow.[15] The Bulgarian Orthodox Church has oftentimes sided with the Russians in its rivalry with the Ecumenical Patriarchate of Constantinople (Istanbul).[16] Patriarch Kirill is frequently in Belgrade. He planned to include Kosovo in his November 2014 visit but ultimately changed his mind because of security concerns. Importantly for Serbian nationalists, the ROC has refused to recognize the breakaway churches of Montenegro and Macedonia. There is a clear parallel with Ukraine, contested by the Patriarchate of Kyiv established in June 1992 following the Soviet breakup. Still, the ROC maintains contact with the Macedonian Church, which no doubt adds to Russia's appeal.[17] Ties with local churches are a useful public relations' tool, in that these are entities commanding a great deal of public trust —in stark contrast with nearly all secular institutions.

The Russian media have made inroads into Southeast Europe as well. A state-sponsored international channel, Russia Today TV (renamed RT in 2009), and the Sputnik agency have been on a mission to shape popular views of Russian foreign policy.[18] Russia Beyond the Headlines (RBTH), a spinoff of the government-owned *Rossiiskaia gazeta*, is available in Serbian, Croatian, Macedonian, and Bulgarian. The print version of RBTH is distributed as an insert in newspaper dailies and news magazines: for example, *Politika* (2012–14), *Geopolitika*, and *Nedeljnik* in Serbia, *Eleftheros Typos* in Greece, and *Duma* (The Word) affiliated with the Bulgarian Socialist Party (BSP).[19]

Despite such inroads into local media, Russian penetration is not as extensive as some might think. Russia has no direct control over a TV station that would allow it to propagate its views directly on world affairs in the region. Despite speculations, RT has failed to launch a channel in Serbian, Croatian, or Bosnian.[20] The closest thing is Sputnik's news bulletin broadcast several times a day by radio stations in Serbia. Successive bids by "Orthodox oligarch" Konstantin Malofeev, included on the Western sanctions' list over his support for the Donbas separatists in 2014, to acquire influential media—Studio B and TANJUG News Agency in Serbia and the Bulgarian channel TV7—have come to nothing.[21] Malofeev and his Balkan proxies and networks have often acted as the advance guard of Russian "soft power." Yet it is difficult to tell whether they work as extensions of the Kremlin or, on the contrary, as privateers carrying the flag with a view to leveraging their "successes" in order to curry favor with Putin. In any event, the Russian state has not put a consistent effort into broadening its footprint in the media sphere. Popular Moscow-based outlets such as *Pervyi Kanal* (Channel One), *Rossiia 1*, or NTV cannot fill the gap, due to the linguistic barrier. By comparison, Al Jazeera Balkans has been in operation since November 2011. Three years later, N1, a twenty-four-hour cable news channel affiliated with CNN, started work from headquarters in Belgrade, Zagreb, and Sarajevo.[22]

Russian business, whether state-owned or not, has been making a more substantial contribution to public diplomacy and soft power. The most straightforward example comes from the field of sport. Lukoil acquired Academic, a basketball outfit from Sofia, in 2000 and is the general sponsor of the Serbian Handball League. Gazprom has been the key sponsor of the popular Serbian team "Red Star Belgrade" since 2010, when the club was running into serious financial problems. In Greece, the Russophone businessman Ivan Savvidis—a member of the Duma between 2003 and 2012 and from the governing United Russia party—acquired a controlling stake in PAOK, a football club based in Salonica.

Russia's Local Networks

Those official channels of influence are just the tip of the iceberg. State-funded public diplomacy bodies, the Orthodox Church, electronic and print media funded by Moscow, are complemented by informal connections that are at times much more effective as instruments of soft power. Unsurprisingly, the border between formal and informal is blurred. There are, for instance, as well as political entrepreneurs such as Malofeev, the Eurasianist Aleksandr Dugin or RISI's ex-head, Leonid Reshetikov, who straddle the divide in the sense that they are both independent players but also act, or pretend to act, on behalf of the Kremlin when networking with various individuals and groups in Southeast Europe. The connections in question reach into local media outlets and opinion makers as well as to political parties and civic groups. Malofeev's contacts, for instance, include prominent personalities such as Panos Kammenos, leader of the Independent Greeks party and defense minister since January 2015 in Alexis Tsipras's coalition government, Milorad Dodik, president of Republika Srpska within Bosnia and Herzegovina, and Nikolay Malinov, publisher of *Duma*—a daily affiliated with the Bulgarian Socialist Party (BSP). Malofeev was, according to reports, involved in the alleged October 2016 coup attempt in Montenegro.[23] Such networks have become much more visible and assertive following the Ukrainian crisis and the deterioration of Russia's relations with the West.

There is a constellation of local proxies, allies, and fellow travellers disseminating official Russia's views of international affairs. The inner circle is formed by a cluster of political parties, with direct links to Moscow. At the 15th Congress of United Russia in June 2016, politicians from Serbia, Montenegro, Bosnia and Herzegovina, and Macedonia signed a declaration calling for neutrality and opposing NATO enlargement.[24] The Alternative for a Bulgarian Renaissance, headed by former President Georgi Pârvanov, attended as well (initialing a separate document with United Russia, the Kremlin's party, acknowledging Bulgaria's membership in NATO and the EU). Russia has close links to another Bulgarian party, the ultranationalist Ataka, which opened its campaign for the European Parliament elections in the spring of 2014 in Moscow, with a promise to take the country out of NATO.[25] The list would not be complete without Vojislav Šešelj's Serbian Radical Party, Golden Dawn, and the Communist Party of Greece (KKE), which is against both the EU and NATO.

The outer circle of Russia's friends encompasses a good number of the mainstream political parties in Southeast Europe, which, in contrast to the radical pro-Russian forces, typically favor both integration with the West and co-operation with Moscow. Examples include the Serbian Progressive Party (SNS), the Democratic Party (DS) and the post-Milošević Socialist Party of Serbia (SPS); the BSP and the center-right Citizens for the European Development of Bulgaria (GERB); as well as virtually all the major Greek parties. Depending on the issue and the moment, Russia could engage and work through either the moderates or the radical anti-Westerners to advance its goals. In March 2014, it was the latter group—Ataka, the KKE, and Serbia's Dveri movement—that sent representatives to monitor the Crimea referendum and give it a veneer of international legitimacy. At the same time, it is the moderates who are in government and could partner with Russia on issues of common interest (see Figure 9).

The fact that Russia has an appeal that spans the political spectrum is hardly unique. As noted by Pomerantsev and Weiss, amongst many others, "[u]nlike in the Cold War, when Soviets largely supported leftist groups, a fluid approach to ideology now allows the Kremlin to simultaneously back far-left and far-right movements, greens, anti-globalists and financial elites. The aim is to exacerbate divides and create an echo chamber of Kremlin support."[26] In Greece, Russia unites the far right, religious traditionalists, socialists, adherents of the pro-Soviet KKE and its one-time Eurocommunist rivals

	Type of pro-Russian position	Political affiliation	Percentage of the vote at most recent elections
Bulgaria			
Citizens for European Development of Bulgaria (GERB)	Moderate	Center-right	32.6 (2017)
Bulgarian Socialist Party	moderate (leadership)/radical (constituents)	Center-left	27.2
Movement for Rights and Freedoms (DPS)	Moderate	Centrist, Turkish minority	8.99
United Patriots (coalition including Ataka)	Moderate/ Ataka – Radical	Far right, populist	9.07 (4.52 for Ataka in the 2015 elections)
Serbia			
Serbian Progressive Party (SNS)	Moderate	Center-right	48.3 (2016)
Socialist Party of Serbia (SPS)	Moderate	Center-left	10.95
Serbian Radical Party	Radical	Far right	8.6
Democratic Party of Serbia – Dveri	Radical	Conservative right	5
Greece			
Coalition of Radical Left (SYRIZA)	Moderate	Left	35.4 (2015)
New Democracy	Moderate	Center-right	28.1
PASOK	Moderate	Center-left	6.2
Independent Greeks (ANEL)	Radical	Conservative right	3.7
Communist Party of Greece (KKE)	Radical	Far left	5.5
Golden Dawn	Radical	Far right	7

Figure 9 Political parties in Bulgaria, Serbia and Greece—attitudes to Russia

that are now part of Syriza. Likewise in Serbia, conservative anti-communists, former Titoists, ultranationalists, and so on find themselves in the same boat. The BSP, DPS, supported by Turks and Muslims, and the xenophobic Ataka have also converged to some degree.

Are friendly leaders and political factions rewarded by the Kremlin in some shape or form? That claim is hard to verify. In April 2015, the Bulgarian Court of Accounts (*Smetna palata*) opened an inquest into donations received by Ataka to the tune of €650,000. Institutionalized party-to-party ties may be even more relevant. United Russia has co-operation agreements in place with DSS (2009), ANEL (2013), and the opposition New Serbian Democracy in Montenegro (2016). And, most importantly, Russian-backed energy projects have generated significant rental opportunities for parties' business clienteles.

Russian influence runs especially strong at the level of civil society, including NGOs, associations, pressure groups, and lobbyists. Some bring together people with roots from Russia and the former Soviet Union. Others cater to the business community: JUGOSOVERO, for instance, a Belgrade-based association with a remit covering the whole of the Western Balkans, the Bulgarian–Russian Chamber of Commerce and Industry, or the Russian–Greek Chamber of Commerce. But there are groups with a distinctly political profile. The Rusofili (Russophiles) movement in Bulgaria boasts that some 12,000 attend its annual gatherings and is closely linked to BSP. The organization helps maintain Soviet army monuments, including the one in the center of Sofia, and sponsors cultural events such as concerts by Liube, billed as Putin's favorite rock band. In Serbia, a report by the Center for Euro-Atlantic Studies lists about twenty pro-Russian associations.[27] Some of them have direct ties to Moscow. The Nashi ("Our People") movement established by Putin's chief spin-doctor Vladislav Surkov had a branch in Serbia, co-operating with local conservative nationalist groupings (Dveri, 1389 Movement). They were present at the blockades of border crossings with Kosovo in 2012. In Greece, an important pool of pro-Russian support is the numerous Russophone community that has been settling in since the 1990s.

Needless to say, all these civil society organizations and networks are a valuable asset for Russian foreign policy. The anti-NATO and anti-EU demonstrations sweeping through Serbia in the run-up to the elections in April 2016 are a case in point. Local media linked the organizers, the so-called Oathkeepers (*Zavetnici*) movement, to the Gorchakov Fund, the Ruski Ekspress (Russian Express) media center close to Konstantin Malofeev, and the Belgrade office of the Russian Federation's Chamber of Commerce.[28] The protests received ample coverage by Sputnik's Serbian branch, as did the anti-government rallies in neighboring Montenegro in October 2015. The anti-NATO movement constitutes a prime example of how Russia's soft power works. Moscow is in a position to rally public support and exercise leverage from within domestic politics, which in turn adds to its bargaining power vis-à-vis the government of the country in question.

In addition to the usual suspects—ultranationalists, anti-NATO campaigners, Orthodox fundamentalists, and conservatives—observers have also raised concern about Russian infiltration of the environmentalist movement in Southeast Europe, pointing to the example of the protests against hydraulic fracturing ("fracking") in Bulgaria and Romania in the winter of 2011–12. The NATO Secretary General, Anders Fogh Rasmussen, went on record in June 2014 accusing Russia of waging a quiet war against shale gas across Europe.[29] In the case of Bulgaria, protests led to a comprehensive ban on exploration and extraction of shale imposed by the government in January 2012. Chevron abandoned its shale gas projects in Romania in February 2015, having left Bulgaria a year before. Although in principle Gazprom was the chief beneficiary of the U-turn—in that it is spared competition from unconventional gas—there has been no smoking gun conclusively linking Moscow to the protests. But it is not unlikely that Russia took advantage of local environmentalists' actions—for example, by providing extra media coverage to maximize their public impact. Kremlin-sponsored media such as RT have been paying a great deal of attention to the issue, blaming the United States, in particular, for a global campaign to force fracking on reluctant countries.

Shaping the Public Debate

The main achievement of Russian soft-power operations is not so much the direct impact on political events—national elections, decisions on energy or security policy, and so forth—as the ability to shape discourse. Local proxies, both on the moderate and on the radical end of the spectrum, are instrumental in spreading stories and messages emanating from Moscow. What is at stake is building a positive image of Russia but equally subverting and discrediting the United States and the EU. The Balkans have proved a fertile soil for the growth of anti-Western narratives, embraced by those who see Russia as a plausible alternative. Thus, NATO's 1999 campaign in Kosovo is at the core of the story about the pernicious effects of American interventions in the Middle East all the way to Ukraine and Georgia. It is usually arrogant America, rather than its European "vassals," that takes most of the blame for all the ills befalling the world as a whole and Russia's friends in Southeast Europe in particular—whether it is jihadi terrorists, asylum seekers pouring into Europe, or Albanian irredentists poised to set light to the Balkans. The West has victimized Serbia and its neighbors in the same way it encroached on Russia and sparked off war in Ukraine, in league with Nazi extremists. The EU for its part has been promoting LGBT (lesbian, gay, bisexual, transgender) rights and exporting its defunct multiculturalism. The false promise of market reforms to encourage European integration are also high on the list of failures blamed on pro-Western elites. Russia, on the other hand, acts in good faith and offers economic opportunities to the common man or woman. It presents an alternative to the bureaucratic diktat by the European Commission or the unfettered neoliberalism preached by the IMF and the World Bank.

These themes, arguments, and storylines are popularized by the media platforms affiliated with Russia's proxies, targeting niche nationalist audiences with a penchant for conspiracy theories. Examples include the Ataka's Alfa TV in Bulgaria, fringe newspapers such as *Dēmokratía* and *Kontra* in Greece, publications like *Geopolitika*, *Pečat* (*The Stamp*), and *Pravda* in Serbia, all featuring recycled content and direct contributions from RT, Sputnik, the RISI, and other Russian entities. The internet and social media amplify the reach of those outlets. Dozens of news portals, websites, blogs, and Facebook pages recycle news and analysis from pro-Kremlin Russian-language media on the hot international issue of the day, be it the war in Syria, Ukraine, or the refugee crisis in Europe. In some cases, such web-based media benefit from a substantial following—though, inevitably, they cannot reach out to a broader audience due to the echo-chamber effect of social media (see Figure 10). Typically, they also have murky ownership, though some are directly traceable to Russia: for example, the NewsFront Agency publishing in Bulgarian and Serbian, amongst other languages, but affiliated with the self-proclaimed People's Republics of Donetsk and Lugansk.

Russia shapes the mainstream media as well. In Serbia and Bulgaria, for instance, Kremlin-friendly commentators are strongly represented in TV and radio talk shows and the opinion pages of high-circulation newspaper tabloids and broadsheets.[30] Rather than bashing the West, the "fascist junta in Kyiv," or America's double standards manifest in the collusion with radical Islam, these commentators simply portray Russia as an amicable power, a respected global player, and force for good in the world. The focus is almost exclusively on foreign affairs, with critical stories about Russian domestic politics and social affairs rarely making appearance. The celebrity figure of Putin invariably dominates the coverage.

Popular Response

The effect of Russian soft power is reflected in opinion polls. A Gallup survey from 2014, funded by the European Commission, showed that Serbian citizens saw Russia as a leading donor, several notches ahead of the EU.[31] The reality could not be more different. Taken together, the EU and its member states have spent €3.5 billion in Serbia alone since 2000. Russia's contribution is hardly a tenth—mostly loans rather than grants—and lags behind that of the United States and even Japan.

Surveys looking specifically at foreign policy tell a similar story. A poll by the *New Serbian Political Thought* (*Nova Srpska Politička*

	Monthly visits (million)	Facebook followers (1,000)	Popularity rank in the country
Bulgaria			
Petel.bg	34	22	60
Bulgarian Times Bultimes.bg	1	24	225
Afera.bg	0.5	5.7	311
Bulgarian Outlook (Bâlgarski pogled) http://pogled.info	0.22	54.7	745
Serbia			
Pravda.rs	1.2	15.8	117
Nedeljnik	0.28	47	547
Informer.rs	2.2	67	49
Novi Standard Standard.rs	0.19	3.9	588
Nova Srpska Politička Misao (New Serbian Political Thought)	0.33	16.2	388
Greece			
Kontra	0.7	1.2	588
Newsbomb	7.6	548	45
Avgi (pro-Syriza)	0.6	21	713

Source: Similarweb.com, Facebook.

Figure 10 Select pro-Russian websites in Bulgaria, Serbia and Greece

Misao), a conservative pro-Russian journal, found in October 2013 that 67.5 percent of Serbians support an alliance with Russia, as against 53.7 percent for EU membership.[32] In December 2015, the pollster Ipsos found that 72 percent of Serbia's citizens hold a positive view of Russia, compared to 25 percent for the EU and just 7 percent for NATO. Vladimir Putin is by far the most trusted foreign politician in Serbia, with one poll placing him ahead of Prime Minister (now President) Aleksandr Vučić (36.1 versus 34.6 percent).[33] The numbers for Republika Srpska are comparable. Support tends to peak around highly publicized events such as humanitarian convoys sent to Serbs in northern Kosovo (December 2011) or Putin's visit in October 2014 (see Figure 11). The pro-Russian consensus in Serbia and Republika Srpska can be contrasted with the divided views in nearby Montenegro. According to a survey from January 2016, 47.3 percent of Montenegrins back NATO membership whereas 37.1 percent do not.[34]

A Russia-friendly outlook is just as common in Bulgaria, a country with notable Russophile traditions. A survey from March 2015 found out that 61 percent of citizens held a positive view of Russia and 30 percent a negative view. The annexation of Crimea in 2014 changed the perspective of 20 percent from a favorable to an unfavorable view, but 6.9 percent went the other way.[35] At the same time, nearly two-thirds of respondents stated they would vote for

Event	Date	Support
Energy Agreement	January 2008	54%
Medvedev's visit	October 2009	53%
Humanitarian aid to Kosovo	December 2011	56%
Putin visit, military parade	October 2014	63%
South Stream cancelled	December 2014	47%
OSCE conference, Foreign Minister Lavrov in Belgrade	December 2015	62%

Source: IPSOS[1]

[1] IPSOS, Istraživanje javnog mnenija – Evropska Unioja, Rusija I Sjedinjene Američke Države u očima građana Srbije [Survey of Public Opinion. EU, Russia and U.S. in the eyes of Serbia's citizens], February 2016, Available at < http://www.ceas-serbia.org/images/CEAS_2016__ipsos_srp.pdf>

Figure 11 Serbian public opinion and Russia

the EU and NATO in a putative referendum and only one-third for alignment with Russia and other post-Soviet states.

The situation in Greece is somewhat comparable. According to a poll from October 2015, citizens see the EU as their main ally, with Russia much lower down the list (44 percent against 12 percent). However, when asked about individual countries, respondents rank Russia second in popularity after France, and well ahead of Germany and the United States. Overall, 58 percent are favorable towards Russia and 34 percent unfavorable.[36]

So What?

The default pro-Russian position in Southeast Europe is that there is no choice to be made between Russia and the West. Countries can have it both ways. Those who argue for a complete rupture with the EU and NATO are usually in minority. The views of moderately pro-Moscow parties and groups find greater resonance. That is certainly true of Greece and Bulgaria, less so of Serbia. But even there the allure of Russia coexists with well-entrenched Western-centric attitudes. An IPSOS survey from 2016 of people aged between eighteen and thirty-five found that the United States and EU remain the prime reference points when it comes to popular culture, lifestyle, fashion, and sports. Russia is barely visible by those measures and there is a general lack of awareness of its history, society, and politics. Whereas 64 percent of respondents supported an alliance with Moscow and 57 percent favored the idea of Russian military bases to be established in Serbia, more than two-thirds preferred to pursue their education and find work in the West. As argued back in 2008 by the Belgrade University professor Miroslav Jovanović, hard-line pro-Russians, just like archetypal Westerners, are a relatively small constituency.[37] Those in between prevail in both numbers and weight.

It is also important to note that the pro-Russian sentiment in the Balkans often rests on incomprehension. This fact was well captured in a comment by none other than Nikita Bondarev, head of the Balkan department at the RISI:

The most ardent Russophiles I had a chance to meet in Serbia have never been in the Russian Federation, many of them don't know the Russian language and form their judgment about Russia after the *Princess Anastasia* TV series. For them Russophilia is, above all, a rejection of Western values and a symbol of a traditionalist and conservative system of values, and Russia is for them the personification of that notion. It is very rare to notice amongst them a true knowledge of Russia, its culture, its realities, or of the processes taking place in Russia and overall of Russian people's life.[38]

This is not much different in Greece, where Russia's popularity draws strength from resentment of the West, the United States first and foremost. In the words of a knowledgeable Greek scholar of Eastern Europe:

When it comes to public Russophilia in Greece, the actual knowledge of Russia is rather limited or elementary. Russia is primarily seen as an actor that can regulate Western influence in a multipolar world order, often coupled with feeble justifications on the basis of Orthodoxy, the Soviet heritage, or a combination of both. In short, Russia's image among the Greek public remains that of a remote, yet not inimical, Eurasian "Other".[39]

These caveats about Serbia and Greece are a welcome reminder that Cold War legacies continue to matter. Greece but also non-aligned former Yugoslavia had much sparser ties with the Soviet Union than Bulgaria or indeed other countries of the Eastern bloc. Thousands of Bulgarians have studied or worked in the former Soviet Union, including at least three prime ministers since 1989. That is in contrast with the Western Balkans. One should not underrate the role played by mixed marriages involving Russian speakers from the former Soviet Union—much more common in Bulgaria and, since the early 1990s, Greece, Cyprus, and Turkey, than in former Yugoslavia. The corollary is that the relationship between the degree of cultural intimacy and foreign policy is anything but linear. The countries most exposed to Russian influence are not necessarily the ones that have resisted integration into the West. In addition, geographic distance from Russia is sometimes a better predictor of how much support Moscow's foreign policy enjoys in a given place.

Conclusion

Soft power is, hands down, one of the most significant—if not the most significant—asset that Russia has at its disposal. Winning over hearts and minds is easier and immensely more cost-effective than bribing governments, maintaining alliances, let alone resorting to hard power. Anti-Western sentiments, nationalism, and positive historical memories of Russia prevail in countries such as Serbia, Greece or Bulgaria. Russia is not in a position to challenge and roll back the EU, draw red lines for the United States, or control the foreign policy of other states, but it can manipulate and rally public opinion in its favor. Influence over domestic politics, whether it conforms with the classical definition of "soft power" or not, awards Russia a symbolic standing on a par with the West. Moscow's proxies in the political domain, civil society, and the media sustain the perception of a power struggle involving two rival poles of equal strength. Ironically or not, the stories of an ever expanding Russian stranglehold over the Balkans, of parties and organizations doing Russia's bidding and governments risking being toppled if they run afoul of the Kremlin, serves perfectly the narrative of Moscow recovering its prestige and clout in European and global affairs. Bearing in mind the limited resources the Russian state has invested, or can bring to bear, that clearly is no mean feat.

Russia's influence over the people of Southeast Europe appears to be rather durable. With no TV channel of its own, the official Russian message of international affairs is as follows: the West is bad and the Balkan nations along with Turkey are, and have always been, its victims; American and EU-promoted democracy and human rights are a facade to cement global dominance; the nefarious alliance of U.S. foreign policy with jihadis and the pursuit of regime change in the Middle East has sown terrorism from Iraq to Bosnia and Kosovo to Germany; America is working assiduously to build "Greater Albania," trampling upon the rights of Serbs, Macedonians, and Montenegrins; Ukraine is just another episode of NATO expansionism, and so on and so forth. There will always be buyers, as there were at the peak of Western might in the 1990s and 2000s. This does not necessarily mean that Russia can obtain the political outcomes it wants—for example, keep a country from entering the EU or make it leave NATO. But it is just enough to muddy the waters and put Europe and, to a lesser degree, the United States under constant pressure in a region that is still vulnerable and is likely to stay that way.

EPILOGUE
Russia's Influence – What's It All About?

Russia's influence in Southeast Europe is real and easily observed. Both before and since the Ukrainian crisis, it affects the region in a multitude of ways. Moscow's rising military might has far-reaching consequences for the security posture of NATO and its members bordering the Black Sea. The Russian oil and gas companies, Gazprom, Gazprom Neft, and Lukoil, still play an enormous role in the local energy markets, despite the headwinds they face and the beefed-up EU legislation aimed at encouraging competition and diversifying supplies. The cult of Vladimir Putin and the celebration of Russia's resurgence on the world stage reigns supreme. Emboldened, Russia has not shrunk from throwing its weight across Southeast Europe, putting pressure on Europe and America, the two guarantors of the security order in the region. The rivalry is intense and it spans one country to the next and across various policy areas. Despite the hopes of détente or even a grand bargain with Russia touted by politicians on both sides of the Atlantic, there is no end in sight to the ongoing contest. For all that, it is important to avoid lazy thinking, put the Russian challenge in perspective, acknowledge its limits, and recognize what it is *not*.

First of all, it is not a return to the Cold War. There are no blocs or alliances poised against one another in Southeast Europe, a clear departure from the recent past. Russia, moreover, has no permanent allies or coherent ideology to export and sustain. Nor is it in a position to build an economic integration unit, for example by expanding the incipient Eurasian Economic Union (EEU) into the Balkans by accepting as members Serbia, Republika Srpska, Macedonia or anyone else. Even Moscow's best friends gravitate to the EU in economic terms and seek positive ties with NATO and the United States. Russia, for its part, has been perfecting the skill of insertion and disruption, without necessarily trying to establish its hegemony over parts of Southeast Europe, a very costly enterprise by all counts.

Second, we are not witnessing a "back to the future" scenario, a return to the classical era of geopolitics, though certain similarities or flashbacks are certainly present. Back in the nineteenth and early twentieth century, Russia wielded much greater clout over Balkan affairs compared to today—thanks to its recurrent military interventions and the very structure and operation of the Concert of Europe. At no point was it an important economic factor. These days, by contrast, Russian energy firms and investments represent a much more effective tool. Whether we consider the South Stream gas pipeline or the 2015 sanctions against Turkey, the economy plays a central role in Russia's relations with Southeast Europe.

What is particularly nothewrothy is that the context is set by the unprecedented degree of interdependence and border permeability in post-1989 Europe. Denser links between societies, financial institutions, businesses, government agencies, media, and so forth, along with the world wide web, have facilitated Russia's infiltration and are essential to the operation of its soft power (or foreign-policy propaganda, depending on one's perspective). Granted, globalization may not be an entirely contemporary phenomenon and there are antecedents in the long nineteenth century. But were Alexander II, let alone Nicholas I, to be miraculously awakened today, would they even recognize the world we live in?

In the Balkans, Russia is not after the establishment of a new political order or an empire, whether formal or informal. Its goal is to undercut and upset the existing institutions and rules set by the West. It is also important to underline the fact that Russia is not acting alone. There have always been willing associates and fellow travelers. They co-operate with Russia to advance their own political and economic interests, always on the lookout for external supporters. Remarkably, some of Russia's associates and partners counted as pro-Western in the not-so-distant past: for example, Milorad Dodik of Republika Srpska, the Turkish President Tayyip Erdoğan, Nikola Gruevski in Macedonia, and so on. Others have made the opposite move, dropping Russia in order to align more fully with the West. That is the case of Montenegro's Milo Đukanović. Russian policy may be, at the end of the day, opportunistic, but the fact of the matter is that there are an endless number of political chancers on the other side too. This, of course, facilitates Moscow's job of asserting its influence, along with the plethora of problems dogging the region such as the painful legacy of wars, pervasive state capture, and the absence of the rule of law.

Russia's footprint in Southeast Europe, which expanded dramatically in the 2000s, became more visible only more recently thanks to the confrontational turn in relations between Moscow and the West. There are divergent factors invoked to account for this downturn: from the Putin regime's quest for internal legitimacy in the face of a stagnant economy and a dwindling public trust in "the system," to the desire to assert Russian interests in a growingly multipolar but also uncertain world, to the anti-interventionist mood within the United States and the EU's chronic malaise. Whether due to the mechanics of power politics, as scholars of a realist persuasion contend, or because of the push and pull of domestic factors, as liberals might argue, Russia is prepared to challenge America and its allies. It wants to be an international agenda-setter, not an agenda-taker. Fears of Western plots to foment "color revolution" and Maidans inside Russia itself mould the foreign-policy thinking of Putin and his inner circle.

Of course, "the near abroad" or, to use Brussels speak, the Eastern Partnership countries, are where Russia's pushback is at its strongest. Yet Moscow has reinserted itself in other regions and political arenas. The military intervention in Syria has broadened its footprint in the Middle East beyond recognition. Even in the

United States itself, the issue of suspected Russian meddling and cyber espionage came to the forefront of the 2016 presidential elections. The Obama administration has styled Russia as a declining regional power. But, in reality, the Kremlin's outreach goes well beyond post-Soviet Eurasia.

Europe is and is likely to remain the key battleground. Yet, as this book has shown in some detail, Russia projects influence far beyond the frontiers of the former Soviet Union. Post-communist East-Central Europe, including former Yugoslavia, is the obvious target. As also is Turkey: Moscow has the means to co-opt Ankara as its relationship with the United States and the EU frays. Western sanctions and the dramatic fall in oil prices have put the Kremlin on the backfoot, but it does know how to play the game of influence and exploit weaknesses and opportunities across Europe's multiple peripheries.

For all that, one should resist the notion that the Kremlin is pulling all the strings in this game. Across Europe, political and civic leaders, governments, and business interests have been more than willing accomplices, enlisting Russia's support to attain all kinds of goals—balancing against external threats, maximizing payoffs and redistributing the spoils, hedging and pushing for concessions from the West, sidelining and outfoxing domestic rivals, muzzling critics. The list goes on and on. This sort of behavior is not unique to Southeast Europe, where historical connections to Russia admittedly play a role. It no doubt has its adepts in many other corners of the continent, including Hungary, the Czech Republic, Italy, Austria, and, not least, Germany. Whatever the weather, there will be always X number of players willing to do business with or to influence Russia.

Is the rival power that Russia has become in a position to undermine the EU from within, starting from its more vulnerable southeastern states? Probably not. For one, despite the belief to the contrary in many quarters, the Kremlin does not appear to have a coherent model that is exportable beyond the post-Soviet space. Neither "the managed democracy" or "sovereign democracy" of Putin's first two terms, nor the more recent praise of conservative values and religion more broadly as well as the celebration of Russia as a unique civilization opposed to global liberalism, quite do the job, irrespective of the fact that there is no shortage of cheerleaders across the EU. From Belgrade to Ankara, from Sofia to Budapest, dysfunctional democracies, state capture, and the backslide to authoritarian politics are, on the whole, homegrown ills, not an outcome of a sinister Muscovite plot. As much as "Putinization" represents a threat, it is worthwhile reconsidering who the real Putinizers are. Even more important, Russia does not appear to have the economic resources for costly ideological crusades nor the will to bankroll friendly regimes. The record in the Balkans proves the point. The EU might be in the doldrums, facing a succession of existential crises, but it still has allure thanks to its market, the sizeable financial transfers, and, to a lesser degree, the power of its foundational narrative.

So what one is left with is a rivalry between an opportunist, which has a clear set of goals though lacks the means to achieve them, and a terminally disoriented West that possesses the power assets but is not of one mind about how to respond to the challenge. This applies both to the EU where member states have always found it difficult to "speak with one voice" on Russia, and the United States where the right balance between containment and engagement continues to be a hotly debated subject. In the meantime, Southeast Europe will navigate the murky waters of this new contest. For the most part, the states of the region will jump on the West's bandwagon but hedge their bets and keep their options open. It would be foolish of Putin to just stand idly by and not take advantage. But, as the saying goes, it takes two to tango.

APPENDICES

Appendix I: Southeast Europe at a Glance

	Population	GDP ($, nominal terms)
Albania	2.774m	4,659.34
Bosnia and Herzegovina	3.829m	4,661.76
Bulgaria	7.265m	7,498.83
Croatia	4.253m	13,607.51
Cyprus	1.141m	25,248.98
Greece	11.03m	21,956.41
Kosovo	1.824m	3,877.17
Macedonia	2.107m	4,838.46
Montenegro	621,383m	7,106.86
Romania	19.96m	9,499.21
Serbia	7.164m	6,353.96
Slovenia	2.06m	23,289.34
Turkey	74.93m	10,971.66

Source: World Bank (2013)

Appendix 2: Former Yugoslavia and Albania

	Population	Ethnic composition	Constitutional model	Relationship with the EU	Relationship with NATO
Albania	2.774m	Albanians (98.8%) Greeks (0.5%) Macedonians (0.16%) Roma (0.14%) Aromanian (0.13) Religious affiliation: Muslims, incl. Sunni and Bektashi (58.9%) Catholics (10.03%) Orthodox (6.75%) Atheists (2.50%) *2011 Census*	Unitary state	Candidate since 2014	Member since 2009
Bosnia and Herzegovina	3.829m	Bosniaks (50.11%) Serbs (30.78%) Croats (15.43%) Others – e.g. Roma (2.73%) not declared (0.77%) *2013 census*	Consociational polity formed by the Federation of Bosnia and Herzegovina, Srpska and the Brčko District	Membership application (2016)	Individual Partnership Plan (2011)
Croatia	4.253m	Croats (90.42%) Serbs (4.36%) Bosniaks/Muslims (0.9%) Italians (0.42%) Albanians (0.41%) Roma (0.40%) *2011 census*	Unitary state	Member since 2013	Member since 2009
Kosovo	1.824m	Albanians (92.9%) Serbs (1.5%*) Roma/Ashkali/ Egyptians (2%) Bosniak/Muslim (1.6%) Gorani (0.6%)	Unitary with large degree of decentralisation and ethnic power sharing	Association Agreement (2015)	Applied to join Partnership for Peace (2012)

*The share of Serbs is higher as the 2011 census lacks data from the Serb-majority municipalities in Northern Kosovo.

	Population	Ethnic composition	Constitutional model	Relationship with the EU	Relationship with NATO
Macedonia	2.107m	Macedonians (64.2%) Albaianis (25.2%) Turks (3.9%) Roma (2.7%) Serbs (1.8%) Bosniaks/Muslims (0.9%) Aromanians (0.5%) *2002 census*	Unitary with large degree of decentralisation and ethnic power sharing	Candidate since 2005	Invitation to join blocked by Greece
Montenegro	621,383	Montenegrins (45%) Serbs (28.7%) Bosniaks/Muslims (11.9%) Albanians (4.9%) Croats (0.9%) Roma (0.8%) *2011 census*	Unitary	Accession negotiations since 2012	Invited to join (2016)
Serbia	7.164m	Serbs (83.3%) Hungarians (3.5%) Muslims/Bosniaks (2.3%) Roma (2.1%) Croats (0.8%) *2011 census*	Unitary	Accession negotiations since 2014	Partnership agreement (2015)
Slovenia	2.06m	Slovenes (83.1%) Serbs (2%) Croats (1.8%) Muslims/Bosniaks (1.6%) Hungarians (0.3%) *2002 census*	Unitary	Member since 2004	Member since 2004

Appendix 3: NATO/U.S. Initiatives in the Black Sea

NATO Initiatives

Ballistic Missile Defence (BMD)	Land-based element (*Aegis Ashore*) was deployed at the Deveselu base, Romania, in May 2016. Consists of a radar and SM-3 interceptor.
Multinational Divisional HQ Southeast	Operating in Bucharest since December 2015. Overseeing contingency plan endorsed at Wales Summit (2014)
Multinational Framework Brigade	Authorised at the Warsaw Summit (July 2016). Contributions from Romania, Bulgaria, Poland

---

Bilateral U.S. initiatives	U.S. Marine Corps Black Sea Rotational Force (BSRF). Deployed since 2010 at Novo Selo (Bulgaria) and Mihail Kogălniceanu (Romania). Strength: 500 troops.
	Armoured Brigade Combat Team (ABCT). M1-A Abrams tanks and Bradley fighting vehicles.

Exercises	*NATO*
	Sea Breeze annual exercises (air, land, sea) since 1997. Co-led by U.S. and Ukraine, with the participation of NATO members, Sweden, Georgia and Moldova.
	Swift Response 15 (August–September 2015). A brigade task force comprising troops from 10 NATO members. Took place in multiple locations across Europe, including Romania and Bulgaria.
	Steadfast Cobalt – NATO Response Force/Very High Readiness Joint Task Force (inaugurated atthe Wales Summit), May–June 2016.
	U.S. Bilateral
	Platinum Eagle - 120 Marines from the BSRF and over 400 Romanian and Bulgarian military forces trained at Babadag Training Area, Romania, in May 2015.
	Bilateral exercises between U.S. and Turkish, Romanian and Bulgarian navies (PASSEX).

NOTES

Introduction

1. Kerry in response to a question by Sen. Christopher S. Murphy (D. Connecticut). See "Sen. Thad Cochran Holds a Hearing on the State Department Budget Request for Fiscal Year 2016," Congressional Quarterly Transcriptions, 24 February 2015. Video footage from the session is available at https://www.c-span.org/video/?324514-1/secretary-john-kerry-testimony-state-department-fiscal-year-2016-budget.
2. EU ministers: Balkans becoming "chessboard" for big powers, *Euractiv*, 7 March 2017.
3. "Würden Sie Krieg mit Russland führen, Frau Merkel?" ["Will you lead a war with Russia, Mrs Merkel?"] *Welt am Sonntag*, 7 December 2014.
4. Formed in August 1989, Gazprom inherited the Soviet Ministry of Gas Industry (*Ministerstvo gazovoi promyshlenosti*, MINGAZPROM). Legally, it is a private corporation, but the Russian Federation government retains a controlling stake. Gazprom ofted acted as a state within a state in the 1990s but was brought under the Kremlin's full control after Vladimir Putin became president. More about Gazprom, its place in Russian foreign policy, and the South Stream pipeline in Chapter 7.
5. The treaty ended the Russo-Ottoman War of 1768–74. It granted, amongst other things, the Ottomans' subjects of Eastern Orthodox faith the right to sail under the Russian flag and allowed for the construction of a Russian church in Constantinople. St Petersburg could also intervene in Wallachia and Moldova, nominally under the suzerainty of the Porte.
6. Sergei Lavrov, "Istoricheskaia perspektiva vneshnei politiki Rossii," ["Historical Perspective of Russia's Foreign Policy"] *Rossiia v Global'noi Politike*, Russian International Affairs Council, March 2016.
7. Vladimir Gel'man, *Authoritarian Russia: Analyzing Post-Soviet Regime Change*, Pittsburgh, N.J.: University of Pittsburgh Press, 2015.
8. Dmitri Trenin, "Getting Russia Right," Carnegie Endowment for International Peace, 2007, p. 76.
9. "The Balkans are the Soft Underbelly of Europe," *The Financial Times*, 14 January 2015.
10. Deutsche Welle, 9 May 2014.
11. Interviewed by DefenseNews.com at the Halifax Security Forum, 29 November 2016. http://www.defensenews.com/articles/interview-president-of-croatia-kolinda-grabar-kitarovic.

12. Barbara Jelavich, *Russia's Balkan Entanglements, 1804–1914*, Cambridge: Cambridge University Press, 1991, pp. 269–70. Jelavich goes on to quote the Bulgarian writer and political activist Liuben Karavelov: "'If Russia comes to liberate, she will be received with great sympathy. But if she comes to rule, she will find many enemies.'"

13. Fyodor Dostoevsky, *A Writer's Diary*, translated and annotated by Kenneth Lantz, Vol. 2, 1877–81, Evanston, IL: Northwestern University Press, 1994, p. 1,202.

14. Ibid., p. 1,200. Further on the period in Jelavich, *Russia's Balkan Entanglements*, Chapter 4. Also Denis Vovchenko, *Containing Balkan Nationalism: Imperial Russia and the Balkan Christians, 1856–1914*, Oxford: Oxford University Press, 2016.

15. More about Leont'ev and his fellow conservatives of the latter half of the nineteenth century in Iver Neuman's classic work, *Russia and the Idea of Europe: A Study of Identity in International Relations*, London: Routledge, 1995.

16. Robert Legvold, "Russian Foreign Policy During State Transformation," in Legvold (ed.), *Russian Foreign Policy in the Twenty-First Century and the Shadow of the Past*, New York: Columbia University Press, 2007.

17. Baron Roman Romanovich Rosen, Russian diplomat and later member of the State Council, in a memo on Russian foreign policy submitted to Nicholas II (September 1912). Quoted in Dominic Lieven, *Towards the Flame: Empire, War and the End of Tsarist Russia*, London: Allen Lane, 2015.

18. Heather Conley, James Mina, Ruslan Stefanov, and Martin Vladimirov, *The Kremlin Playbook: Understanding Russian Influence in Central and Eastern Europe*, CSIS and the Center for Study and Democracy (Sofia), October 2016.

19. Conley et al., *The Kremlin Playbook*, p. 1.

20. COMECON or CMEA (*Sovet ekonomicheskoi vzaimopomoschi*, SEV) was founded in 1949, initially in response to the U.S. Marshall Plan. Until its dissolution in 1991, it brought together the Eastern Bloc countries as well as the USSR's Third World allies such as Vietnam, Cuba, and Mongolia.

1 The Balkans Rediscovered

1. "Situatsiia v Iugoslavii" ["The Situation in Yugoslavia"], *Kommersant*, 29 July 1995.

2. TASS, 28 April 2015.

3. The Yugoslav wars started on 27 June 1991 when the federal army clashed with Slovenia's Territorial Defense and police forces. Spilling over into Croatia, it culminated with the conflict in Bosnia and Herzegovina (6 April 1992–21 November 1995). The next episode was marked by the war in Kosovo ending with NATO's campaign against rump Yugoslavia in March–June 1999 (Operation Allied Force). The coda came with a military confrontation between the Macedonian government and Albanian militants in 2001.

4. Ironically enough, the subject of the piece was the Serbs' rebuff of Russian diplomacy. Chuck Sudetic, "Bosnian Serbs Reject Peace Plan for 3d Time, Defying Russia," *The New York Times*, 2 August 1994.

5. Numerous Soviet experts had built a career denouncing Titoist revisionism—much like Sovietologists in Yugoslavia whose main job was to debunk Soviet imperialism, bureaucratic sclerosis, and dogmatism.

6. Konstantin von Eggert, remark at the conference *Russia in the Balkans*, London School of Economics and Political Science, 13 March 2015. Report available at http://www.lse.ac.uk/europeanInstitute/research/LSEE/Events/2014–2015/Russia-in-the-Balkans/merged-document.pdf (all links accessed 21 October 2016).

7. Mikhail Gorbachev, *Zhizn' i reformy*, [*Life and Reforms*], vol. 2, Moscow, p. 380.

8. The chances were that Kadijević was double-dealing and simultaneously talking to the United States as well. Sergei Romanenko, *Iugoslaviia, Rossiia i "slavianskaia ideia"*, *Vtoraia polovina XIX v.–nachalo XXI v.* [*Yugoslavia, Russia and "the Slavic Idea": From the Second Half of the 19th Century to the Beginning of the 21st Century*], Moscow: Institut Prava i publichnoi politiki, 2002, pp. 386–88. Kadijević fled to Moscow in 2001, fearing indictment by the International Tribunal for Former

Yugoslavia (ICTY). He received Russian citizenship in 2008, dying in Moscow six years later.

9. Kadijević and the YNA were mulling a coup of their own, in collusion with Milošević. See Josip Glaurdić, *The Hour of Europe: Western Powers and the Breakup of Yugoslavia*, New Haven, CT: Yale University Press, 2011, p. 140. See also Kadijević and Jović's memoirs. Veljko Kadijević, *Kontraudar. Moje viđenje raspada Jugoslavije*, Belgrade: Filip Višnjić, 2010. Borisav Jović, *Zašto bih ćutao*, Belgrade: Novosti, 2014.

10. Yeltsin never went to Belgrade, nor was Milošević ever invited to Moscow on an official visit, unlike Croatia's President Franjo Tuđman or Kiro Gligorov of Macedonia. The Serbian president came twice on working visits (1995, 1998). The one in the autumn of 1995 was originally planned as part of a three-way summit with Tuđman and the Bosnian President Alija Izetbegović, which did not take place.

11. What made an impression on Milošević and his allies was the Western powers' reluctance to take a firm stand as well as their insistence on preserving the territorial integrity of the Soviet state—whatever the cost. See Glaurdić, *The Hour of Europe*.

12. James Headley, *Russia and the Balkans: Foreign Policy from Yeltsin to Putin*, London: Hurst, 2008, p. 80.

13. The Federal Republic of Yugoslavia, composed of Serbia and Montenegro, was established in April 1992.

14. Headley, *Russia and the Balkans*, p. 108. Il'a Levin (1995) " 'Neopanslavism': Mutuality in the Russian–Serbian Relationship," in Stefano Bianchini and Paul Shoup, *The Yugoslav War, Europe and the Balkans: How to Achieve Security*, Ravenna: Longo Editore, 1995, pp. 73–82.

15. Headley, *Russia and the Balkans*, p. 106.

16. The CPRF won the largest number of deputies (157) in the second Duma elections in December 1995.

17. The LDP garnered 70 out of 450 seats, having won by far the greatest share of votes. Communists finished third with 65 seats. By comparison, despite trailing behind the LDP in terms of absolute numbers of votes, the pro-Yeltsin Russia's Choice secured 96 seats thanks to the single-member constituencies. The reformist Yabolko obtained 33 seats.

18. Tanjug, 1 February 1994. In 1995, Zhirinovskii concluded a formal alliance between the LDP and the Serbian Radical Party of ultranationalist Vojislav Šešelj.

19. Igor Rotar, "Brotherly Love: Russia and the Serbs," *Jamestown Foundation*, 3 November 1995; http://www.jamestown.org/single/?tx_ttnews%5Btt_news%5D=19103&tx_ttnews%5BbackPid%5D=217&no_cache=1#.VkuoumSrRQI.

20. Romanenko, *Iugoslaviia, Rossiia*, p. 400. See also Gus'kova, *Istoria iugoslavskogo krizisa, 1990–2000* [*History of the Yugoslav Crisis, 1990–2000*], Moscow: Russkoe pravo-Russkii natsional'nyi front, 2000.

21. *Pravda*, 13 January 1992. Quoted in Paul Goble, "Dangerous Liaisons: Moscow, the Former Yugoslavia, and the West," in Richard H. Ullman (ed.), *The World and Yugoslavia's Wars*, New York: Council on Foreign Relations, 1996, p. 188.

22. The survey was timed to take society's pulse at a moment when the Supreme Soviet held a heated debate, for the first time, on policy in Yugoslavia.

23. From 1993 onwards, Grachev and Prime Minister Viktor Chernomyrdin overshadowed Kozyrev in shaping policy vis-à-vis the "near abroad", with consequences for Russian foreign relations more broadly. Neil Malcolm et al., *Internal Factors in Russian Foreign Policy*, Oxford: Oxford University Press, 1996.

24. Goble, "Dangerous Liaisons," p. 193.

25. *Jutarnji List*, 18 February 2017.

26. Presided over by Robert Badinter, a French constitutional judge, the arbitration commission of European magistrates was established in August 1991 by the EC to provide legal advice on the issue of recognition. The opinion regarding the independence of Macedonia, Slovenia, and Croatia was issued on 14 September 1991.

27. Andrei Kozyrev, *Preobrazhenie* [*Transformation*], Moscow: Mezhdunarodnie otnosheniia, 1995, p. 121.

28. The only exception was the short-lived attempt to support the FRY Prime Minister Milan Panić's unsuccessful bid to challenge Milošević in the Serbian presidential elections of December 1992.

29. Andrei Kozyrev, "The Lagging Partnership," *Foreign Affairs*, vol. 73, no. 3, May/June 1994, pp. 65–6.

30. The plan assigned 49 percent of Bosnia's territory to the Serbs, meaning they had to cede land. This was the second time that a Moscow-backed settlement had been torn apart by the Serbs after the plan proposed by the UN's Special Envoy Cyrus Vance and the EU's representative David Owen in 1993. However, Russia was not as heavily invested at that moment. In addition, the Vance–Owen plan was killed not just by a RS parliament vote against it (4 May 1993) but also the U.S. administration's skepticism due to the assessment that the settlement rewarded ethnic cleansing. By contrast, in 1994, Kozyrev invested in the Contact Group proposals, having canvassed both Milošević and Tuđman.

31. Maksim Iusin, "Serby nanosiat zhestokii udar po prestizhu rossiiskoi diplomatii" ["Serbs are Dealing a Harsh Blow against Russian Diplomacy"], *Izvestia*, 20 April 1994.

32. UNSC Resolution 943 of 23 September 1994.

33. Headley, *Russia and the Balkans*, pp. 200–1.

34. S/1994/1358, 2 December 1994, proposed by Bosnia and Herzegovina, Croatia, Djibouti, Egypt, Nigeria, Oman, Pakistan, Rwanda, and Turkey.
     Full text: https://www.globalpolicy.org/component/content/article/196/40064. html. The resolution sanctioned Croatian Serbs for launching attacks into Bosnia.

35. *The New York Times*, 12 August 1995.

36. On 19 November 1994, Russia voted for the UNSC resolution authorizing the extension of air strikes into Serb-held areas of Croatia.

37. During the so-called Operation Storm (Operacija Oluja), the overhauled Croatian forces overran RSK between 4 and 8 August 1995.

38. A delegation from the Russian Ministry of Defense visited RS during the NATO air campaign. Headley, *Russia and the Balkans*, p. 234.

39. Robert H. Donaldson and Joseph L. Nogee, *Russian Foreign Policy: Changing Systems, Enduring Interests*, 5th edn, London: Routledge, 2014, p. 247.

40. Russia highlighted its contribution to the peace settlement—for example, the resumption of gas deliveries to Sarajevo after a meeting between Prime Ministers Viktor Chernomyrdin and Haris Silajdžić in October 1995.

41. The command-and-control mechanism was established by an agreement signed by U.S. Defense Secretary William Perry and Pavel Grachev on 8 November 1995.

42. PIC was established in London in December 1995. It includes approximately forty states and international organizations involved in Bosnia and Herzegovina. Its steering board holds weekly meetings in Sarajevo at the level of ambassadors.

43. Quoted in Richard Holbrooke, *To End a War*, New York: Modern Library, 1999, p. 117.

44. *Kommersant*, 25 September 1997.

45. Headley, *Russia and the Balkans*, pp. 296–7.

46. Leontii Shevtsov, "Russia–NATO Co-operation in Bosnia: A Basis for the Future?" *NATO Review*, vol. 45, no. 2, March 1997, pp. 17–21.

47. See Headley, *Russia and the Balkans*, p. 302ff.

48. Wesley Clark, *Waging Modern War*, New York: Public Affairs, 2001, p. 377. See also Sarah E. Mendelson, *Between Friend and Foe: U.S.-Russian Military Relations Ten Years After the End of the Cold War*, The National Council for Eurasian and East European Research, 2001, pp. 10–12.

49. Strobe Talbott, *The Russia Hand*, New York: Random House, 2002, p. 194.

50. Oleg Levitin, "Inside Moscow's Kosovo Muddle," *Survival*, vol. 42, no. 1, Spring 2000, pp. 132–3.

51. Here is how Egor Gaidar, prime minister of Russia in 1992, reflected on the issue of why Yugoslavia and Kosovo animated Russian sentiments. "It was very difficult to

explain because the perception was that Russians have their own domestic worries. They have low living standards and wages that are in arrears. Why should they genuinely worry about Yugoslavia? Again, do you really think that they are seriously interested in eighteenth-century ties with Yugoslavia and the Orthodox Church? This has very little to do with historical ties and the Orthodox Church. If you ask an ordinary Russian whether he knows the difference between the Karađorđević and Obrenović families and which of the two was sympathetic to the Austrians and which to the Russians, I doubt that he will be able to answer your question." Quoted in Padma Dessai, *Conversations on Russia*, Oxford: Oxford University Press, 2006, p. 98ff.

52. Roy Allison, *Russia, the West, and Military Intervention*, Oxford: Oxford University Press, 2013, Chapter 3.
53. Levitin, "Inside Moscow's Kosovo Muddle," p. 137.
54. Gazeta.ru, 25 March 1999.
55. Boris Yeltsin, *Prezidentskii marafon [Presidential Marathon]*, Moscow: AST, 2000, p. 291. English translation: *Midnight Diaries*, New York: Public Affairs, 2000.
56. A poll conducted by *Ekho Moskvy* radio station showed only 23 percent in favor of the FRY joining. Oksana Antonenko, "Russia, NATO and European Security after Kosovo", *Survival*, vol. 41, no. 4, 1999, pp. 109–10. The idea of adding rump Yugoslavia as a third member to the Russia–Belarus Union State was touted as early as 1998 by Vojislav Šešelj.
57. A military technical agreement signed in Kumanovo, across the border with Macedonia, arranged for the Serbian security forces' handover of control to NATO. In all likelihood, the plan for a deployment in Kosovo had been discussed in advance with Yeltsin and Defense Minister Igor Sergeev. Yeltsin remained incommunicado as the "leap to Prishtina" proceeded, in order to deny any responsibility should the operation go wrong. See Artem Krechetnikov, "Brosok na Prishtinu: na grani voiny" ["The Leap to Prishtina: On the Verge of War"], BBC Russian Service, 11 June 2014 http://www.bbc.com/russian/international/2014/06/140610_pristina_march_anniversary.
58. The then commander of the Airborne Troops, Lieutenant General Nikolai Stas'kov, claimed credit for ordering the operation. According to his account, Yeltsin endorsed it *ex post*. Stas'kov interviewed in *Krasnaia Zvezda* (published by the Russian Ministry of Defense), 28 August 2004.
59. Putin interviewed by David Frost, Breakfast with Frost, BBC, 5 March 2000. Full transcript: http://news.bbc.co.uk/hi/english/static/audio_video/programmes/breakfast_with_frost/transcripts/putin5.mar.txt.

2 Meddling in Europe's Backyard

1. Quoted in Pavel Felgenhauer, "Kosova and the 'frozen conflicts' of the former USSR," *Eurasia Daily Monitor*, vol. 5, no. 3, Jamestown Foundation, 21 February 2008.
2. *Dan* (Podgorica), 5 October 2005.
3. A deal was reached in late December, with Serbia accepting to pay $100 million up front and $100 million by the end of 2015.
4. By that point Russia had only 320 troops in Prishtina, compared to 3,000 at the outset, and 650 in Bosnia. It still left 100 police officers as part of the UN administration in Kosovo (UNMIK). Russian diplomats and military officials went to considerable lengths explaining that the pull-out did not mean Moscow had lost interest in the region altogether. James Headley, *Russia and the Balkans: Foreign Policy from Yeltsin to Putin*, London: Hurst, 2008, p. 462.
5. Interview in *Izvestia*, 10 September 2003.
6. Maksim Iusin, "Solidarnost', no ne bol'she" ["Solidarity but nothing more"], *Izvestia*, 29 October 2001.
7. Dmitri Trenin, *Post-Imperium: A Eurasian Story*, Washington D.C.: Carnegie Endowment for International Peace, 2011, p. 107.

8. Literary Serbian, to give one example, was codified in Vienna in 1850, following a compromise reached by prominent Serb and Croatian intellectuals including Vuk Karadžić. Vuk's reform differentiated Serbian from Church Slavonic, which also widened the lexical distance with Russian.

9. The delegation led by Matija Nenadović, Serbia's first prime minister, received money instead. Barbara Jelavich, *Russia's Balkan Entanglements*, Cambridge: Cambridge University Press, 1991, p. 12. Prince Czartoryski was to become a leader of the Polish Uprising of 1830–1 and, later, patron of the Polish émigré community in the Ottoman Empire.

10. Garašanin kept Serbia neutral during the Crimean War (1853–56).

11. David McKenzie, "Russia's Balkan Policies Under Alexander II, 1855–1881," in Hugh Ragsdale (ed.), *Imperial Russian Foreign Policy*, Cambridge: Cambridge University Press, 1993, p. 257.

12. Yugoslavia did not establish diplomatic relations with the Soviet Union until June 1940. By comparison, Greece had done so in 1924 and Bulgaria and Romania in 1934.

13. In January 2001, another Montenegrin, Danilo Vuksanović, was appointed but he was not backed by either the Serbian government or Podgorica (because he was part of the anti-Đukanović opposition).

14. The Federal Republic of Yugoslavia was officially replaced by the State Union of Serbia and Montenegro, a loose federation, in February 2002. The following month Koštunica ceded his post to Svetozar Marović, a Montenegrin politician. The union was dissolved after Montenegro voted for independence at a referendum in May 2006.

15. Together, Putin and Koštunica called on the West to rein in and disarm Albanian radicals ("terrorists") in Macedonia. After Belgrade, Putin paid a visit to the Russian contingent in Kosovo. CNN, 17 June 2001.

16. *Kommersant*, 7 June 2000.

17. Interview with Economy and Finance Minister Božidar Đelić, *Kommersant*, 12 November 2003.

18. Progresgas Trading (PGT), a joint venture between the Federal Republic of Yugoslavia and Gazprom, collected 1 percent commission of deliveries. In September 1993, the FRY and Russia signed a Memorandum of Understanding to commission PGT to build a connection linking the Serbian grid with Bulgaria and the Transbalkan Pipeline. Milošević boasted that once the Yugoslav conflict ended, Serbia would be importing and moving larger volumes of Russian gas and drawing in considerable investment from Russian companies. Đorđe Padejski, "Srbija i Gazprom—od Miloševića do danas" ["Serbia and Gazprom—from Milošević to Today"], *Peščanik*, 7 February 2011.

19. In 2003, Lukoil paid €117 million for 79.5 percent of Beopetrol and promised to invest an additional €85 million. Siniša Mali, who was dealing with the deal, subsequently left the Privatization Agency to join Beopetrol-Lukoil as director. He was elected mayor of Belgrade in April 2014. Heather Conley, James Mina, Ruslan Stefanov, and Martin Vladimirov, *The Kremlin Playbook: Understanding Russian Influence in Central and Eastern Europe*, CSIS and the Center for Study and Democracy (Sofia), October 2016, p. 59.

20. Tim Judah, "Kosovo: Behind-the-Scenes Hard Talk Begins," ISN Security Watch, 24 December 2005; James Ker-Lindsay, *Kosovo: Road to Contested Statehood*, London: I. B. Tauris, 2009, p. 29.

21. Talks kicked off in February 2006. In July they moved from the technical to political level, with President Boris Tadić and Prime Minister Vojislav Koštunica attending along with their opposite numbers from Kosovo, Fatmir Sejdiu and Agim Çeku.

22. Guiding principles of the Contact Group for a settlement of the status of Kosovo, Yearbook of the United Nations 2005, p. 472.

23. "Decision on Kosovo status should be applicable to other areas—Putin," *Interfax*, 30 January 2006.

24. Ker-Lindsay, *Kosovo*, p. 29.

25. The full transcript of the speech and Q&A is available at http://en.kremlin.ru/events/president/transcripts/24034.

26. Straying from the November 2005 Guiding Principles, the Troika explored a range of ideas, including partition and exchange of territories (floated by Ischinger), an interim settlement on the 1972 agreement between East and West Germany, a version of the Taiwan-China model, and so on.

27. Romania, Greece, Cyprus, Spain, and Slovakia.

28. A remark at the Russia in the Balkans conference, London School of Economics, 13 March 2015.

29. Koštunica lost the parliamentary elections in May 2008 and moved to opposition.

30. *Kommersant*, 21 September 2007.

31. During the vote in the General Assembly, the EU abstained, with the exception of five countries that refused to recognize Kosovo's independence: Spain, Greece, Cyprus, Romania, and Slovakia. The United States also voted against.

32. Russia's deposition is available at http://www.icj-cij.org/docket/files/141/15628.pdf.

33. B92, 30 September 2008.

34. "Why I Had to Recognise Georgia's Breakaway Regions," *The Financial Times*, 26 August 2008.

35. A year after the Georgian war, the Russian prime minister reminded German TV viewers about Bosnia: "In this connection I recalled the tragedy in Srebrenica. In 1995 the European peacekeeping contingent was represented there by the Dutch who chose not to join the fray. . . . They still remember it and are bringing apologies. But people in Srebrenica were killed. What did they expect from us? To behave in the same way and to fail to do our duty to the people whom we had to protect? So, we have no need to apologize to anyone. We are confident that we are right. We are not going to pick a fight or argue; we will work." Vladimir Putin interviewed by the German ARD TV channel, 29 August 2009; http://premier.gov.ru/eng/events/458.html.

36. The ICJ's advisory opinion is available at http://www.icj-cij.org/docket/index.php?p1=3&p2=4&case=141&p3=4. The court declined to address broader questions to do with the right to self-determination or the subject of whether the political process to determine the entity's status had run its course. The Russian judge Leonid Skotnikov issued a dissenting opinion.

37. Padejski, "Srbija i Gazprom."

38. In September 2008, the Serbian government released a report by the auditing firm Deloitte that valued NIS at $3.1 billion.

39. "Russian deal pits Dinkić vs. government," B92, 11 December 2008.

40. Moscow preferred extending a loan instead.

41. The contract was awarded to Centrgaz, a subsidiary of Gazprom.

42. In an interview from 2011, the NIS CEO Kirill Kravchenko complained that due diligence had found that the company was in the red for four years prior to 2008 (the government claimed it was turning a profit). *Kommersant*, 3 March 2011.

43. As of 2015, Srbijagas was €820 million in debt. *Večernje Novosti*, 4 August 2015.

44. Majority-owned by the Russian Central Bank, Sberbank acquired the Austrian Volksbank's operations in Eastern Europe, including Serbia, Bosnia and Herzegovina, Croatia, and Slovenia.

45. Prime Minister Ivica Dačić mulled the establishment of an investment fund with VTB.

46. Poultry and edible waste, some sorts of cheese, white sugar, sparkling wine, ethyl-alcohol, cigars and cigarettes, cotton yarn and fabric, special woven fabrics, some types of compressors, tractors and new and used passenger cars.

47. Republic of Serbia, European Integration Office, Public Opinion Poll, June 2014. Available at http://www.seio.gov.rs/upload/documents/nacionalna_dokumenta/istrazivanja_javnog_mnjenja/opinion_poll_14.pdf.

48. The independent princedom famously declared war on Japan in 1904, out of solidarity with the Russian Empire.

49. Floriana Fossato, "Russia: Djukanovic's Visit to Moscow Seen as 'Turning Point',", *RFE/RL*, 9 August 1999.

50. *Kommersant*, 4 June 1998.

51. Montenegro inherited the FTA concluded between Russia and the Federal Republic of Yugoslavia.

52. Ana Bogavac, "Crna Gora: Strah zbog Putinovog zakona o prodaji nekretnina" ["Montenegro: Fears due to Putin's Law on Real Estate Sales"], *Deutsche Welle*, 19 April 2013.

53. In 2008, Luzhkov gifted the Mayor of Podgorica, Miomir Mugoša, a suspended bridge over the Morača River. It was inaugurated on 19 December, the day that Podgorica marks its liberation in 1944.

54. The Russian daily *Izvestia* published a local edition from the resort town of Budva. Atlas TV, a Montenegrin channel, broadcast a business programme in Russian. The town's high school introduced Russian-only classes to accommodate the newcomers. I am grateful to Srdja Pavlović for bringing all these details to my attention.

55. *Dan*, 1 April 2005.

56. "Oligarch's Battle Clouds and Economy," *The Financial Times*, 17 October 2008. Deripaska's RusAl was prevented from acquiring a coal mine and a thermal power plant at the town of Plevlja.

57. *Reuters*, 3 December 2013. The row was somewhat reminiscent of an earlier case involving the 2004 purchase of the steelworks at Nikšič by Rusmonstil for the symbolic price of €1,000. Having failed to make the investment foreseen in the privatization contract, the Russian company then abandoned the steelworks, leaving it heavily in debt.

58. *BalkanInsight*, 19 December 2013.

59. The MFA spokesperson Maria Zakharova remarked that Montenegro was faced with "[an] internal political crisis accompanied by popular protests." "Deep divisions" on NATO membership made the plebiscite necessary in the interest of democracy. *TASS*, 15 December 2015.

60. Christo Grozev, "The Kremlin's Balkan Gambit: Part I and Balkan Gambit: Part 2. The Montenegro Zugzwang," *BellingCat*, 4 and 25 March 2017: https://www.bellingcat.com/news/uk-and-europe/2017/03/04/kremlins-balkan-gambit-part; https://www.bellingcat.com/news/uk-and-europe/2017/03/25/balkan-gambit-part-2-montenegro-zugzwang.

61. The key witness in the case, anti-Western activist Aleksandar Sinđelić, was not involved in the Serbian volunteer units fighting in Donbas, for instance. Miloš Teodorović, "Živković: Sinđelića nismo hteli u Ukrajini, Rusija me odlikovala zbog Krima" ["Živković: We did not want Sinđelić in Ukraine. Russia decorated me because of Crimea"], RFE/RL, 25 November 2016. See also Damir Marušić, "Did Moscow Botch a Coup in Montenegro?" *American Interest*, 30 October 2016. The story about the foiled plot broke out after a tense election day marred by allegations of fraud and vote-buying as well as by the temporary shutdown of popular messaging mobile applications such as Viber and WhatsApp.

62. RS President Milorad Dodik quoted in Croatia's daily *Večernji List*, 2 January 2016.

63. Ambassador Aleksandr Botsan Kharchenko quoted by *Tanjug*, 27 January 2010.

64. A Russian MFA desk officer for Bosnia and Croatia quoted in a cable from the U.S. Embassy in Moscow, 23 October 2008; https://wikileaksru.wordpress.com/2008/10/23/08moscow3123-bosnia-for-russia-solution-lies-with-the-eu.

65. The EUSR position was established in 2002. Starting with Paddy Ashdown that year, High Representatives also served as EUSR in a "double hatting" arrangement. The two posts were decoupled in 2011.

66. Most recently in an MFA statement on the twentieth anniversary of the Dayton Accords. http://www.mid.ru/en/foreign_policy/news/-/asset_publisher/cKNonkJE02Bw/content/id/1947249.

67. Olja Stanic, "Russia Purchases Bosnian Oil Assets," *The Moscow Times*, 5 February 2007.

68. *The Srpska Times*, 2 December 2014.
69. Major Russian banks like VTB and Sberbank refused to loan money to RS.
70. Bosnia's Membership Action Plan (MAP) is on hold as the two entities failed to agree on registering defense property as owned by the common state.
71. *Al Jazeera Balkans*, 30 August 2016.
72. *Slobodna Bosna*, 7 February 2017.
73. In accordance with the Sejdić–Finci judgment of the European Court of Human Rights obliging Bosnia to give equal rights to members of ethnic communities other than the Bosniaks, Serbs, and Croats, the three "constituent nations" under the Dayton arrangement.
74. Croatia hoped to replace Hungary as the main route to Slovenia and Italy. However, by 2012, it became clear it would host a branch rather than the main trunk line.
75. *Nacional*, 20 June 2010. Vladimir Socor, "Russian Oil Business Targeting EU's Entrant Croatia," *Eurasia Daily Monitor*, vol. 9, no. 20, *The Jamestown Foundation*, 30 January 2012.
76. Between 2006 and 2008, Russia supplied ten Mi-171 helicopters to Croatia. The consignment covered the Croatian share ($65 million) of Soviet debt owed to former Yugoslavia.
77. Russia blamed the reluctance to let Gazprom or Rosneft into INA on American pressure. Maria Grigoryan, "Ruski veleposlanik priča o tome kakvi će biti odnosi Rusije i Hrvatske u 2015" ["Russian Ambassador Speaking about what Russian–Croatian Relations will be in 2015"], Russia Beyond the Headlines, 9 December 2014.
78. Azimov mentioned the prospects of rising numbers of Russian tourists on Croatia's Adriatic coast as well as the potential for investment in the shipbuilding industry. Interview in *Nacional*, 29 March 2016.
79. Adelina Marini, "Russian Money Creeping into Croatia," *EUInside*, 14 July 2016.
80. "Croatia's Agrokor Signs Loan Deal with Russia's Sberbank," Reuters, 2 May 2016; Sven Milekić, "Russians May Take Over Croatia's Agrokor, Economist Says," *BalkanInsight*, 17 March 2017.
81. *The Slovenia Times*, 6 February 2017.
82. *Sputnik*, 31 July 2016.
83. Sintez operates a combined cycle thermal plan running on gas, with state-owned Toplofikacija holding 20 percent. In 2005, Lukoil acquired a network of petrol stations.
84. "Merkel Hat die Länder des Balkans zusammengebracht" ["Merkel has Brought Together the Balkan Countries"], *Frankfurter Allgemeiner Zeitung*, 30 November 2016. Russia's Balkan influence was the subject of talks that CIA director John Brennan held in Tirana in December 2016. *BalkanInsight*, 9 December 2016.
85. See for instance an article by the eminent TV host and Kremlin propagandist Dmitrii Kiselev, "Fond Sorosa podbiraet kadry dlya revolyutsii v Makedonii" ["The Soros Foundation is Choosing Cadres for a Revolution in Macedonia"], Vesti.RU, 24 May 2015. Available at http://www.vesti.ru/doc.html?id=2604657. See also "Moscow Expects Thorough Investigation of Reported Coup Attempt in Macedonia," *Sputnik*, 1 February 2015.
86. The theory originating from the Russian state-owned news portal *Sputnik* had made its way into the Balkan media and was finally voiced by Lavrov on 20 May 2015 during a hearing at Russia's State Duma.
87. "'Greater Albania' ambition setback for Balkans—president," B92, 15 May 2015.
88. Comment of the Press and Information Department at the MFA of Russia on the situation in Macedonia, 3 March 2017. http://www.mid.ru/press_service/video/-/asset_publisher/i6t41cq3VWP6/content/id/2666892.
89. The meeting with Biden was originally scheduled for June but he could not attend because of the death of his son. Nonetheless, Vučić used the opportunity to meet other senior officials, including Susan Rice, national security advisor to President Barack Obama.
90. *Nezavisne Novine*, 17 November 2014.
91. The Serbian Radical Party and the coalition between *Demokratska stranka Srbije*

and the conservative Dveri movement, which had sent observers to Crimea during the 2014 referendum, made it past the threshold.

92. John E. Schindler, "President Trump's First Foreign Policy Crisis: Balkan War Drums Beat Again," *The Observer*, 25 January 2017.

3 Across the Black Sea

1. *Sega Daily*, 23 October 2004.
2. *Ziarul de Iaşi*, 17 September 2005.
3. Statement made on the talkshow *Referendum*, Bulgarian National Television, 24 March 2014.
4. A paraphrase of "With Germany but never against Russia" attributed to King (Tsar) Boris III (1918–43).
5. Agerpres, 24 March 2014.
6. German Marshall Fund, Transatlantic Trends, Key Findings 2012, p. 43.
7. Richard Nixon's visit in August 1968 was followed by one by Gerald Ford in 1975 and Vice President George Bush in 1983.
8. Russia first acquired Bessarabia in 1812. The Paris Peace Treaty of 1856 terminating the Crimean War transferred to the Principality of Moldova the counties of Izmail, Cahul, and Bolgrad. Russia retook them in 1878 on the pretext that the concession had been made to Moldova rather than Romania.
9. The war terminated Russia's protectorate over the Danubian principalities dating back to 1829.
10. The region of Bukovina belonged to the Principality of Moldova until 1775, passing then to the Habsburgs before it was taken by Romania in 1918.
11. The Balkan League of 1912–13 uniting Bulgaria, Serbia, Greece, and Montenegro was championed by Russia as a bulwark against Austria-Hungary and Germany's influence in Southeast Europe. Its collapse during the Second Balkan War was a strategic loss for St Petersburg.
12. Transcript available through the Wilson Center, http://digitalarchive.wilsoncenter.org/document/117430.
13. In all likelihood, the United States was seeking reciprocal support from Moscow concerning the ongoing intervention against General Manuel Antonio Noriega in Panama. *Chicago Tribune*, 25 December 1989.
14. BSP was the new name adopted by the Bulgarian Communist Party (BCP) in April 1990.
15. Neither country's legislature had ratified it, a fact that then Prime Minister Petre Roman would bring up to his own credit in the years to come.
16. Zhelev lobbied Yeltsin to recognize Macedonia's independence in August 1992.
17. PSDR was renamed the Social Democratic Party (PSD) in January 2001 following a merger with a minor group, the Romanian Humanist Party (PUR).
18. Russia's ambassador Leonid Kerestedzhiiants promptly handed a note in protest. Greece, France, and Germany were sympathetic with the Russian view at the time. *Capital*, 10 April 1997.
19. President Iliescu backpedalled after cross-party consultations, fearing—in hindsight, rightly—about his chances of re-election. Public opinion was against the treaty with Moscow.
20. Valerian Stan, "Rusofobia: Un Snobism Pagubos," *Cotidianul*, 8 February 1999.
21. Tom Gallagher, *Theft of a Nation: Romania since Communism*, London: Hurst, 2005, p. 215. The war was unpopular in both countries also because of the losses resulting from the UN sanctions against the Federal Republic of Yugoslavia since 1992. Constantinescu's decision not to run for re-election in November 2000 also had to do with Romania's unpopular involvement in the war against Serbia.
22. Leslie Holmes, "Russia's Relations with Former External Empire," in Amin Saikal and William Maley (eds), *Russia: In Search of its Future*, Cambridge: Cambridge University Press, 1995, p. 134.

23. Dimitar Bechev, *Constructing South East Europe: The Politics of Balkan Regional Co-operation*, Basingstoke: Palgrave Macmillan, 2011.
24. The Yamburg Agreement with Bulgaria was concluded in 1986.
25. A dispute concerned the Krivoy Rog Mining and Processing Works of Oxidised Ore, a joint venture started in 1986 near Dnipropetrovsk. Russia's position was that outstanding claims ought to go to Ukraine. Romania, which remains a shareholder in the non-operational plant, has contributed an estimated $800 million, making this its largest investment abroad.
26. *Dnevnik*, 24 February 2002.
27. The case of Multigroup and its boss, the oligarch Iliya Pavlov, who was assassinated in March 2003, is studied in Misha Glenny, *McMafia: A Journey through the Global Criminal Underworld*, New York: Knopf, 2008, Chapter 1: Death of an American.
28. *Capital*, 24 October 1998. Bulgargaz and Gazprom switched to direct sales only in 2002.
29. The two sides discussed upgrading cross-border infrastructure as well as proposals for bartering Romanian wheat, meat, and cooking oil for gas. See "Romania, Gazprom Plans Gas Pipe to Turkey," Reuters, 26 November 1998.
30. In 1998, it accounted for a full 14 percent of Bulgarian GDP and 8 percent of exports. Adnan Vatansever, "Russian Involvement in Eastern Europe's Petroleum Industry: The Case of Bulgaria," Global Market Briefings, 2006, p. 18.
31. Lukoil took over Serbia's Beopetrol in 2003 and expanded into Macedonia in 2005.
32. Petrotel was originally developed by American investors at the turn of the twentieth century. Neftochim dates back to the 1960s. Still, in 1998, Petrotel was technologically equipped to refine crude oil at a depth of 82 percent, which corresponded to EU standards but was rare in Russia itself. *Kommersant*, 17 January 1998.
33. John Beyerle, "Bulgaria's Most Influential Politician: Great Hopes, Murky Ties, Sofia," 9 May 2006, available at https://wikileaks.org/plusd/cables/06SOFIA647_a.html.
34. CNN, 18 February 2003.
35. The Molotov–Ribbentrop Pact was referenced in a separate, legally non-binding, ministerial statement, a decision rebuked by the opposition. A bilateral commission of historians was tasked to inquire into the question of the First World War's "national treasure." The treaty reaffirmed the party's right to join alliances—vaguely committing them not to "strengthen their own security at the expense of other states."
36. The plan to revive Belene followed from the shutdown during the period 2004–7 of four units at the Kozloduy nuclear power plant, which had been commissioned in 1974. As in other Central and Eastern European countries, the decommissioning formed part of EU membership conditionality and was justified on grounds of safety.
37. Bulgaria stayed out, presumably because the facility across the border with Romania was sufficient to cover its own territory. *Novinite*, 5 May 2011.
38. Polls have shown that 10 to 20 percent of the public support reunification with Romania.
39. He was supported by the local Bulgarian community and had one of their number, Vasile Tarlev, as prime minister.
40. *Capital*, 10 November 2006.
41. *Standard*, 3 February 2006.
42. AES, in which Gazprombank held a 49.8 percent stake, was joined by Siemens and Areva (France).
43. One possible reason was its exclusion from the discussions between Moscow and Sofia on financing the 51 percent stake held by Bulgaria's National Electricity Company. See U.S. Embassy Cable, Bulgaria: Belene Nuclear Power Plant: More Troubles, REF: A. SOFIA 0069 B. SEPTEL, 7 July 2009. Available at https://www.theguardian.com/world/us-embassy-cables-documents/215404.
44. He used the pretext that consultant HSBC had produced a negative feasibility study

whereas the recommendation was for the government to continue the search for a strategic investor to replace RWE.

45. In September 2013, police and the State Agency for National Security (DANS) searched the officers of Risk Engineering, the principal consultant of the Belene nuclear power plant, on suspicions of embezzlement. Bogomil Manchev, the CEO of Risk Engineering, explained the episode as a plot by his competitors. According to a U.S. Embassy cable from 2006, "[Manchev's] power in the [Bulgarian] energy sector was rumored to be all-encompassing." Dirty Energy: Corruption and Lack of Transparency Plague Bulgarian Energy Sector, Sofia, 20 December 2006, available at https://wikileaks.org/plusd/cables/06SOFIA1691_a.html.

46. *Kommersant*, 21 August 2013.

47. The list included a subsidiary of Vodstroy 98, linked to the Movement of Rights and Freedoms (MRF), Technoexportstroy, which was managed by former President Georgi Pârvanov's secretary, and Glavbolgarstroy, which had handled large public contracts during GERB's term in office (2009–12). There was also a company connected to the First Investment Bank, a large lender.

48. The remaining 70 percent of the Bulgarian contribution was to be covered by loans from private banks.

49. Funds were frozen in response to changes in the Energy Act intended to bypass EU legislation and facilitate South Stream.

50. Peevski's appointment as head of the State Agency for National Security (DANS) in June 2013 triggered public outrage and a wave of street protests in Sofia.

51. On KTB's bankruptcy: Matthias Williams and Tsvetelia Tsolova, "Accusations fly in Bulgaria's murky bank run," Reuters, 4 July 2014. Also the investigative website www.ktbfiles.com launched by a coalition of Bulgarian NGOs and watchdogs.

52. Interview with the Interfax and Anadolu news agencies, 13 November 2015. Full text available at http://en.special.kremlin.ru/events/president/news/50682.

53. *Mediapool*, 7 June 2016.

54. In November 2011, Bulgaria and Azerbaijan concluded an agreement for the delivery of 1 bcm per annum. The gas could arrive through the TANAP pipeline traversing Turkey and the Transadriatic Pipeline (TAP), its extension into Greece.

55. *Sega*, 7 November 2016.

56. See Dimitar Bechev, "A Very Bulgarian Drama: What Rumen Radev's Presidential Election Victory Means for Bulgarian Politics," European Politics and Policy (EUROPP) Blog, London School of Economics, 14 November 2016. http://blogs.lse.ac.uk/europpblog/2016/11/14/rumen-radev-bulgaria-russia-president.

57. The early elections were triggered after Borisov tendered his resignation in November 2016, following Radev's victory. In the campaign, Borisov accused the caretaker government of endorsing a greater NATO presence in the Black Sea. Mariya Cheresheva, "NATO Black Sea Plans Cause Dissent in Bulgaria," *Balkan Insight*, 22 February 2017.

58. The PSD-led government of Victor Ponta was ousted by a wave of anti-corruption protests in December 2015. For a year Romania was governed by a technocratic cabinet appointed by President Iohannis and headed by Dacian Cioloş, formerly EU Commissioner for Agriculture.

59. Foreign Minister Meleşcanu: "I have not signed any protocol with Russia's Embassy," *AgePress*, 21 February 2017.

4 Friends with Benefits

1. "Russia and Greece: Co-operation for Peace and Prosperity," *Kathimerini*, 26 May 2016.

2. Takis Michas, "Athens Rekindles Its Russian Romance," *The Wall Street Journal*, 21 January 2015. Sam Jones, Kerin Home, and Courtney Weaver, "Alarm Bells Ring over Syriza's Russian Links," *The Financial Times*, 28 January 2015.

3. Meike Dülffer, Carsten Luther, and Zacharias Zacharakis, "Im Netz der russischen Ideologen," *Die Zeit*, 6 February 2015.

4. Quoted by *Sputnik*, 17 April 2015.

5. Neli Esipova and Julie Ray, "Greeks Oppose Economic Sanctions Against Russia," 25 August 2015. Available at http://www.gallup.com/poll/184811/greeks-oppose-economic-sanctions-against-russia.aspx.

6. Mark Leonard and Nicu Popescu, *Power Audit of EU–Russian Relations*, ECFR, 2007, pp. 27–8.

7. There was an earlier assault in 830 when the Rus plundered settlements off the coast of the Sea of Marmara. The Rus, a mix of Eastern Slavs and Scandinavians (in all likelihood the governing elite), largely manned the so-called Varangian Guard (*Tágma tōn Varángōn*), an elite force attached to the emperor.

8. In 1708, Peter the Great reformed Cyrillic extensively, dropping several Greek characters with no phonetic equivalent in Russian. Peter's civil script (*grazhdanskii shrift*) version forms the basis of the Cyrillic used in Bulgaria and differs from Serbian Cyrillic.

9. The French navy blockaded the port of Piraeus to prevent Greece from joining on the side of Russia.

10. The reigning House of Glücksburg, hailing from Schleswig-Holstein—disputed between Denmark and Prussia—was originally staunchly pro-British and anti-German. Still, Queen Olga of the Hellenes, the wife of the dynasty's founder George I (1863–1913) and mother of Constantine I, was a niece of Emperor Alexander II.

11. Greece participated in the Entente's anti-Bolshevik campaign in Ukraine between 1919 and 1920.

12. In response, Tito closed the Yugoslav border, cutting off supplies to the Greek communist guerrillas. A good part of the KKE stayed loyal to Moscow until the bitter end. Having rejected Eurocommunism in the 1970s, the party continues to enjoy support—winning 7 percent at the national elections in September 2015. Syriza originates from the so-called KKE of the Interior, a Eurocommunist faction.

13. Nikiforos Diamandouros, "Cultural Dualism Revisited," in Anna Triandaphyllidou, Ruby Gropas, and Hara Kouki, *The Greek Crisis and European Modernity*, Basingstoke: Palgrave Macmillan, 2013, pp. 208–33.

14. Following the 1974 invasion of Cyprus, Prime Minister Constantine Karamanlis withdrew Greece from NATO's integrated command.

15. John Loulis, "Papandreou's Foreign Policy," *Foreign Affairs*, Winter 1984–85.

16. *The Sunday Times*, 4 August 1985. Interestingly, the last commander of the Soviet Black Sea Fleet (1985–91), Admiral Mikhail Khronopoulo (Hronopoulos), was an ethnic Greek from Crimea.

17. The $2.4 billion contract envisaged the increase to 2.4 bcm between 1992 and 2002. The cost of the contract was $2.3 billion per year. Per Hogselius, *Red Gas: Russia and the Origins of European Energy Dependence*, Basingstoke: Palgrave Macmillan, 2013, p. 200.

18. *The Financial Times*, 13 August 1984.

19. The plant came onstream in 1986 at Amyntaio, near the northern town of Florina. Energomachexport and Zarubezhenergoproekt took part in the work.

20. Cyprus gained independence in 1960, having been under British rule since 1878. The constitution established a power-sharing system allowing for the political representation of the island's Turkish community. Violent clashes between Greeks and Turks in 1964 made the Cypriot conflict an international issue. In 1974, after a military coup in Nicosia backed by the colonels' junta governing Greece, Turkey intervened to prevent unification and occupied the northern third of the island, including parts of Nicosia. The Turkish Republic of Northern Cyprus proclaimed independence in 1983, but this has been recognized only by Turkey. Negotiations to reunify the island have been underway, in one form or the other, since 1975. Although leaders of the Greek and Turkish community agreed to establish a "bizonal bicommunal federation" as early as 1977, Cyprus remains divided to date. In April 2004, the Greek Cypriots voted down a reunification plan prepared by UN Secretary General Kofi Annan, which had won the approval of the Turkish Cypriots. Days later, on 1 May, the Republic of Cyprus represented by the government in Nicosia joined the EU.

21. The Soviets supported Makarios against General George Grivas, head of the para-military EOKA and subsequently commander of the National Guard. See Augustus Richard Norton, "The Soviet Union and Cyprus," in Norma Salem (ed.), *Cyprus: A Regional Conflict and its Resolution*, London: Macmillan, 1992, pp. 100–13.

22. In March 1996, for instance, Defense Minister Gerasimos Arsenis called for an anti-Turkish coalition comprised of Greece, Armenia, Syria, Iran, Iraq, Bulgaria, and Russia. Athens developed military and intelligence ties with Damascus.

23. The PCA remained frozen until December 1997 because of the First Chechen War.

24. *Athens News Agency*, 25 June 1994.

25. Deputy Foreign Minister Viktor Afanasievskii attended the summit of Balkan heads of state and government in Crete (3–4 November 1997), the first of its kind, which institutionalized the Southeast European Co-operation Process (SEECP).

26. Centrist and even center-right politicians such as Sophocles Venizelos and Spyros Markezinis looked to Moscow as a tactical ally as far back as the late 1950s. Sotiris Rizas, "Domestic and External Factors in Greece's Relations with the Soviet Union: Early Cold War to Détente," *Mediterranean Quarterly*, vol. 24, no. 1, 2013, pp. 57–80.

27. A reference to Aleksii's ecclesiastical title, Patriarch of Moscow and of All the Russias.

28. *Kommersant*, 21 March 2000. The EU accession of Cyprus (2004) and of Romania and Bulgaria (2007) widened the circle of predominantly Eastern Orthodox member states.

29. In the beginning of the 1990s, the population of Greek origin in Armenia was esti-mated at 7,000, in Azerbaijan 2,000, in Georgia 105,000, in Ukraine 150,000, and in Russia 90,000. Panagiota Manoli, "Greece's Engagement with the Black Sea Economic Co-operation," Xenophon Paper no. 2, International Center for Black Sea Studies, 2007, p. 69.

30. *Kommersant*, 12 September 1995.

31. Monteagle Sterns, *Entangled Allies: U.S. Policy Toward Greece, Turkey, and Cyprus*, The Council on Foreign Relations, 1992, pp. 65–6.

32. Interview with Lieutenant General Viktor Samoilov, director of *Rosvooruzhenie*, *Kommersant*, 29 November 1994.

33. Interviewed in 2013, Aleksei Kudrin, finance minister between 2000 and 2011, drew a link between the purchase of the missiles with the Russian government's decision not to toughen rules regarding offshore banking in Cyprus, amidst the 1998 finan-cial meltdown. *Kommersant*, 26 March 2013.

34. BBC News, 16 February 1998.

35. Hogselius, *Red Gas*, p. 234.

36. After a peak of 85 percent in 2005, Gazprom's share actually shrank thanks to lique-fied natural gas imports from Algeria's Sonatrach and, after 2007, an interconnector pipeline with Turkey.

37. Quoted by the Associated Press, 8 December 2001.

38. Moscow settled for 51 percent of the venture, having insisted on 90 percent before. Putin negotiated the deal in September 2006 with Karamanlis and the Bulgarian President Pârvanov during the visit to Athens.

39. Aristotle Tziampiris, "Greek Foreign Policy and Russia: Political Realignment, Civilization, and Realism," *Mediterranean Quarterly*, vol. 21, no. 2, 2010, pp. 78–9.

40. Russia's share would be split between Transneft, Gazprom Neft, and Rosneft.

41. For a snapshot of the internal debates at the time, see Tziampiris, "Greek Foreign Policy and Russia."

42. Halfway through the statement, in between "Switzerland" and "Italy," Putin briefly inspected his necktie's label, eliciting smiles from aides and guests. Anna Smolchenko, "Greece Signs on to South Stream, *The Moscow Times*, 30 April 2008.

43. *Mediapool*, 29 May 2013.

44. The U-turn was probably motivated by the ongoing anti-trust probe carried out by the European Commission. *Kathimerini*, 21 April 2013.

45. Prime Minister Andonis Samaras (ND) lobbied Azerbaijan actively. The DESFA sale ran into difficulties in 2015 when the European Commission ordered SOCAR to surrender 17 percent of the company in order to comply with EU competition rules.

46. *To Vima*, 10 June 2013.

47. RT, 19 June 2015.

48. In the meantime, Greece has been exploring some alternative ideas. In February 2016, the CEOs of Gazprom, DEPA, and Edison (subsidiary of Électricité de France, EDF) signed a memorandum to develop a pipeline route between Greece and Italy. The scheme resuscitated ITGI-Poseidon, an interconnector pipeline originally proposed by DEPA and Edison in 2005.

49. George Christou, "Bilateral Relations with Russia and the Impact on EU Policy: The Cases of Cyprus and Greece," *Journal of Contemporary European Studies*, vol. 19, no. 2, June 2011, p. 230.

50. Emily Young, "Russian Money in Cyprus: Why Is There So Much?" BBC News, 13 March 2013.

51. The treaty allowed capital gains from companies registered in Cyprus to be taxed at 10 percent, half the rate in Russia. Moreover, Cypriot laws made it possible for assets to be freely transferred to other offshore destinations, for example the Virgin Islands.

52. Russia blocked a resolution on financing UNFICYP, unhappy about the increase of its contribution, but endorsed a redraft soon thereafter.

53. *Kommersant*, 23 April 2004. In all likelihood, it was upon a Cypriot request that Russia imposed the veto. James Ker-Lindsay, "Membership and Foreign Policy," in James Ker-Lindsay, Fiona Mullen, and Hubert Faustman (eds), *An Island in Europe: The EU and the Transformation of Cyprus*, London: I. B. Tauris, 2011, p. 125. For a positive appraisal of the veto, Costas Melakopides, *Russia–Cyprus Relations: A Pragmatic Idealist Perspective*, Basingstoke: Palgrave Macmillan, 2016, pp. 78–9.

54. Quoted in Christou, "Bilateral Relations with Russia and the Impact on EU Policy," pp. 225–36.

55. "Voenno-tehnicheskoe sotrudnichestvo Rossii i Kipra" ["Dossier on Military Technical Co-operation between Russia and Cyprus"], ITAR-TASS, 24 February 2015.

56. EU Foreign Affairs Council on 9 February 2015, Kassoulides explained that the agreement concerned solely "the maintenance of Russian military equipment sold to Cyprus in prior years, and the spare market parts according to existing contracts." Russian ships could enter Cypriot ports to undergo repair or be refueled—or indeed to evacuate civilians from Syria. *Protothema*, 9 February 2015.

57. The motion was introduced by AKEL.

58. RT, 31 January 2015.

59. *Greek Reporter*, 19 September 2013.

60. According to the article, Leonid Reshetnikov, head of the Russian Institute for Strategic Studies (RISI), played the go-between. Pavlos Papadopoulos, "O Leoníd, o Aléksis ke o Panagiótis" ["Leonid, Alexis, and Panagiotis"], *To Vima*, 19 July 2015. See also *Greek Reporter*, 21 July 2015.

61. Putin to Hollande: "Tsipras asked to print drachmas in Russia," *To Vima* (English version), 14 October 2016.

62. "Alleged Greek $10bn Plea to Putin for Printing Drachma Not True—Kremlin," RT, 22 July 2015.

63. The statement was made at the St Petersburg International Economic Forum attended by Tsipras and Economy Minister Lafazanis, *Sputnik*, 20 June 2015.

64. *Komsomolskaya Pravda*, 13 July 2015.

65. Elena Tiufaniuk and Elena Zubova, "Krakh Atlantidy: kak Rossiia spasala, no tak i ne spasla Kipr" ["The Crash of Atlantis: How Russia was Trying to Save but did not Save Cyprus"], *Forbes.ru*, 2 April 2013.

66. The Cyprus crisis was one of the reasons why, in May 2013, the Duma introduced legislation forbidding parliamentarians and civil servants from holding bank accounts, stocks, and bonds overseas. The law excluded real estate but introduced tougher disclosure rules.

67. Sara Stefanini, "Cyprus Fears Russia could Wreck Reunification, *Politico.eu*, 14 January 2017.

68. Since 2004, Turkey has blocked parts of the so-called Berlin Plus arrangement between NATO and the EU enabling the Common Security and Defence Policy missions to use alliance assets. As a tit for tat, Cyprus has blocked Turkey's participation in the European Defence Agency and EU structure.

5 The Russian–Turkish Marriage of Convenience

1. Quoted in Oleg Kolobov, Aleksandr Kornilov, and Fatih Özbay, *Sovremennye turetsko-rossiiskie otnosheniia. Problemy sotrudnichestva i perspektivy razvitiia* [*Contemporary Turkish–Russian Relations: Problems of Co-operation and Development Perspectives*], Nizhnii Novgorod: Nizhnyi Novgorod University, 2004, p. 28.
2. Dmitri Trenin, *Post-Imperium: A Eurasian Story*, Washington D.C.: Carnegie Endowment for International Peace, 2007, p. 123.
3. *Hürriyet*, 6 September 2008.
4. In an ironic twist, the Putin–Erdoğan reconciliation summit in August 2016 occurred in the "Greek Room" at Constantine Palace (*Konstantinovskii Dvorets*), named after one of its former owners, Grand Duke Konstantin Pavlovich (1779–1831). The grandson of Catherine the Great and named after Emperor Constantine the Great, he was primed to be the head of a restored Byzantine Empire. The irony was all the more complete because of Erdoğan's strong links to his native Istanbul district of Kasımpaşa, abutting the Golden Horn, from where Sultan Mehmet the Conqueror's navy launched its assault on Constantinople in May 1453.
5. A brilliant essay by the Dutch historian Erik-Jan Zürcher has located the origins of a vast number of members of the Committee of Union and Progress and the subsequent Kemalist generation in a relatively narrow region of northern Greece and today's Republic of Macedonia and Kosovo. "Who were the Young Turks," in *Young Turk Legacy and Nation Building*, London: I. B. Tauris, 2010, pp. 95–110.
6. Ushakov had delivered a series of devastating defeats to the Ottomans in the Black Sea during the Russo-Ottoman War of 1787–92.
7. Russia's navy obtained the right of unrestricted passage into the Mediterranean in 1833, which lasted until 1841.
8. Quoted in Nicholas Gvosdev, *Russian Foreign Policy: Interests, Vectors and Sectors*, Thousand Oaks, CA: CQ Press, 201, p. 324.
9. The wars of 1877–78 and 1914–17 were fought out of necessity. On both occasions, Russia was drawn into a military confrontation because of its allies and clients. Even though it harbored realistic aspirations to take control of the Straits in the First World War, the outbreak came too early—before the Tsarist Empire had developed sufficient naval capabilities to attain that goal. See Michael Reynolds, *The Clash and Collapse of the Ottoman and Russian Empires, 1908–1918*, Cambridge: Cambridge University Press, 2011.
10. Dominic Lieven, *Empire: The Russian State and its Rivals*, New Haven, CT: Yale University Press, 2000, pp. 128–9. Iver Neumann and Einar Wigen have gone a step further, arguing about the presence of a specific state tradition associated with the Eurasian steppe that shaped the politics of the Russian and the Ottoman Empires as well as their successors, the Russia and Turkey of today. See "Remnants of the Mongol Imperial Tradition," in Sandra Halperin and Ronen Palan (eds), *Legacies of Empire: Imperial Roots of the Contemporary Global Order*, Cambridge: Cambridge University Press, 2015.
11. Completed in 1928, the monument also includes the prominent Bolshevik commander Kliment (Klim) Voroshilov, known as "the Iron Commissar." Voroshilov's figure is often mistaken for Mikhail Frunze, another prominent Red Army general who, as ambassador of the Ukrainian Soviet Socialist Republic to Ankara in 1921, had befriended Mustafa Kemal.
12. The extermination of Armenians was justified with the Russian advance into Ottoman territory in eastern Anatolia during the First World War. The then Young

Turk regime viewed the Armenians as a fifth column conspiring against the empire. See Ronald Gregor Suny, "They Can Live in the Desert but Nowhere Else," *A History of the Armenian Genocide*, Princeton N.J.: Princeton University Press, 2015, p. 78ff.

13. Further details in Selim Deringil, *Turkish Policy During the Second World War: An "Active" Neutrality*, Cambridge: Cambridge University Press, 1989, chapters 5–6. Germany could rely only on battleships that had entered the Black Sea prior to the invasion of the USSR. It shipped submarines in part down the Danube to assemble them in allied Romania. Eager to escape occupation by either the Germans or the USSR, Turkey switched sides again in early 1945, joining the anti-Hitler coalition.

14. The Soviet leader wanted the return of the cities of Kars and Ardahan in eastern Anatolia annexed to the Russian Empire in 1878 and then ceded by the Bolsheviks back to Turkey in 1921.

15. Set up with the 1955 Baghdad Pact, the Central Treaty Organization brought together American allies in the Middle East: Turkey, Iran, Iraq, and Pakistan, as well as Great Britain.

16. With the so-called "Johnson Telegram" of 1964, President Lyndon Johnson communicated to his counterpart İsmet İnönü that the United States was not prepared to endorse a Turkish invasion of Cyprus. See Duygu Sezer, "Peaceful Coexistence: Turkey and the Near East in Soviet Foreign Policy," *The Annals of the American Academy of Political and Social Science*, vol. 481, Soviet Foreign Policy in an Uncertain World (September 1985), pp. 117–26.

17. Bulgaria had been supplying Turkey with electricity since the 1970s.

18. In March 1991, Özal, elected president in 1989, signed a co-operation agreement in Moscow with Mikhail Gorbachev, extending the 1984 document.

19. Özal oversaw the setting up of the Turkish International Co-operation and Development Agency (*Türk İşbirliği ve Kalkınma İdaresi Başkanlığı*, TIKA), established in 1992 as part of the Foreign Ministry.

20. Ankara's vocal denunciation of Russian actions in the First Chechen War (1994–96) at international meetings, including the Organization of the Islamic Conference (OIC), irked Moscow. Russia accused Turkey of sending volunteers and material support to the separatists, or at least allowing them to operate freely from its territory. At the G7 meeting in Halifax (June 1995), Yeltsin told reporters that the Chechen leader, General Dzhokhar Dudayev, had been granted asylum in Turkey, a claim denied by the authorities in Ankara. By that point, Dudayev had visited Turkey twice—and even met President Süleyman Demirel in October 1993.

21. Syria hosted the PKK leader Abdullah Öcalan. Greece and Syria concluded a defense agreement in March 1996.

22. Quoted in Tuncay Babalı, "Implications of the Baku–Tbilissi–Ceyhan Main Oil Pipeline Project," *Perceptions. Journal of International Affairs*, Winter 2005, p. 22.

23. In the same zero-sum logic, the Turkish national-security establishment was concerned that Moscow was prepared to use the PKK to sabotage the BTC.

24. President Demirel remained a lone standard bearer of the cause until the end of his presidential term in 2000.

25. Demirel made his way to Moscow shortly after the Armenians had taken over two strategic towns, Shushi and Laichin, and were also closing in on the exclave of Nakhichevan. Turkey was providing arms and advisors to the Azeri forces.

26. *Milliyet*, 11 January 1997.

27. The idea for BSEC dates back to diplomatic consultations by Turkey, USSR, Romania, and Bulgaria in Ankara in 1990. In 1992, the organization brought together all the littoral countries, together with Armenia and Azerbaijan.

28. From November 1992 onwards, a joint Turkish–Russian economic commission started operation.

29. Philip Robins, *Suits and Uniforms: Turkish Foreign Policy since the Cold War*, London: Hurst, 2003, p. 223. Some estimates put the figure as high as $15 billion. Kolobov et al., *Sovremennye turetsko-rossiiskie otnosheniia*, p. 23.

30. Figures quoted in Kolobov et al., *Sovremennye turetsko-rossiiskie otnosheniia*, p. 27; *Izvestiya*, 19 December 2001.

31. Erbakan was amongst the invitees for Aslan Maskhadov's inauguration as president in February 1997. *Hürriyet Daily News*, 3 February 1997.

32. In 2002, Turkey promised Russia it would catch and extradite Movladi Udugov, Chechnya's former foreign minister, who was allegedly hiding on its territory.

33. The drama echoed the 1996 hijacking of the ferry *Avrasya* (Eurasia) in Trabzon. The takeover was carried out by a group of Turks of Caucasian ancestry, a Chechen and an Abkhaz led by Muhammet Tokcan, who was also responsible for the Swissôtel episode. The hostage drama catalyzed a Russian–Turkish agreement on fighting terrorism. However, thousands of Salafis from the North Caucasus continue to reside in Turkey, many of whom have fought in Syria and Iraq, a constant point of friction with Russia. Unlike the nineteenth-century Circassian diaspora, which tends to have secular orientation, these recent arrivals support AKP.

34. Habibe Özdal et al., *Turkey–Russia Relations in the Post-Cold War Era: Current Dynamics—Future Prospects*, Report 13–06, International Strategic Association (USAK), July 2013, p. 21.

35. Öcalan had to leave Russia for Italy and then Greece, to be ultimately captured by Turkish commandos in Kenya in February 1999.

36. Robins, *Suits and Uniforms*, p. 220.

37. Several months beforehand, in April 1997, the two had contracted an additional 8 bcm for the Trans-Balkan Pipeline.

38. As part of the deal, ENI won an informal commitment by Russia to be granted rights over a gas field near the Caspian port of Astrakhan.

39. The BTC had much greater capacity compared to the two other pipelines inaugurated at the same time: from Baku to the Georgian port of Supsa (145,000 barrels/day) and to Novorossiisk in Russia (105,000 barrels/day). Those two projects that failed had originally been a disappointment for Ankara. It had failed to link the conditions of their construction to a commitment by Baku to the BTC.

40. *The New York Times*, 15 December 1997.

41. Robins, *Suits and Uniforms*, p. 224.

42. Duygu Bazoğlu Sezer, "Turkish–Russian Relations: The Challenges of Reconciling Geopolitical Competition and Economic Partnership," *Turkish Studies*, vol. 1, no. 1 (2000), p. 62.

43. *NTV*, 8 September 2010. The pipeline project was subsequently abandoned.

44. Fiona Hill and Ömer Taşpınar, "Turkey and Russia: Axis of Excluded," *Survival*, vol. 48, no. 1 (2006), pp. 81–92.

45. "What Turkey needs precisely is a new quest. I think the best way to deal with that is to be together with the Russian Federation and, if it is possible not to neglect the U.S., to include Iran. Turkey has seen no help from the EU. EU views negatively the issues that are of interest to Turkey." *Radikal*, 8 March 2002.

46. Dugin's book *Osnovy geopolitiki* (*The Fundamentals of Geopolitics*) was translated into Turkish in 2003 and he visited the country more than once—notably on the eve of the failed coup attempt on 15 July 2016. Şener Aktürk, "Fourth Style of Politics: Eurasianism as a Pro-Russian Rethinking of Turkey's Geopolitical Identity," *Turkish Studies*, vol. 16, no. 1 (2015), pp. 54–79. See also Marlène Laruelle, *Russo-Turkish Rapprochement through the Idea of Eurasia: Alexander Dugin's Networks in Turkey*, Washington, D.C.: The Jamestown Foundation, 2008. Ozgür Tüfekçi, *The Foreign Policy of Modern Turkey: Power and the Ideology of Eurasianism*, London: I.B. Tauris, 2017.

47. Perinçek was released from prison in 2014. On the realignment following the coup attempt of 15 July, see Omer Taşpınar and Gönül Tol, "Erdoğan's Turn to the Kemalists," *Foreign Affairs*, 27 October 2016.

48. Nikolai Podgornyi was acting head of state when he visited in 1972. Putin's visit was originally scheduled for September, but the tragic hostage drama in the town of Beslan in northern Ossetia made him postpone the trip.

49. In Sochi, they were discussing Russia's co-operation in the fight against the PKK, following a bomb attack in the resort town of Kuşadası. *Kommersant*, 18 July 2004.
50. Erdoğan was initially not eligible to serve as prime minister because he was prevented from running in the 2002 general election. He took up the position only in March 2003, after winning a by-election in Siirt, a town in southeastern Turkey.
51. That is why the State Department was hard at work to convince Bulgaria and Romania to join Black Sea Harmony. See Black Sea: Romania/Black Sea Harmony and Black Sea Forum, 06ANKARA2482, 5 May 2006, available at https://wikileaks. org/plusd/cables/06ANKARA2482_a.html; Bulgaria: MFA Takes Hard Line on Black Sea Harmony, 20 February 2007, available at https://wikileaks.org/plusd/ cables/07SOFIA87_a.html. On Turkey's assurances that Black Sea Harmony was a bridge to NATO, see a Turkish MFA Official: "NATO Involvement in the Black Sea is our End Game," 4 August 2005, available at https://wikileaks.org/plusd/ cables/05ANKARA2060_a.html.
52. Around 2002, the two militaries intensified contacts. Ankara was visited by the Russian Chief of Staff, General Anatolii Kvashnin, in January. His Turkish counterpart, General Kıvrıkoğlu, returned the call in June 2002. They adopted a "Framework Agreement on Co-operation in the Military Field and Agreement on Co-operation in Training of the Military Personnel." See Şener Aktürk, "Turkish–Russian Relations after the Cold War," *Turkish Studies*, vol. 7, no. 3 (2006) p. 344.
53. At the Bucharest Summit in April 2008, Turkey supported granting Georgia a Membership Action Plan (MAP), but nonetheless it was not eager to push the issue unilaterally against the wishes of France or Germany, who advised caution. Turkey/NATO: Turkey and Our Bucharest Summit Priorities, Cable from the U.S. Embassy in Ankara, 21 March 2008. Available at https://wikileaks.org/plusd/ cables/08ANKARA567_a.html.
54. *Milliyet*, 2 September 2008.
55. One of his objectives was to dispel doubts that Russia was putting pressure on Turkey by delaying truck drivers at its border crossings.
56. Article 18, para D. "In the event that one or more countries without a shore on the Black Sea desire to send naval forces into the Black Sea, for a humanitarian purpose, the said forces cannot exceed 8,000 tons." The general limit instituted by the Convention is 30,000 tonnes for a single country. See Chapter 6.
57. Richard Holbrooke, "The End of a Romance," *The Washington Post*, 16 February 2005.
58. "Both the Karabakh and Turkish–Armenian problems are extremely complicated in their own right," Putin argued, "and I don't think they should be joined together in a package." He continued, "Each problem is hard to resolve even taken on its own, and if we lump them together, any hope of their resolution automatically recedes into the distant future." Quoted in Richard Weitz, "Russian–Turkish Relations, Steadfast and Changing," *Mediterranean Quarterly*, vol. 21, no. 3 (2010), p. 77.
59. Trade between Turkey and Tatarstan exceeded $3 billion. Sergey Markedonov and Nataliya Ul'chenko, "Turkey and Russia: An Evolving Relationship," *Carnegie Endowment for International Peace*, 19 August 2011.
60. On 31 May 2010, Israeli commandos raided a group of six ships carrying humanitarian supplies to blockaded Gaza, killing eight Turkish citizens onboard. The "Gaza Freedom Flotilla" had been put together by the Humanitarian Relief Foundation (*İnsani Yardım Vakfı*), an Islamist NGO close to the AKP. In response, Turkey recalled its ambassador from Israel and cancelled joint military exercises. Although the Israeli prime minister, Binyamin Netanyahu, offered an apology in 2013, encouraged by the United States, it was not until 2016 that ties with Turkey returned to normal.
61. Mensur Akgün, Sabiha Senyücel Gündogar, Aybars Görgülü, and Erdem Aydın, *Foreign Policy Perceptions in Turkey*, Istanbul: TESEV, 2011, and Türkiye Sosyal-Siyasal Eğilimler Araştırması, Farklı Bir Bakış, 2012. Quoted in James W. Warhola and Eğemen B. Bezci, "The Return of President Putin and Russian–Turkish

Relations: Where Are They Headed?" *Sage Open*, July–September 2013, p. 2. Available at http://sgo.sagepub.com/content/spsgo/3/3/2158244013503165.full.pdf.

62. Quoted in Suat Kınıklıoğlu and Valerii Morkva, "An Anatomy of Turkish–Russian Relations," *Journal of Southeast European and Black Sea Studies*, vol. 7, no. 4 (2007).

63. In January 2010 the Council had its first session in Moscow. Taking part with Erdoğan were Foreign Minister Ahmet Davutoğlu, Foreign Trade Minister Zafer Cağlayan, Energy and Natural Resources Minister Taner Yıldız, Agriculture and Rural Affairs Minister Mehdi Eker, and Transportation Minister Binali Yıldırım. Reuters, 11 January 2010.

64. Some estimates of Turkish exports, together with tourism and the turnover of companies operating in Russia, have put the overall exchange at $65 billion. "Turkish Investments Come Under Spotlight as Relations Worsen," *Today's Zaman*, 29 November 2015.

65. By way of compensation and as part of the 1997 deal on Blue Stream, the Turkish government awarded a contract to Stroitransgaz for the expansion of the national gas grid. In 1998, Turkish firms agreed to hire a quota of local workers in addition to the ones brought in from Turkey.

66. Figure quoted by Erdoğan at a joint press conference with Putin in Moscow, 6 August 2009. Transcript available at http://www.turkey.mid.ru/hron/hron_e_29.html. In 2008 alone, Turks carried out projects to the tune of $3.9 billion, making Russia their second most significant market after Turkmenistan ($5.38 billion in 2008).

67. Data in Kolobov et al., *Sovremennye turetsko-rossiiskie otnosheniia*.

68. "Russian Tourists Flooding into Turkey," *Hürriyet Daily News*, 31 October 2014.

69. Under a twenty-five-year contract signed in August 1996 that includes a "take-or-pay" clause.

70. The standoff was resolved in November 2012 when Turkish authorities licensed four private companies, including Bosphorus Gaz that is majority-owned by Gazprom, to contract Russian gas and supply it directly to the domestic market.

71. The pipeline was inaugurated in 2006, with an initial capacity of 8.8 bcm. The consortium included BP and Statoil (25.5 percent each), SOCAR (Azerbaijan), Lukoil, Total, and the National Iranian Oil Company (10 percent each), and Turkey's TPAO (9 percent). BP's share increased to 28.8 percent.

72. In parallel negotiations, the company Çalık Enerji, known for its links to the AKP, signed a three-way deal with Russia's Transneft and ENI for an oil pipeline running from Samsun to Ceyhan (October 2009). The Samsun-Ceyhan Pipeline gave Russia room to maneuver vis-à-vis Greece and Bulgaria, its partners in the Burgas–Alexandroupolis Pipeline. The project was shelved in 2013.

73. Russia meanwhile was exploring ways of bypassing the Turkish EEZ altogether. See Vladimir Soccor, "Moscow Playing with Multiple Options on Black Sea Pipelines," *Eurasia Daily Monitor*, vol. 6, no. 103, Washington D.C.: Jamestown Foundation, 29 May 2009.

74. Volumes started at 7.5 bcm in 2006 and reached a maximum of 14.7 bcm in 2012. The recession in 2008–9 actually saw a decrease of purchases that continued into 2010. The "take or pay" clauses had inflated Turkey's overall bill. The deal further-more extended the 1997 and 1998 gas agreements to 2025 and helped find a compro-mise on the deliveries via the Trans-Balkan Pipeline. See Gareth Winrow, *Realization of Turkey's Energy Aspirations: Pipe Dreams or Real Projects?* Turkey Project Policy Paper No. 4, Brookings Institution, April 2014, p. 7.

75. Two of the main partners in Shah Deniz, SOCAR and BP, hold respectively 58 percent and 12 percent in TANAP.

76. Rosatom's subsidiary, Atomeksportstroy (AES), won the tender as a sole bidder, in consortium with several Turkish partners.

77. Weitz, "Russian–Turkish Relations," p. 70.

78. *RIA Novosti*, 6 August 2009.

79. Aaron Stein and Chen Kane, "Turkey's Nuclear Ambitions," *Bulletin of the Atomic Scientists*, 15 May 2013.

80. *Daily Sabah*, 27 April 2016.
81. "If Russia loses a friend like Turkey with whom it has a lot of co-operation it is going to lose a lot of things. It needs to know this," Erdoğan told reporters. "Syria Conflict: Turkey Tells Russia to Avoid Clash," BBC News, 7 October 2015.
82. *Hürriyet Daily News*, 7 December 2015.
83. In October 2012, Turkey intercepted and forced a Syrian commercial airliner, en route from Moscow to Damascus, to land. The crew and passengers, including seventeen citizens of the Russian Federation, were then searched at Ankara airport. This episode led to the postponement of the pre-scheduled session of the High-Level Co-operation Council.
84. Habibe Özdal and Kerim Has, "Türkiye Rusya: Derin Ayrışma (mı?)" ["Turkey and Russia: Is this (a) Deep Rift"], *Analist 60*, USAK, February 2016, p. 40.
85. On 4 March 2014, several days after "little green men" seized control of Crimea, Erdoğan called Putin to discuss the crisis.
86. A comment made during a workshop on "Implications of the Ukrainian Crisis for Eastern Europe," Ministry of Foreign Affairs of the Republic of Turkey, Ankara, 2 June 2014. Summary at http://sam.gov.tr/workshop-on-implications-of-ukrainian-crisis-for-eastern-europe.
87. B92, 28 December 2015. As large-scale fighting erupted in Nagorno-Karabakh in April 2016, Erdoğan accused Russia of stoking tensions and pledged to support Azerbaijan. However, Turkey did not follow up words with actions. Moscow upgraded its military contigent at the base in Gyumri, Armenia, right next to the Turkish border.
88. *Nezavisne Novine*, 2 December 2015.
89. Reports have credited Cavit Çağlar, a Turkish businessman with connections in Dagestan, and the Kazakh president, Nursultan Nazarbayev, with mediating between Moscow and Ankara. T24, 9 August 2016.
90. *RT*, 27 June 2016. The Turkish government has blamed the Su-24 incident on supporters of the self-exiled cleric Fethullah Gülen whom they accuse of having masterminded the 15 July coup attempt. The AKP animosity against the U.S., Gülen's country of residence, which was seen as complicit in the failed putsch, smoothened the turn to Russia.
91. *Daily Sabah*, 17 July 2016.

6 From a Military Standoff to Hybrid Warfare

1. *Deutsche Welle*, 9 May 2014.
2. Interviewed by Sputnik Serbia, 11 January 2016. https://rs.sputniknews.com/intervju/201601111102429280–Ekskluzivno-intervju-sa-Dmitrijem-Rogozinom.
3. Bobo Lo, *Russia and the New World Disorder*, London: Chatham House, 2015, p. 40.
4. *Dnevni Avaz*, 29 September 2014.
5. David E. Senger and Eric Schmitt, "Spy Agency Consensus Grows that Russia Hacked D.N.C.," *The New York Times*, 26 July 2016.
6. Even Serbia has come to acknowledge NATO's contribution. Upon meeting NATO's Secretary General Jens Stoltenberg in February 2015, Prime Minister Aleksandar Vučić declared: "For us what matters most is the presence of KFOR forces in Kosovo and Metohija as well as the guarantees you have given for the security of Serbs." *Blic*, 6 February 2015.
7. Izmir hosts the HQ of NATO's land forces (LANDCOM).
8. In relative terms, Turkey scaled down expenditure from 2.9 percent of GDP (1988) to 2.1 percent of GDP (2015). Data from the Stockholm International Peace Research Institute (SIPRI) for 2015. www.sipri.org.
9. Russia is also ahead of the UK ($55.2 billion/2 percent of GDP) and France ($50.9 million/2.1 percent of GDP). International Institute of Strategic Studies, *The Military Balance*, London: IISS, 2016.

10. Moscow and Kyiv negotiated a twenty-year lease agreement in 1997. The Khrarkiv Pact was extended in April 2010 for a period between 2017 and 2042. Measured in tonnage, about 80 percent of the Black Sea Fleet has been stationed in Sevastopol and another 9 percent in the port of Feodosia.

11. *Admiral Grigorovich*, the lead ship in that batch, was commissioned in March 2016. Two further frigates were to be added the same year, while the remaining three were delayed as the construction companies needed to find a replacement for Ukrainian-made diesel turbines. The corvettes and two of the submarines have been commissioned too, with the remainder expected to be in service by the end of 2018. Two of the corvettes, *Zelenyi Dol* and *Serpuhov* (launched December 2015), have been part of Russia's operation in Syria. See Oxford Analytica, "Black Sea Fleet Projects Russian Power Westwards," *OA Daily Brief*, 15 April 2016.

12. *The Washington Post*, 29 September 2015.

13. The S-400s were tested in the Kavkaz 2016 exercise conducted primarily in Russia's Southern military district in August 2016. See Sergey Sukhanin, "Counter-Containment: Russia Deploys S-400 Complexes to Crimea," Jamestown Foundation, *Eurasia Daily Monitor*, vol. 14, no. 2, 18 January 2017.

14. Igor Delanoë, "Sootnoshenie *vooruzhennykh* sil v Chernomorskom regione" ["Balance of Armed Forces in the Black Sea Region"], Dossier, *Russian International Affairs Council*. Available at http://russiancouncil.ru/blackseamilitary.

15. Russia ordered the ships in 2010. In the 2014 takeover of Crimea, it relied on a fleet of smaller landing vessels. Turkey has five large landing ship tanks (LSTs) and forty-nine smaller landing vessels, and has an ambitious program to expand its capabilities by the early 2020s. See Delanoë, "Sootnoshenie vooruzhennyh sil v Chernomorskom regione."

16. Janusz Bugajski and Peter Doran provide a helpful snapshot of the state of play as of summer 2016: "Romania's navy is focusing on the Type 22 frigate Phase 2 modernization program and the acquisition of a new class of corvette. The existing combat management system (CMS), electronic warfare (EW) suite, radars, and electro-optical systems are all obsolete and will need to be replaced. The program is also planned to enhance anti-submarine warfare (ASW) and anti-surface warfare (ASuW) capabilities through the installation of anti-ship missiles and the provision of a missile-based air-defense capability." "Sofia is preparing to acquire two new domestically produced patrol frigates worth €400 million ($452 million) in the next three years, as specified in the 2016 state budget, but other similar programs are likely to take longer. The Bulgarian parliament also approved expenditures for refurbishing two of its existing Belgian-made frigates. The country possesses a few other ships, including anti-mining vessels, which are valuable for the region. Sofia has also made a decision (and the parliament approved funding) for updating its air fleet by buying a new escadrille of modern aircraft—either American F-16s or Swedish Gripen fighter jets." *Black Sea Defended: NATO Responses to Russia's Black Sea Offensive*, Center for European Policy Analysis (CEPA), Strategic Report 2, July 2016, pp. 9–10.

17. Interview with a NATO official, October 2016.

18. The ERI earmarked $789 million in 2016 and $3.4 billion in 2017 to strengthen the defense of Central and Eastern Europe.

19. The Montreux Convention on the status of the Straits was signed on 20 July 1936 by Turkey, the Soviet Union, Bulgaria, Romania, Yugoslavia, Greece, the United Kingdom, France, Australia, and Japan. Italy signed, with reservations, in 1938. The United States was not eligible, but has since complied with the Convention nonetheless. It allowed for the resumption of full control of the Bosphorus and the Dardanelles. The Convention limits the time that warships of non-littoral nations can stay in the Black Sea during peacetime to twenty-one days. There is a cumulative restriction of 45,000 tonnes for vessels allowed in at any given time, and no single state can go over the 30,000 tonnes limit—effectively ruling out nuclear-powered submarines and aircraft carriers. Annex II prohibits the passage of aircraft carriers

explicitly. Littoral states, by contrast, enjoy the right of free passage into the Mediterranean. Turkey has refused to sign the 1994 United Nations Convention on the Law of the Sea (UNCLOS) in order to avoid a revision of the Montreux arrangements. See Anthony DeLuca, *Great Power Rivalry: The Montreux Conference and Convention of 1936*, Boulder, CO: East European Monographs, 1981; Cem Devrim Yaylalı, "The Montreux Convention Regarding the Regime of the Straits: A Turkish Perspective," *C4 Defence*, April 2014.

20. The Center was established under a co-operation agreement initialed during President Dmitry Medvedev's visit to Belgrade in October 2009. Its permanent staff consists of ten Russian Federation citizens and twenty from Serbia.

21. Conversation with a former senior American diplomat, Atlantic Council, Washington D.C., December 2015. See also Janusz Bugajski and Margarita Assenova, *Eurasian Disunion: Russia's Vulnerable Flanks*, Washington D.C.: The Jamestown Foundation, 2016, p. 235. The activities of the "Russian Center" have been covered extensively by Radio Free Europe/Radio Liberty (RFE/RL). See Predgrag Blagojević, Ljudmila Cvetković, and Iva Martinović, "RSE u ruskom centru u Nišu" ["RFE in Nish's Russian Center"], *RFE/RL Service in Serbian/Croatian/Bosnian*, 7 March 2016; Iuliia Petrovskaia, "Negumanitarnye ambitsii Moskvy" ["Moscow's Non-Humanitarian Ambitions"], *Radio Liberty*, 24 May 2016.

22. Dnevnik, *RTS*, 2 April 2016. Zakharova's briefing on 25 February 2016. Available at http://www.mid.ru/press_service/video/-/asset_publisher/i6t41cq3VWP6/content/id/2111747#11.

23. "Slavic Brotherhood Exercises Aimed at Crushing Potential Maidan Scenario," Sputnik News, 3 September 2015. Roger McDermot, "Slavic Brotherhood 2015 Rehearses Anti-Color Revolution Operations," *Eurasia Daily Monitor*, vol. 12, no. 160, The Jamestown Foundation, 8 September 2015.

24. The Kremlin mouthpiece *Izvestia* wrote about a prospective $3 billion loan to help Serbs acquire advanced systems such as S-300 missiles and T-90 tanks. "S-300 will Protect the Balkans," *Izvestia*, 31 March 2011.

25. Serbia continues to service the engines of its MiG-29 fighter jets at the Russian Aerospace Corporation (RSK), formerly the Mikoyan-and-Gurevich (MiG) Design Bureau, under an agreement from 2006. In 2015, Croatia repaired the engines of its aging MiG-21s in Ukraine, a deal that has triggered a corruption scandal. Zagreb is currently considering offers for JAS-39 Gripen (Sweden's SAAB) and for surplus F-16s from Israel. Romania phased out its MiGs in 2013 with the purchase of twelve second-hand F-16s from Portugal. In October 2015, the Bulgarian Ministry of Defense signed a deal with Poland to prolong the life of the country's MiG-29s. (Angel Krasimirov and Matthias Williams, "Bulgaria Eyes Poland Fighter Deal to Cut Dependence on Russia," Reuters, 6 July 2015). However, the contract was cancelled in November 2016, following the election of the air-force chief Rumen Radev as president, and Sofia ordered four new and six refurbished engines from MiG, through a Bulgarian intermediary company. In the meantime, prosecutors launched a criminal investigation against the former minister of defense, Nikolay Nenchev, for signing the deal with Poland.

26. The only side payment for the helicopter purchase has been Russia's blanket agreement to invest into a maintenance facility at Batajnica, near Belgrade, which could service Soviet-made helicopters from across former Yugoslavia and Central and Eastern Europe.

27. RFE/RL, 11 January 2016. http://www.slobodnaevropa.org/a/rogozin-vucic-rusija-razmatra-vojne-potreb-srbije/27481267.html.

28. Igor Božinovski, "Russia to Donate MiG-29s, T-72s to Serbia," *IHS Jane's Defence Weekly*, 22 December 2016. The delivery of the fighter jets presented a logistical problem as it was not clear whether Serbia's NATO neighbors, Bulgaria and Romania, would allow access through their airspace. Prime Minister Vučić spoke of an alternative option: a transfer of the planes disassembled in parts. Richard Tomkins, "Serbia to Receive MiG-29 Fighters from Russia," *UPI*, 28 March 2017.

29. Nikita Bondarev interviewed by Branka Mitrović, "Rus će izabrati 'ševrolet' pre nego srpski 'punto': Putinov čovek otkrio tajne srpsko-ruskih odnosa" ["The Russian would Choose a Chevrolet over a Serbian Fiat Punto: Putin's Man Reveals the Secrets of Serbian–Russian Relations"], *Newsweek Serbia*, 19 January 2016.
30. Serbia co-operates with the Ohio National Guard following an agreement dating back to 2006.
31. In 2007, Cyprus sold the S-300 systems to Greece—and received Russian-made TOR-M1 short-range missiles as compensation.
32. Reuters, 26 February 2016. Bugajski and Assenova, *Eurasian Disunion*, p. 266.
33. See, for instance, the insightful debates on the website Warontherocks.com with contributions from Jyri Raitasalo ("Hybrid Warfare: Where is the Beef," 23 April 2015), Mark Galeotti ("Time to Think about Hybrid Defence," 30 July 2015), and Michael Kofman ("Russian Hybrid Warfare and Other Dark Arts," 11 March 2016), amongst others.
34. "Russia Plans a 'hybrid warfare' Campaign Aimed at Destabilising Europe, says Bulgarian President," *The Independent*, 14 November 2015.
35. According to Eurostat data from 2013, Russians make up the largest group of foreign nationals residing in Bulgaria, 12,000, roughly one-third of the total. The number of 300,000, cropping up in Bulgarian media from time to time, appears to be grossly exaggerated.
36. Sofia identified the hacker collective Sofacy as a plausible culprit. Operating since 2007, the group has been linked to attacks against the White House, the German Bundestag, the French TV channel TV5 Monde. *Capital*, 29 January 2016.
37. *Hotnews.ro*, 15 January 2016. Previously, Romania, as well as Bulgaria, were themselves the source countries of cyberattacks.
38. Three Czech generals were forced to resign in 2009 after being implicated by the country's counter-intelligence services. The same year Estonia convicted Herman Simm, a senior official at its defense ministry. "Russian Espionage Targeting New NATO Members," *RFE/RL*, 7 August 2010.
39. Scenesetter for Bulgarian Interior Minister Petkov's meetings in Washington, 2 October 2006. Petkov appointed as advisor to his ministry both Brigo Asparuhov and General Lyuben Gotsev, deputy chief of foreign intelligence prior to 1989 and briefly a foreign minister thereafter, who had been schooled by the KGB in the early 1960s. Journalists have alleged that Gotsev oversaw ties between Bulgaria's security services and the budding organized crime syndicates around the time communism ended. He has denied those claims.
40. Srđan Janković, "Montenegro, Russia and NATO: An Issue of Double Agents?" *RFE/RL*, 21 July 2014.
41. *Danas*, 11 July 2007.
42. Julian Borger, "14 Years a Fugitive: The Hunt of Ratko Mladić, the Butcher of Bosnia," *The Guardian*, 21 January 2016. See also Julian Borger, *The Butcher's Trail: How the Search for Balkan War Criminals Became the World's Most Successful Manhunt*, London: OtherPress, 2016. On Moscow's collusion with international crime, see Mark Galeotti, *Crimintern: How the Kremlin uses Russia's criminal networks in Europe*, Policy Brief, European Council on Foreign Relations, April 2017.
43. Mairbek Vatchagaev, "Another Chechen Émigré Murdered in Turkey," *Eurasia Daily Monitor*, vol. 12, no. 42, The Jamestown Foundation, 6 March 2015.
44. Mark Galeotti, "From Trump's Washington to the Capitals of Europe, Corruption is Russia's Greatest Ally," *In Moscow's Shadows* blog, 3 March 2017. https://inmoscowsshadows.wordpress.com/2017/03/03/from-trumps-washington-to-the-capitals-of-europe-corruption-is-russias-greatest-ally.

7 Playing the Energy Card

1. The Russian flag was originally inspired by that of The Netherlands.
2. Roderic Lyne, Strobe Talbott, and Koji Watanabe, *Engaging with Russia: The Next Phase*, Washington D.C.: The Trilateral Commission, 2006, p. 65.

3. Some 70 percent of Gazprom revenues are from exports, though 72 percent of production is consumed in Russia. Jonathan Stern, "The Matrix: Introduction and Analytical Framework for the Russian Gas Sector," in James Henderson and Simon Pirani, *The Russian Gas Matrix: How the Markets are Driving Change*, Oxford: Oxford University Press, 2014.

4. Statement at the Balkan Energy Summit, 24 June 2007. Transcript available at http:// kremlin.ru/events/president/transcripts/24368.

5. Ivan Nazarov, "Overview of the Russian Gas Industry," in Andrey Vavilov and David Nicholls (eds), *Gazprom: An Energy Giant and Its Challenges in Europe*, London: Palgrave Macmillan, 2013, pp. 38–9.

6. Later on Gazprom became the sole owner.

7. In September 2016, for instance, the Bulgarian, Romanian, Greek, and Ukrainian transmission system operators (TSOs) reached an agreement to offer capacity auctions in reverse mode on the Trans-Balkan Pipeline. I am grateful to Martin Vladimirov for alerting me to this key development.

8. In fairness, it could have been worse. Temperatures were low but not exceptionally so. Industry was not operating at full capacity. Hydropower in the Western Balkans was abundant, allowing for electricity exports. Aleksandar Kovačević, *The Impact of the Russia–Ukraine Gas Crisis in South Eastern Europe*, Oxford Institute for Energy Studies, March 2009. Available at https://www.oxfordenergy.org/wpcms/wp-content/uploads/2010/11/NG29–TheImpactoftheRussiaUkrainianCrisisinSouthEasternEurope-AleksandarKovacevic-2009.pdf.

9. To bring them on board, ENI agreed to transfer 30 percent of the shares. Incentives for foreign partners also included stakes in gas fields to "ship-or-pay" clauses guaranteeing stability of profits.

10. Romano Prodi, head of the European Commission, was reportedly offered the CEO job, but unlike Gerhard Schröder in Nord Stream, turned the Russian proposal down.

11. Nabucco obtained a Trans-European Network (TEN) Strategy in February 2008, with additional support from Austria and Romania.

12. Quoted in James Marson and Joe Parker, 'In Reversal, Neighbors Squeeze Russia's Gazprom Over Natural-Gas Prices', *The Wall Street Journal*, 1 May 2013.

13. Related by Ilin Stanev, editor at *Capital Weekly*. A detailed account of the negotiations is in Ilin Stanev, "Yuzhen potok kato politicheski proekt i kazus na plenenata dârzhava" ["South Stream as a Political Project and a Case of State Capture"], in Atanas Georgiev, Galya Alexandrova, Ilin Stanev, Stefan Popov and Julian Popov (eds), *"Yuzhen potok" i ovladyavaneto na dârzhavata [South Stream and State Capture]*, RiskMonitor, November 2016, pp. 22–43.

14. Gazprom agreed to shift some of the volumes to private companies selling directly to Turkish domestic consumers, including its subsidiaries Bosphorus Gaz Corporation and Avrasya Gaz (owned by Gazprombank). Surrendering market share helped BOTAŞ financially because of the low domestic prices set in regulations. To be able to compete, dependent traders obtained a substantial discount from the Russians. Şaban Kardaş, "Turkey Pursues Mixed Aims over Supply Contract Cancellation with Russia", *Eurasia Daily Monitor*, vol. 8, no. 182, The Jamestown Foundation, 4 October 2011.

15. Sergei Lavrov, "State of the Union Russia–EU: Prospects for Partnership in the Changing World," *Journal of Common Market Studies*, vol. 51, September 2013, pp. 6–12.

16. In 2006, the European Commission listed Nord Stream as a priority project under the Trans-European Network (TEN), which subsequently justified its exemption from the TEP requirements.

17. Jonathan Stern, Simon Pirani, and Katja Yafimava, "Does the Cancellation of South Stream Signal a Fundamental Reorientation of Russian Gas Export Policy?" Oxford Energy Comment, Oxford Energy Institute, January 2015, p. 4.

18. Between 2009 and 2011, Surgutneftgaz held a 21.2 percent in Hungary's MOL, which is the largest shareholder in INA.
19. Lukoil brushed aside its sponsorship of Iurii Luzhkov and Evgenii Primakov's bid for the Kremlin in 1999–2000, and the presence of its grouping, Regions of Russia (*Regiony Rossii*), in the Duma between 1995 and 2003.
20. Thane Gustafson, *Wheel of Fortune: The Battle for Oil and Power in Russia*, Cambridge, MA: Belknap Press, 2012, p. 121.
21. Bobo Lo, *Russia and the New World Disorder*, London: Chatham House, 2015, p. 28.
22. *Bloomberg*, 25 March 2014.
23. Majority-owned by Russian entities, YugoRosGaz controls part of the Serbian grid and trades on the domestic market. It buys gas back from the state-owned monopoly Srbijagas at cheaper, regulated rates than the ones it charges Srbijagas on behalf of Gazprom. In 2013, Srbijagas had to borrow €450 million from the government to avoid bankruptcy. "Ko zarađuje od uvoza gasa" ["Who is Profiting from the Import of Gas?"], *Insajder*, *B92*, 30 September 2013. Also Đorđe Padejski, "Srbija i Gazprom–od Miloševića do danas" ["Serbia and Gazprom–from Milošević to Today"], *Peščanik*, 7 February 2011.
24. Georgiev, Alexandrova, Stanev, Popov and Popov, "*Yuzhen potok" i ovladyavaneto na dârzhavata*, pp. 22–43.
25. In June 2015, the Sofia-based Risk Management Laboratory estimated Lukoil Neftochim had avoided taxes to the tune of €343.5 million over the period 2006–14. Laboratoria za izsledvane na riska, *Osnovatelni sâmneniya za oshtetyavane na bydhzeta na Republika Bâlgariya s tsenata na suroviya petrol* [*Grounded Suspicions of Harming the Republic of Bulgaria's Budget through the Price of Crude Oil*], June 2015. www.riskmanagementlab.com. Lukoil disputes the calculations.
26. Both firms have extensive business connections with Russia. ENI is a partner in the Blue Stream pipeline and played a key part in South Stream. OMV, a market leader in Central and Eastern Europe, was similarly involved in South Stream. The company has stakes in several gas fields in Siberia and was one of the first in Western Europe to import Soviet gas in 1968.
27. Mali has been accused of laundering the money through real estate on the Bulgarian Black Sea coast. Stevan Dojčinović, Dragana Pećo, and Atanas Tchobanov, *The Mayor's Hidden Property: Organised Crime and Corruption Reporting Project*, 19 October 2015. https://www.occrp.org/mayorsstory/The-Mayors-Hidden-Property/index.html.
28. Sanader was sentenced to nine years' imprisonment in March 2009.
29. In-depth study of European energy security, accompanying the document "Communication from the Commission to the Council and the European Parliament: European Energy Security Strategy" (COM(2014) 330 final), p. 9.
30. The reliance of other industries on Gazprom (e.g. petrochemicals, ceramics, glass, steelworks, etc.) provides the Russian company leverage vis-à-vis incumbent national companies that it deals with.
31. Turkey has doubled its wing and geothermal capacity since 2005, and has set a 30 percent renewables target for 2023. Apart from the Akkuyu nuclear power plant developed with Rosatom, the government has signed a deal with Japan's Mitsubishi and the French company Areva for a second plant at Sinop with an equal capacity (4,800 megawatts).
32. "Commission sends Statement of Objections to Gazprom for alleged abuse of dominance on Central and Eastern European gas supply markets," 22 April 2015, http://europa.eu/rapid/press-release_IP-15-4828_en.htm.
33. Under proposed amendments to the Security of Gas Supply Regulation of 2010 (994/2010) already endorsed by the Council.
34. The volume of gas sales based on hub-linked prices rose to 64 percent of the total in Europe in 2015. IGU, *Platts*, 9 May 2016.
35. Martin Vladimirov and Sijbren De Jong, "Deciphering Gazprom's Pipeline Agenda in Europe," *Atlantic Council*, 14 March 2017.

36. "Paying the Piper," *The Economist*, 4 January 2014. In some parts of Europe contract prices are actually below the spot market.
37. For example, by setting aside funds to meet compensation claims and reducing the base price under the LTCs that is not linked to oil. See Jonathan Stern, "Russian Responses to Commercial Change in European Gas Markets," in James Henderson and Simon Pirani, *The Russian Gas Matrix: How the Markets are Driving Change*, Oxford: Oxford University Press, 2014.

8 The Allure of Russia's Might

1. Analyzed in Miroslav Jovanović, "Two Russias: On the Two Dominant Discourses of Russia in the Serbian Public," Monitoring the Russian–Serbian Relations, International and Security Affairs (ISAC) Fund, Belgrade, 2008, pp. 43–53.
2. Joseph S. Nye Jr., "Think Again: Soft Power," *Foreign Policy*, 23 February 2006.
3. Fiona Hill, "Moscow Discovers Soft Power," *Current History*, vol. 30, no. 2, 2006, p. 341.
4. James Sherr, *Hard Diplomacy and Soft Coercion: Russia's Influence Abroad*, London: Royal Institute for International Affairs/Chatham House, 2013.
5. Tomila Lankina and Kinga Niemczyk, "Russia's Foreign Policy and Soft Power," in David Cadier and Margot Light (eds), *Russia's Foreign Policy: Ideas, Domestic Politics and External Relations*, London: Palgrave Macmillan, 2015, p. 98.
6. American media: "Do as we say, not as we do," RT, 26 December 2015. https://www.rt.com/op-edge/327132–media-cnn-propaganda-us-russia.
7. Peter Pomerantsev and Michael Weiss, "The Menace of Unreality: How the Kremlin Weaponises Information, Culture and Money," a Special Report presented by *The Interpreter*, a project of the Institute of Modern Russia, November 2014.
8. See Orysia Lutsevych, "Agents of the Russian World: Proxy Groups in the Contested Neighbourhood," Chatham House Research Paper, April 2016.
9. Agnia Grigas, *Beyond Crimea: The New Russian Empire*, New Haven, CT: Yale University Press, 2016, esp. Chapter 1: The Return of Empire, pp. 1–24.
10. At the Kamchia Sanatorium Complex developed by former Moscow Mayor Iurii Luzhkov and his wife, the businesswoman Elena Baturina, after 2009. There are annual camps on the Greek island of Lemnos hosted by the RISI (see below), as well as in Republika Srpska, which are run in co-operation with Srpski Kod (Serbian Code) and Naša Srbija (Our Serbia) and brings in youth from Russia, Serbia, Transnistria, Donbas, Crimea, etc.
11. In November 2016, Reshetnikov went into retirement and was replaced by Mihail Fradkov, ex-head of the Foreign Intelligence Service.
12. The International Fund for the Unity of Orthodox People, a GONGO under the Patriarch's patronage, has decorated President Georgi Pârvanov and Patriarch Maxim of Bulgaria, Serbian Patriarch Pavle, director Emir Kusturica, top-ranking tennis player Novak Djoković (Doković), President Tassos Papadopoulos of Cyprus, President Kostis Stefanopoulos (Greece), Archbishops Hristodoulos, head of the Greek Church, and Anastasius, head of the Albanian Church. The Russian Patriarch presents the awards each January in Moscow's Christ the Savior cathedral.
13. *Kurir*, 26 July 2013.
14. Russia is partly funding the painting of frescoes inside the neo-Byzantine cathedral, built between 1985 and 2009 as a symbol of the Orthodox revival in post-communist Serbia. It is the largest Orthodox temple in the Balkans and the second largest world-wide. The main cathedral in Sofia, St Alexander Nevsky (built between 1904 and 1912), is even more closely linked to Russia. Named after a Russian medieval prince, it was designed by a Russian architect, Aleksandr Pomerantsev. For a brief period between 1916 and 1918, when Bulgaria and Russia were fighting each other in the First World War, the cathedral was renamed to St Cyril and St Methodius. It was inaugurated in 1924 as a monument to Bulgaria's debt to Russia, represented on the occasion by the White Russians rather than the Bolshevik regime.

15. In contrast to Serbia where a number of metropolitans have read theology at universities in Western Europe or Greece.
16. Most recently in withdrawing from the Pan-Orthodox Council convoked by the Ecumenical Patriarchate in Crete, 16–26 June 2016.
17. In June 2014, work began on a Russian church in Skopje. Holy Trinity is funded by Sergei Samsonenko, owner of the Vardar Football Club. Archbishop Stefan, head of the Macedonian Orthodox Church, was present at the groundbreaking ceremony and offered blessings. http://www.rferl.org/content/macedonia-russian-orthodox-church-skopje/27093507.html.
18. Launched with a presidential decree in December 2013, Sputnik succeeded RIA Novosti and runs in Serbian and Turkish amongst other languages. Its Turkish-language service was temporarily blocked during the tussle between Moscow and Ankara in late 2015 and the first half of 2016, but later came back online.
19. As well as in scores of prominent newspapers around the globe, from *The New York Times* to the *Daily Telegraph* and *Le Figaro*.
20. The internationally celebrated film-maker Emir Kusturica (*Underground*, *Time of the Gypsies*) has been mentioned as a potential director.
21. In 2015, Malofeev, owner of Tsar'grad TV promoting "Orthodox values" in Russia, attempted to buy TV7 and sister channel News 7 along with other assets from Tsvetan Vassilev, head of the Corporate Commercial Bank (KTB). Once the fourth-largest bank in Bulgaria, KTB filed for bankruptcy in 2014 amidst a political scandal involving loans to business cronies and empty-shell companies. Malofeev is believed to be the owner of Art TV, a cable channel in Serbia. Malofeev made headlines during Easter 2015 when he paid for the jet bringing the holy fire from Jerusalem to Belgrade. Malofeev has also been linked to Panos Kammenos, leader of Independent Greeks (ANEL) and defense minister.
22. N1 is owned by KKR, an American-based investment fund. General David Petraeus is the chairman and it is affiliated with CNN.
23. A Putin ally allegedly involved in the Montenegro coup plot, BNI IntelliNews, 3 March 2017. http://www.intellinews.com/putin-ally-allegedly-involved-in-montenegro-coup-plot-116855/?source=montenegro.
24. The Democratic Party of Serbia (founded by Vojislav Koštunica), the ultranationalist Dveri (Gates) movement, the Serbian People's Party (part of the cabinet in Belgrade), the Alliance of Independent Social Democrats (SNSD) of Milorad Dodik, the president of Republika Srpska, and the Democratic Party of Serbs in Macedonia.
25. In March 2014, Ataka led rallies against the EU sanctions ("It was Russia, not EU, which liberated us from Turkish yoke," read the placards).
26. Pomerantsev and Weiss, *The Menace of Unreality*, p. 6.
27. Center for Euro-Atlantic Studies, "Eyes Wide Shut: Russian Soft Power Gaining Strength in Serbia—Goals, Instruments and Effects," Belgrade, May 2016.
28. N. Latković and M. Jasnić. "Tačno je da nam Rusi pomažu. DSS, Dveri, Zavetnici i Treća Srbija rade protiv Srbije u EU" ["It is true that Russians are helping us. DSS, Dveri, Oathkeepers and Third Serbia are working against Serbia's entry into the EU"], *Blic*, 24 March 2016. Available at http://www.blic.rs/vesti/politika/tacno-je-da-nam-rusi-pomazu-dss-dveri-zavetnici-i-treca-srbija-rade-protiv-srbije-u/g9kq9vf.
29. Andrew Higgins, "Russian Money Suspected behind Fracking Protests," *The New York Times*, 30 November 2014; Keith Smith, *Unconventional Gas and European Security: Politics and Foreign Policy of Fracking in Europe*, Center for Strategic and International Studies (CSIS), 2014.
30. Examples include tabloids such as *Blic*, *Informer*, and *Telegraf* in Serbia, together with the broadsheet *Politika*; *Weekend*, *Telegraf*, *24 Chasa*, and *Trud* in Bulgaria. TV channels include Pink, B92, Studio B, the public broadcaster RTS (Serbia), BNT, BTV, and Nova TV in Bulgaria. For a detailed study of pro-Russian discourse in Bulgarian media, see Dimitar Vatsov et al., *Anti-Democratic Propaganda in Bulgaria*, *2013–2016* (Human and Social Studies Foundation, 2017). Available at http://hssfoundation.org/wp-content/uploads/2017/04/REPORT_PART1_EN.pdf.

31. TNS Medium Gallup, "Public opinion on the EU and European integration," February 2014. Available at http://www.europa.rs/upload/Opinion%20poll% 20results% 20for% 20press% 20conference% 20FIN% 20ENG.pptx.

32. Spoljnopolitičke orijentacije, "Južni Tok, I sprsko-ruski odnosi iz ugla srpskog javnog mnjenija" ["Foreign-Policy Orientations, South Stream, and Serbian–Russian Relations from the Perspective of Serbian Public Opinion"], November 2013. Available at http://www.mc.rs/upload/documents/prezentacije/221113_NSPM_ Juzni-tok_Srpsko-ruski-odnosi.pdf.

33. Published by the New Serbian Political Thought Foundation in November 2015. Blic, 22 November 2015.

34. According to a survey by the DAMAR polling agency, Café Del Montenegro, 22 February 2016. Available at http://www.cdm.me/politika/damar-469–odsto-gradana-za-nato-dps-daleko-ispred-svih-partija-sa-409–procenata-podrske.

35. Alpha Research, "Bålgarskata vånshna politika, konfliktåt Rusiya-Ukrajna i natsion-alnata ni sigurnost" ["Bulgarian Foreign Policy, the Ukraine–Russia Conflict and National Security"], http://alpharesearch.bg/bg//socialni_izsledvania/socialni_ publikacii/balgarskata-vanshna-politika-konflikta-rusiya-ukrayna-i-nacionalnata-ni-sigurnost.841.html.

36. Survey by the polling company Public Issue (www.publicissue.gr) quoted by Lóránt Györi, Péter Krekó et al., Natural Allies: The Kremlin Connections of the Greek Far Right, Budapest: Political Capital, 2015. A more recent poll, by ELIAMEP, finds 50.5 percent in favor and 11 percent against. "Greek public Opinion and Attitudes toward FYROM and the Name Issue," October 2016.

37. IPSOS, Istraživanje javnog mnenija. Jovanović, "Two Russias."

38. Nikita Bondarev, "Zašto Srbi ne razumeju današnju Rusiju" ["Why Serbs do not Understand Today's Russia"], Nedeljnik, 8 March 2016.

39. Vassilis Petsinis, "Putin's 'useless idiots' or Signs of a Deeper Pathology? Russophilia and National Populism in Greece," openDemocracy, 29 January 2015.

SELECT BIBLIOGRAPHY

The literature on contemporary Russia's foreign policy, and especially relations with the West, is both voluminous and ever growing. Vladimir Putin's ambition to bring much of the former Soviet Union into a sphere of influence and restore Moscow's power and prestige on the world stage is generating and is bound to generate more and more books, articles, and reports. In addition, the present essay would not be complete without at least a cursory overview of writings on the history and politics of Southeast Europe. Putting together an exhaustive bibliography, therefore, presents a tall order. What follows is more a collection of references and suggestions for further reading that might benefit the inquisitive reader, rather than a full catalogue of any sort. While I give a general preference to works in English, there are also occasional entries in other languages, not least Russian.

A good introductory text on Russia's international politics is Dmitri Trenin's *Post-Imperium: A Eurasian Story* (Carnegie Endowment for International Peace, 2007). Long-time head of the Carnegie Endowment's office in Moscow, Trenin is, hands down, one of the most perceptive, well-informed, and eloquent commentators on Russian foreign policy writing in English. Reflecting the deterioration of relations between Putin's regime and the West in the mid-2000s, *Post-Imperium* highlights the trends and forces driving Moscow's bid to reassert its power in the "near abroad" and beyond. For a more up-to-date snapshot of Russian politics and foreign policy after the annexation of Crimea and the war in eastern Ukraine, readers may consult the special issue of *Foreign Affairs* entitled "Putin's Russia: Down but Not Out" (May/June 2016), which includes essays by a group of eminent scholars and analysts such as Trenin, Stephen Kotkin, Gleb Pavlovsky, Maria Lipman, Fyodor Lukyanov, Sergei Guriev, and Daniel Treisman.

There are plenty of general surveys of Russia in European and global affairs. A must-read list includes Andrei P. Tsygankov, *Russia's Foreign Policy: Change and Continuity in National Identity* (Cambridge University Press, fourth edition, 2016), which stresses the role of ideas in shaping Moscow's external behavior; Bobo Lo, *Russia and the New World Disorder* (Brookings Institution, 2015); Jeffrey Mankoff, *Russian Foreign Policy: The Return of Great Power Politics* (Rowman and Littlefield, second edition, 2011); Nicholas K. Gvosdev, *Russian Foreign Policy: Interests, Vectors, and Sectors* (Cq Press, 2013); and David Cadler and Margot Light (eds), *Russia's Foreign Policy: Ideas, Domestic Politics and External Relations* (Palgrave Macmillan, 2015). On Russia's love-hate relationship with the United States, Angela E. Stent, *The Limits of Partnership: U.S.–Russian Relations in the Twenty-First Century*, second updated edition (Princeton University Press, 2015), which describes the cyclical pattern of rapprochements or "resets" followed by episodes of confrontation that have taken shape since the early 1990s. On EU–Russia relations, and the normative tensions that underlie them: Ted Hopf (ed.), *Russia's European Choice* (Palgrave Macmillan, 2008); Hiski Haukkala, *The EU–Russia Strategic Partnership: The Limits of Post-Sovereignty in International Relations* (Routledge, 2010); Hiski Haukkala and Nicu Popescu (eds), *Russian Futures: Horizon 2025* (EU Institute for Security Studies, 2016). A survey on the tangled relationship with Europe would not be complete without Iver Neumann's magisterial *Russia and the Idea of Europe: A Study of Identity in International Relations* (Routledge, second edition, 2016), a fine study of Russian thought spanning the period since the eighteenth century.

Turning to Ukraine and the period of confrontation with the EU and the United States, *Ukraine Crisis: What it Means for the West* (Yale University Press, 2014) by Andrew Wilson is highly recommended. Wilson has earned recognition as one of the foremost authorities on post-Soviet Eastern Europe, and he is a knowledgeable and engaging writer. Other books of interest in the same genre that delve into the origins and the dynamics of Russia's rift with the West include Agnia Grigas, *Beyond Crimea: The New Russian Empire* (Yale University Press, 2016), Robert Legvold, *Return to Cold War* (Polity, 2016), as well as Steven Rosefielde, *The Kremlin Strikes Back: Russia and the West After Crimea's Annexation* (Cambridge University Press, 2017).

There are plenty of studies in each of the three thematic areas covered by this book (security, energy, and soft power). *The Politics of Security in Modern Russia* (Routledge, 2016), edited by Mark Galeotti, is an up-to-date guide containing chapters on a range of sub-issues, from nuclear warfare to organized crime and terrorism, by first-rate experts in the field. Galeotti, whose blog *In Moscow's Shadows* (inmoscowsshadows.wordpress.com) offers lots of insight into all things Russian, is also the author of *Hybrid War or Gibridnaya Voina? Getting Russia's Non-linear Military Challenge Right*, November 2016 (available online through lulu.com), an original and informative piece of analysis. Russian subversion of foreign countries' democratic system, a topic that has risen to prominence following the American presidential election of November 2016, is at the center of *Deception: Spies, Lies and How Russia Dupes the West* (Bloomsbury, 2012) by Edward Lucas, a journalist who has covered Eastern Europe for *The Economist* since the 1990s. The book follows in the footsteps of *The New Cold War: How the Kremlin Menaces Both Russia and the West* (Bloomsbury, 2008), which has already gone through three editions. For a critical response to Lucas's thesis, see the review of his 2008 volume by the Princeton historian of Russia Stephen Kotkin: "Myth of the New Cold War," *Prospect Magazine*, April 2008.

With the two gas crises in Eastern Europe of 2006 and 2009, energy security has become another subject animating discussions on Russian foreign policy. Energy is a complex matter as it combines and draws on a multitude of disciplines, including politics, economics, law, and even geology and climatology. There are several edited volumes and single-author books that clear the high bar and are therefore worth mentioning, particularly where gas is concerned: Adrian Dellecker and Thomas Gomart, *Russian Energy Foreign and Security Policy* (Routledge, 2011); James Henderson and Simon Pirani, *The Politics of Energy: The Russian Gas Matrix: How Markets are Driving Change* (Oxford University Press, 2014); Andrei Belyi, *Transnational Gas Markets and Euro-Russian Energy Relations* (Palgrave Macmillan, 2015). Marshall I. Goldman, *Petrostate: Putin, Power, and the New Russia* (Oxford University Press, second edition, 2010) is a highly readable, if already somewhat dated, account of the politics of energy in today's Russia. Other titles of interest include Thane Gustafson, *Wheel of Fortune: The Battle for Oil and Power in Russia* (Harvard University Press, 2011), and Daniel Yergin, *The Quest: Energy, Security and the Remaking of the Modern World* (Penguin, 2011), which pays considerable attention to the Russian case. Dieter Helm, *Burn Out: The Endgame for Fossil Fuels* (Yale University Press, 2017) argues that the era of gas and oil is coming to a close and charts, amongst other things, the geopolitical consequences for Russia and Europe (Chapters 6 and 8).

Russian soft power is similarly an issue attracting scholars and policy analysts alike. An early examination of the concept as applied to Russia is Fiona Hill, "Moscow

Discovers Soft Power," *Current History*, vol. 105, no. 693, October 2006. Skeptical voices were never absent: Andrei Tsygankov, "If not by tanks, then by banks? The role of soft power in Putin's foreign policy," *Europe–Asia Studies*, vol. 58, no. 7, 2006. The Ukrainian crisis injected new vigor into the debate. *Beyond Crimea* by Grigas (see above) and Marcel Van Hepern, *Putin's Propaganda Machine: Soft Power and Russian Foreign Policy* (Rowman & Littlefield, 2015) both deal with Russian-style *miagkaia sila*. Russia's use of links to fringe political actors in the West, another hot topic, is studied by Anton Shekhovtsov, *Russia and the Western Far Right: Tango Noir* (Routledge, 2017).

Moving to Southeast Europe, the historical scholarship on the region's links with Russia is truly vast. Barbara Jelavich, *Russia's Balkan Entanglements, 1806–1914* (Cambridge University Press, 1991), an in-depth, nuanced account of St Petersburg's dealings with the Balkan states as well as with the Ottoman Empire, constitutes, by and large, the gold standard. Jelavich is an accomplished guide across the European power politics of the day and regarding Russian decision makers' motives and dilemmas as well as a foremost scholar of the region (see her two-volume *History of the Balkans* published by Cambridge University Press in 1983). Another monograph of note is Matthew S. Anderson, *The Eastern Question, 1774–1923* (Palgrave, 1966). *Russian Foreign Policy: Essays in Historical Perspective*, a 1962 volume by Yale University Press, contains an informative chapter on the Balkans by Ivo Lederer, the book's Zagreb-born editor. In the same genre, in other words the Russia of today seen through the prism of history and of "persistent factors," Robert Legvold, *Russian Foreign Policy in the Twenty-First Century and the Shadow of the Past* (Columbia University Press, 2007). Russia's connections to Southern Slavs and their role in triggering the First World War is discussed at length in Christopher Clark, *The Sleepwalkers: How Europe Went to War in 1914* (Harper, 2014). Also highly recommended is Dominic Lieven, *Towards the Flame: Empire, War and the End of Tsarist Russia* (Allen Lane, 2015), which draws on a wealth of hitherto unpublished Russian diplomatic and personal archives. On the ideological cross-currents and Russian perceptions of the Balkans in the era of the "Eastern Question": David MacKenzie, *The Serbs and Russian Pan-Slavism, 1875–1878* (Cornell University Press, 1967); Charles Jelavich, *Tsarist Russia and Balkan Nationalism: Russian Influence in the Internal Affairs of Bulgaria and Serbia, 1879–1886* (Praeger, 1978); Denis Vovchenko, *Containing Balkan Nationalism: Imperial Russia and Ottoman Christians, 1856–1914* (Oxford University Press, 2016). There are several notable titles in Serbian and Bulgarian: Nikola Popović, *Srbija i carska Rusija* (Službeni glasnik, 2007); Simeon Radev, *Stroitelite na sâvremenna Bâlgariya* (Bâlgarski pisatel, second edition, 1990); Andrey Pantev, *Angliya sreshtu Rusiya na Balkanite, 1879–1994* (Nauka i izkustvo, 1972). The Tsarist Empire's Greek connections are explored in Stephen K. Batalden, *Catherine II's Greek Prelate: Eugenios Voulgaris in Russia, 1771–1806* (Columbia University Press, 1982), and Vasilis Kardasis, *Diaspora Merchants in the Black Sea: The Greeks in Southern Russia, 1775–1861* (Lexington Books, 1998). On Greece more broadly: Stathis Kalyvas, *Modern Greece: What Everyone Needs to Know* (Oxford University Press, 2015), which puts forward the argument that the Greek experience in state- and nation-building has been a qualified success, despite the latest crisis; and Thanos Veremis and John Koliopoulos, *Greece: The Modern Sequel* (Hurst, 2002). Paschalis Kitromilides, *Enlightenment and Revolution: The Making of Modern Greece* (Harvard University Press, 2013), contains plenty of fascinating details about Greek intellectuals and statesmen's ties to Russia in the late eighteenth and early nineteenth century.

The list of works of the Balkans in the twentieth century is long, but those looking for a concise overview should turn to Richard J. Crampton, *The Balkans Since the Second World War* (Routledge, 2002), which pays sufficient attention to Greece, Bulgaria, and Romania, countries often overshadowed by former Yugoslavia. Readers drawn to both the socio-economic as well as political history should turn to John Lampe's *Balkans into Southeastern Europe, 1914–2014: A Century of War and Transition* (Palgrave, second edition, 2014). Surprisingly, there is no survey of the international politics of the region, as opposed to those of former Yugoslavia or of individual countries' foreign policies. Aurel Braun, *Small State Security in the Balkans* (Macmillan, 1983), is such a holistic account, but it concerns a different period, the 1970s and early 1980s. Svetozar Rajak et al. (eds), *The Balkans in the Cold War* (Palgrave Macmillan, 2017), stands out in the scholarship of the era, featuring chapters from eminent diplomatic historians.

Yugoslavia's violent disintegration in the 1990s gave birth to an impressive body of academic work. A recap of the often polarized discussions is contained in Sabrina Ramet, *Thinking about Yugoslavia: Scholarly Debates about the Yugoslav Breakup and the Wars in Bosnia and Kosovo* (Cambridge University Press, 2005), and Norman M. Naimark and Holly Case, *Yugoslavia and its Historians: Understanding the Balkan Wars of the 1990s* (Stanford University Press, 2003). The international efforts to contain the violence are analyzed critically by James Gow, *The Triumph of the Lack of Will: International Diplomacy and the Yugoslav War* (Columbia University Press, 1997), and Josip Glaurdić, *The Hour of Europe: Western Powers and the Breakup of Yugoslavia* (Yale University Press, 2011), amongst many other books. Russia is invariably part of the narrative. Laura Silber and Allan Little, *Yugoslavia: Death of a Nation* (Penguin, 1997), which accompanies the BBC documentary of the same name, is notable because it draws on extensive interviews with the main actors involved in the wars. The Kosovo conflict of 1998–99 is tackled in Tim Judah's *Kosovo: War and Revenge* (Yale University Press, 2002). Peter Siani-Davies (ed.), *International Intervention in the Balkans since 1995* (Routledge, 2003), and Jacques Rupnik (ed.), *The Western Balkans and the EU: "The Hour of Europe"* (EU Institute for Security Studies, 2011), should be consulted as well.

The best and most comprehensive account by far of Russia's involvement in the Yugoslav wars is James Headley, *Russia in the Balkans: Foreign Policy from Yeltsin to Putin* (Hurst, 2008). Headley has done an excellent job in meticulously charting the evolution of Moscow's policies, marshaling diverse sources. His particular strength is the Yeltsin period and the interplay between domestic forces in Russia and international factors. Vsevolod Samokhvalov, *Russian–European Relations in the Balkans and Black Sea Region: Great Power Identity and the Idea of Europe* (Palgrave Macmillan, 2017), taking its cues from the academic discipline of International Relations (IR), is a welcome addition to the debate. The chapters on Russia included in Richard H. Ullman (ed.), *The World and Yugoslavia's Wars* (Council on Foreign Relations, 1996), and Alex Danchev and Thomas Halverston (eds), *International Perspectives on the Yugoslav Conflict* (Palgrave Macmillan, 1996), provide valuable insight into the war in Bosnia as well.

The conflict in Kosovo is, unsurprisingly, the most popular subject in the literature on Russia's Balkan policy. John Norris, *Collision Course: NATO, Russia and Kosovo* (Praeger, 2005), is a lively journalistic account of the politics surrounding the air campaign against former Yugoslavia in March–June 1999. For a more scholarly interpretation, see the respective chapter on Kosovo in Roy Allison, *Russia, the West and Military Intervention* (Oxford University Press, 2013). A handful of journal articles written at the time have not lost their relevance, including Oleg Levitin, "Inside Moscow's Kosovo Muddle," *Survival*, vol. 42, no. 1, 2000, and Oksana Antonenko, "Russia, NATO and European security after Kosovo," *Survival* vol. 41, no. 4, 1999, and Predrag Simić, "Russia and the Conflicts in the Former Yugoslavia," *Journal of Southeast European and Black Sea Studies*, vol. 1, no. 3, 2001. Highly recommended also are the memoirs produced by decision makers involved in the crisis: e.g. Strobe Talbott, *The Russia Hand: A Memoir of Presidential Diplomacy* (Random House, 2002), and Evgenii Primakov, *Vosem' mesiatsev plius* (Mysl', 2001).

Yugoslavia has been the subject of many academic publications in Russian. Elena Gus'kova, a senior researcher with the Russian Academy of Sciences' (RAN) Institute for Slavic Studies, has from early on become a leading voice on the issue. Her *Istoria Iugoslavskogo krizisa: 1990–2000* (A. Solov'ev, 2001) is written from a distinctly nationalist perspective and paints a positive image of the wartime Republika Srpska and of Slobodan Milošević, laying the blame squarely at the West's doorstep. A more balanced account of the war is contained in Sergei Romanenko's monographs *Iugoslaviia, Rossia i "slavianskaia ideia": vtoraia polovina XIX–nachalo XXI veka* (Institut prava i publichnoi politiki, 2002) and *Rossiisko-iugoslavskie otnosheniia v kontekste étnopoliticheskikh konfliktov v Srednei Evrope, nachalo XX veka–1991 god* (Novoe literaturnoe obozrenie, 2011). One should also note Konstantin Nikiforov, director of RAN's Institute for Slavic Studies who served as President Yeltsin's speechwriter between 1992 and 1998. His main works include *Mezhdu Kremlem i Respublikoi Serbskoi (Bosniiskiii krizis: zavershcaiuschii etap)* (RAN, 1999) and *Iugoslavia v 20 veke: ocherki politicheskoi istorii* (co-author, Indrik, 2011). Lastly, Carnegie Moscow has a collection of essays reflecting the Russian debates following NATO's Operation Allied Force: Ekaterina Stepanova (ed.), *Kosovo: Mezhdunarodnye aspekty krizisa* (Carnegie Moscow, 1999).

The role of Russia in former Yugoslavia since the early 1990s has been for the most part a topic of interest of policy analysts: e.g. David Clark and Andrew Foxall, "Russia's Role in the Balkans – Cause for Concern?" *Henry Jackson Society*, June 2014, and Marta Szpala, "Russia in Serbia – Soft Power and Hard Interests," Center for Eastern Studies (OSW), Warsaw, 29 October 2014. There are, however, scholarly publications of note too, such as Aleksandar Fatić, "A Strategy Based on Doubt: Russia Courts Southeast Europe," *Contemporary Security Policy*, vol. 31, no. 3, 2010, or Andrew Konitzer, "Serbia between East and West," *Russian History*, vol. 38, no. 1, 2011. Konitzer, in particular, goes a long way towards deconstructing parts of the mythology related to the Russian–Serbian brotherhood and the perception of Moscow's expanding footprint in the economy. A special mention is due to James Ker-Lindsay's book *Kosovo: The Path to Contested Statehood in the Balkans* (I. B. Tauris, 2009), as it chronicles the (re)emergence of the diplomatic alliance between Moscow and Belgrade in the mid-2000s. More on the same subject in Žarko Petrović, *Russia–Serbia Relations at the Beginning of XXI Century* (ISAC Fund, 2007). Russia's penetration of Balkan economies and domestic politics is discussed in Janusz Bugajski, *Dismantling the West: Russia's Atlantic Agenda* (Potomac Books, 2009) as well as in a recent book he has co-authored with Margarita Assenova, *Eurasian Disunion: Russia's Vulnerable Flanks* (Jamestown Foundation, 2016).

Bulgaria and Romania have been unjustly overshadowed by former Yugoslavia and have caught on only in the past several years, thanks to the Ukrainian crisis. Of course, there is outstanding historical work on those countries' relations with Russia: Barbara Jelavich, *Russia and the Formation of the Romanian National State, 1821–1878* (Cambridge University Press, 1984); Duncan Perry, *Stefan Stambolov and the Emergence of Modern Bulgaria, 1870–1895* (Duke University Press, 1993), along with countless monographs and articles in local languages on the period before 1914. When it comes to the twentieth century, one could learn a great deal from books such as Charles King, *The Moldovans: Romania, Russia and the Politics of Culture* (Hoover Institution Press, 1999), Richard J. Crampton, *Bulgaria* (Oxford University Press, 2007), or Vladimir Tismeneanu, *Stalinism for All Seasons: A Political History of Romanian Communism* (University of California, 2003).

There is also a growing literature on Russian influence on the present-day politics and economies of EU members in Southeast Europe. Think-tank reports such as Heather Conley et al., *The Kremlin's Playbook: Understanding Russian Influence in Central and Eastern Europe* (CSIS, 2016), and Dimitar Bechev, *Russia's Influence in Bulgaria* (New Direction Foundation, 2015), assess Moscow's impact on the economy, domestic politics, and media. Chapters on Bulgaria, Romania, Greece/Cyprus, and Slovenia are included in Maxine David, Jackie Gower, and Hiski Haukkala (eds), *National Perspectives on Russia* (Routledge, 2013). Boyko Marinkov and Biser Banchev (eds), *Ukrainskata kriza i Balkanite* [*The Ukraine Crisis and the Balkans*] (Paradigma, 2017), is a comprehensive effort to map out responses in the entire region, from Albania to Romania and Croatia to Turkey. It is hoped that the collective volume by the Balkan Studies Institute at the Bulgarian Academy of Sciences will find its way to the English-language reader. There is a literature in English concerning Greece and Cyprus, often seen as the EU member states most sympathetic to Russia. Costas Melakopides, *Russia–Cyprus Relations: A Pragmatic Idealist Perspective* (Palgrave, 2016), looks at Moscow's role in the divided island, but is written for the most part in an uncritical, pro-Kremlin key. On Russian influence over the Greek far right, Péter Krekó et al., *"Natural Allies": The Kremlin Connections of the Greek Far Right*, Political Capital, 2015. For an overview of Russian–Greek relations, stressing the role of strategic interests, Aristotle Tziampiris, "Greek Foreign Policy and Russia:

Political Realignment, Civilizational Aspects, and Realism," *Mediterranean Quarterly*, vol. 21, no. 2, 2010. See also the chapters by Konstantin Filis and Nikos Tsafos in Spiridon N. Litsas and Aristotle Tziampiris (eds), *Foreign Policy Under Austerity: Greece's Return to Normality?* (Palgrave Macmillan, 2017). For Russian perspectives on EU members in Southeast Europe: Natalia Kulikova et al. (eds), *Rossia i strany Tsentral'noi i Iugo-Vostochnoĭ Evropy: vzaimootnosheniia v nachale XXI veka* (RAN, 2012); Azhdar Kurtov (ed.), *Rumyniia: istoki i sovremennoe sostoianie vneshnepoliticheskogo pozitsionirovaniia gosudarstva* (Rossiiskii institut strategicheskikh izsledovanii, 2013).

Russia's rich if turbulent relationship with the Ottoman Empire and modern Turkey spanning centuries is the subject of scores of monographs and articles. Dominic Lieven, *Empire: The Russian Empire and its Rivals* (Yale University Press, 2000), contains some fascinating and erudite passages juxtaposing and comparing the Tsarist and Ottoman state. *Imperial Rule*, edited by Alexei Miller and Alfred J. Rieber (CEU Press, 2005), is another exercise in the comparative study of European and Eurasian empires in the era of nationalism. The volume features an insightful chapter co-written by Norman Stone, a renowned scholar and polemicist who has contributed to the study of both Russia and Turkey. Michael A. Reynolds, *Shattering Empires: The Clash and Collapse of the Ottoman and Russian Empires, 1908–1918* (Cambridge University Press, 2010), studies the last chapter of the relationship and, for the most part, concentrates on the two empires' rivalry in the Caucasus. Victor Taki, *Tsar and Sultan: Russian Encounters with the Ottoman Empire* (I. B. Tauris, 2016), explores the "discovery" of the Ottoman state and the role of the Orientalist imagination in the formation of Russia's own identity. The wars of the early nineteenth century as well as the Tsar's patronage and support for the preservation of the Ottoman Empire in the 1830s are covered in Alexander Bitis, *Russia and the Eastern Question: Army, Government, and Society: 1815–1833* (Oxford University Press, 2006). Charles King's *Midnight at the Pera Palace: The Birth of Modern Istanbul* (W. W. Norton, 2014) narrates with elegance and depth the story of another, oft-forgotten encounter between (White) Russians and Turks, taking place in the cosmopolitan milieu of the early 1920s. King is also the author of the captivating *Black Sea: A History* (Oxford University Press, 2005). For a Russian perspective on the Ottomans and their relations with Russia, Svetlana Oreshkova (ed.), *Osmanskaia imperiia: problemy vneshnei politiki i otnosheniia s Rossiei* (Institute for Oriental Studies, RAN, 1996).

Turkish–Soviet relations in the interwar decades and during the Cold War is another vast area of scholarly enquiry, but a good overview is to be found in Bülent Gökay, *Soviet Eastern Policy and Turkey, 1920–1991* (Routledge, 2006), which is a source for the origin and development of the Turkish left as well. Turkey is also covered in Galia Golan, *Soviet Policies in the Middle East: From World War Two to Gorbachev* (Cambridge University Press, 1990). Last but not least, Baskın Oran, Atay Akdevelioğlu, and Mustafa Akşin, *Turkish Foreign Policy, 1919–2006: Facts and Analyses with Documents* (University of Utah Press, 2010), a monumental volume of nearly 1,000 pages originally published in Turkish, deserves special praise.

Turkey's economic and security ties with the Russian Federation and the countries of post-Soviet Eurasia is explored in-depth in Philip Robins, *Suits and Uniforms: Turkish Foreign Policy Since the Cold War* (Hurst, 2003). Another highly recommended text is *Turkish Foreign Policy since 1774* (Routledge, third edition, 2012) by William Hale, the doyen of the study of Turkish politics in Great Britain. Turkologists in Russia and scholars of Russia and Eastern Europe in Turkey have also produced plenty of studies: for instance, Natalia Ul'chenko (ed.), *Rossiisko-turetskie otnoshenia: istoria, sovremennoe sostoianie i perspektvy* (RAN, 2003); Oleg Kolobov, Aleksandr Kornilov, and Fatih Özbay, *Sovremennye turetsko-rossiiskie otnosheniia: problem sotrudnichestva i perspektivy razvitiia* (Nizhnii Novgorod University, 2004); Gülten Kazgan, *Dünden bugüne Türkiye ve Rusya: politik, ekonomik ve kültürel ilişkiler* (Bilgi University Press, 2003). The story of the Russian intervention in Syria since September 2015 and Turkey's response is yet to be retold in a book, whether written by an academic or a journalist.

Finally, one should acknowledge the remarkable work done on Russia and the former Soviet Union at several research centers in Turkey: Bilkent University, the Middle East

Technical University, the USAK think tank in Ankara (sadly, closed by an executive decree following the coup attempt on 15 July 2016), and Kadir Has University in Istanbul. They have been doing the job that RAN's Oriental Studies Institute is doing on the Russian side in studying bilateral ties. Samples include Habibe Özdal et al., *Turkey–Russia Relations in the Post-Cold War Era: Current Dynamics, Future Prospects* (USAK, 2013), Gencer Özcan et al., *Kuşku ile Komşuluk: Türkiye ve Rusya İlişkilerinde Değişen Dinamikler* (Iletişim, 2017), and Mustafa Aydın, *Europe's Next Shore: The Black Sea Region after EU Enlargement* (EU Institute for Security Studies, 2004). Aydın has assembled an impressive team of scholars working on the Black Sea, the Caucasus, and wider Eurasia at Kadir Has. His most recent edited volume is *Kafkasya'da Değişim Dönüşüm – Avrasya Üçlemesi* (Nobel, 2012).

INDEX